The

Road

Story

and

the

Rebel

The

Road Story

and

the Rebel

Moving

Through

Film,

Fiction,

and

Television

Katie Mills

SOUTHERN ILLINOIS
UNIVERSITY PRESS
Carbondale

Printed in the United States of America
09 08 07 06   4 3 2 1

Library of Congress Cataloging-in-Publication Data
Mills, Katie, 1956–
The road story and the rebel : moving through film,
fiction, and television / Katie Mills.
        p. cm.
Includes bibliographical references and index.
1. Road films—History and criticism. I. Title.
PN1995.9.R63M55 2006
791.43'6552—dc22
ISBN-13: 978-0-8093-2709-6 (cloth : alk. paper)
ISBN-10: 0-8093-2709-0 (cloth : alk. paper)
ISBN-13: 978-0-8093-2710-2 (pbk. : alk. paper)
ISBN-10: 0-8093-2710-4 (pbk. : alk. paper)
                                        2005030355

Printed on recycled paper. ♻

The paper used in this publication meets the
minimum requirements of American National
Standard for Information Sciences—Permanence
of Paper for Printed Library Materials, ANSI
Z39.48-1992. ∞

For Jan Mills (1925–1999) and
Irma Mathieu Augusta (1906–2002),
who went on the road,

and for my nieces,
Camille Mills Kitchen and
Marina Mills Kitchen,
who are already making
road stories of their own

Contents

Figures

Preface

> The open road, the dusty highway, the heath, the common, the
> hedgerows, the rolling downs! Camps, villages, towns, cities!
> Here today, up and off to somewhere else tomorrow!
> Travel, change, interest, excitement! The whole world before you,
> and a horizon that's always changing!
>
> —Toad speaking in *The Wind in the Willows*

During the 1950s, few middle-class mothers had careers, but my mom did, as a traveling salesperson, leaving home in her blue convertible Ford Galaxie every six weeks or so to go on the road. Her mother, another unusual person, passed the job down to her, so these two women in my family handled the route between 1951 and 1966, all told. Mom expanded the territory, covering California, Nevada, Utah, Idaho, Montana, Oregon, and Washington by herself in her huge convertible. Every few years, a new Ford replaced the one worn out by my mom's excessive travels. I remember a childhood full of blue Galaxies.

When my mother was on the road, my father and I would sometimes read *The Wind in the Willows* together at night. Filled with images of both Mr. Toad and my mom on the highway, I had the sense as a child that the road was a magical place where highly unusual people were lucky enough to go. I understood all too well that my mother was not typical (but neither was Mr. Toad, for that matter, so it made sense to me). She defied the norm of expected gender roles for the 1950s, as did my father, who put up with her absences from home and her successes in the business world. But he was an art museum director and, as it turned out, a closeted gay man, so we were different from everyone else on so many levels that I lost count. We maintained the appearance of conformity, but inside the safety of 15 Bonita Avenue our idiosyncrasies simply couldn't stay repressed.

My mom's freedom to come and go depended on the constancy of Irma Mathieu Augusta, a lovely and enduring African American woman who took care of us children from the time I was ten months old. She was widowed, with grown sons who had recently moved to Berkeley, California, from Donaldsonville, Louisiana. Perhaps half of the huge Mathieu clan had moved from Donaldsonville to Berkeley, although the family members never stopped traveling back and forth. Well before the turn of the century, Irma's grandfather built the Donaldsonville family homes on property he bought in St. Ascension Parish. Holding down the Berkeley homestead was Uncle Joe, a Pullman porter, who hosted the newly arriving relatives at his house, which he bought in the 1920s, near the Sacramento Street train tracks. Irma and her family reinforced the message for me that the people I loved were highly mobile.

We lived in the type of town where a mother could comfortably leave her family for two weeks at a time while she went on the road, with good schools and plenty of parks. There were not any other families like ours. But because we were one of the few with a swimming pool, plenty of kids were nice to me. From earliest childhood consciousness, it seems, I understood that "regular" people were the neighborhood kids swimming in our pool or the families on television that I watched with rapt attention. Clearly, the inhabitants of my home—my traveling mom, my gay father, my creole Irma, and even my beloved Mr. Toad—were unusual. Rather than being a major problem, this difference from the norm united us all, rooting us outside the mainstream even though we lived in its neighborhood.

A conscious awareness that I had a "connection" to the road genre did not occur to me until 1991, when *Thelma and Louise* hit the nation's movie screens. After seeing the film on opening night, sitting in the dark theater while recovering from an ending I had never anticipated, I realized in retrospect that I have always loved the representation of the road and the genre's stories of transformation. Seeing women occupy the lead roles of a road film made its landscape shots and fateful plot—typical features of *all* road films—suddenly take on new meaning. I was already in my thirties, taking a couple of graduate seminars in hopes of thinking more deeply about pop culture, and that film inspired me on an intellectual journey that now puts me behind the computer or in front of the classroom far more often than out on the road.

My methods as a scholar are shaped by the solace I found in childhood by equating the stories shared with my father about Mr. Toad on the highway with the anecdotes relayed by my mom about her road trips. As a kid who conflated my mother and Mr. Toad, it is no coincidence, then, that I juxtapose popular narrative and historical detail in order to recognize the nuanced subversions possible in daily life.

In this work, I have been fortunate to be nurtured by many mentors, beginning with Hayden White and Stephen Heath as well as my classmates at UC Santa Cruz's History of Consciousness Program, where I was never officially enrolled. For enriching my studies at USC in the interdisciplinary Film and Literature Program, I am grateful to Tania Modleski and Lynn Spigel, and for the unflagging support of David James, Peter Manning, and my chair, Joseph Allen Boone. I have been helped tremendously by the encouragement of Ann Charters, Deborah Martinson, Tom Burkdall, Anne Shea, Rosemary Weatherston, Carol Carter, Paul Casey, Lisa

Kernan, Julie Townsend, Ryan Stark, and Rebeca Ko. My editor at Southern Illinois University Press, Karl Kageff—with whom it is a pleasure to work—is always gracious and insightful. Thanks to my copyeditor, Louie Simon, a whiz in theory and syntax. My brother and sister, Mike Mills and Megan Kitchen, have given welcome support throughout, as did my late parents, Jan and Paul Mills. Most of all, I thank my beloved Rick Bolton, my caring soul mate, who has helped me think through each of these insights and generously traveled many emotional miles with me in the completion of this project.

The

Road

Story

and

the

Rebel

Introduction
What Automobility Offers Cultural Studies

In *Sunset Blvd.* (1950), Norma Desmond bragged about the superior quality of her car compared to those made after World War II. Norma owned quite an automobile, a handsome 1932 Isotta Fraschini, which would have been built up from the chassis to her specifications—including the leopard-skin seats and gold-plated telephone connected to the chauffeur's cab (fig. 1). By contrast, she derided "those cheap new things built of chromium and spit." Yet those two materials, American and low-brow as they are, explain precisely what captured

Fig. 1. Max (Erich von Stroheim) chauffeuring Norma Desmond (Gloria Swanson) and Joe Gillis (William Holden) in Desmond's custom-built 1932 Isotta Fraschini in *Sunset Boulevard* (1950). Directed by Billy Wilder; film copyright © Paramount Studios.

the fancy of the generation that came of age after World War II—the hot rod-ders, lowriders, and bikers of the late 1940s who were imagining a very different type of automobility than Norma Desmond's.[1] These rebels without a cause built upon prewar cars, which they chopped, welded, painted, lowered and raised via hydraulics, then proudly cruised, bringing new glory to old technology—thanks precisely to chromium and spit.

Like the postwar cars created from prewar models by a new generation want-ing to get its kicks on Route 66, so too have road stories been jacked up, dropped down, ripped apart, and recombined—in other words, substantially re-envisioned for a multimedia and multicultural age. We shall see that postwar and postmodern road stories offer a glimpse not only of contemporary automobility but also of the revolution in authority between people clinging to prewar social privileges—to a hierarchy that did not question the power of wealth or seniority, nor buck against patriarchal or white privileges—and those who turned the story of America's open road into a declaration of independence. Insisting on their right to social mobil-ity, many postwar storytellers created from the road narrative a broader vision of autonomy and mobility for all. They are the ones who turned narratives about movement into a genre of rebellion, using whatever medium they could access to tell stories of their differences from the mainstream.

What Norma's disdain for chromium and spit reveals is her objection to the democratization of mobility that characterized the postwar years. The leveling of privilege is at stake in Norma's snobbery—and in the postwar American road story. No longer did one need to be rich to motor around Sunset Boulevard, for the average Joe—as embodied in her companion, Joe Gillis (William Holden)—could scoot up there in a dream car bought on credit, dressed in the image of success even if he were in truth as poor as a pauper. The postwar automobile's shiny chromium surface did symbolize superficial flash, and the spit of the assembly-line workers at "The Big Three" indisputably helped make automobility available to the masses—and herein lies all that Norma resisted, which we ignore at our peril. Road stories chronicle these symbolic changes as well as the evolving face of the storyteller who uses automobility as a metaphor to champion the significant social rebellions of the postwar years. These rebels *with* a cause use any of the mass media available—either the more costly productions like film, the high volume content of television, or the traditional esteem of the novel.

As suggested by *Sunset Blvd.,* the new writers would be not only young, white men like Joe Gillis but also women—like his romantic counterpart, Betty Schae-fer—and eventually minorities, expatriates, gays and lesbians, and members of all sorts of communities that have been marginalized in American society. In 1950, Norma could still lord it over Sunset Boulevard, but further east in Los Angeles, over on Whittier Boulevard, second-generation Mexican Americans were celebrating their hybrid ethnic and American identity by turning old Chevies into lowriders. Through the heart of Los Angeles, Japanese Americans were experiencing racism on the buses of Wilshire Boulevard; and down on Central Street, African Americans were challenging real-estate covenants that kept them segregated there. While the boulevards of cities demarcated barriers between different racial groups and socioeconomic classes, the progressive social changes sparked by the war—including widespread employment of women and the eventual desegregation of the military—can be read in the road stories of the postwar years and still in the transformations of this genre today. Like the tricked-out cars created in postwar barrios and suburban garages, road stories serve as vehicles for Americans' sense of the self as autonomous and mobile, two linked qualities that will be condensed throughout this study in the term "automobility."

ROAD SCHOLARSHIP AND "INTERMEDIARY" METHODS

Postwar mobility is a fact that can be measured by social scientists, but in this study of America's fictions of automobility, the data are more oblique, for popular narrative reflects social change within the realm of fantasy and desire rather than statistics and charts. We shall survey here how writers and directors who want to foreground their autonomy and mobility use the road genre to proclaim an emancipation in social relations that began in World War II but flowered throughout the Vietnam era and continues today. Furthermore, this study traces the media by which these remapped narratives circulate among Americans—in movie theaters, on television as well as video and DVD, in print, on the Internet, and even in video games.

Thanks to postwar technology, the road story flourished in ways that are truly incomparable to its prewar counterpart. We shall consider the road story as a popular narrative form, and find in its postwar remappings and postmodern evolutions the subtext of contemporary identity politics. For this task, we rely upon an interdisciplinary, multimedia approach, which runs counter to the lingering tradition of studying genre by scholarly discipline. Because the methods used in this project are hybrid, this chapter will review the well-trod techniques of each discipline's "road scholarship," then suggest what an "intermediary" approach offers to scholars willing to go off the map. Historiography will help us fill in missing information about women and minority contributors to the road genre.

Hence, this chapter moves from the literary scholars who focus specifically on the theme of the car and road in fiction and nonfiction written works (Dettelbach, Stout, Lackey, Sherrill, Primeau, Paes de Barros) to film scholars working on the road film (Corrigan, Cohan and Hark, Laderman, Sargeant and Watson) by way of genre theories drawn from rhetoric (Devitt, Beebee, Cohen) and media scholars trying to navigate the meaning of our netscapes and sense of self (Morley, Jenkins). This overview provides the road map for my methods in the following chapters, which will move decade by decade through the evolution of the novels, films, and television shows in order to demonstrate that the modern American road story is a multimedia genre that goes through cycles of rebellion and co-optation that affect all of us, even if we have not seen any of the recent road films or played *Grand Theft Auto.*

Literary scholars first acknowledged a road genre, for literature has a deep-rooted tradition in the picaresque as well as the pilgrimage or journey narrative and the African American migration narrative.[2] Even today, many literary scholars cling to the idea that one need only look back at Homer's *Odyssey* or Chaucer's *Canterbury Tales* to understand the modern-day road story, as if it were possible to ignore how electric media alter the narratives that circulate and the diversity of people who purchase and create them.

In 1976, Cynthia Golomb Dettlebach wrote perhaps the first full-length monograph on the theme of the automobile in American fiction and pop culture, for which she found a wealth of examples, especially in the works of William Faulkner and Flannery O'Connor. In 1983, Janis P. Stout followed up with *The Journey Narrative in American Literature,* studying how "the characteristic journeys of American history influenced our literature by providing images and a framework of values associated with movement and direction" (5–6). Literary scholars have recently added to this work, with Ronald Primeau's *Romance of the Road: The Literature of the American Highway* (1996), Kris Lackey's *Road Frames: The American Highway Narrative* (1997), and Rowland A. Sherrill's *Road-Book America: Contemporary Culture and the New Picaresque* (2000), the latter two studying nonfiction books. In 2004, Deborah Paes de Barros focused on the fictional work of women authors in *Fast Cars and Bad Girls: Nomadic Subjects and Women's Road Stories,* as will be discussed later in this chapter. In this thirty-year period of literary study, scholars have moved from the mobilities of the car to the space of the highway to the fluidity of identity as a representation.

Film scholars have only been writing about the road genre for the past fifteen years, although the cult-oriented book, *Road Movies* (1982) by Mark Williams, offered an early compendium of these films. Other books for fans include *Races, Chases and Crashes: A Complete Guide to Car Movies and Biker Flicks* (1994) by Dave Mann and Ron Main, as well as *Two Wheels on Two Reels: A History of Biker Movies* (2000) by Mike Seate and Matthew Gagnon. Jack Sargeant and Stephanie Watson's *Lost Highways: An Illustrated History of Road Movies* (2000) offers a cross between fan appreciation and journalistic insights. More recently, and of central importance to this field, is David Laderman's *Driving Visions: Exploring the Road Movie* (2002), which adds scholarly insights to Steven Cohan and Ina Rae Hark's landmark anthology *The Road Movie Book* (1997). These studies have grown out of the formative discussions of the road film genre found in Timothy Corrigan's *A Cinema Without Walls: Movies and Culture after Vietnam* (1991).

Later in this Introduction, we will consider Corrigan's work within the context of the late 1980s.

Even museums merge the scholarly and popular fascination with American automobility. Shows range from the California Museum of Photography's 2000 exhibit and catalog, *Rearview Mirror: Automobile Images and American Identities,* edited by Kevin Jon Boyle; the Getty Museum's "The Open Road: Photography in America 1850–Now" (2001); and Ulrich Keller's exhibit and catalog, *Highway as Habitat: A Roy Stryker Documentation, 1943–1955* (1986). Back in 1970, *The Highway,* organized by the Institute of Contemporary Art at the University of Pennsylvania, gave some early shape to this work. In all, however, it is plain that the theory to explain this postwar genre has come relatively recently, in contrast to the long-standing presence of road stories in pop culture.

Genre tends to be studied in universities by medium, for few departments are yet interdisciplinary. This modernist practice reflects the goal of the first half of the twentieth century to push each medium to its uniqueness. In rebellion, some artists of the fifties and sixties embraced a philosophy of "intermedia," as we will see in chapter 2, on the Beats. The term "intermedia" describes an artist's use of media that willfully ignores boundaries between film and literature or art or music, in contradistinction to modernism's emphasis on the differences between each medium.[3] Intermedia is a concept that benefits postwar and postmodern cultural studies because it helps us to see how minority groups or marginal communities may be responding to mainstream stories by using less-expensive and more-accessible forms of media production. As such, intermedia opens up methods for these postmodern times, when storytellers and their protagonists travel readily from one medium to another. With the goal of finding a methodology that will account for the ideological uses of narrative in a media-saturated America, we shall review some attempts to apply cultural studies to the magical mystery tour of road stories throughout these postwar decades. Hybrid methods are still being invented forty years after Marshall McLuhan noted: "Program and 'content' analysis offer no clues to the magic of these media or to their subliminal charge" (34).

Rhetorical theory focuses on how genres function among users to create part of a group's identity; in turn, this offers a way to consider how dissenting communities have used genre to frame or constitute their cultural rebellion.[4] In *Writing Genres,* Amy Devitt sums up current genre scholarship as moving away from categories or structural analysis in order to study a genre's "rhetorical purpose and social contexts. . . . As ideological as groups are, so are the functions of their genres" (51). Devitt expands on how genres function:

> Genre, in its role as a social structure, can be seen as tool and agent, both constructed and constructing, always constructed by people but not always by the same people who are acting with it at that moment.

> . . . Cultures and situations, like genres, are constructed by humans responding to material conditions and perceiving similarities [and also perceiving differences]. As people interact with cultures, situations, and genres, they are shaped by those contexts and reaffirm those contexts [or rebel against them]. Even as people use a particular genre to mediate between context and text, they both operate within and recreate that genre.[5] (49)

Hence, we shall see how storytellers use the road genre to recycle certain tropes in order to highlight the differences in identity between a new type of protagonist and its predecessors, or to exploit the similarities. Devitt adds to this concept in noting that people "recognize genres are the roles they are to play, the roles being played by other people" (12). Thus, we will ask what the discourse of "liberty and freedom for all" meant to African Americans as the NAACP organized the Montgomery Bus Boycott of 1955–56, as well as to Toni Morrison as she remaps the road story in *Song of Solomon* (1977) with her politically ignorant black character, Milkman. How are artists responding to political history and cultural tradition via the road genre? This question is especially important when minority and marginal communities have so many more opportunities to influence genre in our multimedia age.

In 1986, rhetorician Ralph Cohen asked "Do Postmodern Genres Exist?", and road stories offer a unique case study for answering with an emphatic yes.[6] We will see throughout this book that postmodern genres have intermediary and multimediary characteristics. Genres reveal themselves as postmodern when they are studied across media platforms. By following changes in road stories in film as well as television and print, for instance, we will discover the debates voiced by storytellers who are alienated from dominant culture rather than merely at odds with its prevailing values. Working with and against genre, subcultural storytellers use it as an ideological space through which their marginalized characters "travel" in order to overturn old hierarchies and assert new meanings. A postmodern genre recognizes its role in identity politics.

Because the road story offers a thematic way of looking at postwar cultural production and postmodern genres, scholars of other genres will hopefully find here some constructive ways to traverse critical theories in their own work. Thanks to the overt theme of mobility and autonomy, road stories explicitly demonstrate the autonomy of storytellers to exploit the mobility of narrative on various media platforms, but these qualities are by no means the exclusive terrain of the road genre. Thus, my intermediary study joins works like David Morley's *Home Territories: Media, Mobility, and Identity* (2000) with a goal of matching "the analysis of modes of communication and of the circulation of messages with the patterns of residence and mobility of the audiences who consume them" (6) by focusing on the social history of peoples and stories. Morley faced many similar challenges in studying the meaning of "home" in our electric age. He also uses adventurous methodology: "It is the articulation of a variety of disciplinary perspectives which is my objective" (6).[7] A similar consideration of transportation and perception shaped the interdisciplinary methods of Wolfgang Schivelbusch's *The Railway Journey: Trains and Travel in the 19th Century* (1977). Increasingly, our genre theories will need to address what Henry Jenkins calls an age of "media convergence":

> We are living in an age when changes in communications, storytelling and information technologies are reshaping almost every aspect of contemporary life—including how we create, consume, learn, and interact with each other. A whole range of new technologies enables consumers to archive, annotate, appropriate, and recirculate media content and in the process, these technologies have altered the ways that consumers interact with core institutions of government, education, and commerce. ("Media Convergence")

Morley apologizes in advance for blurring methodological differences in "my attempt to seek out parallels and analogies amidst such a disparate body of work in different disciplines" (8). Yet he welcomes the debate and critical engagement that will come as interdisciplinary scholars create tools capable of addressing what I will call the "media matrix"—the constellation of medium, message, and messenger—as well as the autonomy and mobility afforded by narrative and genre to the postmodern reader/spectator.

Only through such borrowings and adaptations does critical theory progress, as Edward Said argued in "Traveling Theory" in 1983. But new scholarly approaches inevitably upset traditional modes of understanding. Our aim here will not be to define the road genre, articulate a canon, or stay within the disciplinary borders of any academic department, but to trouble all of these concepts—not for the sake of rebellion, but simply because the contemporary road story, as a uniquely postwar and postmodern genre, requires new approaches before its social significance can be fully appreciated. Through the synthesis and juxtaposition of critical theories, we can open up familiar texts to new meanings by demonstrating what they reveal about technological advances and identity politics, adding this to the aesthetic and commercial influences that most scholars study.

Rather than inventory passages that celebrate the road, then, we shall look at the types of stories told via the narrative device of the road and automobility, the types of new technologies or civil rights laws that alter the genre or open up distribution channels for new audiences, as well as what happens to this genre of rebellion when authors, filmmakers, producers, or critics see themselves as even more marginalized than the rebels who created the earlier road stories. There are many patterns evident, for instance, in the different motives for hitting the highway or the sorts of destinations and dreams pursued en route, which could help build a semiotic study of the genre; yet our focus will be to analyze how those patterns are reinforced or subverted depending on the gender, race, and sexuality of the narrators and authors/directors. We will concentrate less on generic paradigms than on their changes, noting for instance the sexual content of the story and the sexuality of the audiences "poaching" upon the story, or tracing how socioeconomic class serves as a covert subtext to the types of travel or tasks accomplished on the road.

Given the broad scope of this study, there are by necessity many gaps awaiting the work of future scholars. Most notably in need of study is the long history between rock 'n' roll and postwar automobility,[8] as it is also important to survey in greater depth the contribution to the road story made by the Internet, comic books, graphic novels, video games, and children's culture. Although I acknowledge the influence of international films or aesthetic movements, there simply is not enough space here to consider in any detail the international shape of the road genre.[9] Another vital relationship to trace would be the theme of road trips in commercial advertisements and political activism, especially in emerging economies (as in China, where Ford is producing some of the nation's popular TV shows, which feature its cars).[10] Furthermore, each road scholar emphasizes a different set of texts, so this field affords many the chance to contribute new texts, methods, and meanings that build a broader understanding of this multimedia and multicultural genre. This wide-ranging survey of sixty years' worth of road stories is an open invitation to dialogue about genre and cultural studies in the postwar and postmodern years.

IDENTITY POLITICS IN ROAD STORIES AND ROAD SCHOLARSHIP

In *Driving Visions,* David Laderman defines "the fundamental core impulse of the road movie [as] rebellion against constrictive social norms" (1) and "a break away from unwelcoming or downright oppressive social circumstances rooted in modernist rebellion" (2). His book seeks to answer the question, "What does it mean to exceed the boundaries, to transgress the limits of American society?" (2). In contrast, we shall ask a related but qualitatively different question: How does the road story, with its themes of rebellion and transformation, offer certain subcultures at key junctures in American social and technological progress a pretext for revising, remapping, or reimagining the narrative of that group's autonomy and mobility? This work complements Laderman's despite the different questions asked and the variety of media examined. Laderman acknowledges a tension in the road genre's "neomodernist" impulses, "a concurrence of conformity with a suspicious disillusionment with dominant cinematic, cultural, and political institutions" (6). We will find the hallmark of postwar road stories, however, in the embedded debates about the political and ethical significance of using the very conventions that one is criticizing. This study measures disillusionment with any one aesthetic medium by looking at the media matrix—that is, the message, messenger (storyteller or narrator), as well as the medium (including its manifestation in intermedia, multimedia, and/or transmedia interactions).

Consequently, we will focus on *fictional* texts that have been highly significant as cultural milestones—the obvious choices being *On the Road, Easy Rider, Thelma and Louise*—or those unjustifiably forgotten by time.[11] While the characters in such works inhabit the margins and subcultures of America, the bulk of the texts considered here are not marginal or "scarce and unfamiliar," nor are they largely nonfiction, as are the works covered by Lackey in his *Road Frames* (ix). Rather, we will concentrate on novels, films, and television shows that continue to influence the genre today. The power of these texts must be understood not just historically but also in terms of their ongoing impact on subsequent generations. The authority of the mainstream road story is both affirmed and subverted to illuminate the price of autonomy and mobility for the marginalized social group it represents *or* ignores.

Because the Beat vision of the road is at the heart of road stories that still register on the national consciousness, this study is anchored on Jack Kerouac's 1957 novel *On the Road*. Prior to Kerouac, the early postwar road stories put desperate people among average, law-abiding citizens—as is evident in the great *noir* films like *They Live By Night* (1949) and *The Hitch-Hiker* (1953).[12] In contrast, the poet LeRoi Jones (now Amiri Baraka) distinguished the type of characters created by him and his Beat companions, Kerouac and William Burroughs, as

> people whom Spengler called *Fellaheen*, people living on the ruins of a civilization. They are Americans no character in a John Updike novel would be happy to meet, but they are nonetheless Americans, formed out of the conspicuously tragic evolution of modern American life. The last romantics of our age.[13] (*The Moderns* xiv)

The reference is to Oswald Spengler, German historian and cultural critic, who envisioned "history as a picture of endless formations and transformations" (Hundert 104), an image that serves aptly for the study of this postwar intermediary genre. Indeed, even today, road stories largely persist in romanticizing the underdog, especially the type that rose up in the civil rights and women's liberation movements—namely, those who demanded in the postwar years not only representation but also the right of self-representation. Often, these newly emerging voices found in the road genre's tropes of autonomy and mobility a way to speak of their discontent.

By grounding these studies in how minority storytellers alter the road narrative as much as do commodity producers catering to mainstream audiences, this work recontextualizes early studies about the road genre, giving historical perspective to a number of truisms that have already fossilized as truth—especially regarding gender and the road genre. For instance, in 1991 the pioneering film scholar Timothy Corrigan voiced a standard view of road films, that the genre is "traditionally focused, almost exclusively, on men and the absence of women" (143). Such a view made sense when offered in 1991, but now that we study the genre in its full scope, we shall find in the following chapters plenty of contradictions. Because films are the most capital-intensive form of cultural production, they tend to represent dominant groups, and the road film is no exception, despite its gestures towards the "*Fellaheen*"; yet, by looking beyond films to books, which are less expensive to produce and thus more available to minority storytellers who seek to create a road story of their own, we can see that the multimedia road genre is broader and more democratic than heretofore appreciated. In particular, the significant role of women as characters, creators, or producers is likely to surprise many.

Thus, one of the goals of this book is to help complicate some of the early hypotheses about the road genre by situating ahistorical arguments within their historical context. How else to explain repeated overgeneralizations that the road genre features men and marginalizes women? For instance, we will see in chapters 6 and 7 that the road films of most the 1970s, like the "indie" films of the 1980s, use a female protagonist and play up her automobility, even though these films were not feminist in design or impact. By historicizing accordingly, it becomes clear that the road film *does* exclude women in the late 1980s, particularly in films like *Midnight Run, Planes, Trains and Automobiles,* and *Rain Man,* which came out while Corrigan was most likely writing his argument. But Corrigan is not accusing these High Concept, Hollywood road films of being masculinist, for he suggests instead that genre itself is hysterical and that the road genre specifically reflects "male hysteria." Corrigan's essay contains many valuable insights into genre, yet this particular aspect of gender needs to be questioned. For instance, Corrigan states: "the contemporary road movie (and its first cousin, the buddy movie) responds specifically to the recent historical fracturing of the male subject . . . and the hysterical but impossible need to stabilize male identities within history" (138). Why is the need to stabilize identity hysterical? Or masculine?

In the age of identity politics and "historical fracturing" of all sorts of subjectivities, why not study how media help us all to construct or stabilize a twenty-first-century sense of self? Looking back at Corrigan's statements, it seems that hysteria was located not in film genre, but in the discourses of scholars of the late 1980s.[14] Gender *is* in crisis then, but in the academy as much as in the movie theater. Seeking ways to discuss gender and power, scholars revitalized psychoanalysis, especially feminists, who had recently exposed hysteria to be a highly patriarchal diagnosis.[15]

It is important to belabor Corrigan's passages, historicizing them not only within the discourses of postmodernism and feminism but also the road films of the Reagan era, because Corrigan's essay is now excerpted into brief quotes that eliminate his specific close readings to become truisms about the entire road genre—and not just simply road films. Building on a quote from Corrigan, for instance, *The Road Movie Book* states in 1997: "the road movie promotes a male escapist fantasy linking masculinity to technology and defining the road as a space that is at once resistant to while ultimately contained by the responsibilities of domesticity" (Cohan and Hark 3). Writing in 2002, Laderman intervenes in the deepening genre debates by noting:

> Whether in traditional exaltation of machismo or as an exploration of masculine identity crisis, the bulk of the road movie genre seems to presuppose a focus on masculinity. This presupposition often bears patriarchal baggage, which both the feminists and gay road movies of the 1990s explicitly challenge. (21)

As Laderman notes, the recent road films debunk this tendency. Now scholars must do so as well.

Because of the ways in which gender conflicts were discussed in the late 1980s and early 1990s, at the same time the road story was beginning to be theorized, it is perhaps no wonder that some feminists dismissed the road genre as unwelcoming to women. For instance, scholar Janet Wolff, in her 1993 essay, "On the Road Again: Metaphors of Travel in Cultural Criticism," warned against the "vocabularies of travel" (227) used during the 1980s by male cultural critics. She cautions: "Just as women accede to theory, (male) theorists take to the road. . . . The already-gendered language of mobility marginalizes women who want to participate in cultural criticism" (234). Wolff objects to Edward Said's term "traveling theory," James Clifford's notion of theory as travel or "displacement," and Fredric Jameson's idea of cognitive mapping. Wolff rejects these vocabularies because "the practices and ideologies of *actual* travel operate to exclude and pathologize women, so the use of that vocabulary as metaphor necessarily produces androcentric tendencies in theory" (224). Wolff warns that women who use travel metaphors may find themselves frozen into static positions of marginality, pathology, or degradation, despite their conscious efforts to salvage or modify such language. For Wolff, there is no safe passage between representation and experience.

Yet we cannot afford to overlook the road stories and metaphors of mobility created or enjoyed by women and other minorities. Both Wolff and Corrigan fail to see the counter-narratives of female mobility that existed even as they made their arguments. A lesson can be learned from Hélène Cixous' essay "Sorties," which was translated and circulating in America in 1980. Clearly, Cixous played with the metaphoric meanings of the French word "*sortie*" as escape and departure in addition to its military meaning. Cixous notes: "Traditionally, the question of sexual difference is coupled with the same opposition: activity/passivity" (288).

In envisioning a world free of just such oppositions, however, Cixous predicts that "another thinking as yet not thinkable will transform the functioning of all society" (289). This power of the imagination is at the heart of the road story, which serves as an extended narrative metaphor about the alternatives to binaries of active/passive.[16] By studying the postwar road story, we witness protagonists who move past gendered binaries, who find the "*sortie*" in what seems, on the surface, "incalculable" (Cixous 289). We need a critical theory that can address both the *literal* and the *literary* movements of subcultures. Metaphoric mobility is a condition of rethinking representation, a way of gaining the autonomy to ask "what counts as experience and who gets to make that determination?" (Scott 407).

All literature builds upon the power of metaphor, which uses connotative language to move readers from literal meanings to figurative insights and emotion. Mass media also is understood through metaphor—often through the metaphor of the highway, from the nineteenth-century nickname for the telegraph as the "highway of thought" to the present-day "information superhighway," the Internet (Standage viii).

Identity also has its spatial metaphors. According to Guillermo Gómez-Peña, we live in a situation he calls "a new cultural topography":

> For me, the only solution lies in a paradigm shift: the recognition that we are all protagonists in the creation of a new cultural topography and a new social order, one in which we are "others" and we need the other "others" to exist. Hybridity is no longer up for discussion. It is a demographic, racial, social, and cultural fact. (13)

Along these same lines, Susan Stanford Friedman argues that "One axis of identity, such as gender, must be understood in relation to other axes, such as sexuality and race. . . . Identity depends upon a point of reference; as that point moves nomadically, so do the contours of identity, particularly as they relate to the structures of power" (22). The driving force of road stories is questions about autonomy, mobility, and identity, whether that identity be threatened or expanded by being on the road. The road genre offers a pop cultural forum for imagining a fluid self and new genres of relating with others.

In this way, not only do metaphors of travel and the road enrich cultural studies by imagining alternatives beyond an active/passive binary, but so do tales of automobility. Road stories usually narrate a conflict, some disruption in a preexisting power dynamic, which motivates a character to go on the road; consequently, a study of the road genre reveals how conflicts change over time, thereby providing a useful chronicle of changing "power trips." Furthermore, when writers or filmmakers exercise their agency by reinterpreting popular genre in order to reflect their subcultural identity, they often revitalize traditional tropes of autonomy and mobility, falling back purposefully upon those vocabularies in order to speak new meanings.

While road stories often celebrate white automobility, some of the finest examples of the genre, such as *Song of Solomon* (1977) by Toni Morrison, depict people of color. Other novels feature automobility as a narrative tangent, as in Sandra Cisneros's *Caramelo* (2002):

> Uncle Fat-Face's brand-new used white Cadillac, Uncle Baby's green Impala, Father's red Chevrolet station wagon bought that summer on credit are racing to the Little Grandfather's and Awful Grandmother's house in Mexico City. Chicago, Route 66—Ogden Avenue past the giant Turtle Wax turtle—all the way to Saint Louis, Missouri, which Father calls by its Spanish name, San Luis. San Luis to Tulsa, Oklahoma. Tulsa, Oklahoma, to Dallas. Dallas to San Antonia to Laredo on 81 till we are on the other side. Monterrey. Saltillo. Matehuala. San Luis Potosí. Querétaro. Mexico City. (5)

This study will thus problematize ideas like those implied by bell hooks in *Black Looks* (1992), when she warns against the "imperialist nostalgia" inherent in the term "travel." Hooks says: "Travel is not a word that can be easily evoked to talk about the Middle Passage, the Trail of Tears, the landing of Chinese immigrants, the forced relocation of Japanese-Americans, or the plight of the homeless" (173). While travel might be a word easily deployed to evoke middle-class white privilege, it *also* describes, as this project demonstrates, a far more wide-ranging set of people. For instance, there have been Japanese Americans who never stopped relocating after the internment camps closed, as depicted in *The Floating World* (1989) by Cynthia Kadohata, just as there have also been workers like my mother, who was a traveling saleswoman on the road throughout the 1950s and 1960s. What counts as evidence of a genre or an intellectual stance is contestable not only among critics, but also within the road story itself.

The very communities whose movements and spontaneity have been restricted by dominant regimes *nonetheless* have repeatedly deployed the language of mobility in American culture. Furthermore, people at the margins of society who find their freedom curtailed because of gender, class, income, race, or sexual orientation have *always* found ways to "get around," despite the barriers or prohibitions imposed upon them. Critics like hooks and Wolff overstate power's privileges of mobility and overlook the travels, both literal and figurative, of women and people of color.[17] Rather than argue to what degree *"actual"* travel practices marginalize people, we shall see that the *"vocabularies of travel"* reveal how subcultures often use images, metaphors, or narratives of mobility in richly creative ways, crafting tales of agency regardless of the restrictions on their movement. Toni Morrison, for instance, claims she uses expressive language to escape being "preserved in the amber of disqualifying metaphors" (Afterword 216).[18] As important as is the ability to move freely, the uplifting power of *discursive* mobility should not be disparaged as a poor substitute for "*actual*" freedom of movement.[19]

On the other extreme, however, our feminist and subcultural interventions must find some way to transcend the binaries that can swing the other way, toward fantasies of movement and rebellion. Whereas Wolff imagines women paralyzed by the vocabularies of cultural studies, Deborah Paes de Barros more recently argued the opposite view, claiming that "the road woman, the nomad is subversive" (17–18). She states that "not only do women travel, but they also negotiate the road in ways that differ dramatically from traditional masculine strategies of momentum" (4). Paes de Barros thus perpetuates a binary between women travelers and male momentum. Women—"bad girls"—in Paes de Barros's book are as powerful as Wolff represents them to be weak. Paes de Barros says, "nomadic women may refuse this co-option. They stand outside popular narrative. . . . Through subversion and absence they remain at the margins" (183). In this way, *Fast Cars and Bad Girls* (2004) slides the mythology of the creative rebel over to women without historicizing or critiquing it.

Just as Norma Desmond suffered by failing to accept a world in which automobility and television were transforming standards of identity, so too will cultural studies stall if it does not adapt new materials and methods to the changing media environments, not only the "mediascape" of the postwar years but also the "netscape" of the postmodern era and the "transmediascape" upon which narratives will increasingly move. To follow the contemporary road story through its accelerated evolutions in our electric age, we need to discover the "back roads" of these familiar texts, to exit the main highways that all lead to the ivory tower, rigid with disciplinary divisions, in order to find in the margins of these narratives evidence of how we negotiate identity, autonomy, and mobility.

It is time now to move away from studying road films and road fiction as separate entities and, instead, contemplate genre in terms of how its functions and ideologies are altered by people. If we are ever to track the contributions made by minority or marginal storytellers, we need to be able to study how genres move between mainstream and margins in the form of different media—some less expensive to produce than others. Furthermore, we no longer have the luxury of overlooking the low-brow, market-driven evolutions in genre storytelling, where people with fewer resources remap commodity goods in order to express themselves, even though these developments may be as distasteful to traditional scholars as chromium and spit were to Norma. We will see in the following chapters that television and drive-in theaters were disdained by die-hard modernists during the 1960s, but that did not stop these media from contributing to the road genre's evolutions that we now celebrate. Today, PlayStation's *Grand Theft Auto: San Andreas* and other new forms of media offer the next generation of storytellers a chance to expand upon popular genres to tell of their hopes and dreams.

CHRONOLOGICAL DEVELOPMENT OF THE POSTWAR AND POSTMODERN ROAD GENRE

The rest of this book details the evolution of this genre of autonomy and mobility by storytellers ever able to awaken in us just a little bit of restlessness or even a ray of optimism about social change. The migrations caused by the Depression in the 1930s and the overall demographic relocations that followed World War II are important to the development of road stories, but our present-day investment in the genre begins with the publication of Jack Kerouac's *On the Road* in 1957. Thus this study starts with an overview of the multimedia road genre's changes over these past sixty years, as rebels remap the road story and corporations then capitalize on the raw exuberance of automobility. By tracing the genre's metamorphoses through different media, the first chapter shows that storytellers from all walks of life use the road story to encourage others to explore identity boldly in this age of media expansion and social change. The historical grounding of these observations begins in chapter 2, which shows that the Beats used the road story as an opportunity for artistic experimentation, a way to rewrite the tragic narratives of Dust Bowl migration into optimistic postwar transformations. But this is the dawn of the television age, and the next chapter demonstrates that the road story travels from the Beats into the mainstream via the CBS series *Route 66* in the early 1960s, thereby commencing a cycle of commodification that follows each period of innovation. In the early sixties, psychedelic vagabond Ken Kesey and the Merry Pranksters update the road trip with the acid trip, and chapter 4 considers Tom Wolfe's account, *The Electric Kool-Aid Acid Test,* to ask who best tells the story of a transformative journey—the original pilgrim or a storyteller? In chapter 5, set in the mid-sixties, the genre oscillates between art and commodification, as we explore by comparing Kenneth Anger's underground homoerotic film *Scorpio Rising* to Roger Corman's drive-in biker films of the late 1960s.

The turning point of this postwar genre came in 1969 with the tremendous success of *Easy Rider,* for this was when the road *film* finally became aware of itself as a genre *and* an artistic statement of rebellion.[20] This film catalyzed the New Hollywood revolution of young auteurs in the early 1970s, a time when many of America's most famous contemporary directors established their reputations through road films. Chapter 6 details this while also demonstrating the overwhelming presence of female protagonists in this allegedly "male" genre. The 1980s was a period of backlash against rebellion, which clearly affected both Hollywood and independently produced road films, confirming once again the genre's cycles of rebellion and commodification, several of which are detailed in chapter 7. When the topic of race and rebellion returns to the road film in the 1990s, for reasons covered in chapter 8, we see a renaissance of the genre, as rebel storytellers twist the roles and rules of genre by means of gender, sexuality, and race. We end this study by thinking ahead about road stories in new digital media, for people are—for the first time ever—easily able to put themselves into a road story within a virtual environment, over which they have more narrative control than ever before. With this hybrid methodology at hand, we are ready to consider how the road genre remains important as new technologies and new generations remap it again and again.

——— 1

Rewriting Prohibitions with
Narratives of Possibility

> Any understanding of social and cultural change is impossible
> without a knowledge of the way media work as *environments*.
> —Marshall McLuhan, *Understanding Media*
> (1964; emphasis added)

The twentieth century was inaugurated around 1895 by the near-simulta-
neous invention of the automobile and cinema. Here was an entirely new culture
of rampant motion, and this double dose of mobility—both real and represented—offered new ways of situating and experiencing oneself. Soon, automobilists
learned to move autonomously, freed from trolley tracks and train schedules. In
1908, writer Oscar Mirbeau had this to say about the experience of automobility:
"Life rushes upon you, is thrown into disorder, becomes animated with frenzied
movement like a cavalry charge, which vanishes cinematographically like the trees,
hedges, walls, and silhouettes which line the road" (Silk 40).[1]

At the same time, cinema audiences acquired the skills of a new kind of spectatorship, drawn as they were to film's thrilling sensation of first-hand movement.[2]
For their part, filmmakers quickly moved beyond providing mere sensation to create a cinema invested in narrative, encouraging audiences to identify with a given
character's point of view. Even the most primitive movies matched subjectively
viewed shots of the inside of a moving train or automobile with exterior shots of
that same vehicle. This phenomenon, called "suturing," stitches spectators into
stable imaginative positions in the midst of moving pictures.[3]

Together, the motorcar and motion pictures generated new perceptions of self
and society.[4] Nowadays, after more than a century of experience with mass media
and widespread movement, we like to think we have a sophisticated understanding
of mobility, both real and imagined. In the course of a single day, we might interact
with images through car windshields, on movie screens, as well as on televisions,
computers, Xboxes, wireless PDAs, cell phones, and DVD players installed in the
back seat of SUVs. In the postwar years, television first exponentially raised the
visual nature of contemporary storytelling, and now digital technology saturates
our lives with images created by binary code and satellite transmissions. Games

like *Grand Theft Auto: San Andreas* (2004) go far beyond suturing us visually into a medium by allowing the player to control a character and influence the narrative's outcome. Broadcast, broadband, handheld, and wireless have only upped the voltage in which we move every day. Truth be told, we are still negotiating our sense of self amidst all of these swiftly moving images. This negotiation is the focus of this study. Here, we will examine the ways in which the metaphor of travel—of setting out on the road—has come to signify personal and collective transformation, at least since the Beats.

The trope of travel has long roots (and routes)—the Bible contains road stories, as do the works of Sophocles, Virgil, Dante, Chaucer, Whitman, and other canonical writers. But the road genre shifted radically in the years following World War II. The Beats' road stories of the 1950s hearken back to the Transcendentalist-Romantic tradition that exalts the individual, as literary scholars note, but the *significance* of that nostalgia stems from its presence within a media-filled, decidedly post-Romantic moment in American history. The Beats brought Walt Whitman's visions into the atomic age *and* also into the age of the television and the interstate freeway.

Marshall McLuhan famously defined media as extensions of human identity. As we construct the stories of our lives, we do find ourselves weighing our options both within physical landscapes and media environments. This is where the road story comes in, for our desire for autonomy and mobility unite in narratives of automobility. And when we compare one generation's road stories to the next—and in particular, when we trace the road genre between rebel groups and across different media platforms—we find that the road story, with its persistent inquiries into autonomy and mobility, stands as one of the most significant popular philosophical meditations of our day. With this in mind, we set out to understand how the road genre has helped us accommodate the range of new identities that have emerged in postwar and postmodern times.

MANUFACTURING IDENTITY

Beginning in the late 1940s and throughout the 1950s, car culture expanded as Americans adjusted to life after wartime. The earliest postwar road stories (which are not part of this study) were dark, *film noir* depictions of this changing society. On the road, risk takers realized that identity could be faked as well as found, as we see in films like *Detour* (1945), *The Postman Always Rings Twice* (1946), *Gun Crazy* (1949), and *The Wrong Man* (1956). In Flannery O'Connor's short story, "The Life You Save May Be Your Own" (1953), the drifter confronts the malleability of postwar identity:

> nowadays, people'll do anything anyways. I can tell you my name is
> Tom T. Shiflet and I come from Tarwater, Tennessee, but you never

have seen me before: how you know I ain't lying? How you know my name ain't Aaron Sparks, lady, and I come from Singleberry, Georgia, or how you know it's not George Speeds and I come from Lucy, Alabama, or how you know I ain't Thompson Bright from Toolafalls, Mississippi? (174)

One might try to erase a desperate past, escape an onerous future, invent a dead relative, or pass as someone else entirely, but things usually turned out badly. While characters in *films noirs* tend to fall victim to bad fate, heroes in subsequent stories often found that the road offered them a chance to reinvent their past or maximize their future, the opportunity to escape fates otherwise dictated by region, race, family, class, and ideology. For these characters, the automobile, the motorcycle, and even the Greyhound bus served as vehicles of freedom.

Tail fins and television were the necessary technological preconditions for the emergence of this more optimistic postwar road genre. Suburbs sprang up around new highways, filled with ranch homes designed for families that watched television. The white flight and eminent domain that came hand in hand with the construction of the new interstates turned traditional downtowns and vibrant neighborhoods into slums. Civil rights protests—intimately tied to these changes in the urban fabric—were brought nightly into homes via television.

Racial politics during and after the war challenged our national ethos, and long-stable identities of home, family, and tradition were further eroded by a variety of social movements, from women's liberation to the Vietnam War protests. Eventually, the idea began to erode that identity could be essential or fixed forever. Minorities had long been familiar with what W. E. B. DuBois called "double consciousness" in 1903—namely, the gap between a minority's empirical experience of identity and the representations imposed by dominant culture. Half a century later, television promoted a milder double consciousness, feeding Americans a daily stream of images of family and conformity that did not square with the messiness of real life. To get around this stereotyped sameness, both mainstream and minority members learned how to "travel" with some emotional autonomy through these narratives, remapping images and subverting genres in an effort to extend identity into less banal territory.

Postwar and postmodern road heroes investigate how one *constructs* a sense of self—somewhere between the map and the mind, between experience and its representation—rather than how one finds an essential self. Such a subject preoccupies artists and philosophers, but even practical people who don't spend a lot of time with "their noses in books" construct their identities too, which is one reason why the road genre has been embraced by popular audiences. The genre encourages us to imagine new lives, teaching us to rewrite prohibitions into narratives of possibility.

Like philosophy, road fiction contemplates the nature of being and the circumstances of representation, but the road story focuses its speculations in the dramas of the mobile protagonist. The intrepid traveler leaves Plato's cave for a look around, hitching a ride on the metaphors of language, the light beams of cinema, the electrons of satellite communication. "In this electric age," McLuhan taught us forty years ago, "we see ourselves being translated more and more into the form of information, moving toward the technological extension of consciousness . . . we can translate more and more of ourselves into other forms of expression that exceed ourselves" (64).

The road genre encourages exploration, inviting generations young and old to improvise new dance steps to the ageless song of the open road. William Least Heat Moon provides one way of looking at this in his memoir *Blue Highways: A Journey into America* (1982):

> On the old highway maps of America, the main routes were red and the back roads blue. . . . Just before dawn and a little after dusk—times neither day nor night—the old roads return to the sky some of its color. Then, in truth, they carry a mysterious cast of blue, and it's that time when the pull of the blue highway is strongest, when the open road is a beckoning, a strangeness, a place where a man can lose himself.

The very idea of losing oneself contradicts the various "habits" of identity we use to anchor our sense of self and our sense of others. It is those very aspects of modern identity—namely, the limiting terms of race, gender, money, sexual orientation, and conformity—that set the wheels in motion, so to speak, for the conflicts explored in road narratives. Road stories usually celebrate rebels who defy the prohibitions that immobilize others. In Toni Morrison's *Song of Solomon* (1977), for instance, the African American character Pilate traveled extensively, even through the Jim Crow south:

> When [her daughter] Reba was two years old, Pilate was seized with restlessness. It was as if her geography book had marked her to roam the country, planting her feet in each pink, yellow, blue or green state. She left the island and began the wandering life that she kept up for the next twenty-some-odd years, and stopped only after Reba had a baby. (148)

These stories about blue highways or pink states use automobility to establish fluidity between state and self, sensation and sign, authenticity and recognition, loss and discovery, immobility and escape. How one extends oneself vis-à-vis the map and the road is always gendered and embodied, and one's expressions of this experience usually compete against alternative vocabularies of the road. Indeed, road stories call attention to the prohibitions—de facto and de jure—that restrict certain groups, even while the road genre often overturns these barriers. These examples affirm that the road story is intimately tied to the search for identity, offering readers/spectators narrative encouragement to traverse the gap of double consciousness between imposed representations and empirical experience in an age of electronic mediascapes.

This study is organized chronologically, showing how, in the time that has passed since World War II, people in the margins have responded culturally to social change and new opportunity via the road genre. The case studies and close readings that follow treat the scores of American road novels, television shows, and films that have amassed since Jack Kerouac wrote *On the Road* in 1957 as an important archive of evolving ideas about power and agency.

In contrast to the chronological order that structures the rest of this book, this chapter looks holistically across the past sixty years of this genre of rebellion. Self-proclaimed misfits with various motives persistently remap the road story in order to proclaim their emancipation, register complaints, and invent utopic solutions. This exploration of the self can easily be exploited by corporations and even people with tremendous privileges who imagine themselves as rebels, typically for commercial ends. The constant cycling from rebellion to exploitation, from innovation to commodification, is also a key part of the road genre, and in fact, the genre returns persistently to questions about selling out, even while holding out for the modernist dream of inventing something brand new.

By unstitching us from a fixed identity, road stories—more than any other postwar genre—help us see ourselves as agents of our destinies, as protagonists rather than passive characters. As do individuals, subcultures also use the road story to manifest new identities. With each new communications technology and each new political movement, questions arise about autonomy and mobility: Who has the freedom to move? In works of this genre, audiences learn how self-image can be constructed dynamically in response to social movements, media innovations, and political shifts—how autonomy can be retained even while we are utterly enmeshed in a global economy of images, narratives, and commodities. At its heart, then, the road story helps readers balance immediate experience and the nurturing influence of narrative.

NARRATIVE AND SELF IN VARIOUS MEDIA ENVIRONMENTS

As early filmmakers realized, we rely upon narrative to help orient ourselves in the world. We tell stories that help us understand evolving social relations, and these stories help us welcome the future.

Autonomy and mobility are core issues of modern life, which is why they play a key role in literature, film, and popular culture. In both postwar and postmodern times, stories about motorized travel—via car, bus, or motorcycle—have inquired into the changing balance between self and community that informs our increasingly multicultural nation. These road stories have taken up movement as a plot device, passing us through different virtual scenarios in order to produce a well-traveled identity. This transportation by means of film, fiction, and television gives us new perceptions of both our home communities and exotic possibilities. No doubt road stories will continue to prove relevant in the twenty-first century, as social and political changes as well as new storytelling technologies all challenge us to evolve our understanding of people, privilege, and power.

Simply put, a road story shows that experiences away from home—perspectives gained on the road—reveal and even transform identity. The road presents a way to experience life, affect others, and change ourselves—and the road *story* dares us to dream of a better life. Of course, road films or novels are far more complex than this simple definition would suggest. The road story sweetens up our daily routines and responsibilities with a taste of freedom and spontaneity. But the appeal of this genre lies in something more complicated—a hunger for new experience and meaning, a hunger that drove Beat writer Jack Kerouac to claim "the road is life."

The postwar American road genre has an additional challenge. It leads us not only through space but also through a media environment rich with information. This begins with an extension of the self into space, as in Thomas Pynchon's *The Crying of Lot 49* (1965):

> She looked down a slope . . . onto a vast sprawl of houses which had grown up all together, like a well-tended crop, from the dull brown earth; and she thought of the time she'd opened a transistor radio to replace a battery and seen her first printed circuit. The ordered swirl of houses and streets, from this high angle, sprang at her now with the same unexpected, astonishing clarity as the circuit card had. . . . there were to both outward patterns a hieroglyphic sense of concealed meaning, of an intent to communicate. (24)

Yet this projection goes beyond the landscape to encompass the negotiation of identity with others. For instance, in his road novel, *Americana* (1971), Don DeLillo creates a protagonist who speaks of this process of identification with image as self and space:

> When I was a teenager I saw Burt [Lancaster] in *From Here to Eternity* . . . for the first time in my life I felt the true power of the image. Burt was like a city in which we are all living. He was that big. Within the conflux of shadow and time, there was room for all of us and I knew I must extend myself until the molecules parted and I was spliced into the image. . . . That night, after the movie, driving my father's car

along the country roads, I began to wonder how real the landscape
truly was, and how much of a dream is a dream. (12–13)

This molecular intermixing of the self and the image is a key part of road stories
in our electric age. Some narratives consider this to be positive, but many depict
the media environment as nightmarish. In the novel *Going Native* (1994), for
example, Stephen Wright's character loses all sense of self while watching television and attempts to escape in his car, turning the in-dash radio dial as restlessly
as he had channel surfed at home: "Sometimes he imagined he could even feel
the media microwaves bombarding his skin, as if he were being literally baked
by encoded clichés" (282). Protagonists like this hit the road, hoping to gain detachment and autonomy by stepping outside of the range of such media, if that
is indeed possible.

On the road, people have experiences that change them, but are individuals
ever free of the media-filled expectations that drive them out of the house in
the first place? Can one hit the highway, "looking for adventure and whatever
comes our way," as Steppenwolf sang in the *Easy Rider* soundtrack, without any
presumptions about the discoveries one will make? This question is not specifically modern (or postmodern, for that matter); even Don Quixote, besotted by
books so long ago, believed he was meeting on the road the fictional characters
about whom he had read.

Miguel de Cervantes' seventeenth-century road story *Don Quixote* was written
soon after the invention of the printing press had created a new mass medium.
People were learning to live in a world filled with books, particularly tales of
romantic quests churned out by the new publishing industry. Don Quixote is
literally the prototypical fool who seeks on the road everything he has read in
romances and chapbooks. Print, in other words, inspired Quixote to lose his wits.
Provocatively, Cervantes taunts his "idle reader," claiming to favor the protagonist
who is knightly enough to "translate . . . desires into action" (33). Yet his character
Quixote only recognizes experiences that superficially duplicate those he had read
about, and thus his "translations" are faulty and foolish. In this way, Cervantes
crafted a novel that fostered detachment, so clever readers could enjoy stories told
in the new medium and yet, unlike the hapless Quixote, exercise some autonomy
over print's charms.[5] *Don Quixote* emphasizes that every story negotiates between
immediate experience and mediated expectation.

How does reading a novel contrast with traveling through a landscape? Since
we project our own desires onto the world outside us, what sort of transformations can or should a text induce? Can active readers exercise some autonomy over
narrative's magic, and do those techniques of distancing ourselves paradoxically
increase our investment in the fictional world? Does immersion in narrative lead
to madness? Questions such as these might be expected in the seventeenth century,

23

when the first novelists were struggling to differentiate their narratives from the romance genre, but we find the same questions being asked by the "Quixotes" of the twenty-first century, who take issue with films, television, the Internet, and video games. DeLillo's character tries to come to terms with his identification with Burt Lancaster, and Wright's character reminds us of all the times we've felt colonized by electronic advertisements. In 1964, McLuhan suggested that electronic media were even harder to escape than print: "In the electric age . . . it is no longer possible to adopt the aloof and dissociated role of the literate Westerner" (20). How *do* we understand ourselves in space, when the landscape gives way to mediascape, now enhanced by satellite? Who are we in the mediated environment? Such postmodern riddles are often posed in road stories.

The term automobility used here highlights the concepts of *autonomy* and *mobility* with regard to both *physical* and *representational* spaces. One of the main goals of this book is to understand how modern media help us "travel" through different levels of cognition or knowledge as well as in the relations we form with others. In recent years, the Internet—which truly does open the world for us—has provided a range of spatial metaphors, such as "netscape," the "world wide web," and "cyberspace." But we should realize that every postwar generation has been forced to contend with a virtual landscape created through media. In this book, we will distinguish between four periods of mediated landscapes, beginning with the "cinemascape" that the Beats inherited from Depression-era films like *The Grapes of Wrath* (1940). These films powerfully influenced the Beats' image of the road, and informed the ways in which they cast themselves as actors within that psychic space. Secondly, once television became a dominant medium, the virtual space constructed therein will be referred to as the "mediascape" to account for the expanding media networks that envelop us, even if we don't watch TV. Next, there is the familiar postmodern "netscape," which presents us with the myriad worlds available on a personal computer. Finally, there's what I am calling the "transmediascape," to refer to a virtual environment created when a narrative extends over several media environments, like a video game and Internet and TV, for example. All of these "-scapes" have, at one time or another, felt lifelike and three-dimensional, even though they have also always clearly been understood as mere constructions. As we shall see, the full meaning of America's road genre only becomes evident by understanding how the genre has evolved within each of these media formats.

Declarations of Independence

One of the bigger differences between our day and Cervantes' is the toppling of hierarchies of identity in narrative—today the lower-class servant Sancho Panza is as likely to be a hero in a road story as is the privileged Cervantes. (Later on, we will note how author Kathy Acker hijacked this classic tale and transformed

Don Quixote into a female knight in search of an abortion.) McLuhan referred to media only as "the extensions of *man*," but in this book we shall see how "-scapes" are equally strategic for extending and expressing the identities of women, blacks, gays and lesbians, Latinas, Asian Americans, and other minorities.[6] Along with McLuhan's insight that the "medium is the message," this book also explores other "messengers," like Ralph Ellison's Invisible Man, Barbara Loden's hapless Wanda, and Gregg Araki's HIV-positive lovers. These and other variously gendered, raced, and sexed figures travel through mediated landscapes, too.[7] Who do we measure ourselves against? Burt Lancaster? Jack Kerouac? Thelma and Louise? The Lone Ranger?

Transgressive storytellers use the road genre to explore the personalities of all kinds of rebellious characters and to escape the influence of myriad earlier road travelers. In Erika Lopez's *Flaming Iguanas: An Illustrated All-Girl Road Novel Thing* (1997), Tomato Rodriguez takes a road trip soon after falling in love with another Puerto Rican lesbian:

> Ever since I was a kid, I'd tried to live vicariously through the hocker-in-the-wind adventures of Kerouac, Hunter Thompson, and Henry Miller. But I could never finish any of the books. Maybe because I just couldn't identify with the fact that they were guys who had women around to make the coffee and wash the skid marks out of their shorts while they complained, called themselves angry young men, and screwed each other with their existential penises. (27)

Consequently this project is less concerned with the question of auteurism—such as the specific contributions to the road genre made by John Steinbeck, Walt Whitman, Jack Kerouac, or Peter Fonda, for that matter—than it is with how these pioneers stimulated subsequent generations of rebels. In general, these remappings *celebrate* the gap of double consciousness, as characters project themselves into preexisting representations to understand their own historically specific identities and shout out their differences. Author Sherman Alexie noted, "Simply having Indians as the protagonists in a contemporary film [like his road film, *Smoke Signals*], and placing them within this familiar literary and cinematic structure, is groundbreaking" (West and West 29). As a genre, the road story is ripe for remapping.

Newly visible social "outlaws"—whether feminists, drag queens, or American Indians—thus become rebels *with* a cause simply by taking to the road genre. For example, in *Tripmaster Monkey: His Fake Book* (1987), Maxine Hong Kingston reimagines the Beat road story in terms of racial Otherness. Although it is not set on the road, her novel expresses both homage and hostility to the Beat legacy when her male protagonist, the Chinese American man Wittman Ah Sing, thinks: "What do you know, Kerouac? . . . . I'm the American here. I'm the American walking here. Fuck Kerouac and his American road anyway. Et tu, Kerouac.

Aiya, even you" (70). In her documentary *My America, or Honk If You Love Buddha* (1996), Renee Tajima-Peña admires the Beats for defying definition even as she maps the changing landscape of Asian American diversity. The road genre is usually about rebellion, but the heart of the road story comes typically from a desire born of contrasts—the Hells Angel in leather and the gay adolescent who fantasizes about him, or the Indian artist who always felt a kinship with Ginsberg's *Howl*. Kingston, Lopez, Tajima-Peña, and many others move through the "double consciousness" of a genre that fails to recognize their difference, offering en route a canny dissection of generic roles. This is how the road story functions at the edge of entertainment as a deconstruction of America's political investment in "liberty and justice for all." This remapping of previous works of the road genre—rarely as explicit as Kingston's or Lopez's passages above—is part of what *characterizes* this genre.

While most road story remappings imagine the rebel protagonist in the driver's seat, some stories get their power by depicting those who stay stuck by the side of the road. Hisaye Yamomoto's short story, "Life among the Oil Fields: A Memoir" (1979) views the privileged mobility of Zelda and F. Scott Fitzgerald from the perspective of Japanese Americans run down by American racism, not in the internment camps during the war but upon their postwar return to civilian life. After her brother is injured in a car accident, the narrator balances her parents' "helpless anger" at the drivers with her own awe at the power of this couple's mobility: "I gaze after them from the side of the road, where I have darted to dodge the swirling dust and spitting gravel [of their speeding car]. And I know that their names are Scott and Zelda" (95). Leslie Marmon Silko's novel *Ceremony* (1977) also uses a similar trope, as do the films *Gas, Food, Lodging* (1992) and *Tender Mercies* (1983).

Each postwar American generation has sought to redefine for its era America's foundation of liberty—be that the right to free expression, to vote, to rebel, or simply to party or act irresponsibly. In road stories, though, the concept of liberty is most consistently defined as freedom of movement. Free movement is a key political right, and not surprisingly, the centerpiece of the civil rights protests of the 1950s and 1960s—the same dozen years that established the postwar road story as a genre of rebellion (i.e., the years between the publication of *On the Road* in 1957 and the release of *Easy Rider* in 1969). For instance, civil rights leader Lillian Smith discussed the Freedom Rides of 1961 in these terms: "[The young student activists of the Freedom Rides] set up a new way of acting, the beginnings of a new ritual; one of human acceptance, of—*not* freedom (that word is too big)—but *free movement in the public places of the earth*" (emphasis in original, 8). Likewise, when any foundational tenet becomes too big to fathom, narratives like road stories create comprehensible spaces for action wherein characters can work out conflicts over their rights.

History confirms that once a marginalized community gains access to media *or* to transportation, it renegotiates its relationship to America's traditions of freedom, liberty, and justice. In *Harold and Kumar Go to White Castle* (2004), the main characters' investment in America as a "land of plenty" (where one's favorite brand of fast food is available 24/7) pushes the heroes to the film's climax, where they confront racist whites and embrace their own racial differences within the "white castle" of their dreams (fig. 2). The problem in studying this genre of rebellion is that few people see independent films like *Harold and Kumar,* which aims for a college-aged, stoner audience. Low-budget films like this or short stories like

Fig. 2. Kumar (Kal Penn) and Harold (John Cho), driven by the American Dream to finally embrace their immigrant identity, in *Harold and Kumar Go to White Castle* (2004). Directed by Danny Leiner; film copyright © New Line Cinema.

Yamomoto's get lost in the shuffle when the cultural standard is a money-maker like *Smokey and the Bandit* or an award-winner like *Sideways*.

A subculture's struggle for autonomy and mobility reveals its relationship to mainstream power as well as its signature cultural subversions. Studying the road story and its contemporary remappings allows us to trace the evolution of our culture's sense of autonomy, which is often expressed less guardedly in popular narrative than in formal statements. Peripatetic characters bring with them a certain privilege of autonomy, introducing a stranger's viewpoint to a community, a perspective that is not weighed down with the justifications of the status quo. Such stories are an important adjunct to explicit civic debates on authority and power.

By considering multimedia versions of the road genre, we can more easily see the ways in which emerging minority storytellers twist old stories to challenge formal conventions that have excluded them. To recognize how rebels remap the genre, we look at how minorities without access to expensive production tools turn instead to lower-prestige print, performance art, or digital media to create their road stories. All of these examples demonstrate that studying film to the exclusion of other media will result in a study skewed toward white protagonists, for few minority screenwriters have the clout of Sherman Alexie to write *Smoke Signals* or director John Singleton to make *Poetic Justice*—both road films that reflect upon minority automobility; more often, this topic appears in documentary film or on the pages of a novel. This is why it is so important to realize that the road story is a multimedia genre whose full significance can only be grasped by studying its role in all media—film, print, television, and digital forms.[8]

In general, the bigger the budget of a road film, the more likely it is to reflect dominant values and white privilege. More often than not, we will need to read these films against the grain to find the subtext of identity politics. For example, there are few road films that deal directly with the politics of travel in the South during the Jim Crow period, but films from the time, like *It Happened One Night* (1934), are notable precisely in how they *ignore* segregation on interstate buses. Other films, like *The Defiant Ones* (1959) or *Dutchman* (1967), offer atypical portrayals of interracial mobility during the civil rights years. More likely, segregation appears in the revisionary films of the last twenty years, such as *Love Field* (1992), which uses a segregated 1960s as the backdrop for an interracial love affair, or *Driving Miss Daisy* (1989), with its biting scene when Miss Daisy listens to Martin Luther King Jr. speak while her black chauffeur waits outside. In *Get on the Bus* (1996), director Spike Lee doesn't even need to invoke the memory of Rosa Parks, for his bus to the Million Man March carries only blacks (fig. 3). There is constant cycling between the gaps left deliberately by mainstream productions and the rebellions of storytellers working purposefully from the margins—indeed, these cycles are a key component of the genre's cultural negotiations.

Fig. 3. Leaving South Central Los Angeles in *Get on the Bus* (1996) by Spike Lee, for the three-day drive to the Million Man March in Washington, DC. Photo, Lester Sloan; film copyright © Columbia Pictures.

People rely upon genre as a way to organize and understand identity, not just narrative. Not only in travels, but also in the travails of lived human interaction, we have come, in the postwar and postmodern periods, to think of gender, sexuality, nationality, and race as genres, if you will—that is, as cognitive systems that frame experience, systems that can be rebelled against or remapped. Both identity and genre are processes of knowing, of understanding relations between a unique being and its community. Both concepts are heuristic but not fixed. Both inform us with expectations, histories, and possibilities, but since both are not static, their actual contributions are always provisional. In the end, as rhetoricians remind us, "*people,* through genres, mediate, defy, reproduce, alter, and create" (Devitt 50).

Hence, the analytical insights to be gained from studying the road genre come from the dynamic and dialogical nature of this remapping. Working with and against the genre, subcultural storytellers use it as an ideological space through which their characters move in order to upset old hierarchies and assert new meanings. To put this another way, rebel writers recognize genre as a pretext in which others perform their identities in defiance of preexisting prohibitions. Genre can be thought of as a "contact zone," as Mary Louise Pratt defines it, that

> emphasizes how subjects are constituted in and by their relations to
> each other. It treats the relations among colonizers and colonized, or

> travelers and "travelees," not in terms of separateness or apartheid,
> but in terms of copresence, interaction, interlocking understand-
> ings and practices, often within radically asymmetrical relations of
> power. (7)

Pratt continues: "Colonized subjects undertake to represent themselves in ways that *engage with* the colonizer's own terms" (7). (As these quotes illustrate, debates over the terms of identity and rebellion articulated within social sciences sound just like the drama of the road genre.) This becomes very clear in the example of LeRoi Jones's 1965 novel, *The System of Dante's Hell,* discussed in the next chapter; his African American protagonist identifies with white literary greats like James Joyce, and fears that embracing a more native black voice will turn him into an invisible man, lost in the anonymity of a racial collective. But Jones also remaps Dante's epic and even Jack Kerouac's segregated Louisiana back roads by means of his black characters, and in this move he is recognizing literary precedent as both oppressive and liberating.

Most genre studies fail in finding the contact zone because they stick stubbornly to one medium—focusing only on road *films,* for instance—even when their sub-ject wants to take them elsewhere. For example, we recognize and appreciate when a film like *Lost in America* makes an explicit reference to *Easy Rider,* recognizing the joke that hippies become bourgeois as they age, even in their fantasies. However, we tend to roll right over the references to *Easy Rider* in Erika Lopez's road novel, *Flaming Iguanas* (see fig. 4), simply because they appear in a book. Let's stop and consider how genres, identities, and media gain new meaning when combined, by turning to this blurb for Lopez's little-known book:

> Tomato Rodriguez hops on her motorcycle and embarks on the ulti-
> mate sea-to-shining-sea all-girl adventure—a story that combines the
> best parts of *Alice in Wonderland* and *Easy Rider* as Tomato crosses
> the country in search of the meaning of life, love, and the perfect post
> office. *Flaming Iguanas* is a hilarious novel that combines text, line
> drawings, rubber stamp art, and a serious dose of attitude.

This pitch invokes two distinct genres and media, namely, the girl's adventure story and the road film, and recasts the biker protagonist as a Latina lesbian. There's no use comparing *Flaming Iguanas* to another motorcycle book, such as *Zen and the Art of Motorcycle Maintenance* (1974), for Lopez's novel is in dialogue with the road film—not with the discussions on value in Pirsig's meditation. Intermedia is part of Lopez's rebellion.

When artists remap road stories, they not only ask who has the right to travel in certain geographical settings—for example, on a Jim Crow back road—they also ask questions about the mobility permitted within particular genres. Author

Fig. 4. Front cover of Erika Lopez's *Flaming Iguanas: An Illustrated All-Girl Road Novel Thing* (1997), in which Latina lesbians hit the highway. Reprinted with permission from Erika Lopez.

Bobbie Ann Mason demonstrates this in her road novel, *In Country* (1984), by putting her young heroine Sam in conflict with the war story itself. Sam refuses to consider the war genre as the sole territory of men, even when the male veterans tell her she cannot understand their suffering because she did not experience it firsthand. In fact, Sam's father had been killed in battle before she was born, and the war had shaped her identity all her life. The presumptive territoriality of genre also played a role in the popularity of the film *Thelma and Louise* (1991), which broke rules about the outlaw genre by foregrounding women as desperate characters.

31

Genre can legitimate *and* invalidate certain types of experiences and characters. The historian Joan Scott has argued: "What counts as experience is neither self-evident nor straight-forward; it is always contested, and therefore political" (412). Nontraditional protagonists put into a traditional genre thus call attention to the gap between experiences sanctioned by a genre and those that are rebellious. We see this debate even in a classic like *Lolita* (1958), when Vladimir Nabokov's hero Humbert Humbert turns the metaphors of the courtship genre: "I have never seen such smooth amiable roads as those that now radiated before us, across the crazy quilt of forty-eight states. Voraciously we consumed those long highways, in rapt silence we glided over their glossy black dance floors" (139). (In contrast, Nabokov's contemporary Simone de Beauvoir, the French feminist, rejects such poppycock when she describes America's smooth highways "as spick-and-span as the tiled floor of a Dutch kitchen" [8].) As Humbert "dances" his stepdaughter Lolita from the "ballroom" to the bedroom, he in turn insults her metaphors as illegitimate: "The log kind [of motor court encountered on the road], finished in knotty pine, reminded Lo, by its golden-brown glaze, of fried-chicken bones" (147). Humbert views their struggle as a clash between his pedigreed education and her pop cultural corruption, but the novel makes clear that Humbert is the one out of his element in a world of cars, movies, and postwar American girls that had not been addressed by the classics upon which he had staked his identity. In Nabokov's brilliant remapping of the European romance by way of the American road story, Lolita is the model victim—doomed for years to serve her stepfather's sexual needs—and the model rebel—subverting Humbert's control to escape on the road (if only to die in the end). All of this points to *Lolita*'s larger goal of remapping genre—not to fall into a psychological drama about Humbert, but to paint in generic strokes the larger social transformations in power and authority taking place in postwar America.

Minority characters like girls, women, street hustlers, and American Indians learn street smarts not only in nontraditional ways, but often from sources dismissed as inferior. We saw this in how Humbert disparages Lolita's fast-food metaphors of the road, but this is also evident in the following passage from Sam, the young heroine of *In Country,* who brings lowly cultural references to bear upon her empirical experiences of the road:

> On the road, everything seems more real than it has ever been. It's as though nothing has really registered on her until just recently. . . . The feeling reminds her of her aerobic instructor, Ms. Hot-pants—she had some hard-to-pronounce foreign name—when they did the pelvic tilt in gym last year. A row of girls with their asses reaching for heaven. "Squeeze your butt-ox. Squeeze tight, girls," she would say, and they would grit their teeth and flex their butts and hold for a count of five,

and she would say, "Now squeeze one layer deeper." That is what the new feeling is like: you know something as well as you can and then you squeeze one layer deeper and something more is there.[9] (7)

As a retort to Kerouac's riff, "What's your road, man?", Sam's passage demonstrates that road stories tend to contest different sources of knowledge between people in power and those who lack power. In *Midnight Cowboy* (1969), Rizzo's fantasies about taking a road trip to Florida are shaped by radio commercials for orange juice. These road story examples reveal the larger negotiation between the legitimacy of high art and the low-brow nature of commodity culture. As scholar Juan A. Suárez has written:

> Popular culture developed to a great extent in isolation of "legitimate" cultural antecedents; yet its strategies of negation and opposition were analogous to those of the historical avant-garde. Popular forms therefore operated as symptoms of dissent within a society which touted its consensual nature. Marginal communities (teenagers, youth groups, ethnic groups, gays, and other urban subcultures) cemented around these forms, clearing up a *space* of their own within the social practices and rituals accompanying popular music, comics, and film cults. (emphasis added, 109–10)

Disenfranchised characters in road stories always find a way to act—even if only within the commercial spaces in which they are welcomed, like aerobics classes, drive-in movies, and convenience stores. Through these spaces of popular culture, the low-brow protagonist finds the authority to speak up or locate the metaphors for describing transformative experiences.

Of course, that doesn't mean that pop culture spaces are *always* productive for minority remappings. The road story gets caught up in the cycle of rebellion and commodification, as does any genre. Because, ultimately, nobody owns the road genre, it goes through periods celebrating the mobility of rich white people, followed by periods in which rebels subvert narratives of privilege. For every rebellious remapping of the genre, there will be some cool-hunting corporation that appropriates its "look and feel" to attract the very people who resist being absorbed into the fashion economy. While PBS is airing the new season of Roadtrip Nation's *The Open Road* (a documentary that features college grads driving around the nation interviewing interesting people), other networks are airing a new Coke commercial, one with a "documentary" feel, that features young adults driving around the nation interviewing interesting people. It is easy to lament this cycle, but it is more important to understand it. Each twist and turn moves the genre along. Inevitably, the cycle revolves, as in the independent film *The Talent Given Us* (2005), which remaps TV's reality genre road story with its fictional narrative about a real family driving cross-country—thereby replacing the spontaneous Oedipal rebellions of MTV's *Road Rules* with its scripted parody of family structure and psychological transformation.

The road story has evolved into a powerful multimedia genre, in part because changes in our concepts of identity, narrative, and technology have altered the nature of rebellion and added significance to the practice of remapping genre. Because of its content, the road story is a particularly restless genre, perfect for times of change, as new cultural producers and audiences actively construct new identities, remixing the matrix of medium, message, *and* messenger. As we study the genre now in depth—decade by decade, generation by generation—we shall see how road stories have augmented the philosophical search for the self by providing accessible stories that challenge old prohibitions, stories that excite us as readers or spectators (and now, participants) to expect something better down the road.

2

Before the Road Genre
The Beats and *On the Road*

This cultural history begins with the Beats, for their Dionysian celebration of autonomy and mobility set the values that still shape the road story today. In Jack Kerouac's novel *On the Road* (1957), his narrator Sal Paradise represents the perpetual optimism of American youth who hope to slip free of constraint and expand instead into the unknown:

> At this time, 1947, bop was going like mad all over America. . . . And as I sat there listening to that sound of the night which bop has come to represent for all of us, I thought of all my friends from one end of the country to the other and how they were really all in the same vast backyard doing something so frantic and rushing-about. And for the first time in my life, the following afternoon, I went into the West. It was a warm and beautiful day for hitchhiking. (14)

Restless, rebellious, spontaneous, ecstatic, and reckless—the Beats embodied these characteristics in their lives and literature. Their excitement rolls right over the complaints of older road stories, such as the cranky travels of Henry Miller in *The Air-Conditioned Nightmare* (1945), the discontent in John Steinbeck's novel, *The Wayward Bus* (1947), or the ominous tension of *noir* films like Ida Lupino's *The Hitch-Hiker* (1953).

The Beats rejoiced in the "song of the open road," recasting Walt Whitman's passionate nineteenth-century poem as a paean to postwar freedom and twentieth-century automobility. Under their creative influence, the road called out to people to escape the commonplace and immerse themselves in life's grand mysteries.[1] Eager to put the past behind them, the Beats turned their questions about postwar renewal into road quests: "'Whither goest thou, America, in thy shiny car of the night?' . . . There was nothing to talk about any more. The only thing to do was go" (Kerouac, *On the Road* 119). They believed they were exploring an America they were simultaneously creating, for their spontaneous writing—like the road trip—was equally a form of invention and discovery.

The intoxicating quality of the road story arising in early postwar America *is* its portrayal of life as an adventure, waiting to be experienced in "the auto of our fate,"

35

as Allen Ginsberg said in his poem, "The Green Automobile" (*Selected Poems* 25). It was this enthusiasm for transformation that put the Beats on the road, where, in many ways, they remain today. Although the Beats had only a relatively small number of followers between the 1940s and the 1950s, their influence—particularly on the road genre—seems only to grow stronger over time, despite great changes in social relations, media technologies, and aesthetic philosophies.

Two historical accidents stamp the contemporary road genre with Beat values. First, there is the great optimism of the Beats. Finally freed from the burdens of the Depression, which had shaped their adolescence, and also of World War II, for which they had been too young to serve, the Beats were exuberant. For all Americans and expatriates living here, automobility was a way to celebrate winning the war, because the government rescinded wartime curbs on car production, gasoline purchases, and speed limits. Second, contemporary media, especially television, helped turn the Beat road story into a popular genre of rebellion while also making celebrities out of the Beats. Thanks to these two factors—timing and television—*On the Road* became, and remains, one of the most significant road stories in American culture, and a major influence on road stories all over the globe. Kerouac's novel serves as a touchstone even decades later, showing up in discussions of films like *Thelma and Louise* (1991) and as the source of the slogan—"What's your road, man?"—painted on the Winnebago of Roadtrip Nation's first season of *The Open Road* (2004) on PBS. To understand postwar and postmodern road stories, one must reckon with the power of the Beats.

The ongoing relevance of *On the Road* and the popularity of the road genre itself have had the unexpected effect of *obscuring* the qualities that characterize works by Kerouac, Ginsberg, and others of the Beat generation. In the fifties, Beat writing did not yet constitute a road *genre* as audiences and critics know it today. The writers' experiments with language and with the mobility of meaning have distilled over time into set themes—bebop jazz, sexual freedom, male bonding and rivalry—or have been reduced to their bare predictable narrative patterns—escape, rebellion, renewal. In the forties and fifties, however, the Beats trusted their creative power to overwrite the sad imagery of Depression- and War-era films like *The Grapes of Wrath* (1940) and *Sullivan's Travels* (1941), as well as the photographs of Dorothea Lange, Walker Evans, and others—all of which constituted a vast "cinemascape" of the road that the Beats vigorously remapped by their "intermediary mysteries," as we will see.

The Beats were also responding to the growing role of minority cultures in postwar America. Beat authors are notorious for fantasizing themselves as "white Negroes," but in this cross-raced identification lays a formative, if clumsy, insight into the fluidity of postwar identity. This identification also had a tremendous impact on the formal qualities of Beat writing, catalyzing its highly experimental nature, as this chapter will detail. We shall also consider alternative readings of

Kerouac's road—in such works as LeRoi Jones's only novel, *The System of Dante's Hell* (1965), and Joyce Glassman's *Come and Join the Dance* (1961)—that express differences of race and gender in ways that Kerouac's characters could not.[2]

In the end, it may surprise us that the Beats gave up their road stories when they had the chance to collaborate with photographer/filmmaker Robert Frank to create the influential art film, *Pull My Daisy* (1959). John Clellon Holmes once claimed the Beats were "uniqueness seeking an image" ("Name of the Game" 627), but while the road became the key image of Beat narratives, the writers remained more loyal to images than to roads. They eventually became multimedia storytellers, creating their narratives and word play in cinema rather than merely being inspired to write in response to cinema and other intermedia catalysts. In pursuit of "spontaneous prose," as we will see at the end of this chapter, the Beats concluded that the "road is spoken" (Ginsberg, *Selected Poems* 8). Throughout, we will confirm that—despite the clichés to which time has reduced the road genre, it is less a collection of formal or semiotic characteristics than it is the sum of social meanings created by the artists and audiences drawn to these tales.

It is easy to enjoy Kerouac's prose or Ginsberg's poems about the road—passion abounds, as is evident in the opening quote. It is harder to grasp the mobility of social meaning and artistic form that also fascinated these writers—the rhetorical mobility that enabled them to create the "new vision and new voice" for their generation. They put their hearts and souls into exploring avant-garde writing techniques capable of awakening artists to speak "the unspeakable visions of the individual" and "believe in the holy contour of life" (Kerouac, "Belief" 59).

THE ROAD TO *FELLAHEEN* MYSTERY

The Beats flocked to subcultures that manipulated the precarious nature of language to create new and unexpected meanings. Kerouac noticed that African Americans played upon standard English to convey private messages to other blacks; William S. Burroughs wrote in *Naked Lunch* (1959) about heroin addicts who rode the subways, undetectable to anyone but fellow junkies and the police; and in his poem, "In Society" (1947), Ginsberg contrasts "queertalk" from the "hiptalk" of blacks and jazz musicians (*Selected Poems* 3). Furthermore, Kerouac and his friend Neal Cassady personally explored the subculture of men who could have sex with other men without defining themselves as homosexual. Fascinated with the ways in which meaning could be appropriated and subverted, they admired—even glamorized—those minorities who created insurrectionary insights out of the building blocks of the status quo.

This delight in the restlessness of signification explains the Beats' attraction to road stories, which they used to philosophize from constantly moving perspectives. On their road trips, they explored a wide range of subterranean cultures thriving in the margins of America. Speaking of his fellow author, Burroughs noted: "The alienation, the restlessness, the dissatisfaction were already there waiting when Kerouac pointed out the road" (Charters, *Portable Beat Reader* xxxi). Kerouac turned his actual experiences on the road into inspirational fictions, lacing social critique with playful utopianism, as in this scat: "What's your road, man?—holy-boy road, madman road, rainbow road, guppy road, any road. It's an anywhere road for anybody anyhow. Where body how?" (*On the Road* 251). Had Kerouac *not* pointed out the importance of the road in the 1950s Beat literary movement, and had he *not* been memorialized by mass media, then the road story might not have the significance it does today as a genre of autonomy and mobility. But ever since the Beats articulated the spirit of postwar American possibility, and once television broadcast their rebellious creativity, the road has become one of the most powerful metaphors of transformation in American pop culture.

Road stories by the Beats present a view of life at the margins. Even though they had the freedom to return to the mainstream whenever money came in or when they needed to return home to write, the Beats rejected consumerism, which they saw as a symptom of conformity, and found aesthetic freedom in their own financial impoverishment. Like the original members of the avant-garde of the twenties, the Beat artists positioned themselves socially and economically in ways that allowed them to emphasize the exotic "Otherness" they saw as "primitive" and "instinctual" in racial minorities. This romanticization of marginality is problematic, of course, but at their particular historical juncture, the Beats' emulation of minority subcultures also helped to reassert some of the social changes begun by the war, including the demand by minority cultures for representation and the refusal of non-conformists to be labeled "deviant." African American Beat poet LeRoi Jones confirmed this positive aspect of the Beats' embrace of the marginal figure:

> Selby's hoodlums, Rechy's homosexuals, Burroughs's addicts, Kerouac's mobile young voyeurs, my own Negroes, are literally not included in the mainstream of American life. These characters are people whom Spengler called *Fellaheen,* people living on the ruins of a civilization. They are Americans no character in a John Updike novel would be happy to meet, but they are nonetheless Americans, formed out of the conspicuously tragic evolution of modern American life. The last romantics of our age. (*The Moderns* xiv)

Inspired by ethnic and sexual minorities, the Beats appointed themselves as intermediaries who would bridge alienated subcultures and the mainstream masses. Their use of the mutability of voice and meaning helped them in this task, as they spoke out against capitalism, censorship, McCarthyism, racism, sexual inhibition, and other social ills.

The Beats incorporated the subversive techniques of many American subcultures into their artistic practices, giving themselves new ways to attack literary
tradition and question the legitimacy of state and social institutions. To give just
one example: Ginsberg famously declared, "America I am the Scottsboro Boys"
("America," *Selected Poems* 63), taking up the racial injustice of the Depression-
era Scottsboro Boys' trials as a cry of solidarity against all oppressive systems.[3]
Ginsberg's line reveals the fluid imaginings of postwar identity. The Beats insisted
that America—despite its ongoing racial segregation—*is* its minorities and down-
trodden, its *Fellaheen*. As odd as it may seem from today's vantage of identity
politics, when we expect each minority to speak for itself, the predominantly white
and male Beats deserve credit not only for their own work, but also for giving
early legitimacy to black and gay expressions.

BRINGING NEW MYSTERIES INTO THE OLD CINEMASCAPE

For Kerouac, the road story gave narrative shape to his experiments in expression
and identity. His narrator in *On the Road* strolls "in the dark *mysterious* streets [of]
the Denver colored section, wishing I were a Negro, feeling that the best the white
world had offered was not enough ecstasy for me" (emphasis added, 180). Kerouac
often referred to his searches for creative transformation as "mysteries"—his recurring use of this word reveals the Beats' preoccupation with the adventures of
racial difference, liberated sexualities, and a new literacy made possible by film
and radio. This preoccupation with "mysteries" also reveals Kerouac's yearning
for transubstantiation, something that ties together his childhood Catholicism
and his adult Buddhism. Responding in 1961 to a young theology student who
had written him, Kerouac clarified his goal:

> Dean and I were embarked on a tremendous journey through post-
> Whitman American to FIND that America and to FIND the inherent
> goodness in American man. . . . It was really a story about 2 Catholic
> buddies roaming the country in search of God. And we found him.
> (Charters, *Letters: 1957–1969,* 289).

Through their pursuit of mysteries, Kerouac and Ginsberg supplanted the road
stories they knew from childhood—the tragedies and screwball comedies of the
Depression in which the road signified hard times and chastity.

In adopting the road story as a form for their experiments, Beat authors and
visual artists recognized that they were stepping onto a road littered with old
narratives. "Post-Whitman" America lay buried beneath the Depression's many
films and photos of Midwest migrants, like the Joads of the novel and film *The
Grapes of Wrath*. In fact, the road story was on the verge of becoming a hackneyed
American form. Beginning with Kerouac's publication of *On the Road,* however,
the Beats initiated an ambitious remapping that went far beyond the theme of the

road, becoming a radical experiment in the style and syntax of literary expression, which Kerouac later outlined in two essays on writing, "Essentials for Spontaneous Prose" and "Belief and Technique in Modern Prose," published in *Evergreen Review* in 1958 and 1959.

The Beats deliberately set about to respond to the Depression's mass-mediated migration images. They were young enough to have avoided the war's worst hardships, giving them the optimism to crave a new vision, and yet they were old enough to feel paralyzed by the preexisting repertoire of mass-media images from that time. In other words, the landscape traversed by the Beats was no longer a completely open road—it was already a "cinemascape," a landscape defined by prior literary representations and cinematic images. Holmes explained in 1965: "The movies of the [1930s] constitute[d], for my generation, nothing less than a kind of Jungian collective unconsciousness, a decade of coming attractions out of which some of the truths of our maturity have been formed" ("The Name" 627). And so, like Ginsberg's narrator in "A Supermarket in California" (1955), the Beats went "shopping for images" (*Selected Poems* 72), feeding on whatever fit their tastes for building a fresh, postwar American voice.

The Beats realized that the inescapable influence of mass media in the twentieth century puts the road trope into a loop of intertextual images circulating via cinema, photographs, and literature. Yet the cinema was also one of the "mysteries" that inspired them. Kerouac and Ginsberg recognized the impact of this cinemascape and used it to fuel their search for new expressive forms, embracing the increasingly visual nature of American life as a way to modernize their writing. The Beats pushed beyond the traditional novel, poem, and photograph toward what Kerouac called "bookmovie," applying the "intermediary" insights they gained from new media to revitalize literature.

The Beats reinvigorated the avant-garde hope of the 1920s, thereby short-circuiting the Depression of their childhood and world war of their adolescence, with the aim of connecting the riskier aspects of modernism from a previous generation to uniquely modern prose, suitable to their time and technologies.[4] In 1959, Norman Mailer called the Beats "an avant-garde generation—that post-war generation of adventurers" (585), recognizing the link between the past and the Beats' desire to find a literary voice that might disrupt the social conformity of the 1950s. Like their predecessors, the Beats embraced cinema and radio, but they also mined the literary past for American textual authority, adopting Whitman's vision of America's limitless vistas and democratic opportunity. Lionizing American writers like Herman Melville also allowed the Beats to admire writers like James Joyce and T. S. Eliot, yet still remain free of the Euro-Anglican literary legacy.[5] Eventually, because American individualism and introspection were more suitable to their tastes, Beat sutras replaced the manifestos of the historical avant-garde.

With the energy of postwar reinvention and the promise of redemption, Kerouac and fellow Beat writers embraced the immediacy of the open road *and* the familiarity of the mediated road story, confident they could remap that narrative terrain with new aesthetic terms. The Beats were not focused on a new road, or a new genre, but *a new sort of story*, one that balanced, on the one hand, the dictates of a genre, and on the other, the voice of a narrator who refused to conform to those dictates. "All that old road of the past unreeling dizzily," Kerouac wrote, "as if the cup of life had been overturned and everything gone mad" (*On the Road* 234).

REMAPPING THE DEPRESSION ERA'S
SOCIAL REALIST AESTHETICS

When Franklin Delano Roosevelt was elected president in 1932, America was deep in the economic chaos of the stock market crash and Dust Bowl migrations. To rally support behind the progressive social agenda of his New Deal, FDR's administration used techniques drawn from publicity and advertising. From 1935 until World War II, the photographers of the Farm Service Administration (FSA) presented sympathetic portraits of displaced families on the road in search of work. Also giving voice and image to the nation's migrations were James Agee and Walker Evans's *Let Us Now Praise Famous Men* (1941) and Richard Wright's contribution to Edwin Rosscam's FSA photos in *12 Million Black Voices* (1941). These images of national turmoil were powerful icons; a photograph like Dorothea Lange's "Migrant Mother"—which featured a worn, gaunt woman with worry on her face, three children clinging to her—put a human face on the sad pilgrimages taking place on America's highways at that time.

At the same time, Hollywood tried to lighten this dark iconography with screwball comedies set on the road, such as Frank Capra's *It Happened One Night* (1934) and Preston Sturges's *Sullivan's Travels* (1941). However, the film industry also offered noteworthy tragedies like John Ford's *The Grapes of Wrath* (1940) in a social realist style clearly influenced by the FSA's photographic aesthetic, which had become the preferred visual style for inspiring social change. Literate image makers began to treat this style as part of a vast semiotic network. In the opening scene of Sturges's comedy *Sullivan's Travels*, for example, film director Sullivan (Joel McCrea) proclaims that he wants to make a movie "that would realize the potentialities of film as the sociological and artistic medium that it is, with a little sex in it, something like . . ." A producer interrupts Sullivan in mid-sentence to add: "Something like Capra, I know." The producer harangues Sullivan for wanting to make a social film with "tramps, lockouts, sweatshops, people eating garbage in alleys, living in piano boxes and ash cans"—that is, a film with the iconography of FSA photographs and films like *The Grapes of Wrath*. Such images "stink with messages," the producer points out.

Hollywood's self-referentiality is commonplace in this era. The challenge for the Beats was to bring this visual vocabulary into their writing, but in a way that freed them from social realism, allowing them to reinvest the road with the promise of the individual while reinventing social critique. Still, the Beats responded to the visceral impact of those older images. The ghostly memories that darken Beat ecstasy are remnants of Depression cinema, when the road "persecuted" its travelers, and Kerouac described the old bums as "moving Henry-Fonda-like"—referring to Fonda's role as Tom Joad in *The Grapes of Wrath*—"with the same sadness as if their adventure together was *persecuting* them [who] have come and gone like *ghosts* across your eyes" (emphasis added, *Visions of Cody* 7–8). Turning instead toward the energy "rising from the underground, the sordid hipsters of America, a new beat generation," Kerouac envisioned a "madroad" that erases the Oedipal crossroads haunted by Tom Joad or "Old Dean Moriarty, the father we never found" (*On the Road* 55, 310). Similarly, Ginsberg's earliest poems, published in a collection titled *The Gates of Wrath: 1947–1952,* also remap the Joad imagery by playing on the sound similarity of the words "gates" and "grapes." In his epigraph to the collection, Ginsberg himself jumps over the Depression, all the way back to the Romantics, citing William Blake's poem "Morning," containing the lines, "To find the Western path / Right thro' the Gates of Wrath / I urge my way." The ghost of *On the Road* is not old Dean Moriarty, father of the holy con-man Dean; the specters that haunt the novel, as we will now see, are Depression *images*—Fonda's Tom Joad, Lange's "Migrant Mother," Sturges's Sullivan, and other mediated figures of the road.

On the Road recounts how Sal Paradise learns to navigate the Depression's cinemascape of the American road. In doing so, he can finally negotiate the two sides of his yearning—one inspired by movie-fed images about the West, the other by his book-dominated life in the East. Sal is a serious young writer who tells "the part of my life you could call my life on the road," which begins "with the coming of Dean Moriarty" (3). He describes Dean as a "holy con-man with the shining mind" whose exuberant monologues, shameless seductions of women, and ecstatic embrace of life inspire the fearful and ascetically alcoholic Sal to go on the road. Dean's soul, Sal notes, "is wrapped up in a fast car, a coast to reach, and a woman at the end of the road" (230). Kerouac's largely autobiographical mode of fiction leaves no doubt that Sal is drawn from Kerouac's own personality, and Dean is modeled after his friend Neal Cassady, pictured with Kerouac in figure 5. (Although he wanted to be a writer, Cassady served primarily as an inspiration to Kerouac and Ginsberg, as well as to Ken Kesey in the 1960s.)

The promise of the road is to enliven the known by means of the unknown. On his first road trip, Sal leaves home in Paterson, New Jersey, by himself, to go west, which he calls "the Promised Land" (16). His eastern hipster friends seem so

Fig. 5. Neal Cassady and Jack Kerouac. Reprinted with permission from Carolyn
Cassady; image from Photofest.

"tedious" and "bookish" next to Dean's "wild yea-saying overburst of American joy; it was Western, the west wind, an ode from the Plains, something new, long prophesied, long a-coming. . . . I could hear a new call and see a new horizon" (10). Sal projects onto Dean the cowboy mythology of early radio and film: "My first impression of Dean was of a young Gene Autry" (5). Sal's West is pure cinemascape, a landscape already imagined through *Sullivan's Travels,* Autry's Westerns, William Saroyan's writings, and the radio plays of the Lone Ranger. Throughout *On the Road,* Sal realizes that media images of the road haunt and hamper his generation, which must learn to break free of the past: "My whole life was a *haunted* life, the life of a *ghost.* I was half-way across America, at the dividing line between the East of my youth and the West of my future" (emphasis added, 17). Even on the road, one tends to seek out the cinemascape rather than attempt to escape it.

On the Road emphasizes the differences between thinking about traveling, enjoying representations of the road, and actually hitting the highway. Before taking off on his first trip, Sal admits:

> I'd been poring over maps of the United States in Paterson for months, even reading books about the pioneers and savoring names like Platte and Cimarron and so on, and on the road map was one long red line called Route 6 that led from the tip of Cape Cod clear to Ely, Nevada, and there dipped down to Los Angeles. (12)

When, during his first night on the road, Sal learns the folly of such planning in the face of the vagaries of road travel, he concludes: "It was my dream that screwed up, the stupid hearthside idea that it would be wonderful to follow one great red line across America instead of trying various roads and routes" (13). Sal confirms a fundamental truth of the modernist road narrative—namely, empirical experience on the road is far different from its representation. For subsequent postmodern generations, empiricism would lose its privileged place in favor of irony about mediated experiences; but in the postwar years, Sal's careful study of road texts while at home did not prepare him for the epistemological challenges he faced during his road trips. As the novel unfolds, the red lines marked on the map give way to the white lines of the road—material, honest, even holy markers of life's mysteries: "[I] held the car to the white line in the angelic road. What was I doing? Where was I going? I'd soon find out" (138). Going on the road gives one the opportunity to experience the difference between representation and spontaneous discovery, and then to write passionately about that difference.

Eventually, Sal gains the ability to translate between experiences in the empirical landscape and the expectations created via the cinemascape, just as he learned to distinguish between the red lines of maps and the white lines of the road. One such lesson occurs when he visits Cheyenne, one of the many towns trying to capitalize on its western heritage. He views with astonishment its "Wild West Week," in which

> big crowds of businessmen, fat businessmen in boots and ten-gallon hats, with their hefty wives in cowgirl attire, bustled and whooped on the wooden sidewalks of old Cheyenne. . . . I was amazed, and at the same time I felt it was ridiculous: in my first shot at the West I was seeing to what absurd devices it had fallen to keep its proud tradition. (33)

In another pivotal experience in this ersatz West, Sal is carousing with author friends, all of whom are emulating the tired literary style of Ernest Hemingway, when he realizes that the "pearl" he seeks is linked to a new vision and voice. To him, this vision is embodied by his new friends Dean and Carlo: "They were like the man with the dungeon stone and the gloom, rising from the underground, the sordid hipsters of America, a new beat generation that I was slowly joining" (54). It will be among this subculture that Sal discovers the new expressive forms he seeks. In part 1, when "everything seem[s] to be collapsing" (56)—which is the usual signal for Sal to move on—he leaves behind the "*storied,* eager Denver streets" (emphasis added, 58). Arriving alone by bus in San Francisco, Sal refers to himself as a "haggard ghost" (59), thus foreshadowing the ghosts that haunt the novel's next chapters. Sal does not find the true West until he becomes like the "ghost of Tom Joad" during a key detour in California's Central Valley, and this enables him next to exorcise an even older specter from his childhood, what he refers to as the "Ghost of Susquehanna," as he heads east toward the future.

Only by remapping his mental collection of old FSA and Hollywood iconography from the vantage of his own road experiences can Sal begin to reclaim his haunted life and Kerouac find the new voice of his generation. For the power of this cinemascape derived from its tremendous appeal, its atavistic promise of new opportunities and insights. On the first leg of his trip back to the East, a bus ride from San Francisco to Los Angeles, Sal delights in being "on the road again" (79), passing through what he calls "Saroyan's town" (80). Between Bakersfield and Los Angeles, Sal meets Terry, "the cutest little Mexican girl in slacks" (81). He becomes convinced that Terry "was my girl and my kind of girlsoul" (82), and with Terry, he finally inhabits the West that road films have helped him imagine:

> The bus arrived in Hollywood. In the gray, dirty dawn, like the dawn when Joel McCrea met Veronica Lake in a diner, in the picture *Sullivan's Travels,* she slept in my lap. I looked greedily out the window: stucco houses and palms and drive-ins, the whole mad thing, the ragged promised land, the fantastic end of America. (82)

What Terry offers, and Veronica Lake lacks, is Sal's passport to the *Fellaheen.* With Terry as his girl, Sal gains access to a subculture he could not otherwise experience. Finally within reach of a racial mystery he craves more than cinema's cowboys, Sal cancels his trip home. When he and Terry agree to return to her home turf of Central California to find work, Sal notes, "The thought of living in a tent and picking grapes in the cool California mornings hit me right" (89). In the agricultural town of Sabinal, Sal pinpoints his Depression-fed cinemascape of paradise by observing "an SP freight going by with hundreds of hobos reclining on the flatcars and rolling merrily along with packs for pillows. . . . 'Damn!' I yelled. 'Hooee! It *is* the promised land'" (emphasis added, 91).

Together with his Mexican Eve, Sal Paradise walks back in time through the metaphoric "gates of wrath" into the racial Eden of the West. Terry and Sal

> hit the wild streets of Fresno Mextown. Strange Chinese hung out
> of windows, digging the Sunday night streets; groups of Mex chicks
> swaggered around in slacks; mambo blasted from jukeboxes; the
> lights were festooned around like Halloween. We went into a Mexican
> restaurant and had tacos and mashed pinto beans rolled in tortillas;
> it was delicious. (93)

When money begins to run out in Sabinal, Sal picks cotton to support Terry while they live in a tent next to "a whole family of Okie cotton-pickers. . . . The grandfather had come from Nebraska during the great plague of the thirties . . . with the entire family in a jalopy truck" (95). Sal warms to the hard life of a cotton picker, earning just enough money each day to support himself, Terry, and her son for that night. Satisfied after his hard work, Sal says he was

> sighing like an old Negro cotton-picker. . . . I forgot all about the
> East and all about Dean and Carlo and the bloody road. . . . I was
> a man of the earth, precisely as I had dreamed I would be. . . . [The
> Okie neighbors in the next tent] thought I was a Mexican, of course;
> and in a way I am. (97)

Through the mysterious transmutations of language and narrative, the Beats imagine themselves as Mexicans, Scottsboro Boys, and movie stars, by means of what Marshall McLuhan would come in the next decade to call "the extensions of man" characteristic of our "electric age." Before McLuhan theorized this phenomenon, the Beats were describing it in their writings. Within the anchoring trope of the road, they tethered these wild wanderings as a way to balance avant-garde innovations with familiar narratives.

The Beats and their fictional heroes, however, have far greater mobility than the *Fellaheen* or women who inspire them. On the one hand, Sal is not simply pretending to understand the subject position of Mexican or African American workers, for he picks cotton and lives among migrant workers, earning a subsistence income the same way they do. But Sal is free to trade in his "grapes of wrath" for a jug of wine at a poetry reading or a jazz jam at Birdland whenever he wants. And he does so as soon as winter comes. His freedom to leave reveals this "man of the earth" to be standing on muddy ground as soon as he "feel[s] the pull of my own life calling me back" (*On the Road* 98). Unlike Terry or her brothers, Sal can escape once the winter winds howl around the tent corners. It is telling—and damning—that he feels only the excitement of the road: "I hid in the grapevines, digging it all. I felt like a million dollars; I was adventuring in the crazy American night" (100). The *Fellaheen* with whom Sal projects his identity may never have the same feeling, for as Sal pinpoints precisely in this simile, financial autonomy and mobility distinguish him from Terry and her family. He leaves Terry *before* he picks up his aunt's check, thereby avoiding any question of whether he should give her some of his money to help her through the winter. Instead, he says good-bye with the insincere, "'See you in New York, Terry,'" explaining in an aside to readers that, "She was supposed to drive to New York in a month with her brother. But we both knew she wouldn't make it. . . . Well, lackadaddy, I was on the road again" (101).

Thus we see how Sal's "adventure" working in the Central Valley allowed him first to reincarnate the "ghost of Tom Joad" and then to eliminate the same spirit. Before he can rest, however, there is one more ghost to confront, one more story to remap:

> I thought all the wilderness of America was in the West till the Ghost of the Susquehanna showed me different. No, there is a wilderness in the East; it's the same wilderness Ben Franklin plodded in the oxcart days when he was postmaster, the same as it was when George Washington was a wildbuck Indian-fighter, when Daniel Boone told stories by Pennsylvania lamps. (105)

These older images of the East are not cinematic; they come, no doubt, from generic American history textbooks and the classrooms of Sal's youth. By the close of part 1 of *On the Road,* Sal has found the "pearl" of the West to be more imaginary than real. He found his "kind of girlsoul" in racial difference, but also found how difficult it was to feed that fantasy through the hard work of the fields. Sal relinquishes that Steinbeckian narrative for the open possibilities of the road, juggling the past identities of the Depression and the future imaginations of postwar possibility.

Despite his greatest efforts, Sal gets stuck for quite a long time in *On the Road* in prior narratives, accumulating memories as sad souvenirs. Once Sal has confronted the lingering cinemascape of part 1, he wastes many journeys remapping his own road experiences:

> we were passing the place in the railyards where Terry and I had sat under the moon, drinking wine, on those bum crates, in October

> 1947, and I tried to tell him [Dean]. But he was too excited. . . . I
> lay in the back seat, exhausted, giving up completely, and sometime
> in the afternoon, while I dozed, the muddy Hudson zoomed by the
> tents outside Sabinal where I had lived and loved and worked in the
> *spectral past.* (emphasis added, 168–69)

By the end of part 3, Sal notes: "I realized I was beginning to cross and recross towns in America as though I were a traveling salesman—raggedy travelings, bad stock, rotten beans in the bottom of my bag of tricks, nobody buying" (245).

Kerouac finally creates a resolution for the empty restlessness of the road by creating an image of the future. At last, Sal stops looking back, where he kept getting lost in other people's stories. Seeing photos of Dean's wife and child, Sal thinks:

> I realized these were all the snapshots which our children would look
> at someday with wonder, thinking their parents had lived smooth,
> well-ordered, stabilized-within-the-photo lives and got up in the
> morning to walk proudly on the sidewalks of life, never dreaming
> the raggedy madness and riot of our actual lives, our actual night,
> the hell of it, the senseless nightmare road. All of it inside endless and
> beginningless emptiness. (254)

Here, Kerouac has constructed a turning point in the narrative, for images—and the "intermediary" practice of writing about images—offer him some of the same power and mystery that drew him to the road in the first place. Kerouac ends the elegiac remapping of the Depression's cinemascape by embracing what he called the "wild form" of the image. We will define this shortly and see that this power of the image brought Kerouac to collaborate in a short art film of major importance, *Pull My Daisy* (1959), which is notably *not* about the road. His fame after *On the Road* gave him the right to use the intermediary prose he had learned to repress in order to write a publishable version of his road experiences.

SUBTERRANEAN VOICES AND THE LOWER FREQUENCIES OF RACIAL AUTHENTICITY

Although there were minority authors addressing the subject of automobility concurrently with the Beats, they did not share the Beats' romantic portrait of marginality. As Sal's dalliance with Terry demonstrates in *On the Road,* most of the *Fellaheen* who inspired the Beats could not travel so freely. Nor could these minorities express their alienation as unreservedly as did Kerouac, Ginsberg, and other Beat writers like Burroughs, scion of a family fortune, or Gregory Corso, a white poet with a prison record.

A brief survey of Kerouac's contemporaries easily demonstrates the racism their characters faced on the road as well as the prejudice that kept the minority authors themselves from being hailed as the celebrities the Beats were well on their way to becoming. For instance, Ralph Ellison published his novel *Invisible Man* (1952) just five years before *On the Road,* describing the very different road experiences of African Americans traveling by bus from South to North—to Harlem, not Greenwich Village.[6] In the fifties, racial segregation was still enforced in the South on interstate and local buses or trains, despite active challenges first through the 1947 Journey of Reconciliation, sponsored by the Congress of Racial Equality (CORE), then by *Brown v. Board of Education,* the landmark 1954 Supreme Court decision upholding the constitutional legality of desegregation, and finally by the 1955–56 Montgomery Bus Boycott. During these years, writers like Hisaye Yamamoto shared stories about the prohibitions on autonomy and mobility experienced by America's minorities. Yamamoto depicts the psychological fallout after the return of Japanese Americans from internment camps, where they were forced during World War II. Her short story, "Wilshire Bus" (1950), reveals the racism experienced on the bus by a woman whose Japanese American husband had fought for America during the war. Even white women who wanted adventure had difficulty breaking free of social expectations, as Hettie Jones discusses in *How I Became Hettie Jones* (1990), the memoir about her years married to Beat poet LeRoi Jones.

Minority writers and the Beats each sought to create a postwar voice with which to demand one's liberties, civil and aesthetic—although the recognition they thereby received was separate but unequal. In *Invisible Man,* Ellison's protagonist rejected the populist rhetoric he had been trained to use in Harlem as an organizer for a fictional political party resembling the American Communists. The Invisible Man eventually repudiated the party's platitudes because they fail to serve the "dispossessed." He aimed to transform American race relations, inviting all to heed his message by asking, "Who knows but that, on the lower frequencies, I speak for you?" (581). The Beats agreed they could learn from these lower frequencies, for they also shunned speaking in the name of the Depression-era "People" and wanted, instead, to speak for the *Fellaheen,* with whom they felt great affinity.[7] Kerouac wrote, they used "a new language, actually spade (Negro) jargon but you soon learned it" ("Beatific" 572), and with this new voice the Beats felt no qualms speaking on behalf of the dispossessed. In 1959, Norman Mailer even coined the expression "white Negro" to describe this "new breed of adventurers, urban adventurers who drifted out at night looking for action with a black man's code to fit their facts" (587). Feeling they had cracked that code, the Beats howled and "blew the suffering of America's naked mind for love into an eli eli lamma lamma sabacthani saxophone cry that shivered the cities down to the last radio / with the absolute heart of the poem of life butchered out of their own bodies good to eat a thousand years" (Ginsberg, "Howl" 67).[8] The twin voices of love and activism appealed both to Ellison's Invisible Man *and* to the Beat subterraneans, and to many who would follow after them.[9]

49

Despite their presumptions, the Beat writers helped legitimize minorities' protests against the contradictions of the mainstream's rosy portrait of society. Many people, whites and people of color, wanted to escape the conformity of dominant culture and yearned for the transformation of the lower frequencies. Until African Americans eventually demanded the right to speak *for themselves,* as Jones would do in 1967 while changing his name to Amiri Baraka, liberal whites used their privileged position to articulate the problems of the disenfranchised, as is obvious in Sal's often-cited passage from *On the Road:*

> At lilac evening I walked with every muscle aching among the lights of 27th and Welton in the Denver colored section, wishing I were a Negro, feeling that the best the white world had offered was not enough ecstasy for me, not enough life, joy, kicks, darkness, music, not enough night. . . . I wished I were a Denver Mexican, or even a poor overworked Jap, anything but what I was so drearily, a "white man" disillusioned. (180)

The Beats spoke out on behalf of minorities and encouraged the efforts of African American writers like LeRoi Jones, Ted Joans, and Bob Kauffman.[10] They also articulated hopes and fears that inspired people of color, as evidenced by those minority writers who have paid homage to these white rebels with gratitude (even if they later added their own remappings), as we saw in chapter 1. Thus, the Beats' emphasis on the disenfranchised ushered in a monumental shift significant to *all* narratives of the post–World War II period, not just road stories. New Deal propaganda and Hollywood popular entertainments offered a set of populist values painted as universal truths. While this populism abated political extremes—from the left-wing Communists to right-wing Klan members—that had emerged during the turmoil of the early 1930s and war years, it also naturalized and reinforced mainstream privilege. In contrast, the Beats made individualism, dissent, and alienation into something heroic.

Just as radio's lower frequencies brought black voices into segregated spaces, so did Beat road stories bring a romanticized portrait of racial mysteries into the mainstream, giving squares and rebels an alternate view of life in the 1950s. The Beats listened to African American radio shows and, through the power of these programs, felt familiar with black life. In New York, they tuned in Symphony Sid's all-night jazz show and mingled with blacks in jazz clubs; on the road, they sought out the racial mysteries that had intrigued them on the radio. In *On the Road,* for instance, Sal notes that he and Dean heard "a momentous mad thing [that] began on the radio; it was the Chicken Jazz'n Gumbo disk-jockey show from New Orleans, all mad jazz records, colored records" (140). On one trip, they zoom through black enclaves on Louisiana back roads, listening to Dexter Gordon and Wardell Gray on the car radio. When they pass an "old Negro plodding along" the road in a mule wagon, Dean reacts: "'Yes!' yelled Dean. 'Yes! Dig him! Now consider his soul—stop awhile and consider.' And we slowed down the car for all of us to turn and look at the old jazzbo moaning along" (*On the Road* 113). But by turning the "negro streets" into arenas for observing black mobility, Kerouac would be taken to task by LeRoi Jones, as we will soon see.

Despite their sympathies for the *Fellaheen*, the Beats safeguarded their cultural autonomy. Rather than align themselves with any particular political agenda, they banded together only by virtue of their delight in the multifaceted nature of dissent. In 1958, Holmes called this

> passive resistance to the Square society in which he [the hipster] lives, and the most he would ever propose as a program would be the removal of every social and intellectual restraint to the expression and enjoyment of his unique individuality, and the "kicks" of "digging" life through it.[11] ("Philosophy" 635)

Although homosexual and African American communities profoundly influenced them, the Beats pursued their eclectic quests in terms of personal vision rather than collective dissent. Submerged in several subcultures, Ginsberg stressed differences between various minority systems of meaning, seeing in this intermediary approach the legacies of poet William Blake and impressionist painter Paul Cézanne rather than any sort of dilettantism. The social insights behind such "imagined communities" informed both the Beats' road travels and aesthetic wanderings. However, although they sought out myriad minority voices and marginal spaces, they rarely rested for long in any one racial or sexual subculture. Just as the road brought Kerouac's narrators in contact with the bounteous "mysteries" of the *Fellaheen*, it also served to rescue them from these excursions, returning them home whenever experiences became *too* mysterious.

In contrast to the African Americans they admired, the Beats were anything *but* invisible. As soon as Kerouac received favorable reviews of *On the Road*, the Beats themselves became subcultural spokespeople for the media. African Americans perhaps were restricted to the lower frequencies of the broadcast spectrum, but Kerouac appeared during primetime on *The Steve Allen Show*. In *Invisible Man*, for instance, Ellison had summed up the position of the African American in relation to media: "These white folk have newspapers, magazines, radios, spokesmen to get their ideas across. If they want to tell the world a lie, they can tell it so well that it becomes the truth" (143). *Time* and *The Jack Benny Show* mocked the Beats, but only because Kerouac had by that point achieved an uneasy celebrity status: his outspoken sentiments and drunken antics coincided with the early days of television, which thrived on curiosity about the marginal while upholding the authority of the mainstream. And so the Beats quickly became mass-mediated images, unwitting icons of a generation's new voice and vision.

The ways in which the Beats traveled on "negro streets" smacks of noblesse oblige, and television would in the 1960s purge this longing for racial immersion from the road story, through the series *Route 66*. Nevertheless, the Beat road story forms a crucial early chapter in America's emerging postwar minority counter-culture, which would climax in the civil rights movement of the sixties. Their work brought widespread attention to the politics of "voice." As we shall now see, Kerouac's narratives may have eventually goaded LeRoi Jones to develop a racialized voice in his lone published novel, *The System of Dante's Hell,* which remaps a key passage of Kerouac's work. Author Joyce Glassman's novel *Come and Join the Dance* (1961) also responds to Kerouac to present a more realistic and rewarding adventure than the road for her female protagonist.

LEROI JONES AND JOYCE GLASSMAN REMAP KEROUAC'S ROADS

Back in 1959, the African American writer LeRoi Jones lived in a predominantly white Beat world. Jones appreciated *On the Road* and Kerouac's spontaneous prose, so much so that he wrote a thoughtful letter on Kerouac's novel for *Evergreen Review*. In this essay, he offered a close reading of Sal Paradise's road trip on that "two-lane highway to Baton Rouge in purple darkness" (*On the Road* 156), which Jones pinpoints as Kerouac's "jewel center" (Letter 253). Jones praises this section as "poetry," especially this passage of Kerouac's: "where the river's all rain and roses in a misty pinpoint darkness and where we swung around a circular drive in yellow foglight and suddenly saw the great black body below a bridge and crossed eternity again" (*On the Road* 156). Jones explains that such passages display "the consciousness that supersedes or usurps the *normal* consciousness of the creator . . . [when the] *writer's voice* becomes his only voice . . . and the creative act itself is accomplished" (emphasis and ellipses in original, Letter 254). Jones's *Evergreen Review* letter affirms his affiliation with the Beats and his belief at the time that a writer's creative individuality—the writer's "voice"—supersedes race.

But Jones also concedes in his letter that Kerouac is occasionally duped, "when he tries painstakingly and often painfully to *conjure* intellectually. . . . Intellectual conjuring has nothing to do with the creative act as such, though it may certainly be concomitant with it" (emphasis in original, Letter 253). When this conjuring appears in *On the Road,* Kerouac's "prose becomes stiff, awkward and *untrue,*" Jones argues. What is important to note, however, is that Sal's trip on that purple highway led him—just a few paragraphs after the passage Jones praises—to an actual conjurer, that is, to a black man on the road near Deweyville, Louisiana:

> There were *mysteries* around here. . . . [We passed] a Negro man in a white shirt walking along with his arms upspread to the inky firma-
> ment. He must have been praying or calling down a curse. . . . At
> one point we got stuck at a crossroads. . . . We were scared too. We

wanted to get out of this mansion of the snake, this mireful drooping dark, and zoom on back to familiar American ground. . . . This was a *manuscript* of the night we couldn't *read*. (emphasis added, 157–58)

If this black crossroads in *On the Road* signals a landscape that Kerouac's characters "couldn't *read*," then Jones's 1965 novel *The System of Dante's Hell* becomes the *manuscript* of racial mysteries that Kerouac would never be able to *write*.[12] Jones's novel focuses on Roi, whose love of white literature has estranged this African American from his racial community, until Roi successfully trades his "drearily disillusioned" world for the tribe of the ecstatic Negro in the segregated Louisiana township, The Bottom, to which he travels by bus. The Bottom is only about 200 miles from where Sal Paradise was too scared by racial authenticity to stay on the road.

Jones's final chapter, titled "The Heretics," is far more than a one-upmanship of Kerouac, for it is the center of Jones's own transformation to the racial consciousness that led him, also in 1965, to divorce his white wife and, in 1967, to change his name to Amiri Baraka and create the Black Arts Movement (Harris xxxii).[13] In his afterword, Jones suggests that he himself atones for racial heresy: "If we can bring back on ourselves, the absolute pain our people must have felt when they came onto this shore, we are more ourselves again, and can begin to put history back on our menu" (*System* 153–54). In The Bottom, Roi struggles to leave behind what Jones describes in his postscript as the "early legacy of the black man unfocused on blackness" (153). *The System of Dante's Hell* fleshes out the cultural analysis Jones proposed two years earlier in *Blues People* (1963), where he described the blues as "secret and obscure . . . a kind of ethno-historic rite as basic as blood" that was unavailable to white Americans (148).

Jones's inversion of Paradise and Hell is a complex rhetorical and genre-based subversion rooted equally in Dante, James Joyce, and the vernacular black migration genre of "immersion," when northern blacks return home down south—however, the butt of Jones's joke is clearly Kerouac's alter ego in *On the Road*. Sal gets frightened by racial immersion, but Roi finds racial salvation on Louisiana's segregated roads. For this reason, we can read Jones's chapter as his way of *"signifyin'"* on Kerouac's Louisiana crossroads half a dozen years after he had praised them. (Black literary scholar Henry Louis Gates Jr. defines *"signifyin'"* as the intent to "revise texts in the Western tradition . . . 'authentically,' with a black difference, a compelling sense of difference based on the black vernacular" [xxii].) When Roi gets to the segregated juke joint at The Bottom, he transforms:

The dancing like a rite . . . [I] looked at the black faces knowing all the world thot [sic] that they were my own, and lusted at that *anonymous* America I broke out of, and long for it now, where I am. . . . And my history was there, had passed no further. . . . I was nobody now, mama.

Nobody. Another secret nigger. No one the white world wanted or would look at. (ellipses and emphasis added, 129–30)

Living for a few days with Peaches, a dark seventeen-year-old prostitute, Roi inhabits a promised land where he grapples with the push of his desire to lose himself in the anonymity of racial collectivity and the pull of his disgust away from an identity based solely on race rather than literature, culture, and the other forces that seduced Roi away from this tribe in the first place. Roi's confession that he once thought of himself as a James Joyce character shows how fiction has permitted him to extend his identity in ways that have alienated him from blackness: "I'm beautiful. Stephen Dedalus. . . . My soul is white, pure white, and soars. Is the God himself" (140). But unlike Sal Paradise—and by extension, Kerouac—who longs for the heart of darkness, Roi is recognized there as kin. (As with Sal's romance with Terry in Steinbeck's California, Roi uses Peaches to become part of the colored world, then leaves her without a glance backwards. A dozen years later, Toni Morrison's *Song of Solomon* signifies upon Jones's immersion narrative to emphasize gender.)

Jones tests the mobility of a "racial" voice in the realm of the road story. As noted by Farah Jasmine Griffin (170), Jones uses the "immersion narrative" to "shed [Roi] of a past of white Western poets and homosexual encounters" (170). But we can see that in one fell swoop, Jones invokes both Joyce's modernist saga and the black migration narrative, all while remapping Kerouac's black Louisiana landscape six years after he had praised Kerouac's rendition of it. This time, however, he emphasizes the distinction offered by a black writer's voice,[14] discovering a black world that remains invisible to whites, who can only conjure it intellectually and then run from this world when they do find it.

The young white women of the forties and fifties who wanted freedom from conservative gender roles tended to exercise one of two options. Some of them moved to hip enclaves in San Francisco or Greenwich Village—where, perhaps, they became romantically involved with a Beat writer, as did Joyce Johnson (née Glassman), who was involved with Kerouac; Hettie Jones, who was married to LeRoi Jones; and Diane di Prima, who had a child with Jones. All these women have since published their own memoirs and writings. In contrast, other young rebel women went abroad to find adventure. This non-conforming expatriate is portrayed by Jean Seberg's character in Jean-Luc Godard's *Breathless* (1959). Riding around with her short haircut in convertibles stolen by Jean-Paul Belmondo, Seberg no doubt inspired many fantasies.[15] (Minority men, like the homosexual Kenneth Anger and African American Melvin Van Peebles, also went abroad, where their work and identities were better appreciated.)

No wonder Paris—more than the American road—beckoned to many creative women in the postwar period. Until the women's movement gained ground in the seventies, few women authors wrote road stories, but some did write about young women traveling to Europe. Hence, Glassman's *Come and Join the Dance* (1961) serves as a crucial bridge between Kerouac's road stories and those by women that will come in the next generation.[16] Glassman's novel portrays the conundrum faced by restless young women in the 1950s—stay in New York and drive around in the broken-down cars of male rebels who were dropping out of Columbia University, or go to Paris. In this era, parents may have been reluctant to let their unmarried daughters live in Greenwich Village, yet they might have been willing to let them travel to Europe to immerse themselves in tradition and culture.

Glassman's novel generates a stark contrast between the male literary canon and female yearning for experience. It opens with Susan about to graduate from Barnard. She looks out at the walls of the campus, walls that trap in the students of the all-girls college and "shut the college off from the street where cars, unseen, rushed and moaned past. The world remained in order" (3). Susan daydreams during the last exam of her entire undergraduate education: "There were sixty-three girls in the gymnasium. They were all [focused] on Melville. Susan wondered what Melville would have thought of sixty-three girls concentrating on him at once" (3). But she finds that Melville is "unimportant and had nothing to do with what really was going to happen" (4)—namely, her imminent trip to Paris, where she hopes to be free. Her passage is booked, her bags packed. Although she has mixed feelings about traveling alone, Susan also realizes that she is confused about most of her feelings, except for her desire to become a rebel. Rather than stay in America reading masculine tales of adventure, she wants to break through the walls that envelop women in propriety. Betty Friedan would not name the "feminine mystique" until 1963, and it would be eight years before Adrienne Rich advised aspiring female writers to see "writing as revision." A woman like Susan had to find the nerve to write all by herself.

First, however, Susan teaches herself that no boyfriend could offer what she sought, which thus propels Glassman's novel into compelling historical significance. Susan's transformation begins when she leaves the Melville exam early and fails to rendezvous with her predictable boyfriend. Wandering alone on the streets of Manhattan, she meets up by chance with Peter, who seems exciting because his life is filled with turmoil and angst. Peter owns a dilapidated 1938 black Packard, in which he spends more time roaming the country than he does studying. He becomes Susan's entry to the rebellious world of "outlaws . . . a mysterious underground brotherhood" (62), which allows her to realize her secret fantasy of shedding her past and becoming one of "the wild girls" (63).[17] Susan confessed, "She wanted to be set in motion too, to run mindlessly and not feel too much" (70). She does not call Peter and his associates Beats, but her new friends certainly fit the description.

The road does bring Glassman to articulate some deep truths, but not in the heroic fashion forged by the male Beats. Her character Susan goes driving with Peter after the anti-climactic graduation ceremony. She longs to make some sort of romantic or sexual connection with him, but despite her fears of going alone to Paris, she does not force a relationship upon Peter. She waits to see what will unfold. Before they get very far outside Manhattan, Peter's car breaks down. They return to the city, where Susan helps Peter sell the car for scrap. This turns out to be an emotional experience for Peter, because his identity has long been invested in this image of masculine automobility. That night they make love, but when Susan wakes up the next morning, she is not tempted to give up Paris for Peter: "She remembered she had a train to catch, suitcases to pick up four blocks away, and a door to close for the last time. She was slipping away from Peter, just as he was slipping away from her. This was the end of something that had been completed" (171). As they say their good-byes, Peter gives her the fatherly advice that she must never regret anything:

> "I know," she said.
> And then she went. (176)

Susan is an independent young woman who not only walks out on her Melville exam, but also moves quickly beyond the broken-down hipster, who patronizes her with unnecessary advice. By implication, we might say that Glassman and perhaps other female authors are also rejecting the American road narrative in order to recognize—if not to help create—the more welcoming alternatives open to women in those years.

INTERMEDIA AS THE ROAD TO THE "SPONTANEOUS" AESTHETIC

For all its attention to racial difference and sexual transgression, the narrative form in *On the Road* is relatively conventional, as Jones's *The System of Dante's Hell* reveals in comparison. Kerouac's early experiments in writing were too wild for publishers, who would only buy work tamed by linear plots, realistic chronologies, traditional spelling and syntax, and comprehensible characters. Kerouac's noteworthy formal innovation—"spontaneous prose"—only occasionally punctuates the traditional structure of *On the Road,* rather than forming its foundation.

Yet that's only because Kerouac learned to minimize the spontaneous prose that marked his writing during the early 1950s. That's when Kerouac actually wrote five different versions of *On the Road,* the last of which became the famed version published in 1957. We turn now to the earlier, experimental version published posthumously in 1972, as *Visions of Cody,* which demonstrates how Kerouac brings a "bebop" voice fully to bear on the road itself:

> THE MAD ROAD, lonely, leading around the bend into the openings of
> space towards the horizon Wasatch snows promised us in the vision of

the west, spine heights at the world's end, coast of blue Pacific starry night—nobone half-banana moons sloping in the tangled night sky, the torments of great formations in the mist, the huddled invisible insect in the car racing onward, illuminate—The raw cut, the drag, the butte, the star, the draw, the sunflower in the grass—orangebutted west lands of Arcadia, forlorn sands of the isolate earth, dewy exposures to infinity in black space, home of the rattlesnake and the gopher—the level of the world, low and flat. (*Visions of Cody* 391)

This paragraph, lavish in the extemporaneous phrasing that Kerouac extolled, marks the full autonomy of Kerouac's spontaneous prose, moving relentlessly through image after image rather than attending to plot points. In *Visions of Cody,* unlike *On the Road,* Kerouac sustains this spontaneous voice for long passages, which made Ginsberg, back in 1952, warn:

I don't see how it will ever be published. . . . Sounds like you were just blowing and tacking things together, personally unrelating them, just for madness sake, or despair. . . . I can't see anyone, [not a publisher like] New Directions, Europe, putting it out as it is. They wont, they wont [*sic*]. (Charters, *Letters: 1940–1956* 372–73)

Visions of Cody subverts the traditional beginning, middle, and end of the road story by privileging impression over plot. In fact, reading *Visions of Cody* as a coherent narrative is difficult if one does not contextualize it within the plot of *On the Road.*

It would take Kerouac two things to resume his spontaneous prose by the end of the 1950s—first, the authority he gained through his success with *On the Road* and, also, a fortuitous collaboration with photographer Robert Frank, at a time when Grove was publishing the work of both creative giants.[18] This meeting of the minds began when Kerouac wrote the introduction to Frank's groundbreaking book of photos taken on the road, *The Americans* (1958).

With Frank, Kerouac was able to use the free style that had been too avant-garde just a few years earlier. But once he had clout, Kerouac put this same "mad road" paragraph in his introduction for Frank (i.e., years after he'd written it in 1952 and years before it was eventually published in *Visions of Cody*). Thus this "mad road" passage is a landmark for Kerouac's turn toward what I am calling "intermediary mysteries." The term comes from Kerouac's introduction, when he says that Frank

has captured in tremendous photographs . . . the agility, mystery, genius, sadness and strange secrecy of a shadow photographed[,] scenes that have never been seen before on film. . . . *intermediary mysteries.* . . . the humor, the sadness, the EVERYTHING-ness and American-ness of these pictures! (emphasis added, 5)

Intermediary mysteries are those gaps between different media—the incommensurability of literature and film, for example, or between words and images—that inspire an untapped wellspring of avant-garde innovation, and Kerouac only began to publicly and directly express this when he became friends with Frank.

Frank's *The Americans* is, in itself, a powerful and touchstone road story, vital to this history of the American road genre for bringing a unique postwar vision that broke with the FSA aesthetic and equaled Kerouac's prose. Frank carefully juxtaposed his photos into a sequence, revealing his interest in visual, "intermediary" narrative and anticipating his later turn away from still photography to film. In his proposal for the Guggenheim grant that supported his year-long car trip around the country in 1955 and 1956 for *The Americans,* Frank wrote that he aspired to create "an authentic contemporary document, the visual impact should be such as will nullify explanation" (*Robert Frank: From New York* 31). *The Americans* in fact goes even further, becoming a meditation on the possibility of photographic narrative itself, in which words are replaced by a syntax built from visual themes. Each of *The Americans'* eighty-three black and white photographs is printed opposite a page that bears only a mention of the city and state in which the picture was taken.[19] Otherwise, Frank structured the book by focusing on motifs—flags, jukeboxes, cars, and the road. Juxtapositions between Frank's images become dialectical, showing both America's dreams and nightmares as revealed through his attention to icons of youth and death, and through portraits of not only the rich or glamorous but also African Americans, Mexicans, Indians, religious fanatics, and drag queens.[20]

Frank's insistence on artistic vision helped shape America's postwar avant-garde. *The Americans* deliberately interrogated the photojournalism common to popular magazines of the 1950s, such as *Life* and *Harper's,* places where Frank had worked as a freelance photographer upon immigrating to the United States from Switzerland in 1947. Frank confessed that when on assignment for magazines, he felt like a "hack writer or a commercial illustrator" because his images were determined by his editor (*Robert Frank: From New York* 31). Like many avant-garde (and expatriate) artists, Frank rebelled against commercial formulae by asserting personal vision: "[I] wanted to follow my own intuition . . . not make a *Life* story. That was another thing I hated. Those god-damned stories with a beginning and an end" (W. Johnson 37). Frank felt that photography driven by mass media could only generate what he called "anonymous merchandise"; the solution was for him, as an *artist,* to photograph "the things that are there, anywhere and everywhere—easily found, not easily selected and interpreted" (*Robert Frank: From New York* 20)—and the photos that resulted aligned him fully with the Beat aesthetic.

Both Frank and Kerouac were inspired by the "intermediary" possibilities created when one artistic medium—prose, in Kerouac's case, and photography, in Frank's—bent in the direction of another medium. Intermedia is not the same as multimedia but a type of transformation of the artist's expressions in one medium by his or her openness to other art forms—jazz, photography, even the patois of African Americans and homosexuals, as we saw earlier. Intermediary methods rejected—whether or not the artist did so consciously—the tenets of late modernism, such as those expounded by Clement Greenberg, which insisted that each artistic medium should foreground its unique qualities. Kerouac's "miscegenation" of media, then, countered modernism's ideas of purity, as befits the Beats' social and aesthetic philosophies and their own predilection for sexual "mysteries"—and led him eventually to discover his modern and spontaneous techniques. (These intermedia projects were the precursors of what would come to be called Happenings in the 1960s.) Film in fact was a key component of postwar attempts to revitalize old narrative forms—first for the Beat generation, then for underground filmmakers of the early sixties and, finally, for the hippies of the mid- to late sixties. Film scholar David James clarifies this lineage by suggesting that social groups like the Beats and others who wanted "to change America [were] brought . . . into an engagement with film" (25).

For their part, the Beat authors were quick to invent new ways to create "intermediary mysteries."[21] For instance, Burroughs used the newly invented portable tape recorder to cut and splice tape-recorded conversations to create nonsensical sounds, giving new meaning to the babble of daily life. Burroughs also applied similar "cut-up" techniques to filmstrips, collaborating with Anthony Balch in avant-garde films such as *Towers Open Fire* (1962). In fact, major exhibitions of the Beats have foregrounded the intermediary nature of their work (without using this term), as can be seen in the Whitney's *Beat Culture and the New American 1950–1965* (1996) and the Los Angeles County Museum of Art's *Ports of Entry: William S. Burroughs and the Arts* (1996).

MOVING BEYOND THE ROAD STORY

The meteoric success of *On the Road* inspired several studios to approach Kerouac about turning it into a film. None of the deals with *On the Road* panned out, much to Kerouac's disappointment.[22] At this stage, Kerouac still struggled financially, and he fantasized not only about earning a "trust fund" to support his mother and himself, but he actually imagined a Hollywood version of *On the Road* that would use film to spread the spontaneous aesthetic he imagined. He described this in a letter to Marlon Brando, who had expressed interest in playing Dean, as his plan to leave "the camera on the front seat of the car showing the road (day and night) unwinding into the windshield, as Sal and Dean yak" (Martelle). Kerouac then details his goal: "What I wanta do is re-do the theater and the cinema in America, give it a spontaneous dash, remove pre-conceptions of 'situation' and let people rave on as they do in real life" (Martelle). (Hollywood wasn't about to underwrite anything so artistic and experimental; in fact, when MGM turned Kerouac's next novel, *The Subterraneans,* into a movie in 1960, the studio replaced the original story's African American girlfriend with a white character—Kerouac's narrative details were too progressive, let alone his directorial vision.) Yet Kerouac's disappointments in Hollywood opened him up to collaborate with Frank and together, with the help of Ginsberg and others, they created *Pull My Daisy* in 1959.

By lending his fame to Frank's first American book of photos, Kerouac helped the younger artist launch his career. Yet the benefits were clearly mutual, for Frank emboldened Kerouac's intermediary insights and wild form, as when Kerouac described Frank's work as an inspiration to writers to write poems "describing every gray mysterious detail, the gray film that caught the actual pink juice of human kind" (*Americans* 6). When Kerouac says in the book that Frank's photos "suc[k] a sad *poem* right out of America onto *film,* taking rank among the tragic poets of the word" (emphasis added, 9), he intimates that if Frank's camera creates a poem, he, Kerouac, can write a picture.

Kerouac had long sought to do this with his prose, but he also wanted to make a film. For this, Frank was his new guru. This is obvious in Kerouac's correspondence from 1958, as when he wrote to Ginsberg: "Robert Frank is going to be our boy: Robert Frank is greatest photographer on scene . . . and is going to make a movie with me in May in New York wherein I will get my experience for later in the year when you come back we will begin work on our first great movie" (Charters, *Letters: 1957–1969* 100). Kerouac then details both narrative and visual innovations he is concocting in his mind's eye for the film he wants to make with Ginsberg. His correspondence from this period frequently mentions his film ideas. Frank and Kerouac even hit the road together to create a feature for *Life* in spring 1958, although the magazine failed to run the collaboration (*Evergreen Review* ran it in 1970, after Kerouac died.)

Thus we can see that Kerouac's inspiration by Frank and the fantasy of having considerable say over the aesthetics of the film version of *On the Road* (Kerouac was actually casting people in his mind in the letter to Ginsberg, cited above) opened up the intermediary mysteries that had been there in the 1952 version of the novel. But back then, Kerouac's giddy enthusiasm was simply too exotic for its time. In 1952, while finishing *Doctor Sax* and working on *On the Road,* Kerouac wrote that he was sensing "something beyond the novel and beyond the arbitrary confines of the story . . . into the realms of revealed Picture . . . *wild form* . . . my mind is exploding to say something about every image and every memory" (Charters, *Letters: 1940–1956* 366).[23] We can see in retrospect just how important the "revealed Picture . . . *wild form*" was to Kerouac—for it helped him resolve the narrative of *On the Road,* as we saw in Sal's discussion of Dean's photograph depicting "the raggedy madness and riot of our actual lives" (*On the Road* 254).

The road became the centripetal force he used in editing out the wild form in his manuscript of 1952 in order to turn it into the more disciplined form published as *On the Road*. The road trope kept Kerouac from spinning too far off track with his visions, giving him a narrative *dharma* (meaning both duty and path) to which he could return when he began to get too wild. We can also see retroactively that Kerouac remapped the cinemascape in *On the Road* because of his exploding desire "to say something about every image and every memory."

By the late 1950s, however, Kerouac did not need to restrain himself any longer and, instead, he articulated his intermediary technique in two essays on writing published in *Evergreen Review*. Between the publication of "Essentials for Spontaneous Prose," his first essay on writing in the Summer 1958 issue, and his second one, published less than a year later, Kerouac makes a monumental shift in his metaphors, referencing film instead of jazz art and jazz metaphors.[24] The earlier essay makes references to drawing—"sketching (before a landscape or teacup or old face)" (72)—and jazz—"*blowing* (as per jazz musician) on subject of image" (72); "Blow as deep as you want—write as deeply" (72). Just nine months later, Kerouac published "Belief and Technique in Modern Prose," recommending notably different techniques for writing "modern prose."[25] Kerouac lists his insights in the form of simple aphorisms, such as: "26. *Bookmovie* is the movie in words, the visual American form" (emphasis added, 59). The final aphorism is: "30. Writer-Director of Earthly movies Sponsored & Angeled in Heaven" (59). Kerouac's second article came out just a few months after Kerouac had worked on *Pull My Daisy,* and the likely influence of this film on Kerouac's ideas cannot be overlooked. With Frank and with film, Kerouac let go of the road.

The concept for *Pull My Daisy* was to make an art film version of *On the Road;* it evolved into a twenty-seven-minute film about a Beat family at home. Frank brought in the painter Alfred Leslie as his co-director, and when Leslie heard a tape recording of Kerouac reading his work-in-progress, *The Beat Generation,* he decided to substitute Kerouac's *On the Road* with *The Beat Generation* (Sargeant 31). Shooting on *Pull My Daisy* began on 2 January 1959.[26] Kerouac's seemingly unscripted voice-over narrates the return home of an itinerant railroad brake man, Milo, to his wife and son, where they host an evening visit of a bishop and his family, along with Milo's Beat poet friends. Frank's cinematography in this film—grainy black and white images, tilted horizons, atmospheric and spontaneous shots—helped lay the aesthetic groundwork for New American film.

The film title comes from the poem "Pull My Daisy," written by Ginsberg, Kerouac, and Neal Cassady. This poem was put to music by David Amram and sung on the film's soundtrack by Anita Ellis, and its spirit and words permeate the film. The first stanza is:

> Pull my daisy
> tip my cup
> all my doors are open
> Cut my thoughts
> for coconuts
> all my eggs are broken
> Jack my Arden
> gate my shades
> woe my road is spoken
> Silk my garden
> rose my days
> now my prayers awaken
> (Ginsberg, *Selected Poems* 8)

This verse at once recalls and recasts the road metaphors that dominated *On the Road,* where Kerouac had summed up a similar image to describe his vision: "All that old road of the past *unreeling* dizzily as if the cup of life had been overturned and everything gone mad" (emphasis added, *On the Road* 234). Whereas the road stabilized the "wild form" in *On the Road,* the poem "Pull My Daisy" suggests that it is now the film reel itself that offers expressive possibilities for art. The line "woe my road is spoken" may even hint of recognition of the limits of the road story form—it has already been "spoken," or spoken for, and is no longer "open." "Pull My Daisy" implies that the "cup of life" is no longer filled with the "grapes of wrath"—that is, haunted with filmic ghosts like Tom Joad. Rather than return to the past (as Sal realized at the end of *On the Road*), the Beats turn to film and other "intermediary mysteries" to explore the future, hoping to find that mysterious power that would allow them to "suc[k] a sad poem right out of America," as Kerouac had said of Frank's photos in *The Americans.*

The Beat authors' immersion in cinema was part of a larger desire to invent new spontaneous ways of writing. Kerouac advised, "write for the world to read and see yr exact pictures of it" ("Belief" 57). His sense of mystery now overlaps with multimedia images, a fact made apparent in articles he wrote during this period for *Holiday, Esquire, Escapade, Playboy,* and *Nugget.* For instance, in "Beatific: The Origins of the Beat Generation," published in *Playboy* in June 1959, Kerouac had this to say:

> [The Beat Generation] goes back to the inky ditties of old cartoons
> (Krazy Kat with the irrational brick)—to Laurel and Hardy in the
> Foreign Legion—to Count Dracula and his *smile* to Count Dracula
> shivering and hissing back before the Cross—to the Golem horrifying
> the persecutors of the Ghetto—to the quiet sage in a movie about

India, unconcerned about the plot—to the giggling old Tao China-man trotting down the sidewalk of old Clark Gable Shanghai. (71)

Ginsberg also took up Hollywood film images and stars, television, radio, the telephone, and other mass-media images for his poems, as in "I Am a Victim of Telephone" (1964): "Buster Keaton is under the Brooklyn bridge on Frankfurt and Pearl" (*Selected Poems* 141). These examples of "intermedia" show how the Beats worked and re-worked the visual impact of Hollywood films as embodied in "intermediaries" like Buster Keaton, Clark Gable, and Henry Fonda.

Their participation in *Pull My Daisy* signals a transformation of the Beats from passive audience members, which they had been in the Depression as adolescents, to active artists of films. The Beats were no longer individual writers bravely facing Depression ghosts, but collaborative producers finally free of the past. Jonas Mekas—a film critic who was not a Beat—lauded *Pull My Daisy,* especially the ability of Frank's cinematography to "carr[y] life from the *street* to the *screen,*" as a form of spontaneous cinema that "grew out of the postwar realities" (emphasis added, 6). Mekas considered Leslie, Frank, and Kerouac to be "prophets" of a new cinema that would express "its truths, its styles, its messages, and its desperations through the most sensitive of its members" (6). Not only was Mekas championing the film in his columns in the *Village Voice,* but *Life* also mentioned it in a feature story on America's new rebels. *Pull My Daisy* and other films like *Shadows* (dir. John Cassavetes, 1959) catalyzed the "New American Cinema" film movement in the late fifties, which quickly evolved into the underground film movement of the early sixties.

Sexuality, racial romanticization of the *Fellaheen,* and intermediary mysteries fueled the aesthetic and social interventions of the Beats, which they used to repudiate both the populism of the Depression and the persecution of the Mc-Carthy era. Cold war negativity was warmed up by celebrating "that crazy feeling in America when the sun is hot on the streets and music comes out of the jukebox" (Kerouac, *Americans* 5). The Beats brought the road story quite a distance in their travels from the "vast backyard" of bebop America in the late forties, via the green automobile of the imagination, to its full fruition in the wild form of Kerouac's *Visions of Cody.* But by 1959, the leading Beat authors—Kerouac, Ginsberg, Corso, and Burroughs—moved "from the street to the screen," from road stories to intermedia experiments involving film. The dual legacies of the Beats' celebratory road story are its themes of rebellion and automobility. What will get lost in the 1960s, however, as the Beat road story becomes commodified, is its complex interrelationship to the "mysteries" of America's dark side and its motivations for remapping the Depression-era cinemascape with a particularly avant-garde optimism of American writers believing they were creating a new world.

3

TV Gets Hip on *Route 66*

> You'll notice that in ON THE ROAD, unlike the Television cheap imitation of it called "Route 66," there are no fist fights, gun fights or horror of that kind at all.
> —Jack Kerouac, letter to Carroll Brown, 9 May 1961

Halfway into the twentieth century, when suburbs and interstate freeways were being built, rebels like the Beats still believed they could escape the conventionality of the middle classes by avoiding its trappings—especially jobs, wives, and televisions. In his 1960 elegy, "The Vanishing American Hobo," Jack Kerouac notes: "I myself was a hobo but I had to give it up around 1956 because of increasing television stories about the abominableness of strangers with packs passing through" (112). In other words, Kerouac announces that he stopped going on the road "around 1956," just before the publication of *On the Road* (1957), which came after five years of unsuccessful attempts to find a publisher for the novel. Perhaps the appearance of hobos and hipsters on television—and their simultaneous disappearance from the road—made Viking Press and its readers more ready to risk the marginal characters of *On the Road*. Or perhaps the new Interstate 40, funded through the National Highway Act in 1956, helped popularize stories about now-nostalgic adventures on old Route 66 and other American back roads. Yet there is no doubt that television helped demonize abominable hobos *and* popularize the road story in the early 1960s.

While Kerouac was hoping to see *On the Road* made into a movie starring Marlon Brando, he never anticipated that someone else would be so unprincipled as to scoop up his road story and turn it into a television series. In this chapter, we focus on TV's first road program, *Route 66,* shot on location, which appeared on CBS for four seasons—premiering, in fact, early in October 1960, right after one of the famous televised debates of the presidential race between John F. Kennedy and Richard M. Nixon. *Route 66* mirrors the celebratory optimism about the road that the Beats had expressed, although it was predictably more conservative in all ways. In fact, the road story with its hint of Beat rebellion solved a number of problems the television medium was facing in 1960. For TV was growing so rapidly as an industry that programs were often made with too little care about quality and too much reliance on formula and genre—as a consequence, soap operas and Westerns were choking the airwaves and the quiz show scandals of 1959 tainted the entire television environment. Into this wasted cultural space came both John F. Kennedy and *Route 66,* both with an intuitive understanding of how to revitalize the troubled medium.

Soon after he won the election, Kennedy dealt sternly with the TV industry by appointing Newton Minow as chair to the Federal Communication Commission (FCC). In 1961, Minow railed against television's inferior programming by blasting it as a "vast wasteland," invoking T. S. Eliot's famous poem, *The Waste Land* (1922). The symbolism of this modernist masterpiece aptly articulated, as we will see in this chapter, anxieties about the lack of controls in the media marketplace and the cultural impoverishment of TV audiences. Eliot's landscape metaphors of the wasteland fit nicely into Kennedy's reigning Camelot mythology, as both relied upon the central image of rescuing a land from ruin—furthermore, Kennedy often talked of his goals as quests and envisioned the nation in grand, symbolic terms. Thus we will see that landscape metaphors become overdetermined in the early discourses of television; this language affirms what Marshall McLuhan later noted, that media must be understood as an "environment" (26)—and to this analytical vocabulary, this chapter adds the term "mediascape" to refer to the electronic landscape as envisioned by television. Eliot's epic poem became a touchstone for older intellectuals who distrusted the new medium of television and resented the encroachment of the mediascape on the serious spaces of art.[1]

Back in 1956, before the hipster writers were even known as the "Beats," the well-established poet Kenneth Rexroth organized what turned out to be a legendary evening at the San Francisco Six Gallery. That was the night that Allen Ginsberg first read his poem "Howl," a watershed event that brought him to the attention of the literary elite. But by 1960, Rexroth abruptly stopped championing the Beats because of their celebrity status. Rexroth warned that "dissent has become a hot commodity" ("Commercialization" 648). Rexroth's criticism was damning because he had been one of the first influential writers to champion the Beats' "powerful virtues," which he defined in 1957 as "social disengagement, artistic integrity, voluntary poverty." In that earlier assessment, Rexroth had argued that Jack Kerouac "is the most famous 'unpublished' author in America" and that "the avant-garde has not only not ceased to exist. It's jumping all over the place" ("Disengagement" 188, 192–93). Just three years later, Rexroth criticized the now-famous Kerouac for caring that it is a *Cadillac* that his character drives in his novel

> across the country at two hundred and five miles an hour . . . in small
> Iowa towns. . . . Who is this guy working for? I mean values like this
> . . . have nothing to do with a serious separation of the creative artist

from society so that he can gain perspective and work upon the society in a responsible manner.[2] ("Commercialization" 649)

What Rexroth perceives is that the status of the Beats has radically changed between 1956 and 1960, when the once-marginal writers became mainstream celebrities practically overnight. As soon as he became popular with *On the Road,* Kerouac was thrust by the media into the role of spokesperson of the "Beat generation." Kerouac found himself invited to give his opinion on poetry, hobos, television, and the human condition. He began writing for popular magazines and, despite his dislike of the limelight, even appeared on William F. Buckley's *Firing Line, The Steve Allen Show,* and other TV shows. Friend and fellow author John Clellon Holmes observed that *Life* magazine called Ginsberg "the most exciting young poet in America" ("Philosophy" 635) and noted that Kerouac was "treated like Marlon Brando [as] a curiosity, not as a serious man; this inevitably does something to an artist" (Marc 56). In the logic of modernism, in other words, serious artists should not let celebrity go to their heads.

Warning against selling out, Rexroth rages because high modernism's once clear-cut insistence on "art for art's sake" was drastically eroding by 1960—largely because of television. Even during the late 1950s, the intelligentsia took for granted that the divide between profit and protest was inviolable, and they were completely unprepared for the rise of pop art. As is clear to us in the twenty-first century in retrospect, the Beats could not remain at the margins once the media decided they were irresistible, for the televisual culture of the 1960s voraciously sought new content in social eccentrics like the Beats. Another factor breaking down the cultural divide between art and commerce involved the ascendance of the *next* generation of the counterculture, for future hippies began charting out in the early 1960s how they would reject tradition differently from their older Beat mentors, whose road stories were rapidly assimilated into the "mediascape."

ROUTE 66 AS THE INTERSTATE BETWEEN THE BEATS AND THE NEW FRONTIER

To Rexroth and other older intellectuals, this commercialization did not seem inevitable, but dangerous. Rexroth recognized that the new landscape of rebellion had quickly become a territory that Madison Avenue wanted to colonize. Because the literature he had recently championed now seemed formulaic and sensational, Rexroth stoically concluded that the "old forms are obsolete" and "we can no longer afford alienation" ("Commercialization" 649). He believed people were wrongly cashing in with "false merchandise":

An awful lot of people are being deluded. They are thinking that they are reading . . . a trenchant and meaningful indictment of society, and they're just reading cheap sensationalism. It seems to me that all this boxcar, heroin, jungle-drums-in-the-hills literature serves exactly the purpose for the exurbanite father that the cowboy pictures on television serve for his children. They relieve life's tedium. (649)

Although Rexroth does not directly say it, the attitudes of this era suggest that this "exurbanite father" suffers a fate worse than being duped by mercantile novels—namely, this weak man is tied down in domesticity. Dad risks falling prey to the sentimental and melodramatic commodity forms like television genre shows that children—and women, although they are only implied in Rexroth's critique—passively enjoy. To someone who aspired to be hip, being likened to a television viewer in 1960 was a serious insult, one steeped in the Beat disdain expressed in Kerouac's statement: "anybody dont like potry [sic] go home see Television shots of big hatted cow boys being tolerated by kind horses" (*Americans* 9).[3]

The Beats had an avant-garde delight in certain aspects of developing technology, such as film, radio, and the newly available portable tape recorder. Somewhat incongruously, then, the Beats rejected television technology, adamantly aligning TV with the bourgeoisie and rejecting it on that account. Despite their interest in remapping the "cinemascape" of the Depression with the new technologies of their present, the Beats did not trust television to be part of their intermedia experiments, leaving this unexplored medium to the next generation. Beats envisioned the road itself as the antithesis of the domestic television set, that is, as the escape route away from the passive pleasures of home and TV—and the greedy consumer desires of a wife. As Kerouac's novel *The Dharma Bums* (1958) makes clear, the hipster is haunted by "middle-class non-identity which usually finds its perfect expression . . . in rows of well-to-do houses with lawns and television sets in each living room with everybody looking at the same thing and thinking the same thing at the same time" (39). It is the "Daddy-O," in contrast to the "exurbanite father," who flees from the consuming demands of "hag masses," or, as Beat Gregory Corso spells out in his famous poem, "Marriage" (1960):

> a fat Reichian wife screeching over potatoes Get a job!
> And five nose running brats in love with Batman
> And the neighbors all toothless and dry haired
> like those hag masses of the 18th century
> all wanting to come in and watch TV.[4]
>
> (181)

The Beats envisioned themselves as "frontiersmen" who enjoyed the active role of writing poetry and living unfettered: "Dharma Bums refusing to subscribe to the general demand that they consume production and therefore have to work for the privilege of consuming, all that crap they didn't really want anyway such as refrigerators, TV sets" (Kerouac, *Dharma Bums* 97).

The distrust of television among the Beat avant-garde in the early 1960s can be understood by what cultural critic Raymond Williams subsequently pinpointed as television's "deep contradiction" (24)—privatized domestic reception and centralized transmissions, emanating from the three powerful networks that dominated American television in the fifties. During the reign of FBI Director J. Edgar Hoover and Senator Joseph McCarthy (whose anti-Communist hearings were so powerful, in large part, because they were televised), the Beats' place outside the economic, familial, political, and aesthetic mainstream made them justifiably paranoid of centralized transmissions. To the Beats, "Big Brother" might readily use TV to manipulate a brainwashed populace. In his twelve-page poem, "Television Was a Baby Crawling Toward That Deathchamber" (1961), Ginsberg criticizes the "Idiot soap opera horror show we broadcast by Mistake—full of communists and frankenstein cops and mature capitalists running the State Department" (*Selected Poems* 281). Kerouac suspected that TV created conformity: "Real hip swinging cats . . . vanished mightily . . . maybe it was the result of the universalization of Television and nothing else" ("Lamb, No Lion" 560). Between the "hag masses" who passively watched TV and the menacing "State Department," which seemed to control centralized transmissions, television stood for everything the Beats rebelled against.

Clearly, the Beats understood the cinemascape of their past—namely, the Depression-era road films and social realist photography of their youth that influenced their images of the road. What they failed to anticipate, however, was the ongoing evolution of the postwar mediascape, especially the way their own representations of the road and country could be appropriated by others.

For the Beats were not the only ones to grasp the concept of mediated space—television executives recognized the medium's power in the postwar period to create an electronically generated sense of national community. During the 1950s, the networks first laid the coaxial cables that linked the country to New York's (and, later, Hollywood's) centralized television transmissions. This was how television developed from fragmented regional broadcasts and discrete television programs into the brand-new format of nationwide broadcasts. And this was when networks perfected the programming concept of TV "flow" in scheduling shows that attracted and retained audiences, even during the commercials. Viewers were trained to "*stay* tuned" for the entire evening. (These metaphors confirm the spatial dynamics in which television consumption was imagined.) By the late fifties, further technological advances in video helped the networks to suture disparate regions, shot independently in separate locations, into one holistic, on-screen televisual collage of America—a new mediascape unlike anything produced previously by film or by the early days of live TV broadcast, when locations had been limited to the sound stage.

In this "cool" cultural climate of television, then, the series *Route 66* began airing in 1960 as a weekly road story about two non-conforming travelers. As the first series to be filmed entirely on location in a different town each week, CBS'S

Route 66 was an innovative, exciting, even daring adventure in 1960s television programming. Indeed, *Route 66* demonstrates the length to which TV producers went to create new imaginary maps of the nation in these early days of the medium's *commercial* eminence, once it lost some of the cachet of live broadcast, which television promoters had self-importantly likened to Broadway theater. *Route 66* knitted together Beat values and commercial mandates in ways that the masses eagerly consumed. In other words, TV got hip on *Route 66*.

The visual excitement of *Route 66*'s innovative car cinematography, combined with its narrative attention to progressive politics and marginalized communities, helped position *Route 66* as a thematic and aesthetic link between the Beats and the "New Frontier" envisioned by presidential candidate Kennedy. To capture the eyes (and hearts) of the nation, *Route 66* featured two handsome bachelors who combined the non-conformity of the Beats with Kennedy's liberal values regarding the "Quest for National Purpose," a topic dominating media discussions during the 1960 presidential election.[5] The quirky wanderlust of the main characters, Tod and Buz, seemed not only harmless but also hopeful, leading to civic progress and public well-being. *Route 66* positioned these young men as ambassadors of the open road who acted out the role television desired for itself—namely, entering regions and homes whose occupants had been previously suspicious of TV's growing influence. By penetrating hermetic communities and offering new models of masculinity and postwar nationalism, Buz and Tod abetted TV's effort to effect a psychological remapping of America in the early sixties.

As we have already seen, the Westerns designed to attract male viewers were deemed unhip. *Route 66* showed at the prime Friday night spot, when "exurbanite fathers" might be home, watching TV with their families. Once Beats had popularized it as the metaphor of masculine freedom, the road trope offered CBS a way to defray apprehensions that TV was a predominantly "feminine" medium. Female-associated formats like soap operas and commercials about how commodities could transform their lives made people reject television as a wasteland. Now, writers like *Route 66*'s Sterling Silliphant could use the road story to entice family men to watch television, attracting the kind of viewer who envisioned himself as too cool to watch a Western yet hip enough to enjoy *Route 66*'s progressive social content and its focus on automobility. The homosocial highway of this innovative adventure series helped CBS secure TV's promising new demographic frontier—namely, the male and youth markets. *Route 66* naturalized its product placement, moreover, by offering its sponsor Chevrolet a road story based on a Corvette, a status symbol of masculine power and (upward) mobility.

Through the mediation of the series, in other words, the Beat world of jazz, (wander)lust, and adventures popularized by *On the Road* in 1957 could be enjoyed from the comfort and safety of one's own family living room in 1960. Actor George Maharis, playing Buz Murdock, starred in the first two years as *Route 66*'s mercurial force and magnetic attraction. Martin Milner, a veteran child actor always cast in clean-cut roles, co-starred as Tod Stiles (see fig. 6). Similarities between the buddies and the fictional characters of Kerouac (or Kerouac himself), however, stopped at surface characteristics such as Maharis' vague physical resemblance to Kerouac, his affinity for the Method School of acting, and qualities that caused *TV Guide* to describe this black-clad actor as "a rebellious young dissenter in search of a philosophy" ("*Route 66* puts George Maharis" 18). A clear hipster reference, for instance, is found in the series' penchant for dialogue laced with bebop slang, as exemplified in the episode "Play it Glissando" (20 Jan. 1961), in which Buz says:

> "Cool. Like I say to her, baby I don't dig the fuzzy stuff, but the hard bop really knocks me out. Now she tags me for the progressive type. How're you going to gas her if you don't know the difference between a flatted fifth and a raised seventh?"

In fact, *Route 66*'s producer Herbert Leonard vehemently denied that *On the Road* influenced his creation, a claim that seems highly dubious given *Route 66*'s careful attention to detail and its appropriations of Beat style.[6]

Fig. 6. Buz (George Maharis) and Tod (Martin Milner) in the CBS television series *Route 66*. Created and produced by Herbert Leonard and Stirling Silliphant; video copyright © Columbia House Video Library.

Yet, while Buz and Tod talk jive and reject permanent jobs or school, they successfully embody the pop culture contradiction of being responsible mavericks. Unlike the real Beats in *Pull My Daisy* (Robert Frank's 1959 avant-garde film), who overstayed their welcome at a family gathering, Tod and Buz disappeared punctually at the end of the hour, leaving the exurbanite father squarely ensconced in his throne. These "Beat" characters were virtual, not virile. Mainstream, not stream of consciousness, describes the nature of *Route 66,* despite its stylish gestures of dissent.[7]

While the Beats may have been concerned with de-familiarizing the American dream, the *Route 66* series focused on re-*familializing* the American wanderer. *Route 66*'s weekly episodes move Buz and Tod to the edge of Beat-like avant-garde territory; by the end of each hour, however, the show skillfully contains its bachelors within a sentimental family plot. Abandoned as a kid on the streets of Hell's Kitchen, Buz had suffered a childhood that turned him into the dark-haired tough—someone quick to start a fight on behalf of the underdog. In contrast, sandy-haired Tod had enjoyed money and opportunity until his widowed father's sudden death, which left him alone with a bankrupt business and no possessions except the new Corvette. These psychological profiles explain the two men's freedom to move from town to town, and job to job, in the shiny sports car. And despite the men's lack of traditional family structure, their tragic orphan status allows the program's writers to create parental figures out of most of the strangers they meet. Hence, despite all its masculine picaresque intentions, the series primarily focuses on family issues.[8] (After all, Screen Gems' first hit series had been *Father Knows Best,* which aired on CBS beginning in 1952, and it also created *The Donna Reed Show* [C. Anderson 265].)

This showcasing of these two young men who tour viewers around the new national mediascape resonates with the national mood in 1960, with its aura of altruistic political optimism embodied in candidate Kennedy. *Route 66* spoke of healing the societal wounds that give rise to subcultures in the first place—namely, the problems of racism, authoritarianism, and indifference. As in stories of the Depression, the road in *Route 66* once again becomes an iconographic landscape for narratives about reunion, rather than rejection, effectively remapping the Beat values of disengagement, alienation, and anti-commercialism with Kennedy's vision of the "New Frontier."

For instance, the series' pilot, "Black November," implicitly condenses the shameful history of lynching black Americans and interning Japanese Americans with other lingering scars from World War II, then magically resolves the angst within the hour. This debut episode suggests that compassion is the younger generation's solution to the residue of hatred left over from a world war it did not fight. The story begins when Buz and Tod have a minor car accident that requires them to stop over in Garth, a town barred to outsiders for fifteen years (viewers must do the math to realize the town has been sealed off since the end of World War II). Even though they are clearly not welcome in the town, Buz and Tod poke around while the Corvette is being repaired and inevitably uncover the town secret: it had housed a German prisoner of war camp during World War II. Back then, the townsfolk passively stood by while Mr. Garth—the most powerful man in the town, its namesake, owner of all the businesses, and, thus, everyone's employer—lynched two young German prisoners after receiving news that his own son had been killed in battle in Germany. Garth plans on hanging Buz and Tod in a re-creation of the earlier atrocity in order to keep the nosy wanderers quiet. This time, Garth's other son Paul—who, since witnessing the original brutality as a child, has been almost autistic—steps forward and stops his father just as the nooses tighten around Buz and Tod's necks. Paul discovers his inherent masculinity by relinquishing passivity and challenging his father in the name of justice.

Time and again in the first season, *Route 66* asserts its sympathies toward liberal politics. The fantasy of the German prisoner of war camp in "Black November" chiasmatically transposes to the Nazi holocaust the repressed memories of American violence against U.S. citizens of African and Japanese descent. Because it stops the second lynching and surreptitiously refers to the greater horror of Aryan racism, "Black November" creates an allegory about the hopeful healing of America's own racial problems. Airing in the transition period between the Montgomery Bus Boycotts of 1955–56 and the March on Washington of 1963, this initial episode grapples with ways to purge racial hatred by forming a new national identity, one uniquely imagined by the cultural force of television. *Route 66* envisions access to this new world not just for the isolated town of Garth, but for the nation itself, harnessing for its ends a particularly *post*-Beat linkage between heterosexual masculinity and mobility even as it trades on Beat-like signifiers. Rather than repress traumatic wartime memories, or use them to fuel aesthetic and social change, the show invokes them in order to lay the ground for a new chauvinism—an attitude in which national patriotism becomes hip, and road rebels become the type of young men who can uplift family viewers at home.

The "Black November" premiere episode also demonstrates the way the series creates fantasmatic narrative and cinematographic revisions of the Second World War and the Depression to establish itself as progressive. Director Philip Leacock's distinctive visual style directly quotes Depression-era imagery, evident in all the *Route 66* episodes he created. With its static, staged tableaux shots of old men in overalls and young men leaning motionless against fences, "Black November" mirrors the Depression's Farm Service Administration photographs by Dorothea Lange and Walker Evans, sucking them into the mediascape of the 1960s.[9] The mobility of Buz and Tod compared to these older still-photo caricatures clearly distinguishes the young generation moving toward the New Frontier from the over-burdened ghosts of the past.

BEING ON THE ROAD AS A NEW TELEVISUAL MODE OF ADDRESS

These stylistic flourishes emphasize the degree to which *Route 66* used the narrative and cinematographic potential of the road to create for television an emotional, spatial, and temporal psycho-geography of America. Throughout the late 1950s, television experimented with how best to adapt the large-scale blocking used on the theatrical stage and movie set to its smaller scale. *Route 66* truly pioneered the uncharted medium with its range of innovative techniques. Indeed, the newness and hipness of the series' visual trailblazing was as exciting in its time as its narrative attention to marginal characters such as ethnic minorities and rebel women.

As the first series filmed entirely on location, *Route 66* was part of production house Screen Gem's strategy to use "location work to give depth to the little screen" (C. Smith 3) in the period when the corporation became publicly traded on the stock market (C. Anderson 259). Cinematographically, the two young, handsome men sitting in the tight space of a flashy sports car offered a new visual frame uniquely suited to TV's small screen. Filmed through the front window of the Corvette, Buz and Tod sat in close enough proximity to be easily framed together in the same shot; alternately, individual shots of the driver and passenger, each man filling up the frame, could be contrasted in fast-paced editing. The car's relative scale set off the often-dramatic landscape shots, putting into high relief the magnificent height of Arizona mesas, the winding curves of an Oregon mountain stream, or the immensity of Milwaukee factory smokestacks. The dynamism of the sharp focus of a head shot framed by a background that was constantly disappearing in the blur of mobility made for visual excitement, as did the tight shots that featured reflections of lights and shadows off the Corvette's long, luxurious hood. Backed by Nelson Riddle's jazzy score, *Route 66*'s opening sequences are the ancient prototypes of a multimedia mixture that would lead, two decades later, to music videos.

The new cinema vérité style of hand-held cinematography, which the avant-garde filmmakers had recently begun to pioneer, offered another source of cutting-edge visual interest when used in *Route 66*. (Indeed, the vérité documentary *Primary* [1960] by Robert Drew, is set on the road while the two Democratic contenders, Kennedy and Hubert H. Humphrey, campaign in Wisconsin.) In 1960, vérité was new in the art cinema houses, let alone on television, so its use on *Route 66* conveyed Beat-like spontaneity and gave the series a hip sensibility. For example, "The Opponent" (2 June 1961), uses hand-held camera work to open an episode about a has-been boxer who was once a champion and a mentor to a younger, role-model-hungry Buz. By playing off Buz's nonstop emotional reminiscence about his friend, the camera in this *Route 66* episode captures the jostling crowds and vertical skyscrapers of a busy street to give a dynamic sense of the city, keeping time with Buz's staccato-paced monologue. In this way, the aesthetic techniques that originated in documentary and art house film for cost savings became stylistic signifiers of youth, spontaneity, and new vision in *Route 66*.

Furthermore, the series cleverly developed its open road format into a substitute for the immediacy and spontaneity of the esteemed but old-fashioned practice of live transmission. Live broadcasts had been the distinctive quality of the television medium until new telefilm tape technology was developed in the mid-fifties. *Route 66* began airing just as filmed prime time shows in 1959 and 1960 outnumbered those in the live broadcast format—the latter exemplified by such respected dramatic offerings as *Playhouse 90;* this programming shift caused some viewers to worry that TV was losing its authentic, theater-like, serious art qualities to lowbrow "character programs" (Boddy 190). Moreover, the spontaneity inherent in the road trope indirectly counteracted the damage done by the rigged quiz shows, which had cynically abused the spirit of authenticity and immediacy that early TV audiences imbued upon the medium.

The fact that *Route 66* featured a different American town each week lent the show, as television commentator Gilbert Seldes wrote in a *TV Guide* review, a note of "something real" (4). He said of the production team:

> The truth is that *Route 66,* whether it captures the exactly right tone for your city or not, does have a tone of its own. You get the impression that each city does something to the people who go there. . . . [The writers] bring an eye for the place, a curiosity about what makes one city different from another. (4)

Viewers found this change of location to be a compelling mode of address; each week, they could check if that week's featured location corresponded to their personal experience of that particular mediascape. Instead of the *temporal* simultaneity of television's then-disappearing live broadcasts, in other words, *Route 66*'s on-location shooting sutured the audience to the series in *spatial* terms. *Route 66* also adapted the cinematic technique of flashback to its television show, thereby taking advantage of new narrative opportunities that had been considerably more difficult to construct during a live broadcast.[10]

Route 66's unique twist of integrating Chevrolet cars within the story line skillfully addressed the desire of sponsors for input on script content—a once-common practice coming under fire in 1959, as television scandals erupted into the quiz show hearings in Congress. For instance, *Variety* noted that each episode of *Route 66* featured a particular facet of the American economy and lauded the fact that the show provided "an excellent built-in plug for sponsor Chevrolet, by the way" ("Black November" 34). Television critics frequently commented on sponsors' commercials in the early sixties, and Chevrolet's spots consistently received good mentions in the *Route 66* reviews. *Variety* ran a very favorable piece on *Route 66*'s third season premiere, noting "one of the Chevy commercials on Friday's preem was worth singling out," then went on to describe its impressive helicopter camera work ("One Tiger to a Hill" 13). No other show could blend content and commerce in quite such a convincing fashion in 1960. By that time, Chevrolet backed many programs, including *The Dinah Shore Show, My Three Sons, Roy Rogers and Dale Evans,* and *The Chevy Show,* but none incorporated a Chevrolet into a plot as naturally as *Route 66.* Chevrolet provided the starring sports car and most of the other vehicles used in the show. The camera would zoom in on the car radio's Chevy logo whenever its passengers eagerly listen to a news bulletin in the episode, for instance. Often the viewfinder fixed on the car manufacturer's brand insignia as the car moved into the horizon.

Toward the end of its first season, *Route 66* was developing even more dynamic plots and pictorial compositions than it had at the time of its premiere in the fall of 1960. Allusions to the nation's past became less frequent by the spring of 1961. The focus shifted to individuals' attempts to mend personal scars, as the plots moved away from the initial episodes' preoccupation with the nation's need to recover from collective pain. Many of these new episodes reflected liberal moral stands, such as a woman's right to freedom from an abusive husband or her right to be respected as an ethnic minority (both themes are considered in "The Newborn," for instance, which centers on a child conceived when a white man raped an Indian woman). Mirroring both the Beats and liberal politicians, *Route 66* empathizes with subcultures disenfranchised from mainstream society.

The series admirably embraced characters usually harshly stereotyped by television, in large part because these outcasts were safely mediated by the comparatively more wholesome presence of Buz and Tod. For instance, episodes featured a heroin addict who tries to steal the Corvette, then goes cold turkey with Buz's help ("Birdcage on My Foot"); a non-conforming "biker chick" ("How Much a Pound is Albatross?"); an insanely jealous trumpet jazzman ("Play It Glissando"); and, an Edith Piaf-type singer tyrannized by her macho, womanizing manager ("Mon Petit Chou"). In 1961, just one week after television covered the riots that erupted in Mississippi when Governor Barnett attempted to block James Meredith's enrollment at the all-white University of Mississippi, a memorable *Route 66* episode brought together renowned African American jazz musicians Ethel Waters, Coleman Hawkins, and Roy Eldridge in "Good Night, Sweet Blues" (6 Oct. 1961). In the narrative, all the old-timers had played jazz together thirty years earlier and were reunited with the help of Buz and Tod as the last request of the dying singer, Jennie (Waters). Besides the narrative about successful African Americans, this episode boasted striking visual compositions that elegantly allow the music to upstage television's typical plot-driven formula.

These few examples show how the show's creators, writer Stirling Silliphant and producer Herbert B. Leonard, worked to make *Route 66* meaningful. They attempted to offer an alternative to the melodramas and romances that had turned television into what many considered a female-oriented medium; they injected liberal social values into their prime-time plots in a show of sympathy and a bid for relevance.

Yet the representation of social issues brought interference for Silliphant and Leonard from CBS executives, who criticized the deviation from television's reliable romantic formula. The executives' attempt to dictate content was revealed in hearings held in 1962 by the Senate Subcommittee on Juvenile Delinquency.[11] The senators subpoenaed CBS's files of *Route 66*, which revealed that CBS President Jim Aubrey had mandated in private correspondence that *Route 66* contain more "broads, bosoms, and fun" (Barnouw 154). *Route 66* creator Leonard was extremely powerful—he was the second-largest TV producer in Hollywood, at a time when Leonard and Silliphant simultaneously produced the popular *Route 66* and *Naked City;* in 1959, Leonard's shows alone "had earned $22 million in syndication" (C. Anderson 264). Leonard protested Aubrey's interference, especially Aubrey's attempt to make *Route 66* into "'nothing more than an hour situation comedy or an ordinary action show,'" despite the CBS president's threat to discontinue the show if Leonard disregarded "'repeated and emphatic suggestions on the proper approach for this series'" (Watson 50). With such evidence in hand, the Dodd hearings showed numerous ways that CBS tried to control *Route 66,* even though advertisers seemed satisfied with the show (Watson 41). Yet in the face of the "dictates" handed down by CBS president Aubrey, Leonard's adventures in civic engagement yielded to romantic and sexual stereotypes.

The liberal politics of *Route 66* had been an attempt to avoid television's clichéd sexual politics. Because the financial imperatives of early network TV demanded mass audiences, network executives opted to attract them by dictating predictable narratives that tended to deliver larger numbers of viewers. Whereas Silliphant and Leonard tried to use social outcasts as a narrative alternative to romance, the networks' efforts to attract more men relied upon such male-oriented gimmicks as fast cars, macho conflict, and big-busted actresses. Kerouac himself commented on such tactics in 1961, as noted in this chapter's epigraph, calling *Route 66* a "cheap imitation" of *On the Road* because of its "fist fights, gun fights [and] horror of that kind" (Charters, *Letters: 1957–1969* 288). CBS's demand that *Route 66* add rumbles and romance, if not outright sexual titillation, brings us to the "wasteland" phase of TV's gender politics in the early 1960s and to the important cultural work performed in these discourses by metaphors of the road.

KNIGHTS-ERRANT IN AMERICA'S MODERN WASTELAND

As noted above, the premiere of *Route 66* immediately followed the second of the televised "Great Debates" between presidential candidates Nixon and Kennedy on 7 October 1960. In broadcasting live a presidential debate for the first time in history, television began to realize the tremendous power of the new medium, for Kennedy's telegenic presence is now a legendary contrast to Nixon's sweaty face and shifty eyes. In a self-serving editorial, *TV Guide* credited the Great Debate "series" as possibly "the greatest contribution to our democracy by a communications medium since the founding of our country" ("As We See It" 4). In the next paragraph, *TV Guide* predicts that historians will view the 1960 election "as a turning point in the *road to intelligent rather than emotional* voting" (emphasis added), thereby exposing the anxiety surrounding the feminized constituency of the new medium, the legitimacy of television entertainment, and the hope that the broadcast of serious political events might counteract TV's bad reputation.

Election coverage promised to move public perception of television away from a Pandora's box of melodramatic soap operas, corporate meddling, and quiz-show scandals. The goal was to move toward a highly efficient box of rationality—an up-to-the-minute, computerized, futuristic medium capable of expertly and intelligently delivering the nation into the new decade and a new administration. Minutes after Nixon and Kennedy debated domestic political concerns, Buz and Tod carefully tiptoed around TV's more home-bound "domestic" connotations in order to deliver the masculine market desired by Chevrolet and the CBS network. In these ways, *Route 66* is the ideological intersection between the "vast backyard of America" that Kerouac memorialized in *On the Road* and the "New Frontier" that Kennedy envisioned for America during his bid for the presidency.

In making his "New Frontier" pronouncements, candidate Kennedy tapped into the same public craving for meaning and authenticity that had fueled the Beats' experiments in the avant-garde. What Beat poet Lawrence Ferlinghetti characterized in 1958 as the need for "a *new* symbolic western *frontier*" (emphasis added, 49) in his poem "I Am Waiting" uncannily anticipates the rhetoric of Kennedy's New Frontier, even though Kennedy envisioned democratic activism whereas the Beats championed disengagement. Metaphors of the journey and mobility also abound in Kennedy's campaign slogans. In *Life*'s issue on "national purpose," the candidate wrote: "Quest has always been the dominant note of our history, whether a quest for national independence; a quest for personal liberty and economic opportunity on a new continent from which the rest of mankind could take heart and hope" (Kennedy, "Hilltop" 70B). Clearly, Kennedy's metaphors of the heroic quest resonate with the rhetoric of the Camelot myth that will soon empower his presidency as well as the *Waste Land* allusions used by his FCC chairman.

During his 1960 campaign, in an address to the television industry reprinted in *Telefilm Magazine*, Kennedy urged broadcasters "not [to] be afraid to be literate," then predicted "more literate campaign speeches, much as in the Presidential campaign of 1856, when the Republicans sent three brilliant orators around the campaign circuit: William Cullen Bryant, Henry Wadsworth Longfellow and Ralph Waldo Emerson" ("Broadcasting" 27). The most erudite reference to come from the Kennedy administration occurred one year later, after the new president appointed Minow to chair the FCC. It was at the 1961 Annual Convention of National Broadcasters that Minow assessed television as a "vast wasteland." Television had enjoyed unbridled expansion during the 1950s, filling the public airwaves with genre Westerns, soap operas, and corrupt game shows. As a consequence, Minow took the earliest opportunity to condemn the industry, using T. S. Eliot's influential poem *The Waste Land* to describe the mediascape's sterile offerings. His appropriation of the title of Eliot's 1922 poem sums up a typical diagnosis of the ills of television by the intelligentsia of the times, thereby revealing the conflict between elite literary culture, on the one hand, and mass cultural tastes, on the other. Minow's metaphor echoes the same fear expressed by the Beats that broadcast media encouraged conformity and curbed male mobility. However, Minow painted Kennedy's FCC intervention in television programming as if it were a wild West rescue: "broadcast's new frontier" would be "sheriffed," Minow promised, by officials who scorned crass commercialism.[12]

Despite the considerable ideological differences between the two groups, both the Beats and the Kennedy administration used similar rhetorical devices to criticize television via images of quests, democratic vistas, new frontiers, and Manifest Destiny. These landscape metaphors suggest that action and control are key issues, indicating perhaps that these intellectuals imagine only two options for spectators in response to TV's empty offerings—either passive reception or passionate rejection.

Minow's reference to *The Waste Land* has implications, moreover, that extend beyond the title of Eliot's poem.[13] Eliot's post–World War I masterpiece meditates on symbolic frontiers and ponders how to refashion meaning out of "a heap of broken images." The poem stages bitter gender conflicts structured around a frustrated quest theme to show how the power of myth has been fragmented by mass culture and world war. Eliot pits masculinity, which is represented as productive and effective, against a wasteland plagued by women's follies, including female voices of reproach, women's numbed sexual activity, and their mechanistic cravings for commodities. As the quintessential modernist, Eliot set a tone for much of the twentieth century, not only in specific works of literature, but in the aesthetic standards used to assess cultural work. Therefore, criticism from voices as varied as Kerouac and Minow about television suggests that Minow's metaphor of the "wasteland" summed up the era's anxiety about what Beat poet Corso had called "hag masses," namely, a feminized viewing audience intent upon nagging would-be heroes into jobs simply to satisfy their desire to purchase domestic appliances (which were another booming postwar phenomenon). Furthermore, TV critics were likely to perceive the innuendo in Minow's reference since some of them (including Gilbert Seldes and Marshall McLuhan) had originally been Eliot scholars.[14] Because television shared with Kerouac and Kennedy the desire to shape the new symbolic frontier—and with it a "new," which is to say less "feminized," audience—*Route 66*'s producers turned the road into a potent symbol of authenticity, spontaneity, and masculinity, remapping a modernist *and* Beat trope in order to lure the same elusive male viewers whom TV was simultaneously enticing via the more reliable tactics of "broads, bosoms, and fun."

The active, masculine road story becomes a recurring antidote to scenarios of passivity, but even more important is the fact that the road story obfuscates the sexual politics at stake in such literary devices. Women would have to wait for 1964 until a criticism of television's gender policies was voiced by Betty Friedan, who blamed TV for contributing to the "feminine mystique." Friedan said, "Beneath the clichés of the feminine mystique, television plays consciously to this tedium, and to the resentment it engenders—narcotizing woman's very capacity to act and think into a passive, sullen, vengeful impotence" ("Television" 96).[15]

Unconsciously, if not explicitly, the condescending attitudes expressed by Rexroth in 1960 about the "exurbanite father," who is passively glued to the television, resonate with the troubled gender relationships haunting Eliot's *The Waste Land*. Eliot's themes of seduction and hysteria suggest that a similar kind of postwar "gender panic" surfaced in the 1960s among television's predominantly male critics. As exemplified in *TV Guide*'s editorial describing the 1960 election as a contest between "intelligent" versus "emotional" voting, the TV industry responded to such threatening connotations with rhetoric laced with masculine tropes signifying rationality, technology, distance, action, independence, control—and mobility.

Eliot's ongoing influence in the 1950s and 1960s remained considerable, but in case broadcasters had not seen the interviews routinely published in the literary and popular press, *Telefilm Magazine,* a TV trade journal, reprinted his award-winning essay on the "*Frontiers* of Criticism" in January 1961, just four months before Minow's speech (emphasis added, 16). Referring to *The Waste Land* was thus Minow's—and, by implication, the Kennedy administration's—tactic for signaling independence from the powerful television industry, which had been caught in too many corruption scandals. Without TV, of course, Kennedy might not have become the president piloting the quest into the 1960s, since the televised debates and his campaign's TV commercials helped him win the election. But by calling TV a vast wasteland, the Kennedy administration demonstrated to the public that it was neither indebted to nor "feminized" by the industry's deep pockets or its naked genre formula of "broads, bosoms, and fun."

The transition from Beat to the New Frontier values is particularly transparent in the *Route 66* episode about Vicki, the biker chick. Titled "How Much a Pound is Albatross?" (9 Feb. 1962), it starred Julie Newmar (and was written by

Silliphant and directed by David Lowell Rich, a veteran director on *Naked City* and *Route 66*). The episode begins like a cross between the films *The Wild One* and *Rebel Without a Cause* when Vicki single-handedly disturbs the whole town by speeding down Tucson's main streets at over ninety miles per hour, just to enliven a policeman's day. She is treated sympathetically at the police station, despite being a Zen-quoting non-conformist. The fact that the camera reveals a photograph of President Kennedy behind the police chief's chair suggests that this episode is self-consciously attempting to negotiate the gap between the road stories of the 1950s and the New Frontier attitudes of the 1960s. At the end of the episode, when Vicki is finally brought before the judge to account for herself, the patriarch chastises her "bizarre and bohemian behavior" and "dedication to non-conformity" as something that might be expected from "the most recidivist vagrant," but that is "unforgivable" when displayed by a girl with "wealth, education, and advantages available to few." The judge concludes:

> If all of us practiced your lack of restraint, young lady, the very freedom you profess to seek would be destroyed and the maturity we've achieved as an organized society. . . . It's a lovely thing to seek the basic deeper meanings of life, but respect for each other and the law that protects us from each other cannot be flouted.

Clearly, the show comes down on the side of the New Frontier rather than the Beat landscape of rebellion, and it panders to traditional gender roles, which ties it to the "wasteland" gender politics being negotiated in this road story television series.

About a year after Minow's NAB address, Philip Booth wrote an intelligent analysis of *Route 66* in the new scholarly journal, *Television Quarterly,* which picks up on Minow's *Waste Land* allusions. Clearly a fan of the series, Booth notes that Buz and Tod "are, fallibly, modern knights-errant in the *wasteland* of contemporary America, searching for human meaning through the desert stretches and signboard cities of *Route 66*" (emphasis added, 7). Then Booth describes TV as "an adolescent girl" (5), making legible, finally, the unvoiced subtext about the feminine terrain of television, unveiling the gender anxiety being voiced in the widespread use of "wasteland" metaphors in the 1960s. Only by piecing together such fragmented, sublimated sexual innuendo can we recognize how shows like *Route 66* worked to remap the mediascape as a chauvinistic space.

The naked aggressions of TV's gender wars are overtly discussed in another essay, appearing in the exact same issue of *Television Quarterly* to which Booth contributed. In an ironic, insightful, and utterly misogynist analysis titled "TV's Womanless Hero," Joseph Golden observes the trend toward prime time heroes placed in "an essentially womanless society." Golden suggests this is a reaction to what he calls "the conspiracy of women to establish a rigidly matriarchal society" (17). Golden continues: "Clearly, some radical action was needed, not only to keep the trend of man *moving* ahead, but to assure the multi-million television viewers that . . . there were still men who could live simply, live strongly [and be] symbol[s] of a sterner, more patriarchal society than we now enjoy" (emphasis added, 17–18). This reign of patriarchy to which Golden alludes presumably pre-dates the new medium of television now enjoyed by those "exurbanite fathers" who stay home to watch TV shows selected by their wives.

Golden's patriarchal theory of the womanless hero of television pinpoints what many critics of *Route 66* noted even before CBS's Aubrey dictated more "broads, bosoms, and fun."[16] In the first season, Buz and Tod rarely got romantically involved with women, even though they occasionally showed signs of wolf-like interest. The scholarly fan Booth regrets Buz and Tod's "apparent refusal to com-mit themselves to their sexual opposites," despite their "fraternity which left no question of heterosexual aptitude" (9). In contrast, however, his hostile colleague Golden makes an observation that reveals the degree to which he conceived the wifeless or motherless male hero as a tonic to the feminizing force of TV and gynocentric formulae:

> The *Donna Reed Show* type[s] of husband are basically contented men whose romance is limited to occasional flirting with their wives. They are sentimental, not romantic, men, not with a capital "R" at any rate. To qualify as a Romantic Hero—instant or long brewed, a man must hear the sad and enduring echoes of a lost voice, must suffer aching nostalgia, must surrender part of himself forever to the past while valiantly jousting with the present. (14–15)

Golden's description aptly pegs Buz and Tod as Romantics. With its rhetoric of chivalry, Golden's analysis suggests his preoccupation with the flooding, feminiz-ing aspect of TV that threatens to drown men (thereby echoing Eliot's trope of the drowned man and the impotent Fisher King). Like Odysseus strapped to the mast to navigate the treacherous straits where the female sirens sing, Buz and Tod have been lashed, so to speak, to the road story in order to stay manly through the wasteland of prime-time television.[17]

Examples of the show's sexism can be chosen at random, so frequently do they appear in any *Route 66* script that has a love interest; the dialogue clearly demonstrates the gender negotiations at work in television shows aimed at men in the early 1960s. In "How Much a Pound Is Albatross?", for instance, when Buz presents the "biker chick" (Newmar) wearing leather motorcycle pants with an outfit he considers to be more appropriate—a sexy dress—she makes the unlikely transformation into a pussy cat. "When I turn into a girl, I do all kinds of foolish and impulsive things," Vicki purrs, as she rubs seductively against Buz. Later, when Tod is stranded in the desert with Vicki, who still sports her new cocktail dress and precarious high heels, he says, "I'm glad I'm not one of those men who stops feeling like a man when a woman starts acting like a man should." In the end, however, the "blonde tornado" refuses to travel with Buz and Tod and drives into the sunset alone on her motorcycle. Perhaps this is a proto-feminist triumph, but more likely it frees up Buz and Tod for their next Romantic drama.

Most of the time, however, the "tornadoes"—as women are repeatedly referred to in Silliphant's scripts, especially after they deliberately included more sexual references—frequently recover from their insistence on independence and learn to sit nicely between the boys in the Corvette. For instance, in "Love Is a Skinny Kid" (4 April 1962), young Miriam (Tuesday Weld) returns to her hometown to confront her mother for having previously committed her to a mental institution. Buz finally breaks through Miriam's icy shell when he uses this analogy, stated while the two of them listen to frogs croaking in the night air: "The female frog," Buz says, "she doesn't have a voice, except for one cry, 'Help!'" Buz's princely protection of a damsel in distress characterizes the show's toady chivalry toward women. Rather than having the power to liberate the prince metamorphosed into a frog, as in the traditional fairy tale, the girl in *this* particular *Route 66* scenario requires patriarchal protection.

While *Route 66* begins its first season by explicitly using the geopolitics of World War II to ameliorate racist moments in American history, it ends the season through guerrilla tactics to bring men into the mediascape via damsels in tight-fitting dresses and spiked heels. Bachelors Buz and Tod seek the trail that will allow themselves and other "real men" to blaze through television's "wasteland" and, via the prime-time adventure genre, to establish the potency of the medium while generating a fecund mediascape that will generate a cash crop greater than anything the Grail Knight ever dreamed.

The *Route 66* episode "I'm Here to Kill a King" coincides with the shift in television's overall role in the mid-sixties, which then contributed to the eventual demise of *Route 66* and this "wasteland" phase of the 1960s road story. Scheduled for 29 November 1963, the episode's uncanny focus on the plotted murder of a political leader meant "I'm Here to Kill a King" never aired, because President Kennedy was assassinated one week earlier.

In one sense, the debate over television as a "vast wasteland" was rendered irrelevant by Kennedy's death. Television redeemed itself with its stately coverage of the funeral and Vice President Lyndon Johnson's swearing-in. Consequently, FCC Chairman Minow pronounced television to be now "sensitive, mature, and dignified. We always hear that television is a young medium. If so, it grew up in a couple of days" (Castleman and Podrazik 170). The medium no longer needed to justify itself and its formats, as it had when *Route 66* was conceived by Leonard and Silliphant in 1960. Partially as a result of these changes, *Route 66* ended in the spring of 1964 with Tod getting married. Along the way, the program had adapted with the nation's changes. When Maharis left the show in 1963, the series replaced Beat-like Buz with a new sidekick for Tod: Linc Case (Glenn Corbett) was introduced on the 22 March 1963 episode called "Fifty Miles from Home." The mere fact that Case was a Vietnam veteran attests to the fact that the social issues fueling the series were changing.

Yet the cast change from Buz to Linc also gave the network a chance to do some damage control. CBS had originally helped create Maharis's flamboyant personality by touting him as a sexy bachelor. Whereas Maharis's star persona was focused on his sexual availability, his replacement Corbett is represented in *TV Guide* in exactly the terms of an "exurbanite father." The article explains that Corbett's "wife made profound changes" in the formerly reckless ladies' man: "Judy was a pusher, and she knew what was good for Glenn. She wanted to marry him and she did." Judy settled her rebel down with "permanency, a home, and eventually children" (Whitney 12). Corbett also explains that, despite sympathizing with the Birmingham racial protests, he cannot march in support because he might punch somebody. In contrast, the character Buz would have gladly punched someone for being racist or unfair to minorities. The article ends with a quotation from Corbett: "Marriage brought me an ordered life. Television brought me a future" (Whitney 13). Clearly, the Beat sympathies of the early show were entirely whitewashed out of the storyline and erased from the actors by 1963.

In being the first to bring the Beat road trip to the screen—the television screen—Herbert and Leonard demonstrate the problems within the studio system at the time, when Hollywood left the exploding youth market to television and drive-in movie production houses. Kerouac hated *Route 66,* but the series inspired a generation of youngsters who had grown up watching television with their "exurbanite dads" to later fantasize about leaving home. Until MTV produced *Road Rules* in 1995, no subsequent TV show set on the road achieved the longevity or impact enjoyed by *Route 66.* The cool medium and the coolness of the road story kept the Beat version of automobility alive for the future, for reincarnation in other television shows about mobility, including *Then Came Bronson* (1969–70), which aired on NBC for one year. Michael Parks starred in the hour-long drama as a disillusioned young man riding around the country on a motorcycle. A short-lived road story about a widowed father and his two sons, *Three for the Road,* ran from September 1975 to November 1976. By the middle sixties, TV had shifted away from rebels and roads to outer space, with *Star Trek,* whose pilot film was made in 1964 (the series began airing in 1966). Castleman and Podrazik call *Star Trek* a "Wagon Train to the stars" (195), which underscores how outer space shows may have replaced both the Western and the road story as the new quest genre.

Route 66 symbolizes the cultural interstate between the Beat road and Kennedy's Camelot, balancing precariously between the modernist purism of art for art's sake and the commercialized wasteland of television. Sure, Kerouac hated it, but he was struggling to get Hollywood to buy the movie rights to *On the Road* when slick TV producers were able to bring Buz and Tod's road trip to national attention every Friday night. When *Route 66* went off the air in 1964, the format of the road story was squarely part of popular culture, already generating yet another phase of remapping in the hot rod and biker films shown at the drive-in theaters.

Route 66 would be just the first of many road stories following the Beats' stupendous success, and most of the gendered metaphors about commodification will—unfortunately—become relevant again. By 1964, the narrative of the open road was well on its way to becoming a multimedia genre, despite the Beats' resistance to this fact. For the rest of the book, in fact, we will see the road genre cycle between phases of commodification and dissent, between rebels who remap its original utopianism and slick producers who capitalize on the profitability of the rebel image. In fact, the cycles themselves are part of the genre, something our theories must accommodate, for they are part of what attracts minority storytellers and major studios back, again and again, to the autonomy and mobility of the road story.

4
Kesey's Quixotic Acid Road Film

"WE BLEW IT!" (368)
　　　　—Tom Wolfe, *The Electric Kool-Aid Acid Test* (1968)

"We blew it."
　　　　—Captain America (Peter Fonda), *Easy Rider* (1969)

In the early days of the psychedelic era, Timothy Leary championed Hermann Hesse's *The Journey to the East* (1932) as "the history of a real-life psychedelic brotherhood" (186), for Hesse is known to have experimented with drugs. Following Leary's lead, devotees of psychedelic or hippie experiments tucked Hesse's novel into their knapsacks alongside *On the Road* (1957) or *The Doors of Perception* (1954) by Aldous Huxley before heading down the highway in search of a countercultural community. And of course the most famous of psychedelic brotherhoods—Ken Kesey and the Merry Pranksters—read it as they planned their own bus trip east in 1964:

> There is another book in the shelf in Kesey's living room that everybody seems to look at, a little book called *The Journey to the East,* by Hermann Hesse. Hesse wrote it in 1932 and yet . . . *the synch!* . . . it is a book about . . . exactly . . . the Pranksters! And the great bus trip of 1964! [. . .] It was like the man had been on acid himself and was *on the bus."* (emphasis in original, Wolfe, *Electric* 128)

One goal of the Pranksters' road trip was to expand their expressive possibilities by making a film while on the road, to push further than the novel in order to break through to new expressive and artistic forms. The larger historical and cultural significance of this film, *The Merry Pranksters Search for the Kool Place,* has been overlooked because it was never finished.[1] Kesey spent thirty years and hundreds of thousands of dollars trying to edit it but never quite got the sound to synchronize with the film. Consequently, Tom Wolfe's New Journalistic account *The Electric Kool-Aid Acid Test* (1968) colors all understanding of Kesey and the Pranksters' road film. Yet it turns out that Hesse's *The Journey to the East* predicted precisely the troubles the Pranksters would face in failing to tell their own story of their journey east.

By following here the film's evolution and influence, both as a countercultural film as well as a road story, we shall discover that it played a pivotal role in lacing the Beat-era road trip with the hippie-era acid trip, quite possibly influencing the Beatles' *Magical Mystery Tour* in 1967 and perhaps even *Easy Rider* in 1969. Since what we know about *The Merry Pranksters Search for the Kool Place* comes from Wolfe, we will see that Wolfe's own writing was shaped by Hesse's and Kerouac's novels, thus creating a hybrid road story that is crucial to the postwar history of the American road genre.

On this trip, the Beat belief in being *on the road* evolved into the Prankster philosophy of being *on the bus,* where that next generation mixed Allen Ginsberg's howls with Timothy Leary's highs and aimed postwar avant-garde innovations toward Marshall McLuhan's galaxies. The word "trip" took on a double meaning that was part of the era's playfulness with language—to travel as well as to take LSD or to blow one's mind. In the Pranksters' league, the two became one. They painted the bus they named "Furthur" in DayGlo colors, then Kesey and a dozen Pranksters embarked on 14 June 1964, journeying east from their La Honda, California, commune to the World's Fair in New York City (with a stop at Leary's psychedelic brotherhood at Millbrook, as seen in fig. 7). They were driven by the famous Beat insider, Neal Cassady, the one who had inspired Kerouac to create his character Dean Moriarity in *On the Road.* The Pranksters hoped the film would help the masses to seek higher consciousness and thereby enhance human potential. Instead, the sheer magnitude of Kesey's Sisyphean efforts to finish the film created the impact he had hoped the film itself would have. Although *The Merry Pranksters Search for the Kool Place* was never fully finished, it nevertheless stands as a testament to the 1960s' utopic visions of expression, enlightenment, and experiment.

Of the many uncanny parallels between Hesse's *The Journey to the East* and the Pranksters' drive to New York in 1964, none is more resounding than the struggle to tell the *story* of a transformative journey. The road trip, for the Pranksters, was an exercise in "living art," which therefore made it elusive to represent retrospectively in either words or film, even though all the action was filmed "in the now." How to craft the document of those past moments was a conundrum they never solved. Likewise, *The Journey to the East* is narrated by the traveler named only "H.H.," who was once an initiate to the secrets of "The League" and a pilgrim on the famous Journey. Decades later, realizing the hollowness of the life he had led after leaving the brotherhood, Hesse's narrator desires to write the history of the League's trip. Reflected in the narrator's struggle to put into mere words the wealth of experiences he had faced, we find Hesse's poignant message about the difficulties of expressing the insights one gains on the road or during enlightenment. In retrospect, this narrator asks:

Fig. 7. Timothy Leary and Neal Cassady on the Merry Pranksters' bus, named "Furthur," in 1964. Photo, Allen Ginsberg; reprinted with permission from Allen Ginsberg Trust.

> But how can it be told, this tale of a unique journey, of a unique communion of minds, of such a wonderfully exalted and spiritual life? I should like so very much, as one of the last survivors of our community, to save some record of our great cause. . . . the images and memories of which will disappear with him if he is not successful in passing some of them on to posterity by means of word or picture, tale or song. But through what expedient is it possible to tell the story of the Journey to the East? (46)

In 1964, the Pranksters were confident of how they would tell their story, for they felt sure that tape recorders and film cameras would enable them to harness the truly spontaneous expressions and new forms of meaning they would experience on their journey. But like Hesse's narrator, they found the task to be far less straightforward than they had imagined. And so, forty years after their famous bus trip, the Pranksters still struggle to pass on to posterity their own road story, to add their voices to the masterful account by Tom Wolfe in *The Electric Kool-Aid Acid Test*.

Throughout the bus trip, the Pranksters filmed everything, for they believed *The Merry Pranksters Search for the Kool Place* would revolutionize everyone—squares and heads. And why not? Kesey was a breakthrough writer with his best-selling 1962 novel, *One Flew Over the Cuckoo's Nest,* which was made into a Broadway play in 1963, plus he was on the verge of publishing his second novel, *Sometimes a Great Notion* (1964). His artistic and financial successes emboldened him to set the goal of going *beyond* the novel, working collectively with the Pranksters in film as a way of escaping the constraints of writing, somewhat as the Beats did in 1959 when collaborating on the art film, *Pull My Daisy.* The Pranksters intended to make

> the world's first acid film, taken under conditions of total spontane-
> ity barreling through the heartlands of America, recording all *now,*
> in the moment. The current fantasy was . . . a total breakthrough in
> terms of expression . . . but also something that would amaze and
> delight many multitudes, a movie that could be shown commercially
> as well as in the esoteric world of the heads. (ellipses and emphasis in
> original, Wolfe, *Electric* 122)

Prankster Paul Perry described it thus: "With this film, the Pranksters set about, as one of their tribal songs went, to 'change the course of time'—and perhaps someday earn some pranking capital" (Perry and Babbs 47). In the sixties, it did not seem naïve to believe that film used by creative and enlightened people could revolutionize mainstream expression. The hippie generation was less vulnerable to modernism's moral separation of art from commerce; this was, after all, the era when Andy Warhol's pop art was becoming influential and radical breakthroughs were being sought.

What we do know about the great bus journey of 1964 thus comes mostly from Tom Wolfe's account of the Pranksters, first published in two Sunday newspaper articles in January and February 1967, then as the finished book *The Electric Kool-Aid Acid Test* in August 1968. Wolfe's account is the definitive record of the Pranksters' road story; without it, the great Prankster journey of 1964 would never have become as important as it is. Even Kesey's son Zane admits he used Wolfe's book to keep track of the stories his father told him.[2]

Yet *The Electric Kool-Aid Acid Test,* Wolfe's shining triumph of "New Journalism," is boon and bane to the Pranksters—and to scholars—because it is, after all, only one person's perspective. Wolfe was never "on the bus" physically or psychedelically, yet he was, like Kesey, an aspiring writer seeking to surpass the novel. His ambitions for writing may have been far less utopic than Kesey's and the Pranksters', but Wolfe succeeded in his goals to go beyond the novel when he helped create "New Journalism," a distinctive new style of writing. *The Electric Kool-Aid Acid Test* has gone into over thirty printings, has been translated into more than a dozen languages, and has revolutionized several genres of writing. Thanks to Wolfe, not Kesey, strangers understand that to be "on the bus" means to have awareness, to be among "those who had had the experience of being vessels of the divine" (Wolfe, *Electric* 116).

Guests at Prankster events might have glimpsed segments of *The Merry Pranksters Search for the Kool Place,* but the public did not have access to these film archives until 1998, when Kesey made them available for sale over the Internet.[3] The task of editing forty-five hours of film had been technically overwhelming until the nineties when nonlinear digital editing became available. The problem was synching up the sound with the visual—the 16 mm camera had run on battery power, but the reel-to-reel audio had been hooked up to the bus's generator, making the two recordings run at different speeds.[4]

During the psychedelic years, making a finished product did not matter much to the Pranksters, nor did the dominance of Wolfe's account. After all, Leary once chided:

> Many who have made direct contact with the life process through a psychedelic or spontaneous mystical experience find themselves yearning for a social structure. Some external form to do justice to transcendental experiences. Hermann Hesse again provides us with the esoteric instructions. Look within. The league is within. So is the 2-billion-year-old historical archive, your brain. Play it out with those who will dance with you, but remember, the external differentiating forms are illusory. The union is internal. The league is in and around you at all times. (188)

Now that they are senior citizens and Kesey has died, the Pranksters are still dancing, but they also recognize the mortality of the *brains* that had been on the bus (after all, even Leary had his brain frozen at his death for the sake of posterity). Unlike human brains, it is clear, the archive does not merely evolve—it must be shaped, fed by first-person accounts as well as retrospective insights. While their artistic anarchism has distinguished them throughout the years, it meant that someone else was always telling the Pranksters' story or was inspired to create new stories by their example. Like Hesse's narrator H.H., the Pranksters finally recognized by the 1990s that "the creations of poetry [may be] more vivid and real than the poets themselves" (Hesse 118). Today, the Pranksters have lawyers—not to bail them out after a drug bust, but to negotiate copyrights, permissions, and licensing fees. Since 1990, they have been selling road stories of their own.[5]

In 1990, Pranksters Paul Perry and Ken Babbs published a retrospective retelling of the 1964 journey, *On the Bus: The Complete Guide to the Legendary Trip of Ken Kesey and the Merry Pranksters and the Birth of the Counterculture.* Promoted in conjunction with the twenty-fifth anniversary of *The Electric Kool-Aid Acid Test,*

Perry and Babbs's book builds on the images and tropes of Wolfe's work rather than challenging them. It offers a valuable adjunct to Wolfe's account, a chance to see familiar stories from different perspectives. In addition to oral histories of the participants and excerpts from previously published material, *On the Bus* offers a wealth of color photographs by Prankster Ron "Hassler" Bevirt, Allen Ginsberg, Gene Anthony, Ted Streshinsky, and others, as well as forewords by Hunter S. Thompson and Jerry Garcia. Timed in conjunction with Thunder Mouth Press's publication of *On the Bus,* Viking simultaneously released Kesey's *The Furthur Inquiry,* a screenplay in the form of a mock trial of Neal Cassady that includes stills from the film footage of the 1964 bus trip, supplemented with photos by Ron Bevirt. Even more important to scholars or devotees of the Pranksters, videos of the trip have been available for purchase since about 1998 from Kesey's home in Eugene, via Key-Z Productions' web site.[6] Kesey, his son Zane, Prankster Ken Babbs, and Babbs's son Simon edited two episodes based on the 1964 bus trip footage, and a third is expected.[7]

Episode 1 of the Key-Z videos is titled "A Journey to the East," linking once again to Hesse and underscoring the fact that road stories are always in dialogue with those that preceded them—not only for the Pranksters, but for all of us. Rather than seeing road trips as discrete events, we must consider the vast constellation of road stories—the influence of *Journey to the East* and *On the Road* (as well as *The Electric Kool-Aid Acid Test*) on the Pranksters' plans for *The Merry Pranksters Search for the Kool Place*—and then that quixotic project's effect on the acid road films that were finished in the sixties, namely *Magical Mystery Tour* and *Easy Rider.* The belated availability of memoirs and videos made by the Pranksters raises questions about the privilege and place of the pilgrim in telling the story: in what ways does the original participant-observer have a greater right or responsibility to tell the story than an outsider? How valid is the contribution made by a journalist (or a scholar) to articulate a counterculture's attempts to speak against the norm, especially if—as with the Pranksters—the rebels are unable or unwilling to do so? What sort of story comes from the moment, and what comes in retrospect, driven perhaps by nostalgia or profit? Finally, how can we understand the impact of Kesey's dream, Wolfe's writing, or the acid road film if we remain stuck within academic disciplines rather than considering the interconnections of film, fiction, and prose? We will not fully appreciate the intermixing of these accounts until we recognize the affinities between all of these texts.[8]

FROM KEROUAC'S "BOOKMOVIE" TO KESEY'S "CINEMA NOVEL"

Each generation remaps the road stories it inherits from its elders. Yet Kesey faced the most powerful predecessor of the postwar years—Jack Kerouac—whose style in *On the Road* so revolutionized writing that up-and-coming avant-garde authors expected that they too would make rebellious breakthroughs in form. The roots of the Merry Pranksters' 1964 road trip reach back to Kerouac's 1957 novel as well as to his search for techniques that would overcome the limitations of syntax and narrative.

In 1958, Kesey began his first novel, *Zoo,* about the North Beach Beat scene told from the viewpoint of a rodeo rider's son; he continued working on this homage to the Beat lifestyle during his first year as a Woodrow Wilson Fellow in the Stanford Writing Program.[9] Understandably, Kesey built upon the postwar modernism of the Beats, which encompassed techniques like using drugs to alter consciousness in order to write freely as well as relying on tape recorders and film cameras to capture words uttered freely. (Many do not realize that Kerouac had used tape recorders for sections of *Visions of Cody,* as well as in the making of the short film, *Pull My Daisy*). In 1959 Kerouac outlined in *Evergreen Review* his hope of finding both a "belief" and "technique" to revitalize modern prose. Toward that end, he proposed the "bookmovie" as a model for writers to create "the movie in words, the visual American form" ("Belief" 57).

But Kesey pushed further; equipped with LSD and Marshall McLuhan's theories about hot and cool media, he catapulted Kerouac's writing rebellions into the 1960s. Leaving behind Kerouac's open road to create the closed psychiatric ward of Patrick McMurphy, Nurse Ratchett, and Chief Broom, Kesey found in lysergic acid diethylamide the breakthrough he had once sought in the Beats' techniques. During the summer of 1959, as is legendary, Kesey volunteered at the Veterans Hospital in Menlo Park as a human subject for experiments with psychedelic drugs. Kesey also worked there at night as an orderly in the psychiatric ward. This is where he situated his new work, which he had begun calling *One Flew Over the Cuckoo's Nest,* and which he continued to work on in Malcolm Cowley's writing class when the fall school semester resumed.[10] By the time Kesey graduated from the Stanford program, he was already on the road to success with this novel. Thanks to the royalties from *One Flew Over the Cuckoo's Nest,* Kesey could support a community of artists and free spirits—they called themselves the Merry Pranksters—dedicated to exploring new avenues of literary expression and mental expansion.

On the book jacket of *One Flew Over the Cuckoo's Nest* Kerouac offered an enthusiastic blurb about the novel and predicted that the young author was "a great new American novelist." Kerouac could not have guessed, however, that Kesey would replace him with breathtaking rapidity as the new guru of the postwar's avant-garde novel. Kerouac's heavy drinking in the years before his death in 1969 only hastened his retreat from the literary scene. Kesey's role as heir apparent to Kerouac was secured symbolically when Neal Cassady joined the Pranksters as driver of the bus Furthur. Prankster Ken Babbs, nicknamed the "Intrepid Traveler," notes:

> The Psychedelic Revolution was flooding the whole universe, not just a few acid minds, a medium through which the wavelength travels. The torch had been passed from the Beat to the Psychedelic, with Cassady as the driver, the tour guide, the swing man, foot in both eras, the flame passing from Kerouac to Kesey. (Perry and Babbs 85)

During the sixties, Beat poet Allen Ginsberg often joined the Merry Pranksters, keeping apace with their psychedelic experiments. Kerouac was the only one of the Beats who did not flow from the 1950s to the 1960s with the Pranksters, as is painfully obvious when watching the footage in episode 2 of the Key-Z Production's video, "North to Madhattan," when the Pranksters join Kerouac, Ginsberg, Leary, and others at Millbrook. Onscreen, Kerouac is visibly angered by the pranks and psychedelic energies of Furthur's passengers and confused by the fact that they wore the American flag as costume.

On that bus trip of 1964, Kesey and his collaborators planned to progress postwar writing from Beat experiments in literature to new expressions of voice and chance through their road movie. They found magic in electric interfaces—those in the brain that could be altered by LSD as well as those on film and audio tape—which they used to challenge the novel as an artistic form. For instance, as Leary noted, it was "historically inevitable" that the "modern technology producing psychedelic drugs mass-market" should combine with "electronic amplification of sound" (Perry and Babbs xix). Clearly, Kerouac's progressive 1959 idea about "bookmovie" held little relevance by 1964 for a generation raised watching television. Rather than flaunting "'individual personal expression,'" the "new sensibility" was "drawing on the popular arts. . . . A new non-literary culture exists today," argued journalist Susan Sontag in 1965 (298). The Pranksters wanted to capture life via recording devices rather than plodding through techniques to aid them in writing spontaneously. Babbs describes the transition from novel to film experienced by Kesey's mobile community:

> Before the bus trip we were talking about "rapping" novels out instead of typing—because typing is so slow. We were going to take acid and stay up all night and rap out novels and tape record them. . . . Finally, we started talking about getting the movie cameras and filming it. So we were very swiftly going from a novel on a page to novels on audio-tape to novels on film. (Perry and Babbs 90)

Instead of settling for Kerouac's techniques of the "bookmovie," Kesey advocated what he called the "cinema novel," since he was far less optimistic than Kerouac about the malleability of narrative: "'Writers . . . are trapped by artificial rules,'" Kesey declared in an interview, "'We are trapped in syntax'" (Wolfe, *Electric* 136).

The Pranksters immersed themselves in new media, a fact that symbolizes the further shift during the sixties from Beat *techniques* to psychedelic *technologies,* a move away from the modernism of Kerouac's road narratives to the wilder energies of psychedelic "trips" as a better way to find an authentic voice. Kesey said:

> I found that no matter how hard I tried to find new areas of my mind or another person's mind in my writing, I would be walking through territory and see that there is Shakespeare's sign. . . . He set a standard and everything since then has been redoing the same thing, with just changing the plots and the emotional play just a little bit. . . . So I started going out and taping with tape recorders and filming, and going back to look over what I had filmed and taped to see if people talked like they did in novels, and they don't. A tape-recorded conversation doesn't look like anything you read. A moment-to-moment account of what goes on doesn't look like any novel that you come across. (Perry and Babbs 58)

Echoing some of the same values espoused in the fifties by Kerouac, Prankster Ron Bevirt said: "The filming was all kind of connected to some of our evolved philosophy, which was simply trying to 'be in the now.' We were trying to be spontaneous and record things as they spontaneously occurred" (Perry and Babbs 56). Where they differed from earlier innovators was in their total reliance on film. Searching for "something wilder and weirder out on the road" than Kerouac had known (Wolfe, *Electric* 90), they captured "the U.S. nation stream[ing] across the windshield like one of those goddamned Cinemascope landscape cameras that winds up your optic nerves like the rubber band in a toy airplane" (Wolfe, *Electric* 92).

For Kesey and his creative collaborators, the road story needed retelling, not because the road had lost its meaning but because the road *novel* had. The Pranksters wanted to enlighten others, not only through LSD and their "acid tests" but also through America's primary mechanism of altered consciousness—the movies. Rather than abandon the road story as an art form, they tried to push expression to do double duty, that is, to revitalize the road trip by means of the acid trip. Two trends helped transform Kerouac's artistic aspirations to the psychedelic age; first, the perpetuation of Beat faith in spontaneity as the means by which one could find new art forms, and second, a similar reliance on new media to capture spontaneous expression, using technology that the Beats had only begun to pioneer in 1959 with their art film *Pull My Daisy,* in order to find the authentic voice that Kerouac had long sought. The Pranksters embraced all broadcast media, even television, as capable of generating revolutionary perceptions for masses of people—as long as artists like themselves intervened. Six years before he died, Kesey continued to feel this way: "The novel is a noble, classic form but it doesn't have the juice it used to. If Shakespeare were alive today he'd be writing soap opera . . . or experimenting with video. That's where the audience is" (Faggen).

Although Leary had pioneered psychedelic drug use, the Pranksters wanted to discover its creative possibilities. Leary was an analytical scientist, whereas they were extroverted artists. By building on Kerouac's road, they were also disproving Leary's typically ascetic comment, "External migration as a way of finding a place where you can drop out and turn on and then tune in to the environment is no longer possible. The only place to go is in" (356). The Pranksters wanted both journey and insight, the chance to *prank* out in the world rather than staying sequestered in some quasi-spiritual community that focused only on the mind. The Pranksters wanted to go out in order to turn others on.

The Pranksters had caught underground films at Midnight Movies whenever they visited San Francisco or Los Angeles.[11] However, despite having this exposure to experimental films, they did not adopt the techniques of auteurs like San Francisco's Bruce Baillie, New York's Stan Brakhage, or Los Angeles's Bruce Connors, who were then challenging Hollywood values with their artisinal, experimental, structural filmmaking. The Pranksters' goal with *The Merry Pranksters Search for the Kool Place* seems to have been to tell a relatively conventional narrative (even if fantastical) based on their road trip rather than to question the established formal elements of narrative filmmaking, as were the underground film artists of the day. Thus they were challenged when faced with forty-five hours of poorly shot footage. Rather than using voice-over the way Kerouac had in his art film *Pull My Daisy,* the Pranksters were stumped by not being able to synch the audio tape with the film footage. In addition, much of it was out of focus. The main camera person had been stoned, or the bus had been moving, or random people had picked up the camera erratically. Furthermore, there were few establishing shots, in keeping with the new aesthetics of rebellion: "But who needs that old Hollywood thing of long shot, medium shot, close-up, and the careful cuts and wipes and pans and dolly in and dolly out, the old bullshit" (Wolfe, *Electric* 122).

But it seems that Kesey did secretly crave that "Hollywood thing" of power and creative control, for he visited Hollywood studio executives several times in search of a deal.[12] Furthermore, he periodically hired professionals to help him edit *The Merry Pranksters Search for the Kool Place;* we will see that Wolfe recounts how Kesey hired Norman Hartweg to edit the film, plus the Pranksters recall that Kesey later hired others to help.[13] Despite their own bravado and the input of experienced editors, the Pranksters could not make the footage work as a (Hollywood) film, nor did they seem to want to revolutionize film praxis as did the underground filmmakers. They wanted to be profitable and popular, too.

After returning from the bus trip, the film initially seemed to be a productive creative challenge. Kesey made his artistic investment clear: "First, let me make it understood I am not a writer. I haven't written anything since I wrote those last drafts of *Notion* and I don't intend to write anything else. I have many reasons for this, the main one being that to continue writing would mean that I couldn't continue my work [on the film]" (Perry and Babbs 55).

Babbs added: "Kesey's mind was on a different medium—film. Time was being spent trying to make sense of the 45 hours of film that had been shot on the bus trip. Not only were we tripping on acid, but we were tripping on film, too" (Perry and Babbs 124). Despite the fantasy of making their acid film a "commercial success," with Kesey investing at least "$103,000 of his own money on the movie" (Perry and Babbs 59, 110), the Pranksters had little to lose even if they failed to finish the project. In contrast to filmmakers like Bruce Baillie and Kenneth Anger, who made considerable financial sacrifices in order to produce their underground films, the Pranksters faced few negative consequences from shooting thousands of dollars of unusable footage, thanks to Kesey's seemingly limitless royalties and the era's aesthetic philosophy of experimentation, which did not consider the creation of a legacy or a product to be a priority.

Hence the preeminence of Wolfe's *The Electric Kool-Aid Acid Test.*

WOLFE GOES BEYOND THE NOVEL WITH NEW JOURNALISM

When asked by Robert Faggen in 1994 what he thought of Wolfe's account, Kesey remembers: "I had no major problems with the book then, though I haven't looked at it since." While none of the Pranksters speak badly of Wolfe, neither do they seem to embrace his account. Kesey added, "It's his memory and not mine."

But Wolfe's account reads as if it *is* Kesey's memory as well as the Pranksters', for Wolfe gets inside all their heads, communicating their thoughts, doubts, visions. In writing *The Electric Kool-Aid Acid Test,* Wolfe says he tried to "re-create the mental atmosphere or subjectivity reality" (*Electric* 371). Indeed, this is his signature style—making innovations in words and mercurial shifts in perspective that were inspired by having embedded himself with the Pranksters in 1966, two years after the bus trip. Yet Wolfe's New Journalism covertly competes against Kesey's writing experiments in the "cinema-novel," as becomes clear by close readings of Wolfe's work. Because Wolfe's descriptions of Kesey's film most likely affected the Beatles' *Magical Mystery Tour* and possibly even Terry Southern's contribution to *Easy Rider,* we see in this section how Wolfe—more than Kesey—remapped Kerouac's *On the Road,* turning Kesey's artistic failures into his own writerly accomplishments. To Wolfe, Kesey becomes his equivalent of Kerouac's Cassady—the muse too busy living life to write. Without Wolfe's powerful writing style and homage to Kerouac, Kesey's dream of the acid road film may not have had the significance it does in fact have on the evolution of the postwar road story.

Wolfe explored his nascent new style of writing with the Pranksters, for their communal lifestyle and sense of acid-like "mutual consciousness, intersubjectivity" (Wolfe, *Electric* 53) made them openly accept strangers. Wolfe had the access he needed to write with an ethnographer's intimacy. In these efforts, he had Kesey's considerable help (Wolfe, *Electric* 371), thus making Kesey's comment to Faggen (above) a bit disingenuous, but also showing how Prankster attitudes changed toward Wolfe's book over time. In addition to talking extensively with Kesey and each Prankster, as he acknowledges in his "Author's Notes," Wolfe used "the Prankster Archives in the form of tapes, diaries, letters photographs and the 40-hour movie of the bus trip" (*Electric* 371). Clearly, his opportunity to preview the film afforded Wolfe the insider's view that gives *The Electric Kool-Aid Acid Test* its juice.[14]

Now that the videos are available through Key-Z Productions, it is clear that Wolfe captured the scenes so aptly in words that the long-unavailable film footage seems nearly redundant. Episode 1 of the videos, for instance, the one titled "Journey to the East," depicts the famous scene of Gretchen Fetchin the Slime Queen, which was the first "acid of the trip [and] their first major movie production." The bus had stopped at Wikieup, "an old Wild West oasis out in the Arizona desert along Route 60" (Wolfe, *Electric* 66). Actually seeing it on video feels so familiar, because Wolfe really did succeed in inventing a new style of writing to "capture the now" and to provide readers with a literary contact high:

> the three of them, Babbs, Kesey and Paula, go running and kicking and screaming toward the lake and she dives in—and comes up with her head covered in muck and great kelpy strands of green pond slime—and beaming in a way that practically radiates out over the face of the lake and the desert. She has surfaced euphoric—
>
> "Oooooh! It sparkles!"
>
> —pulling her long strands of slime-slithering hair outward with her hands and grokking and freaking over it—
>
> "Oooooh! It sparkles!"
>
> —the beads of water on her slime strands are like diamonds to her, and everybody feels her feeling at once, even Sandy—
>
> "Oooooh! It sparkles!"
>
> —surfaced euphoric! euphorically garlanded in long greasy garlands of pond slime, the happiest slime freak in the West—
>
> —and Babbs is euphoric for her—
>
> "Gretchen Fetchin the Slime Queen" he yells and waves his cane at the sky.
>
> "Oooooh! It sparkles!" (*Electric* 67)

In truth, Wolfe's words transform the shaky home movie into mind-expanding text, masterful in catching the moment and creating euphoria from the mundane.

What the videos *do* offer that no words can convey is Neal Cassady's personality and manic monologues. Although Wolfe tries to capture them in words, it is a far different experience to actually see and hear them on video. Cassady's rap transformed the Pranksters' experiences into adventures. Watching the videos, one can imagine how his constant murmurings and non sequitur pronouncements made each Prankster feel as if she or he was in a movie; in contrast, Wolfe could not convey this feeling merely by saying, "They were all now characters in their own movies or the Big Movie" (*Electric* 69). Still, despite a thirty-year anticipation, the video releases of *The Merry Pranksters Search for the Kool Place* add only minute details to the archive offered by Wolfe's account. No new revelations. No big surprises. Just an animation of the stories Wolfe had written down so many years ago.

There is no doubt about it, Wolfe's writing sparkles, and *The Electric Kool-Aid Acid Test* is a fabulous account, with the added bonus that Wolfe had been meticulous as a journalist to consult the archive as well as to bring it to life. Wolfe also makes the Pranksters into the stars of their movie in ways they could not have accomplished themselves. Wolfe's style gives readers the impression of being there on the bus, largely because Wolfe was able to create what Kerouac had described as "bookmovie," his "movie in words, the visual American form" ("Belief" 57).

Although Kesey downplayed the influence of Kerouac on his own writing style,[15] Wolfe never did. Wolfe credits the Beats for inspiration: "I was one year short of the beatnik era" (*New Journalism* 26). In fact, although we have seen that Babbs talked about Cassady as being the "swing man, foot in both eras" (Perry and Babbs 85), that title rightly belongs to Wolfe. His description of how he wrote his 1963 breakthrough article, "There Goes [Varoom! Varoom!] That Kandy-Kolored Tangerine-Flake Streamline Baby," sounds exactly like Kerouac's own methods for writing modern prose:

> I just started typing away . . . I just started recording it all, and inside of a couple of hours, typing along like a madman, I could tell that something was beginning to happen. By midnight this . . . was twenty pages long and I was still typing like a maniac. About 2 AM or something like that I turned on WABC, a radio station that plays rock and roll music all night long, and got a little more manic. I wrapped up . . . about 6:15 AM, and by this time it was 49 pages long. (*Kandy-Kolored* 4)

Wolfe here embodies Kerouac's famous advice from 1958's "Essentials of Spontaneous Prose": "Time being of the essence in the purity of speech, sketching language is undisturbed flow from the mind of personal secret ideas words, *blowing* (as per jazz musician) on subject of image" (72). Wolfe's account of "recording it all" during an all-night stint while listening to the midnight radio mirrors Kerouac's legendary three-week writing of *On the Road,* except that Wolfe was listening to rock 'n' roll rather than to the Beats' beloved jazz. Even Wolfe's notorious punctuation—his use of dashes and exclamation marks!—is rooted in the Beat era, as Kerouac once advised: "No periods separating sentence-structures already arbitrarily riddled by false colons and timid usually needless commas—but the vigorous space dash separating rhetorical breathing (as jazz musician drawing breath between outblown phrases)" ("Essentials" 72).

Beyond procedure and punctuation, however, Wolfe seems to have found in Kesey the same type of muse Kerouac once found in Neal Cassady. Consider, for instance, the similarity in both authors' descriptions of their heroes. Kerouac wrote:

> Dean's intelligence was every bit as formal and shining and complete [as narrator Sal Paradise's New York friends], without the tedious intellectualness . . . it was a wild *yea-saying* overbust of American joy; it was Western, the west wind, an ode from the Plains, something new, long prophesied, long a-coming. (emphasis added, *On the Road* 10)

Likewise, Wolfe described Kesey as a

> Western intellectual, Western U.S. , that is. That makes him unique to start. There is no Western intellectual tradition. Intellectuals on the West Coast have been Eastern, at bottom, drawing upon the styles and concepts of the literary worlds of New York and Boston. . . . Kesey's intellectualism includes a kind of Dionysian *yea-saying* tied in with the buoyance of life on the West Coast. (emphasis added, "Super Hud" 12)

Through the repetition of a key phrase like "yea-saying" and the similar delight of two New York authors in vibrant Western intellectualism, we have some circumstantial evidence that Wolfe's relationship to Kesey reflected Kerouac's to Cassady. These passages suggest that Wolfe's high regard of Kerouac influenced his techniques, if not his unique writing style. Furthermore, other mirrorings of *On the Road* in Wolfe's book position *The Electric Kool-Aid Acid Test* as Wolfe's own remapping with Kesey as his Dean, but various narrators taking the place of Kerouac's Sal Paradise. In other words, Kerouac and Wolfe were both catalyzed by their charismatic acquaintances, whom they eventually surpassed as writers. Indeed, in *The Electric Kool-Aid Acid Test,* Wolfe accomplished what Kesey had wanted—to go beyond the novel.

For the Pranksters, the bus trip *was* the movie, but for Wolfe, writing was the journey. Unlike Kesey, Wolfe retained his hope and belief in writing as a technique, as suggested in his comments in 1974: "There's so much *terra incognita* that novelists should be getting into that they could easily be wholly concerned with the social fabric, the social tableau. . . . I've completely relished this *terra incognita,* these subcultures, these areas of life that nobody wanted to write about" (Bellamy

39). The undiscovered *terra* waiting to be known, if I correctly interpret Wolfe's viewpoint, is not found on the American road, where the Beats once sought it, or in the mind, as the Pranksters believed, but in what Wolfe calls "these subcultures" of true believers who could not put their own stories down on paper—perhaps these are similar to what the Beats once called the *"Fellaheen,"* only these seem to be stoned white kids with a graduate education rather than poor "Negroes" or New York junkies. Wolfe added: "All these novelists always talk about changing the consciousness of their times, but they're not even going to come close to it in the kinds of novels they're writing now" (Bellamy 42). In other words, *The Electric Kool-Aid Acid Test* accomplished what *The Merry Pranksters Search for the Kool Place* was supposed to have done.

Wolfe transformed writing in the 1970s by calling himself a journalist, but he used the techniques then rejected by novelists like Kesey:

> [I] use stream of consciousness so that I can present the mind of Ken Kesey—as I try to do in a number of chapters of *The Electric Kool-Aid Acid Test*—to get completely inside Kesey's mind, based on interviews, tapes that he made, or letters that he wrote, diaries, and so on. It's still a controversial thing to use, but I was not at all interested in presenting my subjective state when confronted with the Pranksters or whatever they had done. It was rather to try to get Kesey's completely. (Bellamy 45)

While avant-garde authors might only be preoccupied with "'the intracranial activity,'" Wolfe notes, "The audience desperately wants to be able to make a pattern out of what it really is they're looking at" (Bellamy 48). Wolfe provides the pattern, brings form and order to the *terra incognita* of Kesey's mind and the Pranksters' bus journey. In the process, *he* writes the road story as New Journalism, not avant-garde literature or ground-breaking film.

The pattern Wolfe brings to the Pranksters' raw adventures is not all that different from *On the Road*. The plan for each road trip, in both Kerouac's and Wolfe's narratives, is always utopic—what *On the Road*'s narrator Sal Paradise called "the pearl" (11); yet, the journeys perpetually fail to live up to expectations. Wolfe and Kerouac each portray Mexico as where the road trip fails, loyalties break, and heroes disappoint. Just as Kerouac's Sal Paradise finally loses faith in Dean, leaving Dean alone in the rainy night as he goes off to the opera with his girlfriend, so too does Wolfe end his account with Kesey appearing a bit pathetic, standing on stage without an audience and singing "WE BLEW IT," over and over again (367–68). By ending *The Electric Kool-Aid Acid Test* on this note, the near-invisible Wolfe slyly ascends as journalist just as Kesey plummets as a visionary. Wolfe goes "further" than the novel, whereas Kesey has only talked about doing so. After an epilogue that tells of Kesey's trial and Cassady's death, Wolfe's book ends with his "Author's

Notes," giving him the last word as he muses on his craft. Thanks to Wolfe's account, the countercultural journey continues in the sixties—not only in Wolfe's record of the Pranksters' all-consuming *The Merry Pranksters Search for the Kool Place* but also through Wolfe's revitalization of Kerouac's road tropes by means of his spontaneous—even psychedelic—prose.

Within *The Electric Kool-Aid Acid Test,* Wolfe ponders outwardly how to tell a story of Pranksters who had moved beyond words. In a crucial chapter, "The Unspoken Thing," Wolfe reports that the Pranksters mistrusted words: they "made a point of not putting it into words. That in itself was one of the unspoken rules. *If you label it* this, *then it can't be* that" (112). In contrast, Wolfe the careful writer wonders aloud about which words to use: "How to tell it! . . . the current fantasy. I never heard any of the Pranksters use the word *religious* to describe the mental atmosphere they shared after the bus trip and the strange days in Big Sur. In fact they avoided putting it into words. And yet—" (ellipses in original, 111). Even as he stands on the sidelines in a different time and space than the Pranksters, hearing the words the Pranksters did and did not use, Wolfe crafts the words those writers refuse to name. In the midst of this chapter on "The Unspoken Thing," Wolfe writes about the movie as a "monster": "But The Movie was a monster, as I say" (122), a "great morass of a movie, with miles and miles of spiraling spliced-over film and hot splices billowing around them like so many intertwined, synched, but still chaotic and struggling human lives, theirs, the whole fucking world's" (131). And because *The Electric Kool-Aid Acid Test* is alive with apt choices, inspired passages, enlivened descriptions, there is an unmistakable triumph in *Wolfe's* self-portrait as author.[16]

More often, Wolfe stays in the background—observer more than participant, reporter rather than narrator, removed instead of present, letting others speak for themselves. Thanks to Wolfe's technique of writing as if he is inside the Pranksters' heads, it's easy to overlook his role as omniscient narrator in his own story. Thus Wolfe is distinct from the other writers he represents in *The Electric Kool-Aid Acid Test,* who are "on the bus" literally with Kesey and the Pranksters and thus become Wolfe's major sources of information.[17] Some authors are mere footnotes in Wolfe's book, but others "go native" and cross the line to take the "acid tests," like Norman Hartweg and Claire Bush. Wolfe recounts how Hartweg, onetime writer for the *Los Angeles Free Press,* was invited by Kesey to come to La Honda to meet Neal Cassady, whom Hartweg had long heroized, as a reward for helping Kesey edit the film. Wolfe turns Hartweg into a proxy narrator for several chapters of the book, saying of Hartweg, "All right, Film Editor, Article Writer, Participant-Observer, you're here. On with your . . . editing writing observing" (*Electric* 140). But like all the writers in *The Electric Kool-Aid Acid Test* besides Wolfe, Hartweg is not able to do what Wolfe could: "[Hartweg] wanted to see the whole film first, a whole run-through, so he could see where he was going"

(*Electric* 144). When Hartweg tries to pull back to observe, when he asks to view the entire movie or poses questions to the Pranksters, Mountain Girl makes fun of him (*Electric* 142). While Wolfe does portray himself as an outsider whose "black shiny FBI shoes" reveal him as being decidedly off the bus, he always seems to out-perform the writers he mentions in the book and upon whom he relies for his compelling "on the bus" voice.

Hesse's *Journey to the East* helps Wolfe to cast Hartweg as a narrator as well as to explain Hartweg's departure from Wolfe's narrative. But it also draws attention away from the fact that Wolfe turns next to *On the Road* to structure the sections after Hartweg leaves the Pranksters (Wolfe, *Electric* 255), thus leaving him without a proxy narrator. For instance, Wolfe notes the "weird divide" of the group after Kesey became a fugitive in Mexico, comparing it to the departure in *Journey to the East* of both the League's leader and the tale's narrator, "H.H." Wolfe writes: "Things got more and more bitter [in *Journey to the East*], and the narrator 'H,' left after the Morbio Inferiore [a place in Hesse's novel]. And the narrator, Hartweg, left after" (Wolfe, *Electric* 238). By calling Hartweg the narrator, Wolfe no doubt refers to the fact that he relied on extensive tape recordings of Hartweg's memories of this time (*Electric* 371). But this *"synch"* between Hesse's novel and Hartweg's departure helps Wolfe's own role as narrator disappear behind the triumph of his ability to piece together eyewitness memoirs plus literary and philosophical tropes to succeed where so many others had failed, catching in words "the unspoken thing." Once Hartweg leaves, Wolfe takes the narrative to Mexico as chapter 21, "The Fugitive," opens with Kesey in Puerto Vallarta. Once Wolfe describes the move of the Pranksters to join Kesey in Mexico, Hesse's *Journey to the East* becomes irrelevant, for Wolfe once again must focus on the "non-leader," Kesey, rather than a narrator like Hartweg. Yet he also relies upon—consciously or not—*On the Road;* like Kerouac, Wolfe portrays Mexico as the place where everything goes wrong. Because Wolfe writes with such immediacy, it is easy to overlook the influence legible in his text of various writers, especially Kerouac.

As much as Kesey ever did, Wolfe pondered and pontificated on the state of the novel and its function as an art form. Not only was Wolfe a reflective writer like Kerouac, but he was also as ambitious as Kesey in wanting to go further. Whereas Kesey attempted to accomplish this goal by using film to surpass the novel, Wolfe succeeded in using Kesey's film and Kerouac's techniques to invent a nonfiction, "intermediary" prose style that felt dynamic, fresh, alive—thereby remapping Kerouac's postwar American road story with electric-inspired New Journalism.[18] In an interview, Wolfe predicted "there's not going to be much difference between the best novels and the best nonfiction" (Bellamy 42). Previously, as Wolfe describes the history of journalism, a reporter was nothing more than a "would-be novelist or simple courier of the great" (*New Journalism* 8); however, New Journalism, according to Wolfe in the forward to his anthology with that title, was "dethroning the novel as the number one literary genre, starting the first new direction in American literature in half a century" (*New Journalism* 5). Clearly, Wolfe was making room for himself on the dais, pushing aside Kerouac and Kesey.

As a journalist, working in this "low-brow," long-ignored form without much tradition, Wolfe felt himself to be free of the anxiety of influence that caused novelists (like Kesey, although Wolfe never directly says this), "who have a romantic view of their role," to become mired in "this second-convolution avant-gardism" (Bellamy 42, 39). Talking with interviewer Joe David Bellamy in 1974, Wolfe described the burden faced by novelists in the postwar period:

> this frantic, hassling, speeded-up search for the new form. I think people are unconsciously selling themselves short when they want to make the form do the work. . . . The fact that there might be something new in content, or new in *comment,* is not anything that impresses people once they get into this frame of mind that the avant-garde is on the frontier sheerly of form. (Bellamy 38)

His focus on content, Wolfe insists, moves him beyond "these poor, frantic, little exercises in form. I really have had so little competition" in writing about the way people live now (Bellamy 40). In many ways, Wolfe presents an alternative yet contemporaneous view of the novel to Kesey's, with Wolfe having had the advantage of observing Kesey's experiments and his failures. Even though it would take decades for the Pranksters to view Wolfe's story as competition, we cannot ignore Wolfe's own rivalry with Kesey in *The Electric Kool-Aid Acid Test.* While Kesey is undoubtedly the protagonist of Wolfe's book, the hero is Wolfe himself, the writer who not only documented the Pranksters' great Journey to the East but who also succeeded in ushering in a new, vibrant, and influential style of writing, which went further than the novel's frantic, romantic exercises in form.

THE MAGICAL MYSTERY SIMILARITIES

The Pranksters had high ambitions for their film. We have already seen that they intended to make

> the world's first acid film, taken under conditions of total spontaneity barreling through the heartlands of America, recording all *now,* in the moment. The current fantasy was . . . a total breakthrough in terms of expression . . . but also something that would amaze and delight many multitudes, a movie that could be shown commercially as well as in the esoteric world of the heads. (Wolfe, *Electric* 122)

Contrast this with another passage of Wolfe's in *The Electric Kool-Aid Acid Test:*

Early in 1967 the Beatles got a fabulous idea. They got hold of a huge school bus and piled into it with thirty-nine friends and drove and wove across the British countryside, zonked out of their gourds. They were going to . . . make a movie. Not an ordinary movie, but a totally spontaneous movie, using hand-held cameras, shooting the experience as it happened—off the top of the head!—cavorting, rapping on, soaring in the moment, visionary chaos—a daydream! A black art! A chaos! They finished up with miles and miles of film, a monster, a veritable morass of it, all shaky and out of focus—blissful Zonk!—which they saw as a total breakthrough in terms of expression but also as a commercial display—shown on British TV it was—that might be appreciated even outside the esoteric world of the heads—THE MOVIE. (189)

By repeating his words between these two passages, Wolfe links the Pranksters' *The Merry Pranksters Search for the Kool Place* with the Beatles' *Magical Mystery Tour*, which premiered in December 1967. Here we turn to the question of the influence of the Pranksters' bus trip film on the Beatles' own acid road film. The many similarities between these two creative communities show the push in this era to expand upon the Beat road story by means of psychedelic visions and cinematic visuals. Both the Pranksters and the Beatles worked in similar ways, fighting the narrative conventions upon which commodity films relied even while hoping to strike gold as filmmakers. Although the Beatles succeeded in finishing their film, their rejection of popular film form in favor of the avant-garde hurt the reception of their film by mainstream audiences. The acid road film took years to evolve.

While no scholar seems to have definitively established a connection, journalists have long suggested the Pranksters' 1964 journey east influenced Paul McCartney, who came up with the idea for the Beatles' self-produced, self-directed acid road film, *Magical Mystery Tour*. In *The Beatles Movies* (1997), for instance, Bob Neaverson notes that McCartney, flying home from America in April 1967, could easily have encountered Wolfe's first articles on the Kesey bus trip, published in *World Journal Tribune* in January and February of 1967 (Neaverson 52, 66). The Pranksters like to claim credit for this inspiration—they seem genuinely happy for the Beatles' success with what may well have been their idea.

Like the Pranksters, the Beatles eschewed scripts in favor of recording "in the now" (Dennis Hopper had wanted to do the same thing while directing *Easy Rider*). *Magical Mystery Tour* had no shooting script, just a large crew out on the road. The film centers on a cross-country bus trip featuring Ringo and his Aunt Jessie, so the bus tour provides what little narrative center there is to the film. In keeping with the underground and psychedelic aesthetics of 1967, many of the sequences are non-narrative, playful, and expressionistic.

Alongside these bold intentions, however, the Beatles also hoped to create an acid road film that would appeal to a "potentially massive audience" (Neaverson 70), just like the Pranksters were still hoping in 1967 to achieve. Despite this intention, *Magical Mystery Tour* was pitifully unpopular with both critics and fans when it first aired on BBC1 on Boxing Day, 26 December 1967. Paul ended up defending it on television, saying: "There was no plot, so it was pointless trying to find one. It is like an abstract painting. . . . We did it as a series of disconnected, unconnected events" (Neaverson 72). Yet the Beatles' methods were criticized by Denis O'Dell, their director of Apple Corps in 1967; in his memoir, he blames the band for these failures: "Unfortunately film production requires financial and logistical problem-solving skills, commodities the Beatles sorely lacked. And their shortcomings in this department would eventually be their undoing [in *Magical Mystery Tour*]" (67). But unlike the Pranksters, the Beatles did succeed in getting a finished film to the marketplace, no doubt because they had producers like O'Dell who kept them from losing themselves entirely in drugs, ideas, and alternative pursuits (at least during the sixties the managers could accomplish this; by the seventies, of course, the Beatles split up as a group).

If indeed the Beatles were sparked by the Pranksters' bus trip, they made *Magical Mystery Tour* fully their own. As a collaboration between all four of the musicians, *Magical Mystery Tour* took far more risks in form than the Pranksters seemed ready to imagine for *The Merry Pranksters Search for the Kool Place*. The film also combines knowing homages to earlier film texts, from the surrealist film *Un Chien Andalou* (1929) to Hollywood's Busby Berkeley musicals. Unlike their first two films, *A Hard Day's Night* (1964) and *Help!* (1965), the Beatles did not play themselves but fictional characters (who never explicitly take drugs; the psychedelic aspects of this film are stylistic, not literal).

While it would be interesting to solve the mystery of whether or not the Pranksters' bus trip and the idea of their film influenced the Beatles, the important point is that both groups had the same philosophy about making acid road films. The Pranksters and the Beatles each functioned as collectives of wildly successful creative souls, people who had demonstrated themselves to be masters of one medium—fiction and music, respectively—and therefore believed it would be easy to slide those established talents into filmmaking. O'Dell observed in retrospect: "The Beatles had supreme self-confidence that they could master any medium. In most respects their previous forays into new areas of creativity had been justified and legitimized by some astonishing successes" (67). This confidence is understandable given the technologies and aesthetics of the time: cameras and sound equipment in the sixties were more mobile than ever, being simple enough that the lay person could use them. Furthermore, all the artists sought out methods of spontaneity and serendipity, and they enjoyed the whimsical results of such methods. Finally, they all invested in the concept of "intermedia"—the idea that one art medium was only artificially distinct from another—for they believed instead that concepts like medium or genre only restricted artistic endeavor.[19] Whereas Kerouac had called for writers to create the "bookmovie," and Kesey experimented with the "cinema novel," the Beatles took pleasure in seeing their musical talents spill over into other arts such as film, writing, and acting.

Whether or not caused by the Beatles' carefree attitude about making the film, *Magical Mystery Tour* flopped in England when it first aired on BBC1. No one quite seems to understand why it was broadcast in black and white when the entire film was shot in color, although the fact remains that color televisions were still not in the majority of UK households in 1967. O'Dell felt the film would have performed better had it aired instead on BBC2 during a later slot when artsy work was typically broadcast; but when *Magical Mystery Tour* re-aired in color ten days later on that desirable channel, O'Dell notes that the damage had already been done, for the re-screening generated "little enthusiasm" (72). While there are some other contributing factors, including an ill-timed release of the accompanying album, Apple Corps was so skeptical of the film's success in America that it released the film to universities rather than general distribution (72). O'Dell also criticized the Beatles' commitment to premiering this avant-garde film on British television, yet their decision may reflect McLuhan's ideas about the cool medium, which could have opened up performance-based artists like the Pranksters and the Beatles to the idea of enlightening the masses via mass media.

What anchors each avant-garde .experiment in form is the Pranksters' and the Beatles' decision, perhaps unconsciously or intuitively, that an acid road film should be the format through which they would illuminate the public. Because the road film did not become a self-aware genre for a few more years (not until after *Easy Rider* in 1969, as we will see), the late 1960s is the time this genre took root—growing from the faded majesty of Kerouac's *On the Road* by means of the technologies and sensibilities of psychedelic gurus and collaborating artists. The Pranksters may have been the first to navigate this remapping, but the Beatles were certainly not the last. The struggle to create a popular and revolutionary road film has obvious contradictions, yet *Easy Rider* would juggle each by romanticizing them, thereby pulling the acid road story from the edge of the avant-garde to the more solid commodity terrain of melodrama.

WE BLEW IT

While *Magical Mystery Tour* was in its final stages of post-production during December 1967, novelist and screenwriter Terry Southern began helping Dennis Hopper and Peter Fonda, the director/producer/actor team, to write their screenplay of *Easy Rider*. Southern was so hip that he had already appeared on the Beatles' famous album cover for *Sgt. Pepper's Lonely Hearts Club Band* in 1967. He protested against the Vietnam War with Beats like Allen Ginsberg and William

Burroughs (Hill 176); like them, he wrote for Grove Press and *Evergreen Review.* Like Kesey and many other writers of the time, Southern leapt enthusiastically into film as the preferred medium, once saying: "The only excuse for writing a novel is if it can't be done as a movie" (Hill 141). During December 1967 and April of 1968 (that is, spanning the time when Wolfe's newspaper articles appeared but before his book was published), Southern wrote an early screenplay for *Easy Rider,* using the storyline verbally conveyed to him by Fonda and Hopper (Hill 166).[20] Southern is a likely candidate for contributing to *Easy Rider* some key lines that seem to have come straight from *The Electric Kool-Aid Acid Test.*

Because these lines concern the ethical dilemma of capitalism, we turn first to the influence of the money men on *Easy Rider* in order to understand the context before considering the lines themselves. Any film that would have the sort of cultural significance imagined by the Pranksters and the Beatles would be, by definition, a commodity; yet making a film capable of being bought and sold in the marketplace was a hurdle that the Pranksters—and, to a lesser extent, the Beatles—could not (or would not) overcome. In contrast, Hopper and Fonda aligned themselves with producers focused more on profits than cultural revolutions, thereby assuring that their investors would intervene when necessary to free the film from their own artsy ambitions.

What unites all of these acid road films is their search for a balance between art and commerce. Even in the most crudely commodified film, *Easy Rider,* the theme of "selling out" freedom for financial profit recurs throughout, just as it influenced the film's title.[21] Wyatt and Billy travel by motorcycle, first to Mexico to pick up a load of illegal drugs, then journey through the American South with the plan to sell the lot and retire as rich men. En route, they encounter people who all give them different insights about freedom, capitalism, and the alternative economy of a commune. This is the context for evaluating the key line that appears in both *Easy Rider* and *The Electric Kool-Aid Acid Test,* when Wyatt announces one night, "We blew it, man." Left cryptic, it's not clear what they blew or why. Instead of articulating any strengths or weaknesses about the outlaw machinations of drug dealing, Wyatt acts as if any cogent examination of what actually went wrong when he and Billie became outlaw capitalists would betray this drug-induced social critique.

The weird "synch" if not outright homage comes from this line, for these are the very words Kesey repeats again and again after the acid graduation while on stage performing music with the Pranksters—"WE BLEW IT!"—the very line by which Wolfe ends *The Electric Kool-Aid Acid Test* (368). If Southern or anyone else had indeed been inspired to use those same words as Wolfe, the context of each is radically disparate. Rather than adopting the Pranksters' antic social deconstructions, *Easy Rider* romanticizes the trope of the outlaw, reducing it to tragedy without reflecting upon its function in the American counterculture. In contrast, Kesey's sense of the "cops and robber movie" was more sophisticated: "[Kesey] is in the cops' movie now, the Cops and Robbers Game, and eventually they will win, because it is their movie—*Gotcha!*" (Wolfe, *Electric* 311). In fact, Fonda's characters throughout his 1960s films utter cryptic expressions of rebellion, as we will confirm in the next chapter.

In effect, *Easy Rider* criticizes Wyatt and Billie for being "bought and sold" while simultaneously making them all the more precious for symbolizing the impossible dream of being free from the marketplace. While willing to play martyrs in the film, neither Hopper nor Fonda wanted to be revolutionary enough to destroy the studio system, for they aimed to be *auteurs* who profited from the very system they criticized. In truth, Kesey hoped for much the same financial success, but he was more of an outsider to Hollywood than Henry Fonda's son and James Dean's co-star, just as he was also more of a rebel and artist. Perhaps if Kesey had had the production teams behind him that had helped the Beatles and Hopper/Fonda finish their projects, *The Merry Pranksters Search for the Kool Place* would have come out before Wolfe's *The Electric Kool-Aid Acid Test* did.

The "We blew it" pronouncement of Wyatt and Kesey, therefore, signifies different types of blame. Kesey's chant seems to have been more of a critique about the evening's performance or perhaps even the Pranksters' grand experiment, whereas the *Easy Rider* plaint seems aimed as much at "the system" that forces people to desire wealth as at Billie and Wyatt's dream to become rich. Mouthed by Wyatt, *Easy Rider*'s more famous "We blew it" is far more cynical. This is the dilemma faced by all who aspired to make an acid road film, from the Pranksters in 1964 through to the Beatles in 1967 and culminating in *Easy Rider* in 1969—hold fast to a psychedelic aesthetic process and risk never finishing the project or releasing it under less than desirable circumstances, although the alternative seemed to be making something whose popularity comes at the price of catering to mass appetites for melodrama. Fonda and Hopper opted for the latter, and the impact of *Easy Rider* was indeed far reaching.

Easy Rider succeeds as one of the most influential films of the psychedelic revolution. Although Fonda tells a story of the evening when the idea came to him for *Easy Rider* (Fonda 241), in fact this film is the product of years of trial and error through a succession of psychedelic collaborations, as we have seen. The year 1969 also saw other experiments with the LSD road trip, from Rudolph Wurlitzer's well-respected road novel *Nog*, called a "headventure," to more exploitative and insincere novels like *Thumb Tripping* by Don Mitchell, which was also made into a movie in 1972.[22] When the long-held fantasy of the popular acid road film finally culminated as *Easy Rider,* it came from the same set of circumstances that had inspired *The Merry Pranksters Search for the Kool Place* and *Magical Mystery Tour*—namely, first-time filmmakers experimenting with spontaneity, drugs, and nontraditional film techniques who also wanted to make a profit.

The driving force behind these road films was optimism about the power of expanded consciousness, which could be accomplished by means of drugs, electronic and film recording equipment, and philosophies about *going in* (as Leary espoused) and/or *pranking outwardly* (as Kesey preferred). Today, a long forty years after Ken Kesey and the Merry Pranksters took their famous road trip east to attend the 1964 World's Fair in New York, Hesse's *Journey to the East* continues to be a trippy metaphor of not only the Pranksters' collaborative experiments with words, nonsense, and representations, but also the conundrum of telling their own story of this journey. By staying preoccupied with THE MOVIE, a visual document of events, Kesey staved off the "dreadful doubt" experienced by Hesse's narrator:

> And now that I want to hold fast to and describe this most important thing [i.e., the journey east], or at least something of it, everything is only a mass of separate fragmentary pictures which has been reflected in something, and this something is myself, and this self, this mirror, whenever I have gazed into it, has proved to be nothing but the uppermost surface of a glass plane. I put my pen away with the sincere intention and hope of continuing tomorrow or some other time, or rather to begin anew, but at the back of my intention and hope, at the back of my really tremendous urge to relate our story, there remains a dreadful doubt. . . . "Is your story capable of being told?" It also asks the question, "Was it possible to experience it?" (48–49)

The Pranksters' long delay in telling a road story of their own raises the question—Who owns a road trip? Is it the people who travel, the ones who immortalize it in words (or pictures), or those who serve as part of the static human landscape passed through by Pranksters or film crews? In the Depression era, writer James Agee and photographer Walker Evans fretted in *Let Us Now Praise Famous Men* (1941) over this very question when creating a document of their road trip into the impoverished South—they called themselves "spies" (7), as if stealing secrets from the families they visited while on their road trip. We have seen that Kesey claimed that *The Electric Kool-Aid Acid Test* consists of Wolfe's memories, not his, but it is more likely that Kesey's memories changed with time, for he avoided holding up a memoir of the 1964 bus trip to the scrutiny of the 1990s. Did Wolfe steal those memories from the expanded Prankster minds, or did he do us all a favor—from the Pranksters to scholars—by transcribing it all "in the moment"?

Although tardy and unfinished, the Pranksters' acid road film has indeed been influential. Like a unicorn, the romantic symbol of an ideal risking extinction, *The Merry Pranksters Search for the Kool Place* just may have been as powerful in its unrealized form as it could ever have been if finished. While Kesey and the Pranksters spent more than half their lives trying to realize the vision of the film in a form they could share with others, the mere idea of this film has nevertheless had a huge impact that persists even to this day.[23] Thanks to the Pranksters' whole-hearted commitment to it, the film became a central component of Wolfe's *The Electric Kool-Aid Acid Test,* plus it most likely inspired the Beatles in their *Magical Mystery Tour,* and may well have shaped some key lines from *Easy Rider.* Along the way, *On the Road* and the postwar liberatory road trip was remapped by the acid trip, as is directly evident in some similarities between Kerouac's novel and Wolfe's account. Looking back, the Pranksters' fantasy of the famous bus film fed many creative minds capable of exploiting the idea, taking up the opportunity lost by the Pranksters when they focused on the NOW instead of on a finished product. However, by staying in the realm of concept rather than commodity, the Pranksters never sold out. It's hard to create a worthy acid road film, whose DayGlo inspirations don't fade or whose predictions don't prove false with the passage of time. But it's even harder to create such a powerful idea about a film. The influence of the Pranksters' dream is revolutionary indeed. For this, the Pranksters can thank Wolfe and *The Electric Kool-Aid Acid Test* as well as their own perseverance in pursuing this quixotic ideal.

In the final analysis, *The Merry Pranksters Search for the Kool Place* is the ultimate prank—it even pranked the Pranksters, who actually thought they would finish it. The Merry Pranksters have *earned* their kool place in cultural history. It turns out that the dream of a revolutionary acid road film inspired people to want to be "on the bus" as much as any actual film might ever have.

5
Road Film Rising
Hells Angels, Merry Pranksters, and Easy Riders

A television plays the old movie, *The Wild One* from 1953, starring Marlon Brando as Johnny, a leather-clad outlaw whose motorcycle gang terrorizes an entire town with its drinking, fighting, and automobility. This TV set is itself in a movie, the landmark underground film, *Scorpio Rising* by Kenneth Anger, made in 1963.[1] This scene details television culture in the early 1960s, reflecting TV's trend to broadcast films licensed from Hollywood studios or owned by television networks. (Rerunning these old films offset the high costs of producing new television programs like *Route 66*.) More purposefully, *Scorpio Rising* reveals how TV viewers indulge in private fantasies, for television *reception*—unlike its centralized broadcasts—cannot be controlled by executive dictates, government mandates, or modernist disdain for TV as a thoroughly commodified medium. Thanks to the rising number of postwar road stories and the simple fact that they could be remapped with personal meaning and private desire, *Scorpio Rising* is the first of many biker films in the sixties that culminated in *Easy Rider*. Given the popularity and persistence of road stories in the postwar years, it is surprising that a road film genre only becomes embraced by Hollywood's main studios in 1969 with *Easy Rider*, but the delay is explained by the changing terrain of film, television, and art production that this chapter will examine.

Scorpio Rising coincides with a full-scale paradigm shift in the road story between 1964, when CBS's television series *Route 66* went off the air and Ken Kesey and the Merry Pranksters filmed their road trip to the East, and 1969, when *Easy Rider* rocked Hollywood studios with the profitability of the rebel image. The metamorphosis of the road story accelerates in the 1960s, traveling through mainstream audiences and marginal subcultures, picking up along the way new rebels to feature and new market niches to satisfy. *Scorpio Rising* introduces this chapter because it underscores the fluidity of road stories that characterize the sixties, particularly the way narratives about automobility move between different media, from film to TV and back again, and between different audiences, back and forth between the underground film cognoscenti and drive-in theater teens. We will pick up from the previous chapter the link to Kesey and the Pranksters, who were the first to get the notorious biker gang, the Hells Angels, to experiment with LSD.

Paralleling the work of this creative subculture is the biker genre's development in the commercial world of "B" films, particularly by filmmaker Roger Corman and two of his protégés, Peter Fonda and Dennis Hopper, who climax this transformation with their smash film *Easy Rider*. By analyzing underground films alongside exploitation films, this chapter calls attention to their similarities—in content, formal style, and financial implications—thus confirming that the cultural work of the road story is to update familiar tropes of rebellion for subsequent generations, technologies, and economies. This can occur on the fringes of marginal culture or at the center of crass commercialization, as we will see.

As these diverse examples of road stories will show, the car or motorcycle carries great meaning in the semiotic systems of the 1960s—from the Corvette in the *Route 66* television series sponsored by Chevrolet to the Harley-Davidsons of the many sixties biker films. The new importance of the vehicle stems from two related factors: first, the visual emphasis of the road story as it moves from print to film and TV in the sixties, and, second, the rival aesthetic philosophies between modernism and Pop Art regarding rebellion, commodity, and spectacle. All these sixties road stories are, in one way or another, about buying freedom or rejecting capitalism's constraints over freedom. This moral conundrum preoccupied artists and business people alike, since these were the years when modernism's strict separation of art and commerce twisted into the hybrid products of Pop Art and camp irony. Yet people at the time pretended the vehicle was not important, thus amping up the mythical quality of the road story's characters; for instance, Frederic Tuten said about *Easy Rider:* "the bikes are incident, they might as well be horses. . . . *Easy Rider*'s strategy is founded on the paranoiac dread that innocence is crowded out, exterminated, like the buffalo" (36, 40). Don't believe it—the bikes carry more weight than the buffalo. Given the bipolar project of using vehicles to signify rebellion, the commodity fetish of this era becomes, literally and metaphorically, a sort of sexual fetish, given the overlap in these years of social rebellion and sexual revolution. Most film scholars realize that Kenneth Anger understood this very well, but we will see by the end of this chapter that Roger Corman, Dennis Hopper, and Peter Fonda did too.

THE UNDERGROUND'S "BAUDELAIREAN" SENSIBILITY IN KENNETH ANGER'S *SCORPIO RISING*

The underground film movement of the early 1960s emerged from the film *Pull My Daisy,* the collaboration between Beat novelist Jack Kerouac, poet Allen Ginsberg, painter Alfred Leslie, and photographer Robert Frank, as discussed earlier. Not only were a vast range of filmmakers making "lyrical" 16 mm films in the 1960s, but there were more art-house movie theaters than ever before, up to eight hundred to distribute the artisinal and underground films that began to be made (Hillier 14). To describe "the changing *frontiers* of cinema" (emphasis added, 67), film critic Jonas Mekas repeated the same language in 1963 of "disengagement and new freedom" (85) he had used two years earlier to discuss the Beats:

> The modern American film, however, is, like poetry and prose, created by new men with new sensibilities. . . . The young actor of today doesn't trust the will of a director any longer. . . . He merges with his part entirely, it becomes a moral problem for him, and a problem of existence. Thus, he doesn't trust any will but his own . . . only distant, deep waves, and motion and voice and groans of a Marlon Brando, James Dean, Ben Carruthers—waiting, listening (the same way Kerouac is listening for the new American word and syntax and rhythm in his spontaneous improvisations; or John Coltrane; or Alfred Leslie). (27–28)

Mekas also noted the changes happening in the early 1960s: "Until now cinema could move only in a robotlike step, on preplanned tracks, indicated lines. Now it is beginning to move freely, by itself, according to its own wishes and whims. . . . new times, new content, new language" (49).

Thus free to go wherever it wants, underground cinema focuses on polymorphous perversity or "ambisexuality," defined as openness "to all sexual practices and objects" (Dyer 118). Citing the influence of Burroughs, Mekas called this new wave of 1960s art films "Baudelairean Cinema," noting that they

> all contain homosexual and lesbian elements. The homosexuality, because of its existence outside the official moral conventions, has unleashed sensitivities and experiences which have been at the bottom of much great poetry since the beginning of humanity.[2] (86)

Because the gay liberation movement would not erupt until the end of the 1960s, "Baudelairean Cinema" seemed more tied to the adventurous sexuality initiated by the Beats in their fascination with the mobility of identity than part of any sort of gay separatist movement. Richard Dyer confirms in *Now You See It* (1990), "gay underground films did not claim to be gay at all, they claimed to be personal"; such films provided pleasure by exploiting "the exhilarating *instabilities* of the necessary *fiction of identity*" (emphasis added, 173). Revealing a queer "double consciousness," *Scorpio Rising* persistently destabilizes identity, overturning such binaries as Hollywood versus underground film or macho biker versus male homosexual, perverting mainstream pop culture through its deliberate misreadings by sexual minorities.

Scorpio Rising's sympathy toward television and other aspects of popular culture fits underground cinema's camp sensibility in the early 1960s. These 16 mm filmmakers and their audiences embraced the role of "perverse spectators," to borrow Janet Staiger's useful phrase, using pop culture to distinguish a deviant,

"Baudelairean" sensibility that differed from—even rebelled against—Kerouac's avant-garde focus on prewar imagery.[3] For instance, the film includes a segment in which Scorpio (Bruce Byron), a gay biker, watches Johnny/Brando on the TV in his room, where James Dean photos adorn the walls. Film artist Anger, himself homosexual, exposed the mechanisms by which masculine identity was constructed in Hollywood idols like Brando and Dean in *The Wild One* and *Rebel Without a Cause* (see figs. 8 and 9).[4] The most transgressive message of *Scorpio Rising* is that a text cannot hold its meaning steady when a viewer invests it with desire, and what we have seen so far and will continue to find is that viewers continuously revitalize the road story with private and communal fantasies that are also historically specific.

Fig. 8. Screen grab from the underground film *Scorpio Rising* (1963). The director Kenneth Anger remapped biker icons, like Marlon Brando and James Dean, with homoerotic desire. Film copyright © Kenneth Anger.

Fig. 9. Marlon Brando embodying postwar automobility and rebellion in the classic *The Wild One* (1953). Directed by Laszlo Benedek; film copyright © Columbia Pictures.

113

Scorpio Rising is not a road film per se, but it does play a vital role in our understanding of motorized rebels by playing against the hypermasculinity of the male loner and revealing how a subculture, in this case the gay community, can undermine a dominant power simply by remapping an image. The twenty-nine-minute film has thirteen separate segments that focus on gay biker scenarios set to popular songs that played on the radio in the 1950s and 1960s. Most of these songs have an explicitly heterosexual narrative, which thus provides an ironic commentary to *Scorpio Rising*'s loose plot centered on homosexual, sacrilegious, and sadomasochistic scenarios between bikers. For instance, the song "Blue Velvet" plays while one motorcyclist dresses in leather to go out, making the pronoun "she" carry double duty. Similarly, the film subverts the meaning of fraternity depicted in inserted footage of the biblical film *The Road to Jerusalem* and Anger's use of comic strips featuring boy cartoon characters. Yet *Scorpio Rising* simultaneously ruptures any easy recuperation of these recontextualized images by mixing them with emblems of Jesus, scorpions, Nazism, and other powerful symbols. Anger's tone moves from camp to vicious aggression in its depiction of sadistic male bonding rituals: for example, Nazi flags are edited into religious scenes, a biker gang's hazing turns into a homosexual rape, and images of Jesus are juxtaposed with Hitler's photo. (Even this, it turns out, emphasizes the polymorphous nature of meaning, for a member of the American Nazi Party felt himself to be victim to Anger's manipulations of this symbol and had the print confiscated, according to Hutchison [136].)

Proclaiming his interest in the "masculine fascination with the Thing that Goes" (Sitney 116), Anger literalizes the mobility of identity, foregrounding the vehicle as a prop of desire, the film star as object of sexual fixation, and the gay biker as the new rebel. Most motorcycle clubs may have been heterosexual, even homophobic, but bikers were part of gay fantasy, imagined regularly in the homoerotic magazine *Physique Pictorial* as early as the 1950s (Suárez 156). Like the African Americans of the Beat era, gays overlaid transparent or standard messages with "underground" meanings. Anger worked with what he called "a definite *eroticization* of the automobile, in its dual aspect of narcissistic identification as virile power symbol and its more elusive role: seductive, attention-grabbing, gaudy or glittering mechanical mistress paraded for the benefit of his [the baby boom teen's] peers" (Sitney 125). The slippery homoerotic underside of language and machines provides rhetorical opportunities for Anger's musical and visual subversions.

By recasting Dean and Brando as icons of homosexual desire, Anger calls attention to the homoerotic aspect of the rebel spectacle. *Scorpio Rising* examines what Anger calls "the Myth of the American Motorcyclist. . . . Thanatos, in chrome and black leather and bursting jeans" (Sitney 116). Anger's caressing pan shots foreground the sexual aspect of the motorcycle's mechanical power and mobility, emphasizing the ritual nature of both bike culture and homoerotic fantasy. He also portrays the alienation and aggression that are realities of living in America's margins—where sexual rebels are vulnerable to ridicule or even rape, thus necessitating them to confront the differentials of power. Anger eroticizes power and its precariousness.

Furthermore, in focusing on the commodity nature of the pop songs, the movie stars, the motorcycles, and the studded leather clothes, *Scorpio Rising* meditates on the vast "machinery" of outlaw production in the early 1960s. By deliberately misreading a text's heterosexual intentions, perverting it in the realm of reception, Anger calls attention to the very notion that anything could become imagined as the "outlaw machine," which was how Harley-Davidson marketed the motorcycles in its huge sales boom of the 1960s. Anger explores the "fetishes" of mobility—the motorcycle itself, as well as the leather and denim clothes of the biker—providing apt self-reflexivity at the dawn of the road film genre, for these same fetishes were commodities that bourgeois swingers could buy or sell. (The British film, *The Girl on the Motorcycle* [1968], sexualized the riding clothes as well.)

REBELLION BOUGHT AND SOLD

The biker trend had begun parallel to the Beats' pioneer writings, for the Hells Angels and other motorcycle clubs also set out in 1947 to remap the same highways and back roads that Kerouac called the "vast backyard" of America (*On the Road* 14). Sensationalist news accounts reported from Hollister, California, in 1947 inspired the script of *The Wild One;* another infamous event in 1963 and another in 1965 brought bikers back into the media glare, where they stayed for much of the 1960s. Popular legend posits that bikers were fighters returned from World War II still hungry for wartime's adventure, speed, and danger, which they found by taking up motorcycles. Except for their mutual love of mobility, this rebel image differs considerably from that of the Beats. Bikers were slightly older; they were not artists; and they were more rejected by the postwar economy than rejecting of it.

The Wild One gave at least one motorcycle club a sense of identity when members attended *en masse:* "[We] cheered like bastards. We could all see ourselves right there on the screen. We were all Marlon Brando" (Thompson 62). In this quote from Hunter S. Thompson's ethnographic *Hell's Angels* (1966), we can appreciate the thin line separating heterosexual celebrity cults and homosexual fantasy—as well as the bold deconstruction of identity and identification undertaken by Anger in *Scorpio Rising.* Anger's underground film was one of the first social commentaries on how the rebel image could be appropriated—here, by gays—but Anger's insights could extend to gonzo journalists and drive-in movie directors.

Like the Beats during the fifties, bikers suddenly became celebrities in the sixties, the voracious media's favorite new bad boys. Compared to the superstars Brando and Dean, however, bikers helped "democratize" the rebel image, for they appeared as a generic type rather than a brand name, known by their clubs' names and colors, but anonymous for all practical purposes, with nearly universal nicknames like "Loser" or "Skip."[5] Articles about the Angels were published in the *Nation, Time, Newsweek,* the *New York Times,* and many other prominent places, plus noted "gonzo" journalist Thompson published his book-length study *Hell's Angels* in 1966.[6] The press answered the Angel's beck and call for briefings, and an entire genre of drive-in movie films was dedicated to their outlaw imagery. Journalist Thompson and also directors Anger and Corman each spent time with Hells Angels clubs as part of their research, all becoming "slowly absorbed" into the gang romance rather than remaining detached (Thompson 46). When the Angels began hanging out with Kesey and the Merry Pranksters, Ginsberg wrote poems to and about the bikers. But by 6 December 1969, the Angels lost their "fifteen minutes of fame" as celebrities when they failed as security guards at the famous Rolling Stones concert at Altamont Speedway, contributing to the murder and mayhem that marred the event.[7]

While their celebrity status was still on the rise, the Angels loved and hated their popularity. Thompson reported: "Shortly after the news magazines made them celebrities they began to talk about 'getting rich from it all,' and their fear of being wiped out soon gave way to a brooking resentment over being 'used' to sell newspapers and magazines" (53). As the Beats had learned in the late 1950s, rebels put in the limelight by mass media must eventually come to grips with their status as mere curiosities—even as commodities "bought and sold in the marketplace," to mirror the famous line from *Easy Rider.* In the 1960s, the difference between rebel subject and object was blurring as ambiguously as the one between art and commodity. The Beats, the bikers, the Pranksters—all hoped to outrun the fate of being used to sell products or magazines, but *Easy Rider* is the first text to run toward it and proclaim the nation's spiritual poverty while cashing in on rebellion's financial profitability.

In the 1960s, everyone is hustling a little profit out of rebellion—even the rebels—as well as the filmmakers and "New Journalists" like Thompson and Tom Wolfe, with their respective journalistic accounts, *Hell's Angels* and *The Electric Kool-Aid Acid Test* (1968). The rising trend of participatory journalism and its stylistic innovations are very important to the development of the road story. Because the biker films are not really road films per se, the journalistic accounts of Thompson and Wolfe become, at heart, the road stories of the mid-1960s.

Whereas the journalists performed the crucial cultural work of articulating various rebel phenomena, the ambiguities of underground film artists like Anger were purposeful. The "Baudelairean cinema" did not aspire to pin down any specific or clear messages about identity, sexuality, or representational systems—for the point is the transportability and double consciousness of subcultural identification. Anger invented a symbolic cinematic "language" with his use of editing, pans, pop music, and appropriated film footage, but—like the Beats before him—he portrayed "mysterious" adventures of sexuality rather than a politically specific agenda. The collages that Anger assembled help "to speak what cannot be directly said—here, most obviously, the revised models of sexuality" that include homosexuality, yet also refer to the general instabilities of sexuality and masculinity (D. James 155).

Yet ambiguity will become a way of avoiding the political ramifications of the cult of rebellion. We will see that the drive-in theater films repeat the looseness of articulation that Anger skillfully uses to interrogate masculinity and desire, but biker genre does so in order to *avoid* a social critique, rather than to challenge dominant sexuality. *Scorpio Rising* stresses the kicks of subverting dominant sexuality. In contrast, the hero of the drive-in biker genre feeds the class frustrations experienced by heterosexual white men who lack education and decent job opportunities—and who wish to assert their dominant, not marginal, identity *as men,* despite their lower-class status.

FROM GAY TO STRAIGHT, FROM RECEPTION TO PRODUCTION

Back in the suburban tracts, a very different type of audience for motorcycle films was growing up and fueling demand for drive-in movie theaters, which screened low-budget exploitation films to teens with access to cars. These genre films included "biker" and hot rod films that aimed at quite different audiences than Anger's, who came to see portraits of homoerotic risk and sadomasochistic power. Once director Roger Corman is drawn to the Eros and Thanatos of motorcyclized outlaws, he reinstates heterosexual power and female risk.

The films considered here were produced by American International Pictures (AIP), formed in 1954 with the partnership of Samuel Z. Arkoff and James Nicholson. AIP was a major low-budget producer of youth-oriented flicks that relied on the formulaic genres of horror, motorcycle, gangster, and science fiction; they were made cheap and fast, with sensationalist scripts delivering regular doses of titillation. These exploitation films constitute an important niche of their own.

AIP directors like Corman espoused a radically different ideology of sexuality and masculinity than did underground artists like Anger, but they all share an insistence on remapping the 1950s films of teen mobility with the sexual freedoms of the 1960s. In fact, the camp sensibility of gay underground filmmakers is the flipside of AIP's generic formulations. The shared outlaw tropes and similar aesthetic rawness in Corman's *The Wild Angels* and Anger's *Scorpio Rising* point to a surprising parallelism that is significant to the evolution of the road story and its cycling between rebellion and commodification.

While underground filmmakers explored the dynamics of cultural reception, AIP directors focused almost entirely on production—for their challenge was to make profitable films, not art. Growing markets in the late 1950s for television and low-budget entertainments such as drive-in movies meant there was tremendous demand for enough product to satisfy the fragmenting audiences, and TV production houses like Raybert and independent studios like AIP shifted into high gear. Despite the formulaic scripts created under such circumstances, these products of the 1950s and early 1960s significantly eroded the market share that film had previously enjoyed. Would a teen prefer *The Love Bug* (1968) or Russ Meyer's *Motor Psycho!* (1965) at the drive-in during a hot summer night? Sinking movie profits only exacerbated the already existing cultural rivalry between glamorous Hollywood films and TV's "feminized" or drive-ins' "low-brow" productions. For self-preservation, the film studios emphasized the prestige and high production values of their creations, while commodity-driven studios filled the niche for exploitation films.

Despite their own financial and pop culture successes, producers of television and other "kitsch" forms felt themselves to be marginalized in the media rivalry they themselves waged with Hollywood's major studios. Having been influenced by the Beats and films like *The Wild One* and *Rebel Without a Cause,* some of these low-budget directors identified their position vis-à-vis the industry as that of the "rebel" operating from the margins. For instance, Corman argued that

> No two films in my career reflect more vividly my natural attraction for stories about the outsider or the misfit than *The Wild Angels* and *The Trip.* . . . I was drifting further from the Hollywood mainstream. My filmmaking instincts, like my stance in politics, were growing more radical. In the process, these films put me together with . . . Peter Fonda, Dennis Hopper, Jack Nicholson, Bruce Dern—who would become known for their portrayals of alienated antiheroes and who, in the 1960s, were part of a vibrant new counterculture in Hollywood. . . . Their work helped turn those films into two of the most controversial and most commercial projects of my career. (129)

Corman's comments also reflect the "auteur" philosophy about film that had begun filtering from France via the journal *Cahiers du Cinema* to New York City, where it cropped up in film reviews in the *Village Voice.* Auteurism holds that directors imprint their signature or vision onto a film, especially commodity films made under industry constraints. It is under these circumstances of commercial imperatives that a visionary misfit might be recast as an auteur. Corman's point of view also helped influence the emerging philosophy of the "art film," which aimed to combine the "artisanal practices of the aesthetic and political avant-gardes" with commercial profits (D. James 282). AIP directors like Corman funneled their alienation into the motorcycle genre, which provided them a vehicle for exploring their own marginality in Hollywood while simultaneously proclaiming their ability as auteurs.

Roger Corman is perhaps the single most influential individual in turning the postwar road story into a film *genre,* both via the motorcycle films he himself directed and the opportunities he created for the generation of directors whose road films in the early 1970s would help raise them to prominence—and again for young directors in the 1980s. Corman inspired not only Dennis Hopper and Peter Fonda but also the "Movie Brats" who will be discussed in the next chapter, including Peter Bogdanovich, who worked extensively on *The Wild Angels,* as well as Frances Ford Coppola, Martin Scorsese, Monte Hellman, and many, many others. At AIP, the prescriptive but frequently profitable films about the socially outcast motorcycle gangs churned out included *The Wild Angels* (dir. Roger Corman, 1966), *Hells Angels on Wheels* (dir. Richard Rush, 1967), *The Glory Stompers* (dir. Anthony M. Lanza, 1967), *The Savage Seven* (dir. Richard Rush, 1968), *The Cycle Savages* (dir. Bill Brame, 1969), and *Run, Angel, Run* (dir. Jack Starrett, 1969). Until 1969, when Hopper and Fonda successfully combined in *Easy Rider* Corman's low-budget leanness with the underground film movement's aesthetic innovations, the biker genre constitutes a key stage in the evolution of road films during the 1960s.

As in any genre of exploitation films, a certain charm can be found in the blatant aggressions born out of the speed and efficiency with which low-budget films must be made. However, their profitability is the main reason these films merited emulation in the 1960s. The financial success of the wild motorcycle rebel genre was assured with Corman's *The Wild Angels,* starring Peter Fonda and Nancy Sinatra, for it only cost $360,000 to make, yet grossed more than $10 million over the years. *Variety* ranked it the thirteenth top film of 1966, making it the highest grossing low-budget picture of its time (Corman 143). Using vérité techniques, *The Wild Angels* and other biker films were shot on location, with real Hells Angels serving as paid consultants (Corman 135–37).

The Wild Angels tells the story of a motorcycle gang run by the charismatic character, Heavenly Blues (Fonda). The club learns that Loser's (Bruce Dern) bike has been stolen by Mexican police, so the bikers ride across the border and steal it back. They leave behind their old ladies, Blues's girl Mike (Nancy Sinatra) and Loser's girlfriend Gaysh (Diane Ladd). In Mexico, Loser recovers his bike but is shot by the police while escaping and winds up in a hospital south of the border. His pals rescue him, only after they rape the black nurse who has saved his life. Loser dies en route, so Blues and the others hold a funeral for him back home, yet all hell breaks loose during the funeral when the bikers stage a riot and perpetrate a rape on the altar. The film ends with the bikers on the run from the police, but Blues has grown increasingly introspective and moody. Instead of escaping with his gang, he stays and waits for the police to arrive, philosophizing that there's nowhere to run anymore.

In contrast to the wholesome portraits in the older motorcycle film *The Wild One,* Corman's work attempted to unveil the primal sexual tensions underlying what that 1953 film had passed off as prim heterosexual love. Desiring to undo what he called "obviou[s] sexual sublimation" (Mason 311), Corman later admitted that he had unintentionally glamorized the violence of the Angels, having fallen sway to their allure when spending time with them to gather material for his films (Mason 312). Corman and the other AIP directors turn bikers into unmitigated outlaws, whose machismo presumably offered a catharsis to working-class youth who felt alienated from both Kennedy's "New Frontier" and Lyndon Johnson's "Great Society."[8] These characters yank back the biker image from gay fantasy to straight society, presenting a virulent heterosexuality that titillated teen audiences at the dawn of the sexual revolution. The films were vehemently sexist, to the point that men's rape of women becomes a standard feature of the genre—we will return to this trope in the next chapter when we consider the feminist response. The few nonwhite men appearing in the biker films are reduced to the roles of drug dealers or incompetent Mexican policemen. In this form of the biker genre, the patriarchal bully asserts his rebelliousness by lording over women and Mexicans, even as experimentation with drugs helps him become somewhat "sensitive" or "artistic" (especially in the roles played by Fonda), as befits the emerging hippie archetype.

Indeed, the drive-in biker films popularized a backlash against the very "mysteries" that the Beat road story had championed—namely, homosexuality, racial difference, and an intermixture of literary and visual qualities in the avant-garde. (In contrast, Route 66 used but defused these Beat themes by translating them into New Frontier tropes.) When new generations remap a road story, that impulse can serve a conservative function as readily as a progressive one, and a close reading will reveal that Corman's use of sadomasochism and rape in The Wild Angels is far more reactionary than the same motifs in Anger's Scorpio Rising.

In particular, the rape scenes in each The Wild Angels and Scorpio Rising clearly show the difference in the politics of subversion of Anger and Corman. In the tenth segment of Scorpio Rising, for instance, the visceral collision of sex and nihilism that occurs during the pop song "Torture" by Kris Jensen is strikingly similar to a scene in Corman's film. Scorpio Rising cross-cuts shots of religious objects, first, with Nazi symbols and, next, moves into a scene in which the fraternal hazing of one biker crosses quickly to what looks like male-male rape. Images of Christ with a crown of thorns are juxtaposed with clips of Brando in The Wild One, thus linking the bikers in this film to the defilement of all that stands "holy" in American society, including religion, anti-fascism, movie stars, and heterosexuality. As film critic Lowry notes of Scorpio Rising, "The New Age is to be born upon the altar of the Old" (45).

Anger's use of sacrilege and Nazi imagery in Scorpio Rising is no less disturbing than Corman's, yet the two filmmakers achieve quite different visions of the new age on their altars. Rather than reinterpret The Wild One, as Corman's title suggests, *The Wild Angels* repeats the same rebellions of young versus old, simply updating them for the 1960s by undoing the sexual restraints of Brando's film, adding rape, drugs, and rock 'n' roll. The Hells Angels in his *The Wild Angels* also stage the death of the Old via a very different rape, one that takes place on an altar—in this case, during Loser's funeral. After the lead character Blues rails at the funeral's minister that his generation just wants to be free to take drugs, the bikers bust up the church. Figure 10 reveals the Nazi flag and mayhem on the altar. While taking drugs and fighting, two of the bikers decide to rape Loser's girlfriend and pull her down behind his coffin on the altar. No one tries to stop them, although Blues intervenes right afterwards when some bikers begin using hard drugs. The clear message—rape is expected, heroin is taboo. In contrast to Anger's campy perversions, Corman fantasizes the takeover by the younger gang of the lone, middle-aged funeral director, thereby perpetuating an Oedipal view of the succession of power within a patriarchal hierarchy. In contrast, *Scorpio Rising* suggests a major upheaval of the established order, not a succession as much as a total capitulation.

Fig. 10. Bikers rioting on the altar at Loser's funeral, adding the Nazi flag, and raping Loser's girlfriend under the approving gaze of their leader, Heavenly Blues (Peter Fonda) in Roger Corman's *The Wild Angels* (1966). Film copyright © American International Pictures.

Underground cinema used ambiguity to explore the mobility of sexual identity, but the inarticulate nature of the biker genre means something quite different. There is no clear goal that Peter Fonda's characters can articulate in either *The Wild Angels* or the other films of the late sixties that he distinguishes with his persona, especially *The Trip* and *Easy Rider*. For example, the funeral scene prior to the rape in *The Wild Angels* sums up the ennui of the bikers, and the formulaic biker genre in general, when Fonda's character Blues jumps up and demands that the Angels just "want to be free." The minister presiding over the memorial service asks Blues what he wants to be free to do, and Blues responds:

> Well, we want to be free, we want to be free to do what we want to do. We want to be free to ride our machines without being hassled by the Man. And we want to get loaded, and we want to have a good time, and that's what we're gonna do. We're gonna have a good time. We're gonna have a party.[9]

Whereas Anger's "Baudelairean" aesthetic had let its homoerotic remapping constitute the sum of its social critique, the emptiness of the rebellion voiced by Fonda's character, here and in *Easy Rider,* reveals the problem with commodity-oriented filmmakers appropriating avant-garde film techniques. The critique must be vague so as to appeal to the largest possible audience.

PSYCHEDELICS AND THE BIKER FILM

During the early- to mid-1960s, the road story manifested in distinctively mass-media forms that fed the predictable pleasures of genre formulae, which we have considered in examining television's *Route 66* and the drive-in theaters' biker films. Simultaneously, the avant-garde underground film movement was at its height, offering a counter-voice to these commodified images. Still another faction of the mid-1960s avant-garde was grounded in the psychedelic movement, where many hippies ended up after having been inspired by the Beats in their adolescence. Even as early as 1962, the Beats were only a "whiff" in the bars of San Francisco's North Beach, according to artisinal filmmaker Bruce Baillie,[10] who also used the figure of the motorcyclist to center his lyrical film, *Quixote* (1968). Scholar Paul Arthur observed: "For the wanderer setting out in '64, all sorts of options were closed down and had been for some time" (33).[11] We have seen how Ken Kesey and the Merry Pranksters used their cross-country bus trip to open up the possibilities for remapping Kerouac's "bookmovie" with their "cinema novel" and to walk through what Aldous Huxley called "the doors of perception" while on the open road. Following the Pranksters' vision, young heads migrated to the Haight Ashbury district, where they purposefully tried to go "furthur" than Beat culture, which was suddenly on the square side of the generation gap by the mid-1960s.

Still, the fact that the Pranksters failed to finish their acid road film, *The Merry Pranksters Search for the Kool Place,* left a gap in the archives of the evolving American road story, filled, ironically, by Corman's drive-in commodities. In particular, *The Trip* (1967) turns out to be the first psychedelic film to hit the mass market in 1967 (followed by *Head,* directed by Bob Rafelson in 1968). Corman's films, *The Trip* and *The Wild Angels,* play a major role in the metamorphosis of the rebel road story from a Beat relic into its hippie reincarnation as *Easy Rider.* A minor detail in *The Trip* signals its place in the transition from the Beat to the hippie generation: the camera catches a glimpse of *On the Road* in the bookshelf of the home where people take their acid trips.

The Trip brought together the key players who would make *Easy Rider:* it starred Dennis Hopper and Peter Fonda, and its script was written by Jack Nicholson—all three of whom went on to achieve fame as the stars of *Easy Rider.* Hopper and Fonda began to collaborate as film artists in *The Trip,* for Corman let them direct the segments that subjectively portray the acid experiences played by Fonda's character. *The Trip* is where Hopper and Fonda first deliberately blurred the boundaries between the artisanal film and the commodity genre. They made arty sequences with a 16 mm camera they borrowed from Corman, who inserted them into his film.

These acid sequences earned the praise of many film critics as being the innovative portion of an otherwise commercially oriented film. However, some modernist champions of underground film resented the bold appropriation of art film techniques; for instance, Parker Tyler called *The Trip* a "popularized, literally Hollywoodized version of an Underground film . . . ineligible as Underground—or, for that matter, as avant-garde. . . . *Drugs* have made pure fantasy into a Hollywood *commodity* at last" (emphasis added, 64, 68). In one sense, the subsequent creation of *Easy Rider* interrogates attitudes like Tyler's, which assume that the underground film movement must remain strictly segregated from Hollywood. Importantly, the famous acid sequence in *Easy Rider,* when Wyatt and Billie drop acid in the New Orleans cemetery, clearly derives from their first tentative explorations as filmmakers in *The Trip,* for it also was shot in 16 mm format, in a spontaneous and informal manner, then inserted into the 35 mm film. These acid scenes mark the attempt of Hopper and Fonda to plant one foot firmly in the underground and the other, defiantly, in Hollywood.

Having experienced Corman's filmmaking pragmatics and his box office successes, Hopper and Fonda set out in *Easy Rider* to challenge the hierarchy that relegated the underground to poverty and Hollywood directors to conventional filmmaking techniques. After he met Fonda and Hopper on Corman's *The Trip,* Nicholson recommended they seek financial backing for *Easy Rider* from Bob Rafelson and Bert Schneider, whose firm Raybert had strong ties to the television production firm of Screen Gems and to its parent company, Columbia Pictures. Nicholson was simultaneously collaborating with Raybert to make the era's *other* major psychedelic film aimed for general release, *Head.* Hopper and Fonda had been negotiating with AIP to produce *Easy Rider,* and Corman had agreed to serve as executive producer (Fonda 249), but Raybert ended up partnering with Fonda's Pando Productions and convincing Columbia to back *Easy Rider.*

For nearly a decade, Schneider and Rafelson influenced the look and feel of both TV and film—especially the road films that would emerge in "New Hollywood" in the seventies, after they parlayed their television success in *The Monkees* into producing *Easy Rider* and other key road films of the seventies. As Fonda noted in his autobiography, "*Easy Rider* money is Monkees money" (252). Likewise, Rafelson reported that his and Schneider's partnership on *The Monkees* show was merely a first step into filmmaking: "We began with a TV series because that was a foot in the door. It was easier to get a pilot of a TV series made than it was to get a movie made" (Lefcowitz 7).[12] Enthusiasm in the psychedelic movement for new media had eased the artistic vanguard's suspicions about mass media, thus opening up TV and exploitation films like Corman's as the backdrop upon which young filmmakers were willing to stage their rebellious visual experiments. Lauding the television series *The Monkees,* for instance, Timothy Leary noted in *The Politics of Ecstasy* that youngsters are "skillful and experienced at handling the media and psychedelic drugs" (Lefcowitz 35), for the two often went hand-in-hand. For these young producers in an increasingly postmodern culture, there was no irony in abandoning the earlier avant-garde desire to walk through the "doors of perception"—which Aldous Huxley had suggested would open when people used psychedelic drugs—in order now to desire getting "a foot in the door" of a Hollywood studio.

Back in 1968, Columbia Pictures gave Raybert just the break it sought when the studio engaged Rafelson to direct the psychedelic film, *Head,* starring the Monkees, thanks to the smash success of Raybert's weekly television series with the band. *Head* was highly self-reflexive and inspired by psychedelic visuals. Typical of the commercial ventures of the time that aspired to be hip, a spirit of spontaneity and improvisation marked the creation of *Head*—as, indeed, improvisation had shaped the TV series *The Monkees* (Lefcowitz 12, 18). Rafelson brought in his friend Jack Nicholson, who had starred in many Corman films but was contemplating giving up acting, to write the script for *Head.* In a technique similar to that pioneered earlier by the Merry Pranksters, all the actors, producers, and creative team of *Head* brainstormed together on a tape recorder, which Nicholson crafted into a script.[13] The finished film baffled Columbia executives with its irreverence and incoherence, so when the early, limited-release screenings of *Head* received mixed reviews, the studio abruptly canceled its general release

(Lefcowitz 58). Only one year later, however, Columbia radically shifted gears and gave Rafelson and Schneider almost anything they wanted, because they had brokered the partnership between the studio and Fonda and Hopper to produce *Easy Rider,* whose success made revolutionary profits (Hill 21).

In *Easy Rider,* then, we see both the psychedelic film and the biker genre film find their artistic zenith, for Hopper as director and Fonda as producer successfully unite Corman's strictly budgeted filmmaking approach with underground film tropes, and add a psychedelic energy stemming from Ken Kesey's psychedelic experiments. Costing $400,000 yet eventually grossing $50 million (Hugo 67), *Easy Rider* not only proved the profitability of youth-oriented, low-budget films, but also, importantly, demonstrated the ongoing power and deep appeal of the road story as a genre of youthful rebellion.

While Raybert brought to *Easy Rider* its links to Columbia Pictures, Hopper added the sensibility of the new "art film" movement in his attempt to bridge Hollywood and the underground. Hopper and Fonda were well poised to do so, since Fonda was powerful as Henry Fonda's son, yet had the rebel badge of having been busted for possession of pot. Hopper had roots in all the rebel factions, from the Beats to the underground, from the avant-garde filmmakers to Hollywood: in the 1950s, he had taken photographs that appeared in Beat exhibitions (in fact, Beat poet Michael McClure accompanied Hopper and Fonda when they pitched the idea of *Easy Rider* to Raybert). As a young actor, Hopper got his start by playing minor parts alongside James Dean in *Rebel Without a Cause* and *Giant* (1956). Hopper had also appeared in the biker film, *The Glory Stompers* (dir. Anthony M. Lanza, 1967), wearing a swastika. But Hopper was also well connected in the avant-garde: he appeared in one of Andy Warhol's screen tests. Around that time, Hopper had fantasized about an intimacy between art and commerce: "Bruce Connor, of all the so-called 'underground movie-makers,' is the most original talent. . . . What a great idea for a major company to hire Connor" (9). In 1969, Hopper clarified the Oedipal type of rebellion he envisioned:

> Film is an art-form, an expensive art-form, it's the Sistine Chapel of the Twentieth Century. . . . [The new filmmakers will appear] when it's their turn to change the balance of power in the good old American Way; then my generation will have its say. . . . Can we fill the movie-gap? And take back our invention? And surpass the Europeans? Yes, when that Individual comes to town. Remember him? The Individual? (11)

Here we see the distinct shift away from the psychedelic philosophy of collaboration to the accelerating romance of the American film auteur, whose talent is measured in rebellion.

Fonda's character Wyatt in *Easy Rider* is like the grown-up son of the "exurbanite father" whom anarchist poet Kenneth Rexroth had disdained in 1960 for watching cowboy genre shows on television (see chap. 3). Fonda's character Wyatt serves as an intergenerational challenge to his father Henry's roles as Wyatt in *My Darling Clementine* (1946) and Tom Joad in the film version of *The Grapes of Wrath* (1940). Between Tom Joad and Wyatt, from Henry Fonda to his son Peter, the self-styled auteur's road rebel in the 1960s seems to be fighting an Oedipal battle in Hollywood—which signals a far different type of insurrection than the one undertaken in the late fifties by the Beats, who wanted to exorcise the ghost of Tom Joad in order to remap the road story so as to tell a new type of story altogether.

Historians like David James distinguish the art film from the alternative film, which had failed to make an impact beyond small circles of the autonomous avant-garde. In contrast, the art film emerged between the "extremes [of] the underground on the one hand and . . . independent industrial productions and eventually even 'anti-establishment' studio features like *Bonnie and Clyde* and *Midnight Cowboy* on the other" (280). James includes *Easy Rider* in this category, arguing that art films constitute a genre, rather than a "mode" or "institution."

Although art films address myriad themes, the road trope is central to the most significant films that constitute the art "genre." Hellman's *Two-Lane Blacktop* (1971), Arthur Penn's *Bonnie and Clyde* (1967), and John Schlesinger's *Midnight Cowboy* (1969)—all exemplary instances of the art film's "radical vision," according to James—also share the underlying theme of "automobility." In this manifestation, the road as a trope clearly continues to offer a landscape of rebellion to this generation of countercultural artists, but the road now additionally offers a means of mending the rift between counterculture and commerce.[14] In the form of *Easy Rider,* the road narrative not only transcended the division between the artisanal and the mass market, but its principals succeeded in moving beyond their roots in television and the drive-in theater form to establish the "art film" as a genre, which then, in turn, helped transform the rebel road story into a full-fledged Hollywood product in the 1970s.

In many ways, then, *Easy Rider* reincarnates the celebratory Beat road story for the hippie generation nearly a decade after the road story was co-opted by television. However, because of the shift in the younger counterculture's attitude toward the commercial sphere, *Easy Rider* deliberately attempts to negotiate the tensions between the older Beat philosophy of "disengagement" and the new one of "beating the system." Specifically, the hippie road film conflates the "social outlaw," as the Beats liked to consider themselves, with the Hells Angel outlaw that Fonda and Hopper had each played in biker films. Whereas the Beats had denigrated the capitalist system, the *Easy Rider* characters Wyatt (a.k.a. Captain America) and Billie try to exploit it by importing drugs from Mexico and selling them in the United States. In the famous speech before he is beaten to death by rednecks, George (Nicholson) explains to Billie why they frighten the rural hicks they encounter, for the freedom of the rebels makes the compromises of the people all the more shameful—"It's hard to be bought and sold in the marketplace."

Billie and Wyatt hope they can *use* the system to finance their forays in counterculture, perhaps the way Rafelson, Hopper, and Fonda believed they could participate in the counterculture *and* work in Hollywood to make what Fonda called in 1969 an "honest" film (Campbell 32). At this level of meta-commentary, *Easy Rider* offers an anxious, if somewhat cynical, document of the quixotic dreams of its filmmakers that mythologized their own complicity in the system. Since Billie and Wyatt are selling drugs in order to retire comfortably *within* the capitalist economy, George's speech, in a sense, condemns the folly of the two easy riders for being bought and sold, but it does so with a sense of futility, as if critique were pointless. Fonda explained this philosophy of *Easy Rider* in 1969 in a *Rolling Stone* interview:

> I am representing everybody who feels that freedom can be bought, who feels that you can find freedom through other things, like riding motorcycles through the air or smoking grass. . . . My movie is about the *lack* of freedom, not about freedom . . . Liberty's a whore, and we're all taking an easy ride. (Campbell 28)

The slang term "easy rider" is important here: it refers to a man who lives off the earnings of his prostitute girlfriend, as her freeloading boyfriend, not her pimp. This term creates the sense that some sort of criticism about easy money is being rendered by a film willing to cash in on vague social insights.

However, what disappoints film scholars in *Easy Rider* is not its attempt to commercialize counterculture, but the contours that attempt takes. The film exploits the outlaw trope, simplifying and celebrating it without exploring its limitations. In other words, the film avoids taking on the responsibility of revitalizing the outlaw stance as a viable option of social change. Instead of articulating any strengths or weaknesses in the outlaw "machinery" of film, Wyatt simply states, "We blew it, man," as if any cogent examination of what actually went wrong when he and Billie were on the road would betray this drug-induced insight. Fonda explained his intentions in 1969: "We don't give out any information through dialogue. We have a very loose plot, nothing you can follow" (Campbell 28). The closest explanation comes in George's famous speech that freedom and being free are two separate things, implying that defining what constitutes freedom in the 1960s serves little function, especially since freedom often amounted to taking drugs (as Blues's rant in *The Wild Angels* suggested). Rather, the more ineffable state of "being free" is the only worthwhile goal. As did the Merry Pranksters' failure to create a document from their footage of the 1964 "acid test" bus trip, *Easy Rider* confirms for the hippie generation that the ephemeral gesture may serve as content.[15]

Yet *Easy Rider* bears so many similarities to details of *The Electric Kool-Aid Acid Test* that they surely both tapped a basic zeitgeist of the era (or else Terry Southern, screenwriter of *Easy Rider,* read Wolfe's early publications). It is easy to sense a resonance between Kesey's Prankster persona as "Captain Flag" (Perry and Babbs 51), the spiritual leader who draped himself in the American flag and searched for new expressive forms, and Fonda's as Captain America, who wore flag clothes and decorated his custom Harley in flag patterns and searched for America—a quest far more solipsistic than Captain Flag's. But the biggest overlap, discussed in some detail in the previous chapter, is in Captain America's cryptic message to Billie, "We blew it." In a weird coincidence that Tom Wolfe might have called *"the synch!"* (*Electric* 128), these are the very words Kesey utters after the acid graduation while on stage performing music with the Pranksters: "WE BLEW IT!" (*Electric* 368). The difference between these two utterances is significant, for Kesey's pronouncement is anchored in self-awareness, whereas Fonda's signals the debt owed by Wyatt and Billie for their faulty dream of freedom.

Easy Rider succeeds in eliciting in viewers the exhilarating feeling of just "being free," which is a measure of its importance as a pop culture text. For *Easy Rider* offers a sensory experience that celebrates automobility *as* autonomy and mobility, thanks to its soundtrack and the dynamic visual images of the landscape blurring behind the speeding motorcycles, as well as its melodramatic ending. In its use of popular rock 'n' roll songs of the 1960s, *Easy Rider* truly succeeded in marrying the commercial and the cultural. Indeed, the *Easy Rider* soundtrack album was one of the first collateral products of film marketed to the counterculture; such a product is now a standard component in the "transmedia" marketing campaigns of films.

As the ecstatic road experience reminiscent of the Beat years entered the mass market in the form of *Easy Rider,* the evolving postwar road story gestures toward social commentary yet invests its energy in cinematography, mise-en-scène, music, and editing. In the end, the new filmmakers reject the position of social critic in order to be film *auteurs,* who leave a palpable trace of their artistry in a narrative about social protest. For instance, *Easy Rider* could have examined why the rebel of the 1960s cannot live in "voluntary poverty" the way the Beats did and thus must sell drugs in order to be creative or authentic, or why the rebel must grapple with capital even if only as an outlaw who is complicit with dominant power. Instead, the film toys with the antitheses of the counterculture and marketplace without seeking a dialectic, and settles for the easy ride of the outlaw as martyr of "the system." In effect, *Easy Rider* punishes Wyatt and Billie for being "bought and sold" while simultaneously making them all the more precious for having sought an impossible dream.

As a landmark road film in postwar America, *Easy Rider* combines a relatively conventional narrative form with avant-garde techniques like the film's subjective sequences, vérité footage, and disjunctive edits. It is *Scorpio Rising*'s director Anger and other underground filmmakers like Bruce Conners or Bruce Baillie who inspired the formal techniques that cemented *Easy Rider*'s "rebel" reputation in popular culture, except that even as *Easy Rider* retains Anger's pan shots of motorcycles and pop music soundtrack, it totally eliminates the gay references of *Scorpio Rising*. By stripping the formal underground techniques from the context of their social critiques, *Easy Rider* helped turn the rebel road film into a generic set of motifs that have, so to speak, nowhere to go.[16]

Although *Easy Rider* is conservative compared to the underground films it emulates, its attempt to make a cultural statement is obviously more ambitious than the social inquiries found in any films made for the drive-in theater market. Of course, Hopper and Fonda were situated quite differently from Corman, with secure backing from Columbia Pictures and Raybert productions, the power of the Fonda family name, and Hopper's ties to the Beats and the underground, not to mention their audacity as young men in what seemed to be the dawning of a New Age. However, despite its gestures to the underground, *Easy Rider* demonstrates the difficulty of combining the socially critical with the commercially viable.[17]

The middle road that *Easy Rider* navigates between the mainstream and the margins, however, marks a turning point in the film industry and the road story. As we will see in the next chapter, the film's financial success brings the art film genre into the 1970s as an auteur-driven "New Hollywood" tries to usurp the Old. The contradictions of *Easy Rider*'s goal to "commercialize counterculture" may be evident in retrospect but, in the late sixties and early seventies, the road genre was born from this dream. The prescient soundtrack of *Easy Rider* accompanying images of Hopper and Fonda flying down the road on their Harley choppers, leather fringe and long hair blowing in the breeze, absolutely captivated young America, the way *On the Road* had a decade earlier. But, with its conservative narrative closure, *Easy Rider* did little with the emotions it incited except to suggest that while mobility was fun, autonomy was dangerous, and unintelligibility was spiritual.

Even given its failures, however, *Easy Rider* offers an intriguing record of just what aspects of the underground film movement were jettisoned in order to bring the biker film into the movie theaters of America. Tellingly, *Easy Rider* erases the homoerotic potential of the buddy story and transforms people of color from a Beat "mystery" into despicable pests, useful only as a source of drugs. Aside from a few vague criticisms, *Easy Rider* represses any understanding of how rebel culture both resists *and* traffics in the ideology of power. In contrast, Kerouac's and Anger's characters explored in greater depth the sexism, racism, and homophobia that was the dark side of the Beat "mysteries." We might not like the racist and misogynist confessions found in Kerouac's *The Subterraneans* or the fascism of *Scorpio Rising*, but we recognize in these works a social critique with substance.

Easy Rider thus embodies the contradictions of the art film as a form of critique when it is bought and sold in the marketplace.

MIDNIGHT COWBOY AS SOCIAL CRITIQUE

In contrast, *Midnight Cowboy,* another important film of 1969 that opens and closes on the road, depicts the dark side of the American dream while also interrogating traditional components of filmmaking, including narrative and mise-en-scène. *Midnight Cowboy* was British veteran director John Schlesinger's first American film and won the Oscar for Best Picture, despite its "X" rating and explicit treatment of homosexuality. Whereas *Easy Rider* uses the road story to get the audience's adrenaline going, *Midnight Cowboy* uses the journeys undertaken by its marginalized characters to illustrate the failure of modern-day America to bring them any closer to their dreams.

The framing bus trips in *Midnight Cowboy* represent idealized quests for an escape from dead ends, but they only bring about a loss of the hope that had hitherto sustained the main characters. At the beginning of the film, Joe Buck (Jon Voight) escapes his dead-end existence in small-town Texas by taking a bus to New York, where he hopes to get rich as a hustler servicing rich women. At the end of the film, Joe, having failed as a hustler, brings his dying friend Rizzo (Dustin Hoffman) by bus from New York to Florida, where Rizzo imagines the sun and surf will soothe his urban ailments. But Rizzo dies on the bus before reaching his "promised land." The final scene, filmed through the bus window, shows the frightened Joe Buck with his arm around the dead man, as reflections of the Miami cityscape bounce off the window pane. The two bus trips in *Midnight Cowboy* reveal the impossibility of autonomy and the futility of mobility for unheroic outlaws, hustlers, and rebels who, more often than not, are immobilized in their marginal lives.

The film teases out the issues that lay dormant in the 1960s biker narratives, especially *Easy Rider,* by deliberately exploring the relationship of the marginalized rebel-figure to commodity culture. For example, in *Midnight Cowboy,* the relation of street people like Rizzo and Joe to American consumerism painfully, yet humorously, comes into focus when the two are shown shivering and shuffling against the cold in their living space, dancing to a jingle on the radio from an orange juice commercial. All of Rizzo's images of his fantasized Florida, from the posters on his walls to the song for Florida orange juice, come from advertising, thereby rendering an ironic view of how people in the margins interpret commodity messages in highly idiosyncratic ways. In an earlier scene, while Joe seduces a floozy living in a penthouse, they make love on top of the (newly invented) television remote control, which flips the TV from channel to channel in the background. *Midnight Cowboy* thus shares with *Scorpio Rising* a kindred use of the medium of film to look awry at mainstream culture.

130

A second issue *Midnight Cowboy* more forthrightly addresses is homosexuality and the potential for homoerotic unruliness behind dominant codes of masculinity. If Joe Buck embodies the trope of the hustler common to gay novels that explore urban alienation, as argued by Richard Dyer in *Now You See It,* his ambiguous sexuality also bespeaks a Beat legacy as well. Indeed, Dyer claims that "the Beats' stress on the spirituality of sexuality is not to be found in the sixties gay underground [films]" (140); rather, Dyer notes, it turns up in novels like James Baldwin's *Another Country* (1962), John Rechy's *City of Night* (1963), and James Herlihy's *Midnight Cowboy* (1965). Dyer argues that each of these stories tells of a male loner who goes in search of America, testing himself without much introspection because of his "uncertainty about his masculinity and heterosexuality. It is not that he wants to find out if he is gay or what that means, but that he wants to prove that he is masculine" (140). Dyer's formulation describes *Midnight Cowboy*'s frank scrutiny of masculinity.

Like the urban novels listed by Dyer, the film version of *Midnight Cowboy* also illustrates with accuracy and poignancy the plight of New York City's lower economic classes, who hustle to stay alive in the streets outside the high-rise penthouses of the wealthy elite who ignore those "below" them. The disparity between the johns and the hustlers in the film pointedly reveals the exploitative side of America's celebration of freedom. *Midnight Cowboy* dialectically deconstructs social hierarchies and fantasies about the potential collaborations between art and commerce, especially in the contrast between the scene when the underground film artists from Greenwich Village film Joe Buck and the filmmakers' party in the Village, in which Joe and Rizzo gorge themselves on the food because they are starving.

Representing a man who sells his sexual services, the hustler trope in *Midnight Cowboy* consciously calls attention to the interrelationship of commerce and rebellion, far more so than does the device of *Easy Rider*'s heroes as drug runners. As mentioned, the slang term "easy rider" refers to a boyfriend who lives off his girlfriend's earnings as a prostitute, which makes us wonder what to call Rizzo, who cannot survive on the poor earnings of Joe Buck, a hustler who fails even with his homosexual clients. *Midnight Cowboy* explores the price of masculine postures, especially the sexualized "macho" role, as embodied in the cowboy type (which *Brokeback Mountain* [2005] unravels). This examination is both literal, as we see Joe Buck "bought and sold" in the hustler marketplace, as well as symbolic, for we also see their restrictive gender roles interfere with the expression of platonic *or* sexual love between Joe Buck and Rizzo. In contrast, *Easy Rider* blends the masculine codes of the biker, outlaw, and cowboy while repressing the homoerotic potential inherent in these American myths of masculinity and ignoring what it means to pose as a rebel, like Joe Buck does, in order to eke out a living on the street. Another important way *Easy Rider* oversimplifies the social problems on which it trades can be seen when Billie and Wyatt die at the hands of dumb rednecks, whereas Rizzo dies because of more elusive enemies—poverty and poor health. While *Easy Rider* has no obligation to address the "crisis" of masculinity or the "price" of freedom, the film shirks any clear and specific position about rebellion, masculinity, or commerce. With its tone of celebration and lack of analysis, *Easy Rider* sets the pace for many of the road films to follow in the seventies.

The paradoxical mix of art and commodity in the road story of the 1960s began with the bold experiment of *Route 66* on television from 1960 to 1964 and came full circle with the motorcycle TV series, *Then Came Bronson,* which ran on NBC between 1969 and 1970. Motorcycles evolved into a symbol of the philosophical introvert, with not only *Then Came Bronson* but also Robert M. Pirsig's *Zen and the Art of Motorcycle Maintenance: An Inquiry into Values* (1974), a memoir of Pirsig's travels with his son in the form of a "Chautauqua" (15)—part philosophy and part narrative—about the need to return to values of "individual integrity, self-reliance and old-fashioned gumption" (358). The loud roar of the choppers in Roger Corman's drive-in biker films displaced the need for any interrogation of the rebel's social function, unlike those offered in *Scorpio Rising* and *Midnight Cowboy.* When Raybert joined forces with Hopper and Fonda to produce *Easy Rider,* custom Harley choppers became the hybrid symbol of aspiring auteur filmmaking. Artist-producers who tried to balance critique and commerce may not have been cynical, but that may be because drugs gave a purple haze to their profit ethics. What is important to see is the travels the road story takes in the 1960s, among rivalrous media, jealous filmmakers, and angry young men. Although many road stories of the 1960s helped foster the transformation of Beat themes into their stripped-down signifiers, *Easy Rider* is the one text that, above all others, marks an end to the era of the avant-garde road *story* and a beginning of the contemporary road *genre* of commodity films.

6

Genre and Gender in 1970s'
New Hollywood

> The cultural treasures . . . have an origin which . . . cannot
> [be] contemplate[d] without horror. They owe their existence
> not only to the efforts of the great minds and talents who have
> created them, but also to the anonymous toil of their contempo-
> raries. There is no document of civilization which is not at the
> same time a document of barbarism. And just as such a docu-
> ment is not free of barbarism, barbarism taints also the manner
> in which it was transmitted from one owner to another. . . .
> [Thus, we learn to] brush history against the grain.
> —Walter Benjamin, *Illuminations* (1940)

> The spectacle is the epic poem of the strife [of each individual
> commodity]. . . . Of arms and the man the spectacle does not
> sing, but rather of passions and the commodity.
> —Guy Debord, *The Society of the Spectacle* (1967)

The financial success of *Easy Rider* rocked Hollywood, causing a revolution now referred to as "New Hollywood," so named to draw a distinction between
the old studio system and the auteur-driven projects of the early 1970s. Francis
Ford Coppola, Peter Bogdanovich, Martin Scorsese, Steven Spielberg, and other
directors each established his name in New Hollywood at least in part through
a film about a woman on the road—*The Rain People* (1969), *Paper Moon* (1973),
Alice Doesn't Live Here Anymore (1974), *The Sugarland Express* (1974), *Two-Lane
Blacktop* (1971), *Badlands* (1973), plus others—establishing each director's cred-
ibility and opening the door to greater opportunities. These so-called Movie Brats
championed innovative techniques and crafted unconventional business alliances
with the Hollywood studios, and some have become the most powerful film
artists in the business today. Yet the epic histories written about these directors
who emerged during this period overlook what Walter Benjamin would call the
"anonymous toil"—in this case, of both genre and gender. These directors are
typically portrayed—and typically portrayed themselves during the seventies—in

terms of individual artistic rebellion against the studio system, ignoring (if not obfuscating) their contribution to a collective genre.

It's time to brush the mythology of the New Hollywood auteur against the grain. As these grandiose stories typically go (and they *do* constitute a genre of their own), a talented and rebellious young visionary comes from film school to triumph in the marketplace, legitimizing Roger Corman's low-budget techniques while Americanizing the innovations of the French New Wave. All these filmmakers had gotten their first chance by contributing to drive-in theater films, thanks to mentoring from director and producer Corman. Nevertheless, this up-and-coming generation of directors did not intend to settle for making B movies. Rather, their passionate commitment to auteurism underscores their ambitions to work in Hollywood without relinquishing their rebel stance. Thus, this chapter will reveal that New Hollywood depended utterly upon the road genre and the appeal of female automobility, as had many drive-in films produced by American International Pictures (AIP). Auteurism masked the interdependence of gender and genre in the early 1970s by adding some European prestige. Along with these auteurs, the contributions of a few influential Hollywood women were critical to the development of the road genre during this time, yet this fact is overlooked in the mythology of New Hollywood. Successful actresses like Goldie Hawn and Ellen Burstyn brought legitimacy to the road films made by neophyte directors like Spielberg (*The Sugarland Express*) and Scorsese (whom Burstyn selected to direct *her* project, *Alice Doesn't Live Here Anymore*). Furthermore, girlfriends and wives contributed much to this era, as we shall see with *Alice Doesn't Live Here Anymore* and *Paper Moon. Wanda,* the only road film of the era directed by a woman, was made by Barbara Loden, an actress married to director Elia Kazan. In sum, genre *and* gender worked together to shape New Hollywood, although the histories ignore this by focusing instead on the auteurism of these young men.

Not that these films or filmmakers were feminist—they definitely were not—but there was growing curiosity about the sexual revolution and growing pressure to represent women as more than just wives. In these films, the heroines' premarital or extramarital sexual adventures allude to the period's larger social rebellions without committing the director to any specific political statement. David Laderman notes that early seventies road films "*minimize* overtly rebellious gestures against society" (84), and we will see here that the centrality of women in these films helps put rebellion under restraint. The filmmakers of this era wanted to distinguish themselves as artists, not social activists, and this was done, in part, by replacing specific social critique with aloof inquiries into the autonomy and mobility of these middle-class white women. In the process, however, these directors gave coherent shape to the road genre, developing road films into respected commodities shrouded by the mystique of auteurism.

Each mobile heroine helps the director marry his rebellious artistry to marketplace demands. This insight was made clear in 1970 by Joan Didion in her novel, *Play It as It Lays,* which offers a sophisticated look at exploitation films that trafficked in women, showing that the endless circulation of naïve starlets between male directors came at a considerable cost. *Play It as It Lays* explicitly places film genre alongside the gender politics of auteurism, revealing the New Hollywood woman to be a sort of commodity—a "trophy wife" caught between the promises and pitfalls of women's liberation.

Both male auteurs and feminist critics got a lot of mileage out of the road genre in this era. Betty Friedan and other feminist writers were turning their attention to popular culture, and their negative reviews contributed to the road film's reputation as a sexist genre. These writers were intolerant of what Friedan called "Hardy Boy" road films, those films centered on male-male buddies like *Easy Rider* and the studio knock-off *Little Fauss and Big Halsy.* Often, these feminist writings lacked a nuanced critique of the director or Hollywood marketplace, condemning the entire road genre while overlooking the contributions made by women. This chapter will show that, to the contrary, some women helped shape the road genre, and that its portrayal of heterosexual relationships reflects the weaknesses of the early seventies rather than those of the genre.

NEW HOLLYWOOD'S GENDERED DIVISION OF LABOR

Play It as It Lays lays bare the gendered division of labor in New Hollywood, wherein the men got famous while their showcase wives fell into anomie, even madness. Didion's heroine Maria is a trifling actress who stars in an underground art film and a biker film before marrying the man who directed both. Maria's husband, aspiring auteur Carter Lang, was modeled on biker film director/producer Roger Corman, or one of his protégés.[1] We learn that Carter gained his reputation, at least initially, by capturing Maria's raw emotions in his film, *Maria.* He obtains this moving footage by forcing Maria to speak on camera about difficult personal experiences, such as her mother's death in a car accident. Didion's fictional account corresponds to anecdotes about New Hollywood auteurs who eagerly capitalized on the emotional "reality" provided by their girlfriends or wives. For example, Henry Jaglom describes how he created a scene in his BBS-produced film *A Safe Place:*

> While I was going with Karen [Black] at one point in our relationship as boy and girl friend, she started telling me some story about lights in the eyes, and I remember getting out my pencil and writing it down. She was crying, and I was writing it down, and then I used that in my movie. (Crane and Fryer 101)

135

Carter's profitable biker film, *Angel Beach,* also stars Maria.[2] The biker genre film always includes a rape, and Carter's compliance with this formula gives Didion the chance to press home multiple meanings of the gambling expression that serves as her title: "play it as it lays." Maria is also expected to "play" offscreen by being a sexually available "lay" for studio bosses. Didion thus expands the biker genre's rape formula to serve as a metaphor for women's exploitation in New Hollywood.

Maria represents the price paid by women for their role as the "medium" upon which New Hollywood turns, onscreen and off. Maria is numbed by the life she faces as the wife of an up-and-coming director, a life that includes shopping with women who hate one another, taking drugs, and sleeping around. When Maria becomes pregnant, all her lovers meld together indistinguishably to form "a single sexual encounter, one dreamed fuck, no beginnings or endings, no point beyond itself" (67–68). In addition to her aimless excursions and trips to visit Carter on location in the desert, she discovers the secret geography of abortion when she is driven to the Valley for the then-illegal procedure. The theme of abortion filters Didion's representation of New Hollywood, not only as a metaphor of the barrenness of the exploitation film industry, but also more literally, with abortion presented as yet another male-run enterprise. Just as she examines the split between the male filmmaker and the female muse, Didion traces the gendered division of labor in the illegal commerce of abortion. By association, *Play It as It Lays* shows both auteurs and abortionists as profiting from the bodies of women, for whom they have little respect. The novel explores the wounds left by these two occupations on Maria's body and soul. Didion's journalistic detachment veils her political stance; only the accumulation of the novel's many tropes—the biker genre rape, the auteur's calculated career trajectory, the trophy wife, and the illegal abortion—reveals Didion's critique of the female condition.

Before all that, however, Maria takes to the road to distract herself from the illegal abortion Carter pressures her to have. The freeway segments offer a noteworthy contrast to Maria's overall paralysis in Hollywood, which stems from her belated refusal to feed her emotions to cameras *or* the auteur. The road offers solace, meaning, and direction: "She drove the San Diego to the Harbor, the Harbor up to the Hollywood, the Hollywood to the Golden State, the Santa Monica, the Santa Ana, the Pasadena, the Ventura. She drove it as a riverman runs a river, every day more attuned to its currents, its deceptions" (13–14). Still, her automobility fails to provide her with any real escape from the Hollywood commodity system, which her sexuality helps lubricate.

In short, then, Didion's novel aptly predicts how the road films of the 1970s reveal a struggle of epic proportions between on-screen narratives that focus on female mobility and the off-screen histories about the New Hollywood auteurs themselves, which focus on the men. For this reason, the road films of New Hollywood embody the era's larger conflicts between sexual freedom and domestic responsibility, rebellion and nihilism, mobility and stasis, protest and passivity. Further, there is considerable anxiety among auteurs about making a film that is too commercial, as Peter Biskind's book *Easy Riders, Raging Bulls* (1998) shows again and again. We might say that many auteurist filmmakers from this time displaced their worries about the commodity status of their films onto the women they cast in those films.

FRANCE'S NEW WAVE AND AMERICAN GENRE

The French New Wave philosophy migrated to Hollywood in the form of *Bonnie and Clyde* (dir. Arthur Penn, 1967), a gangsters-on-the-road film that François Truffaut was initially slated to direct. *Bonnie and Clyde* had tremendous influence on the aesthetic style and narrative substance of the auteurist road genre, including the importance of female automobility.

During the fifties and sixties, rebellious French filmmakers like Truffaut and Jean-Luc Godard offered insight into American genre films while popularizing cost-saving formal innovations—their films doubled as entertainment and bold meditations on cinema as an art form.[3] Along with this new aesthetic outlook came the French filmmakers' fervent belief in auteurism, which lauded the signature styles of individual directors. This philosophy was disseminated in the United States during the sixties via film columns in the *Village Voice* and other publications, and it became a standard symbol of rebellion against the studios.

Godard's important film *Breathless* (1959) was partially an homage to the genre of American gangster films, and partially a revolution in formal style that emphasized spontaneity. With many of its segments featuring the road and "automobility," *Breathless* also explored the themes of autonomy and mobility, and the relationship between France's postwar youth and American genre films exported to France after World War II.

Here in America, *Bonnie and Clyde* was one of the first American films to pay homage to the French New Wave, extending the revisions to the gangster genre visible in *Breathless*. But it also capitalized on the uniquely American themes of Depression bank robbers and rural heartlands, along with the romance of the open road and the defiant outlaw. (The film was made even more appealing by the notoriety of the actual bank robbers, Bonnie Parker and Clyde Barrow, played by Faye Dunaway and Warren Beatty.) As we have seen, the Beats in the 1950s worked to uncouple the road story from Depression-era symbols, especially the "ghost" of Tom Joad in *The Grapes of Wrath*, but *Bonnie and Clyde* eagerly reclaimed the Dust Bowl as part of the American cinemascape. Just as Godard did in *Breathless*, director Penn used the "on the lam" sequences of *Bonnie and Clyde* to reflect on the ways in which mass media shape public attention, although Bonnie and Clyde actively solicit media attention and shape it by providing the press with their own photos and poems. *Bonnie and Clyde*'s mixture of European art film rebelliousness and American outlaws metaphorically spilled over into the auteurist fight against "the system."[4]

The success of *Bonnie and Clyde* in 1967 and *Easy Rider* in 1969 suggested to many observers that the United States might be positioned to develop its own "New Wave," a hope mirrored in the moniker "New Hollywood." The low-budget techniques and high-minded concepts of American auteurs sparked a homegrown countercultural movement in the 1970s that rivaled the French New Wave's influence in the 1960s. Taken together, the road and the rebel became the foundational motifs of New Hollywood.

Whereas French New Wave directors consciously interrogated the link between film genres and their generation, New Hollywood filmmakers deemphasized any contributions to genres they might be making. The American cult of auteurism focused on an artist's stylistic innovations rather than on the formulae shared with others. For example, Monte Hellman, the director of the road film *Two-Lane Blacktop,* cites European film theory to demonstrate that his interest in the road story was an aesthetic bid for spontaneity rather than a function of genre. Hellman refers to Siegfried Kracauer's idea that the street is "a place where the flow of life is bound to assert itself" (72).[5] Hellman claims the road and the cars in his film are "just a cultural appendage . . . side effects. A way to augment the reality" (Walker 37).

By virtue of the preoccupation of these filmmakers with New Wave formalism, the road film emerged as a genre uniquely aligned with the aesthetic of the time—the hand-held shots, editing techniques, and telltale "coincidences" interjected in the mise-en-scène (such as a news brief about Vietnam on the car radio). The road setting offered a creative location to budding auteurs, who valued the cinematic attributes of spontaneity and vérité. For instance, Coppola shot *The Rain People* without a script, and Hellman released the script of *Two-Lane Blacktop* just pages at a time to the actors in a bid to make their performances more spontaneous. Despite the universal recognition of *Easy Rider* as an influential—even revolutionary—film, each additional film in the early seventies that featured the road may well have seemed unique to its director. While studios and critics perhaps understood that they were witnessing the birth of Hollywood's road genre, auteurs preferred to see their work in more personal and philosophical terms, feeling that their films just *happened* to be road stories. No matter the point of view, the seventies produced a noteworthy body of road films that address issues of autonomy, mobility, and alienation in highly idiosyncratic ways.

Bonnie and Clyde also contributed to the New Hollywood revolution by showcasing Bonnie's viewpoint and voice, a shift that reflected the growing impact of the women's movement. Bonnie's insights defy the "blind hubris and stubborn resistance of the traditional gangster" (Man 23), distinguishing *Bonnie and Clyde*'s revision of the gangster genre by means of its unexpected portrayal of gender. The French New Wave films certainly included women, but America's New Hollywood films truly focused on them, using them as symbols of progressive politics, albeit without any coherent gender philosophy.

Indeed, this landmark film owes much of its power to its representation of Bonnie as a transgressive female. Bonnie's delight in autonomy, along with her penchant for crime and her thrill in running from the police, all mark her as a threatening woman. Prior to 1967, Bonnie might have been portrayed as a femme fatale, like the criminal women in *noir* road thrillers like *Detour* (1945) or *Gun Crazy* (1949). But as reimagined in the sixties, Bonnie emerged as an outlaw martyr. The scale of violence within the film was unprecedented, but the on-screen murder of Bonnie in particular, filmed in slow motion, achieved iconic status in film history. Her brutal fate on-screen was seen as a condemnation of trigger-happy state power, serving as Penn's rebuke to the war in Vietnam. Yet the political allusions *Bonnie and Clyde* may have conveyed during the Vietnam War did not carry over to the other mobile heroines in the seventies New Hollywood. This character type would reappear in the road films of the nineties, but in the sixties and seventies, Bonnie was an exception rather than the rule—far too self-assured to be a model of gender, too excited by crime to have been a feminist. Bonnie helped put women into the road film, but once there, the female characters exemplified Maria's passivity rather than Bonnie's power.

MATERNITY AND MOBILITY

Because they controlled the financing, the established Hollywood studios considered films to be commodities over which they had complete jurisdiction.[6] But first-time director Dennis Hopper and producer Peter Fonda wanted to change this with *Easy Rider*. Using low-budget techniques they had learned while working with Roger Corman, they minimized the costs of *Easy Rider* and thus maximized their freedom from studio interference; this was how they created a defiant film that drew from the innovations of underground filmmaking, the very antithesis of commercial film. Hopper and Fonda's previous work with Corman made them more comfortable with the notion of working within a genre, even though they were still invested to some degree in the auteurist myth of creative rebellion. They wanted to stage a revolution, but they also wanted it to be *in* Hollywood, not relegated to the screens of drive-in theaters of America's suburbs.

Initially, *Easy Rider*'s success catapulted its principals into a great negotiating position for contracts with the studios. Columbia, for instance, signed *Easy Rider*'s producers Bob Rafelson and Bert Schneider to "an unusually liberal multi-picture production deal" for films budgeted under $1 million (Hill 58). Rafelson and Schneider added Steve Blauner to their company, converting Raybert into BBS (for Bob, Bert, and Steve). Their new production company went on to create many of the films that established the "open-ended . . . naturalistic, less overtly dramatic" style of New Hollywood—films shot on location that frequently included key road segments, even if they were not all explicitly road films (Grimes 60, 61).[7] By 1971, each of the stars of *Easy Rider*—Fonda, Hopper, and Nicholson—had also directed a feature film. Although these three men never successfully moved from acting into directing, New Hollywood grew into a fascinating network of directors, actors, cinematographers, producers, and studios—all involved at one stage or another in the creation of road films.[8]

Prior to the rise of these maverick directors, the studio system had been losing a significant amount of money throughout the 1960s on lavish musical productions and Technicolor epics. Studios were focused on "roadshow" distribution, aimed at differentiating movies from TV: "Roadshowing, with the advance, reserved seating, limited showings, and 'epic' film subjects, attempted to shift the act of moviegoing into a special occasion: an event" (Wyatt, "Roadshow" 72). While this mode of distribution made sense for films like *Funny Girl* (1968), the studios' films and distribution strategies did not connect with the growing youth market. Thanks in part to productions and input from BBS, Columbia began to make headway in developing films specifically aimed at the youth, such as *Alice's Restaurant* and *Medium Cool* (both 1969), *M*A*S*H* (1970), *Carnal Knowledge* (1971), and *American Graffiti* (1973) (Wyatt, "Roadshow" 72–73). Distributing new films like these out to this new audience took some time for the studios to learn: "The confusion allowed for an incredibly rich period of filmmaking which, while still responding to the economic imperative of the film industry (i.e., to maximize box office revenue), failed to constrain the filmmakers substantially" (Wyatt, "Roadshow" 73).

Like Hopper and Fonda, Francis Ford Coppola first worked for director Roger Corman (who also served as producer on Coppola's *Dementia 13* in 1963). Having made the leap from B movies to the big budget *Finian's Rainbow* (1968), Coppola used his newfound clout to form American Zoetrope, his own production company, in the hope of gaining more creative control over his work. *The Rain People* (1969) was American Zoetrope's first effort.

Coppola gained great fame as a director for his film *The Godfather* (1972), but as crucial as that film was in the formation of the New Hollywood, so was his earlier road film *The Rain People*. Film historians rarely discuss *The Rain People,* although it embodies all the characteristics of New Hollywood film. It was shot on location from an unfinished script that incorporated improvisation and serendipity on the road to create the desired spontaneity. The cast and crew traveled in station wagons, with Cinémobile trucks in the posse, through eighteen states (Goodwin and Wise 89). The shooting schedule extended for an incredibly long four months. Critics and audiences rejected *The Rain People,* and the film lost $700,000. Despite the film's problems—the narrative does stall at some points—the desired spontaneity is quite evident in the finished film, an unpredictable and intriguing narrative about a woman on the road.

Whereas *Bonnie and Clyde* was the first to play up the significance of the female road rebel in New Hollywood film, *The Rain People* confirmed her importance two years later. While Bonnie is an outlaw, however, Coppola's heroine Natalie represents a far more innocuous type, the female road rebel the auteurs would come to favor in the 1970s, a rebel for whom motherhood is a motive for going on the road. Like Maria in *Play It as It Lays,* Natalie (Shirley Knight) in *The Rain People* becomes pregnant and wants to exert some control over her life by taking off in the car. She leaves her husband one morning without saying a word, driving off in the family station wagon (after stopping off to say good-bye to her parents). Natalie calls her husband sporadically from turnpike phone booths, first to announce that she is pregnant and then to discuss her desire for an abortion, which her husband does not want her to have. Natalie does not have a destination, but she suspects that a child will curb her autonomy, and so she keeps moving.[9]

In 1969, the politics of abortion could be conveniently slippery, perfect for the thin line the auteurs were attempting to walk between the political and the personal. Abortion signified progressive politics, yet it was also such a mainstream issue that it could hardly be considered radical in Hollywood. (Until 1973, abortion was under the jurisdiction of individual states, many of which made it illegal. The 1973 Supreme Court decision, *Roe v. Wade,* took the decision out of the states' hands and made it a national right for adult women.) The need to cross state lines to obtain an abortion in a legal state was one reason many women took road trips in the 1960s and early 1970s.

Although Natalie goes on the road to avoid motherhood, she quickly finds herself caring for a childlike character. She picks up an attractive young hitchhiker, Kilgannon (James Caan), intending to enjoy him as a casual sex partner, but her trip quickly becomes derailed by his problems.[10] Natalie learns during her seduction of Kilgannon—nicknamed Killer for his athletic prowess—that a football accident has left the young man brain-damaged. His university had paid him off and abandoned him, despite the fact he clearly cannot survive on his own. Conflicted yet compassionate, Natalie takes Killer on the road with her and tries to find him a home and a job. At each bend in the road Natalie encounters increasingly claustrophobic terrain, as she is forced into maternal relationships that might be described as "aborted."

She is running from marital and family commitments, but Natalie is not an updated version of the Beat road hero—spontaneous and irresponsible. Nor is she a hippie chick out of *Easy Rider.* Although she is young and sexually liberated, Natalie is clearly a middle-class housewife, an unlikely rebel. Natalie's flight toward freedom is inhibited by a conflicted sense of obligation to the hitchhiker as well as her husband. (Even her name, with its root word *natal,* emphasizes her maternal role.) In the sexual realm, where she appears to pursue desire without guilt or inhibition, Natalie repeatedly picks up partners who are damaged and inevitably curb her sexual autonomy.

Natalie provides an early example of the way in which New Hollywood auteurs *avoided* the very feminist politics they evoked. The New Hollywood road films channeled the alienation of the female protagonist toward broad protest, transforming her into a cipher by which the director could offer vague allegorical comments on America. Natalie may symbolize a woman in motion during the era of the women's movement, but she is paralyzed by the "children" of American institutions who need care. The film in the end aims to reveal the failure of "the system," which left football star Killer Gannon on the side of the road, where he meets his death at the hands of a motherless child, whose home in an immobilized trailer suggests the stalled family institution. In contrast to the Beats' optimistic vision of postwar automobility, this doomed view of mobility speaks of failure. (Natalie might also be read as a symbol of America's failing involvement in Vietnam at that time. Like America, Natalie tries to do well, but she only becomes bogged down in her role as protector and caretaker.)

THE TREND OF FEMALE APATHY AND AUTOMOBILITY

The title character in Barbara Loden's independent road film *Wanda* (1970) is a working-class "floater" whose aimlessness undermines both the American dream *and* the fantasy of rebelling against it. Even though the plot involves her participation in a bank robbery, Wanda is the antithesis of the women seen in postwar gangster films. She is neither the femme fatale of *Gun Crazy* nor the ecstatic outlaw of *Bonnie and Clyde,* nor, for that matter, is she the surrogate mother of *The Rain People.* Wanda is perhaps even more insidious than an armed criminal precisely because she lacks passion and vision. Early in the film, Wanda (played by Loden) shows up late to the custody trial and indifferently relinquishes her two infants to her ex-husband, testifying that they will be better off without her. She drifts down the road, from man to man, seeking nothing beyond a meal and a place to sleep. She does not require respect from the men with whom she has sex. One boyfriend (Michael Higgins) forces Wanda to call him Mr. Dennis. He keeps her around to help him stage a bank robbery, but Wanda has so much trouble with the simple task of driving to the crime scene that she misses the heist altogether. When she arrives late at the bank, she learns that the police have killed Mr. Dennis as he waited for her to arrive with the getaway car. The police do not suspect the confused Wanda to be an accomplice, and somewhat reluctantly, she gets off scot-free. The last shot of the film, which shows her drinking with servicemen alongside other barfly girls, suggests that Wanda will continue to bumble along.

As the director, author, and star of *Wanda,* Loden embodies the auteur philosophy (Taylor 15). She made this quirky, moody film about a mobile, sexually available woman, and she made it outside the film industry by shooting it for under $200,000 in 16 mm in conjunction with Foundation for Filmmakers (Schickel 432). Yet, as the wife of Elia Kazan, the powerful "Old Hollywood" director who cast her in two films before marrying her, Loden also incongruously incarnates the real-life version of the casting couch ingénue who becomes the trophy wife of the powerful film director.[11] Because Loden died young, she never made another film nor did she achieve auteur status. *Wanda* screened in only a few theaters; it owes what reputation it has to its premiere at the Venice Film Festival of 1970, where critics extolled Loden's promise as a director. Despite the film's obscurity, *Wanda* disproves the statement that the road genre in the seventies is entirely male-directed.

Loden's portrait of indifference is hardly a call to arms for women. As reviewer John Russell Taylor noted in 1970: "[Wanda] is, absolutely, the woman as object; the militant ladies of American will no doubt be very indignant about her plight" (15). The fact that Loden created an apathetic female character for her directorial debut sheds another ray of light on the state of affairs between men and women in New Hollywood. Rather than bucking the system like male auteurs, Hollywood women in this era were expected to float from the arms of one director to another, according to Biskind's *Easy Riders, Raging Bulls.* Sexual liberation was assumed for these women, but not gender rebellion. Loden rejected the privileges of being the trophy wife in order to make her film, but her working-class character Wanda survives only by being sexually available. While Loden's reasons may not be known, we should assume she understood the complexity of the themes she was using given how hard she had to fight the tide to make this film.

Both Loden and Didion built their stories around unresponsive women. Being passive-aggressive might not be healthy, but it *can* be a rebellious stance for women who feel they have few options other than to withhold the emotions everyone seems to expect from them. Rather than be the source of pathos and catharsis, these women choose to be numb instead. These road stories would not be called feminist, since these heroines do not achieve their goals or move independently of men, but Didion and Loden do twist the road genre to offer a portrait of female automobility that resists the heroic tropes of male rebellion. (It's worth keeping in mind that New Hollywood was full of passivity at the time—in fact, the male heroes of 1970s New Hollywood films, especially those played by Jack Nicholson—tended to display the same apathy and insanity as the female characters of the day.)[12]

Monte Hellman's *Two-Lane Blacktop* (1971) offers an intriguing juxtaposition here. Like most auteurs of this time, Hellman had gotten his start with Corman and AIP Studios, and like many directors, he was inspired by French New Wave films.[13] In *Two-Lane Blacktop,* Hellman improvised upon the male buddy film to make a picaresque story centered on a languid and mostly silent "Girl" (Laurie Bird), who climbs wordlessly into the back seat of a souped-up '55 Chevy to go on the road with two hot-rod racers, namely, "The Mechanic" (Dennis Wilson) and "The Driver" (James Taylor) (see fig. 11). *Two-Lane Blacktop* fully revises the hot-rod genre films of the 1960s, turning the generic focus of these films from the men to the enigmatic girl who affects them (much as Didion did with the biker genre in *Play It as It Lays*).

Unlike *Play It as It Lays* or *Wanda,* however, *Two-Lane Blacktop* was famous even before its release. *Esquire* magazine published Rudy Wurlitzer's entire script for the film, along with a cover photograph of "The Girl" hitchhiking. Touting the work of New Hollywood directors, the magazine christened *Two-Lane Blacktop* "the movie of the year" before it ever opened. The machinery of New Hollywood publicity clearly favored the men in New Hollywood rather than the women like Didion or Loden, in part because the publicists were cogs in the wheels of this cult of auteurism, themselves trying to work their way up the New Hollywood food chain. *Two-Lane Blacktop*'s publicist Beverly Walker, for instance, exemplified in her own life the pressure on women to sleep with rising auteurs; she told Biskind, "'In Hollywood, men put enormous pressure on women to fuck them, even it it's only once,' she says. 'It's like the dog that pisses on the lamppost. They want that kind of connection to you, and then maybe they can relax'" (Biskind 234).

Unlike other heroines in road films of this time, the passivity of the Girl in *Two-Lane Blacktop* carries different implications. She is the foil that reveals the inability of her male companions to escape the shallowness of their own reality, which is racing cars. Her quiet presence is enough to push the men to recognize their emotional shortcomings and their failure to ask for what they want. She eventually leaves them both, climbing onto the back of a motorcycle with a young stranger. Once again, the Girl's role is not feminist, but it subtly deconstructs masculinity in the film. The men dictate that she sit in the back seat, and she complies, but not without accusing them of imposing a "masculine power trip." In the triangulated romance that develops between the two racers and the woman, the men mutely hint at their private desires—but the Girl is the only one who acts. Unlike Maria and Wanda, this young hippie "floater" wants to do something, even though what she wants is never clear.

"GTO" (Warren Oates), another character in *Two-Lane Blacktop,* illuminates further the shortcomings of the laconic Driver and Mechanic. GTO is an older man who has recognized his need to break out of isolation and is willing to take risks to do so. GTO may feel as self-important as the younger racers, but he differs from them in being aware of his vulnerability. His irrepressible character contrasts sharply with the silence of all three young characters. As GTO races across the

Fig. 11. The Girl (Laurie Bird) in Monte Hellman's *Two-Lane Blacktop* (1971), an example of female automobility often depicted by the New Hollywood auteurs. Courtesy of the Academy of Motion Picture Arts and Sciences; film copyright © Universal Studios.

country, he offers yet another romantic option for the Girl, who begins to display some agency and desire as she moves from man to man. In the end, the Girl tires of each man's shortcomings and leaves all three of them—without speaking a word, of course. She joins a young man on his motorcycle, a "younger" form of mobility meant to contrast with the "older" values symbolized by the GTO (a Detroit production car) and the superstock Chevy (a remnant of the hot-rod movies made by directors like Corman).

In short, the mysterious, apathetic female occupies center stage in the road stories of early New Hollywood. Another road film that bears out this trend is *Badlands* (1973), Terrence Malick's directorial debut starring Sissy Spacek and Martin Sheen. From *The Rain People* to *Badlands,* these road films all share a minimalist approach, not only in their portrayal of female characters, but also in their uses of stark landscape and the alienated beauty of the vérité cinematography.

While it is true that the politics of these films was muddled, it is important to acknowledge that these auteurs approached both gender and genre in more interesting ways than contemporaneous studio-based directors. Commercial efforts like *Little Fauss and Big Halsy* and *Cannonball Run* were formulaic films that perpetuated reactionary notions of gender and romance, as we will see.

A ROAD MOVIE OF ONE'S OWN

The box-office failures of *The Rain People* and *Two-Lane Blacktop* signaled to the studios that they needed to reassert control over the new auteurs. Paul Lewis, producer of many of the New Hollywood road films, noted: "The freedom that we were allowed was over with *The Last Movie, The Hired Hand,* and *Two-Lane Blacktop.* The end of the '70s began at the beginning of the '70s" (Biskind 137).

The beginning of the 1970s was also the time during which feminist film critics began to gain a voice in print. *Ms.* magazine began publication in 1970, as did several other magazines aimed at supporters of the women's movement. The mainstream press also started publishing editorials and film reviews by feminists like Betty Friedan and Joan Didion. Many of these women writers began to speak out against the sexual politics of New Hollywood films and the road genre, and *Two-Lane Blacktop,* in particular, generated significant response. In the *New York Times,* Sherry Sonnett Trumbo complained about the

> rash of "tell it like it is" movies—all with men. . . . Characters like Bobby in *Five Easy Pieces* and the driver in *Two-Lane Blacktop* give their male audience a model and a starting point [for leaving the System]. . . . But where is the movie about a woman going through the same processes? Where is the movie that shows us what alternatives and possibilities are open to us as women? (149)

Feminist reviewers at that time felt that women were being passed over in New

Hollywood, but critics like Trumbo ignored the female lead characters in auteurist road films, precisely because these reviewers were searching for masculine tropes of rebellion familiar from the 1960s. Trumbo's essay reveals the lack of tolerance among feminist audiences for the enigmatic qualities of women in road films.[14] In the *New Yorker,* Pauline Kael argues that the problem facing women in rebel road films was not a lack of roles, but that their roles were burdened with futility. In her review of *Two-Lane Blacktop* and *Drive, He Said* (dir. Jack Nicholson, 1971), she wrote:

> The commonplace that America is having a national crackup is taking its toll on cinema writing and acting. . . . The romanticism of breakdown has affected the style of good actresses in another way: they have so often been called on to play jittery kooks and, for sentimental purposes, retarded drunks and speechless chicks going wherever the wind blows that they have had to perfect a technique for making muddleheadedness seem piercing and sweet. ("Split" 56)

The malaise affecting these characters, Kael also points out, has something to do with America's "national crackup"—its larger sense of futility at home and in Vietnam.

Although feminist reviewers complained about misogyny in road films, their analysis of the genre tended to take much for granted. In the *New York Times* film review section, for instance, Friedan discussed the "rage in the American dream house" of Hollywood:

> Movies in this country are, of course, made almost completely by men. . . . In one after the other of the sickly slick latter-day Hardy Boys that have filled the Best Ten movie lists and occupied the movie houses the last few years ("Easy Rider," "Midnight Cowboy," "Little Fauss and Big Halsy," etc.), aging boys toddle two-by-two down the vacant road to nothingness—a road somehow as void of any sense of human life or human value as it is devoid of women. . . . These movies, in their simultaneous cynical, cheap pandering to the youth market and hard hats, by that convenient poignant bullet through the long hair, seem to be obscene. They wallow in the non-life, non-love that is drowning us in America—and helping to drive us to vicious violent destruction in the world, without a ray of that transcendence which is art. (15)

Friedan's righteous indignation befits the early stages of a new movement like feminism. Yet the "nothingness" Friedan disparages in these films is not fully explained by the male dominance of production. We have seen that female auteurs Didion and Loden used this very "non-life, non-love" sensibility as the focus of

147

their road stories. Rebellion became tied up with passivity in the 1970s, perhaps as a precursor to the loss of faith in rebellion we will see in the 1980s. We need to search further to ascertain the links between gender and genre evident in the New Hollywood road films.

With the benefit of hindsight, we can see that the real problem was not simply that road movies were made by men; rather, the turmoil of changing gender relations gets acted out in the era's road films—and passivity or numbness was a noncommittal coping strategy of not only the commodity marketplace of films but also of the human beings caught in the indeterminacies of social change. It is clear from Biskind's *Easy Riders, Raging Bulls* that these directors were as troubled about selling out as they were about not becoming famous, and that all this turmoil is reflected in their personal relationships. It is no wonder that "the movie brats . . . were not into prescriptive, politically correct cinema" (Biskind 314) and, instead, this anxiety is legible in the portrayals of gender in their films. Unlike many other film genres in the postwar years, the relatively new road genre accepts the destruction of traditional gender roles as a given and portrays the awkward search for new roles between the sexes. We're seeing here evidence of a time of real confusion. That's why the road genre in the 1970s never heralds what we would recognize today as a feminist stance. Despite the genre's willingness to explore, its representation of women's changing roles remained disappointingly conservative—the clearest politics in these road films champion the sexual revolution, not women's liberation per se. The problem is male dominance in the industry and the poverty of social roles for women in 1970s' Hollywood—the films reflect the times.

MALE EXPLOITATION FILMS

There is probably no surprise in finding that the most interesting filmic representations of gender during that time deconstruct masculinity, as in *Midnight Cowboy, Duel,* and *Thunderbolt and Lightfoot.* Nevertheless, the road genre of the seventies approached gender in ways that are important to both men and women. The "Hardy Boys" road films of 1969 and 1970 that Friedan criticizes did prioritize male automobility, but these works still deserve more than a categorical dismissal. For instance, *Little Fauss and Big Halsy* has been called an "*Easy Rider* rip-off" (Biskind 152), but such a description fails to convey its total lack of art film sensibility or commonsense humanity.

Although Hopper and Fonda hoped to cash in with *Easy Rider,* their commercial goals were moderated by their sense of film as an artistic medium. While auteurs were clearly prima donnas, the commercial directors were more likely to deliver trite portraits of male-female relations, using genre as a way to dismiss feminism altogether. (In other words, even while I am acknowledging its limits, I must clarify that auteurism has a certain utility for studying the road films of New Hollywood—as long as the dynamics of genre and gender are folded in.) Thus, it is possible to distinguish the films in the "Hardy Boys" category according to the division between self-appointed auteurs and directors with strictly commercial ambitions. Paramount Pictures hired the latter type in British filmmaker Sidney J. Furie to direct *Little Fauss and Big Halsy*.[15] The studio's belated attempt to graft the AIP-style exploitation biker genre onto this film, without any insight into gender or genre, separates *Little Fauss and Big Halsy* from both *Easy Rider* and *Two-Lane Blacktop*. *Little Fauss and Big Halsy* rescripted the "folk resentments"[16] of the AIP biker genre for Paramount's more mainstream audiences. The studio recycled the reactionary portrait of the nihilistic male biker typical to AIP films, even though *Little Fauss and Big Halsy* was a film about motorcycle racing, not a biker film per se. Instead of the rape and robbery scenes usually found in biker films, the film gives us presumably more palatable scenes of sexual promiscuity and petty theft. In its ambition to reach a broad spectrum of male viewers, the film becomes mundane, eliminating all egregious offenses save misogyny. By falling back on banality, the film alienated audiences, critics, *and* feminists in one fell swoop.

Like the biker films, *Little Fauss and Big Halsy* stresses an overtly heterosexual narrative to compensate for any homoerotic tension elicited by the male buddy story. A blonde woman who has had sex separately with each of the men introduces this tension by referring to them as each other's "boyfriends." For the most part, however, the film depicts Halsy (Robert Redford) and Little (Michael J. Pollard) treating women as sex objects. Halsy speaks frankly to Little about his trouble with women, whom he refers to as dogs, pigs, hurting whores, gland cases, and trophy girls. Introspectively, Halsy muses: "Sometimes when I'm drunk I really think they're princesses, when I wake up they're just pigs." Little responded: "I just figure you like pigs." *Little Fauss and Big Halsy* is full of the formulaic sexism that the "Movie Brats"—to their credit—avoided in their road films.

The recurring theme of pregnancy is an interesting point of connection between *Little Fauss and Big Halsy* (which *does* include a female road traveler, despite Friedan's description) and the auteurs' road films. Pregnancy seems an unlikely subject for a male-oriented film like *Little Fauss and Big Halsy* until the film's conventional sexual politics are taken into account. A naked young woman, Rita (Lauren Hutton), jumps into Little and Halsy's truck one day while having a drug experience (she carries a copy of Burroughs's *Naked Lunch*). After the predictable triangulation of affections between the two men and Rita, Redford's character just as predictably prevails as the romantic partner, which causes a predictable rift between the two rivals. The two reconcile much later, when Rita is eight months pregnant. In private, Halsy admits to Little that he couldn't hustle the money for "an operation" until it was too late. The film ends on a freeze-frame shot of Halsy fixing his bike; this frozen end to a story about mobility—plus the overall misogyny of the film—reveals the great distance between *Little Fauss and Big Halsy* and the auteurist road films lumped with it by Friedan, *Easy Rider* and *Midnight Cowboy* (both discussed in the previous chapter).

Another male-focused film from 1971 worthy of mention is *Duel,* a movie made for television by director Stephen Spielberg. *Duel* suggests the road is the terrain where strangers battle to the death as a function of their inherently male and aggressive nature. A salesman (Dennis Weaver) drives on a back road through the desert near Los Angeles, listening to radio talk shows whose on-air callers all have something to say about gender roles. This henpecked husband keeps flashing back in memory to an argument he had earlier with his wife. He stops at a roadside Laundromat to call her, but she is bitter and preoccupied by the kids, who in turn are preoccupied by the blaring television set. In a memorable framing shot, the salesman is seen through the circular door of the dryer, as he talks on the phone, as if he is trapped by domesticity even while out on the open road. After this small but significant interaction with his wife, the salesman must contend with interactions between men. He soon encounters an archetypal "man's man"—a "rogue cowboy" who slowly draws the salesman into a deadly duel on the highway.[17] The rogue driver's truck is large and menacing, and the driver himself is never seen. The contest turns into a life-and-death battle of wits, one the salesman eventually wins. At the end, the salesman sits on a ridge, battered but alive, watching the sun go down; he is proud and relieved that he was able to trick the anonymous driver into careening off the cliff.

MEN AND WOMEN TOGETHER ON THE ROAD

After 1971, the "Hardy Boy" style of buddy films gives way to narratives about male-female couples on the road. Even AIP moved away from the biker genre it had pioneered to create an exploitation road film with a lead female character in *Dirty Mary Crazy Larry* (1974), which features two veterans of the biker years—Peter Fonda and Adam Roark—who both mistreat the girlfriend, played by Susan George. TV director John Hough made *Dirty Mary Crazy Larry,* which ends in the same way as the cult film *Vanishing Point* (1971), with everyone blown to bits, a trademark of the post–*Easy Rider* rebellion. But even the tony Grove Press tiptoed into film production and distribution in the 1960s and 1970s (distributing many films, including Jean-Luc Godard's *Weekend* in 1967), and producing *Road Movie* (1974) by art film director Joseph Strick; the latter a far more interesting triangulation than AIP's film. In *Road Movie,* a hooker with a heart of gold on the road lets herself be taken full advantage of by two truckers. The road films by Richard Compton, director of *Macon County Line* (1974), and former photojournalist Dick Richards, director of *Rafferty and the Gold Dust Twins* (1975),[18] also stand out as interesting exceptions in their portrayal of female autonomy. Clint Eastwood shows his persistent preoccupation with the mechanization of masculinity and male desire in his road film *Gauntlet* (1977), which features Eastwood and his wife at the time, actress Sondra Locke.

In 1972, Didion's novel *Play It as It Lays* was finally made into a film directed by Frank Perry. But the popularity of the novel did nothing to offset the critics' rejection of the movie version. For instance, Pauline Kael hated the work of Didion and Perry, stating in the *New Yorker* that "Perry hasn't found a 'visual equivalent' for the famished prose [of Didion's novel], but maybe this high-class-whore-house style of moviemaking is the *true* equivalent" ("Current Cinema" 156). Kael blamed scriptwriter Didion for enjoying *too* much control over the film version of her novel. Didion *did* in fact have an unusual amount of power for a woman in Hollywood—she selected Frank Perry to be the film's director and co-scripted the novel's adaptation with her husband, John Gregory Dunne.[19] Her brother-in-law, Dominick Dunne, co-produced the film with Perry. Kael suggests Didion chose Perry because "he had already glorified the suffering little-girl-woman in *Diary of a Mad Housewife* [1970]" (156), which was written by his wife, Eleanor Perry, from a novel written by Sue Kaufman.[20] In this one review, Kael trivializes the accomplishments of the few women with substantial creative input in New Hollywood. In his review in the *New York Times,* however, Vincent Canby was more sympathetic to Didion's novel, which he felt evoked pity, while "the film is more likely to evoke pure, unadulterated envy" due to the chic, elegant touches added by visual consultant and Pop Art painter Roy Lichtenstein ("Review" 36). Similarly, critic Foster Hirsch compared Tuesday Weld's acting to the film's "hifalutin' camerawork, the fractured editing, and the smug halo lighting," and accused Weld, who once "played variations on . . . Lolita," of becoming "a high-fashion model, posing for Frank Perry's glossy lay-outs" (9).

Even hack, sexist films like *Little Fauss and Big Halsy* did not generate as much gender-oriented rhetoric from mainstream reviewers as did *Play It as It Lays.* Clearly, *Play It as It Lays* affronts the ethos of critics championing New Hollywood, and causes them to respond in highly gendered terms. Here is where my epigraphs' references to epic—"Of arms and the man"—at the beginning of this chapter come in, for they suggest there is much at stake whenever any history is written of great men. The Marxist Situationist writer Guy Debord said, "Of arms and the man the spectacle does not sing, but rather of passions and the commodity" (43), suggesting that heroism masks the role of passions and the commodity—which we see here are all rolled up into the women who are a crucial part of New Hollywood's road films. The passive characters like Maria and Wanda are refusing to deliver the passion required of epic, passion produced in New Hollywood by the gendered division of labor. By obliquely calling attention to the interdependencies of gender and genre, Maria fails to stay invisible and "anonymous," to recall Walter Benjamin's passage. This might be one reason for the highly charged—and gendered—words slung about in reviews.

Play It as It Lays, in fact, breaks the unwritten rules of auteurism by calling too much attention to gender and genre—just as Maria did in Didion's novel of New Hollywood. Perry's style is perhaps too close to the auteurs', who distinguish themselves from the hacks by virtue of female automobility, hand-held camera-work, and other art film influences.[21] Clearly, something about *Play It as It Lays* pushes these auteuristic signatures too close to generic banalities. The spiteful attacks on the film seem motivated less by Perry's work than by the collision of New Hollywood auteurism with Didion's cool parody of it.

Seen from today's vantage, the film version of *Play It as It Lays* seems to effectively use the trademark style of New Hollywood, rather than inadequately mimicking it. The film's quick editing, voice-overs, and interjection of actresses' screen tests and Carter's art film *Maria* all offer depth to the film narrative, creating an intelligent adaptation of the novel. Shots of Los Angeles streets, highways, and billboards exemplify the formalism of the 1970s' road films. Furthermore, the casting choices of Tuesday Weld, seen as Maria in figure 12, and Adam Roarke to play Carter show how conscious the film's creators were of the *types* of characters expected in the road genre. Tuesday Weld was already affiliated with the BBS ensemble, having starred in Henry Jaglom's *A Safe Place* the previous year with Nicholson and Orson Welles. Adam Roarke was the veteran of several AIP motorcycle films.

There is more evidence that the gender-laced rhetoric condemning *Play It as It Lays* is not exceptional. Road films featuring women were often described in pejorative terms. For instance, Phoebe Adams of the *Atlantic* said that Martin Scorsese's road film, *Alice Doesn't Live Here Anymore* "outsuds any soap opera" (Feldman 124). *Variety* also criticized Scorsese's now-signature moving camerawork in *Alice*—"the nervous camera-creeping telegraphs immediately that something's wrong with the script: that's a dead giveaway outside of mystery-suspense pix" ("Rev. of *Alice*" 17), even though this is more of the same quirky camera work that was hailed in *Mean Streets* (1973) as evidence of Scorsese's skill. The use of terms like "soap opera," "whorehouse," "high-fashion" in reviews of female-oriented road films reveals the deep-seated gender turmoil provoked by such films.[22]

FICKLE FEMINISM

Casting a girl—instead of a grown woman—offered directors a way to highlight female autonomy without invoking feminist politics, as we can see with *Paper Moon* (1973). Director Peter Bogdanovich was yet another former apprentice to Corman who was also close friends with French New Wave directors, and he embodies all the best and worst qualities of the New Hollywood auteur. (Indeed, his personal

Fig. 12. Tuesday Weld as Maria Wyeth, who drives the Los Angeles freeways to gain a feeling of control in *Play It as It Lays* (1972). Adapted from the popular novel by Joan Didion, the film, directed by Frank Perry, was panned. Courtesy of the Academy of Motion Picture Arts and Sciences; film copyright © Universal Pictures.

life is a notorious example of New Hollywood's gendered division of labor—again, Biskind's book is full of the details.) *Paper Moon* won an Academy Award for its female actress, ten-year-old Tatum O'Neal, who played the supporting role to her father, Ryan O'Neal. Her character Addie is ambitious, fiercely independent and competent, but she is also completely devoted to the man with whom she travels—her father, or rather, the man she believes to be her father (played, of course, by the actress's real father). As is evident in its setting in the Depression years, the film offers a nostalgic portrayal of female autonomy and mobility. The road trip—a familiar setting for family conflict—in this case ends in laughter and a few happy tears, sending an upbeat message about the endurance of family.

After *Paper Moon*'s Oscar win in 1973, two road films won Oscars the next year, demonstrating that automobility offered great opportunities for advancing the careers of directors and actors. In fact, Ellen Burstyn used the influence she had gained from her starring role in *The Exorcist* to package a film project specifically tailored to win an Academy Award. She accomplished that goal with the road film *Alice Doesn't Live Here Anymore,* which earned her the coveted prize of Best Actress in 1974. The tentative explorations of female automobility that began with *The Rain People* and *Wanda* culminated in *Alice* just five years later.

Unlike the characters of those earlier films, Alice has a destination and travels with her twelve-year-old son. Widowed at age thirty-five, Alice decides to leave Albuquerque and drive with Tommy to Monterey, California, to fulfill a long-standing dream to work as a singer, a dream she gave up when she married. En route, she briefly takes a job singing in a Phoenix bar, leaving town when a new boyfriend (Harvey Keitel) becomes violent. Alice ends up in Tucson, working as a waitress and falling in love with David (Kris Kristofferson), a rancher she meets in the diner where she works. Instead of going to Monterey, she and her son stay in Tucson to see how the relationship with David will work out. The film's story was partially shaped by Burstyn: "Her first order of business was to change the screenplay," making the script better fit "the woman's point of view" while working in tandem with the director's "sense of the dramatic line" (Keyser 45). Given these stated goals, it is surprising that Burstyn did not have the authority to end her story as she wanted, which was for Alice to keep traveling on the road rather than stay with her new boyfriend, David.

Even more important than Burstyn's influence on the script is the fact that she chose her own director, a young auteur named Martin Scorsese, in a sequence of events that have become legendary. She wanted a director who could do justice to the script's portrayal of a mobile woman, and reportedly considered Barbara Loden (presumably because of Loden's experience directing *Wanda*) (F. Kaplan 34). Burstyn asked Coppola to recommend a director, and he advised her to see Scorsese's *Mean Streets* (1973).[23] After doing so, and perhaps after reading the praise of the ever-powerful champion of Scorsese, *New Yorker* reviewer Pauline Kael, Burstyn hired Scorsese.

As we have already noted, the girlfriend of an auteur often influenced the portrayal of gender in a given film. Scorsese's collaborator and girlfriend, Sandy Weintraub, is said to have read the script first and urged it upon Scorsese (Keyser 49).[24] Weintraub helped in the production in many ways, as she had in his earlier *Mean Streets.* After the focus on men and violence in *Mean Streets,* Scorsese and Weintraub saw Burstyn's big-budget picture as a chance to show that he could make a commercial film and that he could direct women. In an interview, Scorsese stressed the significance of including women in the production, noting that an

> important idea on *Alice* was to use women in the crew—Sandy Weintraub was associate producer, Toby Rafelson [wife of director Bob Rafelson] our art director and Marcia Lucas [then wife of director George Lucas] my editor—to help us be as honest as possible. But

we never intended it to be a feminist tract. It was a film about self-responsibility and also about how people make the same mistakes again and again. (Scorsese 51)

Including the wives and girlfriends of auteurs in the production of *Alice* was as political as Scorsese was willing to get, however. Even though he claims he wanted Alice to continue on down the road without David, Scorsese feared "that such a powerful ending would paradoxically be misinterpreted as feminist propaganda" (Keyser 57). Although he saw himself as an auteur, Scorsese didn't want to be seen as a feminist, and on this score he chose his battles cautiously. He accepted the studio's aversion to a feminist ending, and fought instead for the expensive and highly stylized introduction that pays tribute to the women's genre films of the forties.

The director was not the only one to soften the gender politics implicit in the film. Even a reviewer like Vincent Canby, who liked *Alice,* took it upon himself to warn audiences not to be put off by the reputation that *Alice*

> is a woman's picture, which makes the movie sound as if it were going to be terribly solemn and humorless, and perhaps even a little chauvinistic about women's rights. Dramatized Gloria Steinem, it's not. It's a clear-eyed, tough-talking, often boisterously funny comedy about women *and* men. ("Terrific" 13)

Despite such disavowals, the road genre was now more dependent on women on the screen and women behind the scenes than ever before.

The contradictory goal of the film, to speak to women *without* delivering a feminist message, was obvious to most viewers. As Kael observed, for instance, in her *New Yorker* review: "*Alice* is like *It Happened One Night* played at the wrong speed. . . . it's the romance itself that's in trouble, and it's the institution of marriage that's in slapstick, role-confusion chaos. . . . the Problem is women trying to figure out a way to be independent without giving up men" ("Woman" 74). The female road rebel may leave home, but it seems she can never leave love—let alone patriarchy—too far behind. (This was also true in *It Happened One Night.*) These road films illuminate all the contradictions of the time—its freedoms and its unacknowledged debts. This body of work may not be historically as important as the *Godfather* trilogy, *Jaws,* or the *Star Wars* films, but the road genre was an important rite of passage on the road for the directors of New Hollywood. We will see in the next chapter that this genre remains an inspiration to each new generation of aspiring auteurs.

For some, the male-buddy exploits of *Easy Rider* might represent the quintessential road film, but rebels take on unlikely forms in New Hollywood. The diversity of road travelers in new films informs us that the road film is maturing as a genre—in just two years, we see a young girl, a middle-aged mother, and an old man each take to the road, their performances all rewarded by Oscars. For also in 1974, *Harry and Tonto* (dir. Paul Mazursky) provided veteran television actor Art Carney with an Oscar for Best Actor for his portrayal of Harry, a seventy-two-year-old traveling across country with his cat, Tonto. The genre itself has traveled a great distance since the "wild angels" and "easy riders" of the 1960s, let alone the Beats in the 1950s. Rather than pandering to a male audience, as Betty Friedan had impugned, the road genre in 1973 and 1974 was tugging at the heartstrings of Middle America.

COUPLES ON THE LAM

The variety of road rebels in these films does not dispute the fact that, in terms of sheer quantity, heterosexual couples on the lam typify the commercial formula of road films. Between 1972 and 1974, fugitive lovers were the subject of films by new auteurs like Terrence Malick, Stephen Spielberg, and Michael Cimino, as well as by established film artists like Sam Peckinpah and Robert Altman. Uniformly, these films find ways to "disarm" their female characters—none of these women on the road are as threatening as Bonnie had been back in 1967.

By turning the issue of female automobility into the problems of couples running from the police, directors lessened the chance that their work would be confused with feminist politics. In *The Getaway* (dir. Peckinpah, 1972), *Thieves Like Us* (dir. Altman, 1973), and *Badlands* (dir. Malick, 1973), the women are laconic partners who keep their cool while the men perpetrate crimes. *Badlands* gives the storytelling power to the young woman, Holly (Sissy Spacek), a high school majorette who lives at home. She goes on the road with her delinquent boyfriend Kit (Martin Sheen) after he murders her father. Holly is enigmatic; she lacks affect and seems to be "going along for the ride." She guides the viewer in a monotonous voice-over, one of the most chilling aspects of the film because it emphasizes her apathy rather than her agency. Even though Holly makes the decision to leave Kit in the end, her coda informs us that she married the lawyer who had defended her, thereby suggesting that she goes with whichever man leads the way (as do the women in *Two-Lane Blacktop, Wanda,* and *Little Fauss and Big Halsy*.) Because Malick shot *Badlands* on location, it has the quality and feel of an auteur's road film, in contrast to the polish brought by established directors Peckinpah and Altman to their road films.

Veteran directors in need of a career boost were tapped by studios jumping on the road film bandwagon. In Peckinpah's *The Getaway,* the wife (Ali McGraw) is quiet but warm-blooded, committed to her husband (Steve McQueen) but sexual, able to stay calm under the pressures faced by any couple that robs banks (unlike the chaos between the married robbers in the 1949 *noir* classic, *Gun Crazy*).[25] Previously respected director Robert Altman was down on his luck in Hollywood when he made *Thieves Like Us* (1973; a remake of the 1947 road film *They Live By Night*), about a young fugitive couple in the Depression who struggle to integrate the husband's career as an outlaw into their marriage and plans for a family.

Less frequently than these silent women, a loud and obnoxious woman is cast as a lead, as in Steven Spielberg's next road film, *The Sugarland Express* (1974). In contrast to his first road film, *Duel,* which is about a husband's autonomy, *Sugarland* examines a woman's rightful place as a mother. When the young, lower-class Lou Jean (Goldie Hawn) is released from jail, she cajoles her husband Clovis (William Atherton) into breaking out of *his* jail so they can travel together to reclaim their infant from his foster home. They kidnap a policeman (Michael Sacks) and force him to drive them across Texas to Sugarland, where their baby lives. Followed by television camera crews and police helicopters, the husband-wife team garners statewide sympathy. They are seen as trying to protect their nuclear family from governmental power. Although Lou Jean is not a very sympathetic character, the young Spielberg made a smart move by casting Goldie Hawn, the highly visible TV actress who won an Academy Award in 1969 for Best Supporting Actress in *Cactus Flower.* Some reviewers dismissed Spielberg as a "shameless" young hack (Farber 11), although Kael, known for championing auteurs, loved the film. Stephen Farber, who decimated the film in his *New York Times* review, accused Spielberg of creating a "misogynist" portrayal of the character played by Hawn (11). Clearly the seventies were tough on women—and on reviewers, many of whom felt obligated to comment on gender portrayals in the blunt terms typical of an early moment of consciousness raising.

By the mid-seventies, a pattern emerged: the female character is either a mute, numb woman who is sexually unfulfilled, or she is an intolerable female chatterbox. The former type is found in *Badlands* and *The Getaway,* in the earlier films *Wanda* and *Two-Lane Blacktop,* as well as in the myriad of voiceless pregnant women in *Play It as It Lays, The Rain People, Thieves Like Us,* and *Little Fauss and Big Halsy.* The latter—the woman who cannot shut up—is seen in *Five Easy Pieces, The Sugarland Express, Dirty Mary Crazy Larry, Slither, Rafferty and the Gold Dust Twins,* and *Bonnie and Clyde.* In the dramas that include loud women, few male partners escape death—Bobby (Jack Nicholson) in *Five Easy Pieces,* who leaves his girlfriend (Karen Black) behind without a word, hopping on a truck like old Tom Joad, is one.

Michael Cimino's directorial debut subverts the growing dominance of the couple on the lam. *Thunderbolt and Lightfoot* (1974) places two male leads, played by established stars Clint Eastwood and Jeff Bridges, into the clichéd couple formula. The chatty young Lightfoot (Bridges) looks up to the older, laconic Thunderbolt (Eastwood) in a relationship that goes beyond mentorship to display the stereotypical habits of heterosexual marriage. Homosexual relations never evolve, but neither does the homophobia that plagued *Little Fauss and Big Halsy,* despite the fact that Bridges disguises himself in women's clothing during the heist. True to fugitive film formulae, one of the two partners dies in the end—interestingly, it is the feminized character, Lightfoot, even though women rarely die at the end of films with couples on the lam (*Bonnie and Clyde* and *Gun Crazy* being exceptions). The unusual gender dynamics make *Thunderbolt and Lightfoot* a good example of an early deconstruction of masculinity within the mainstream road genre.[26]

The close appearance of so many similar road films led critics to recognize that a self-reflexive genre was emerging. Feminist scholar Marsha Kinder accused the male buddy road film of being part of a backlash "to counter the forces of Gay Lib and the Women's Movement," condemning *Easy Rider, Midnight Cowboy, Thunderbolt and Lightfoot,* and *Two-Lane Blacktop* as male-oriented films. Linking male buddy road films to Kerouac, to the success of *Bonnie and Clyde,* and to cop movies prevalent in the seventies, Kinder argued that the outlaw heterosexual couple reveals changing views about rebellion: "even their rebellion is culturally determined; like the police, the outlaws merely reflect the society and its limitations" (10). During the seventies, the female protagonist on the road tamed rebellion at the very same moment this genre of rebellion was established, suggesting that the genre's expansion (and the auteur's epic status) came thanks to the expedient use of female automobility to construct an apt but apolitical commodity. The road films that followed in the wake of *Easy Rider* reveal the double tensions of gender and genre being negotiated in New Hollywood, both in the on-screen depictions of female mobility and in the private lives of the auteurs and their female companions. The decade's explosion of road films registers the cataclysmic changes in gender and sexual relations coinciding with the aesthetic rebellions of auteurism.

GENRE AS A FUNCTION OF GENDER AND GENERATION

While the increasing presence of women in New Hollywood road films suggests a degree of social change, their roles ultimately helped young male directors to imprint the mark of *their* power over the studio bosses with whom they were locked in an Oedipal battle between generations of men. Although the road genre focuses on gender, these films raise the riddle of femininity without the solution of feminism. The heroine's rebellion instead usually takes the form of sexuality, titillating viewers rather than challenging them. For the most part, these films avoid making any feminist statement that might alienate the mass market. Amazingly, it would take another twenty years before a film directly portrayed women on the road because they were angry about patriarchy.

Yet the fact of the women's movement and the evolution of feminist criticism helped keep the New Hollywood insurrection from being *merely* an Oedipal crisis, one in which the sons usurp their fathers or earn the acclaim once bestowed on the New Wave directors. Feminism may have been just one of the several liberation movements affecting these directors and the women with whom they were involved, but it galvanized the era, leading directors to define autonomy in terms of female automobility. Unlike the road stories of the Beat and hippie decades, the road genre film in the early seventies conveyed a mixed message regarding rebellion: the plot that portrayed a woman as a rebel simultaneously dampened any suggestion that her marginality was due to her gender. The heroine could be wild and eccentric, but her sexual freedom would ultimately be trumped by middle-class values. In other words, along with the feminization of the postwar road rebel comes domestication and cliché.

These female road characters *were* pathologized by their numbness and muteness but, in truth, so were most of the male companions in these auteuristic films. All in all, New Hollywood filmmakers may have been responding to changing gender roles, but these auteurs purposefully depoliticized the circumstances that put women on the road, using only vague references to abortion rather than taking a stand on any ongoing debate. In the five years between *Easy Rider* and *Alice Doesn't Live Here Anymore,* New Hollywood remapped the road story, recasting the road rebel from the heterosexual con man of the 1960s biker film into the blonde sexually available young mother informed by an apathetic and easily capitulated form of rebellion. For the rest of the 1970s and through most of the 1980s, the road film falls into the pattern of recycled formulae rather than active remapping. As we shall see in the next chapter, the "High Concept" phase of studio production will soon supplant the freewheeling era of New Hollywood, and the road genre will shift from rebellious auteurism to naked commercialism, with its success measured in box office profits.

7

Back to the Family, or Rewinding the Postmodern Road Story

> "Roads? Where we're going, we don't need roads!"
> —Doc Brown in the final scene, *Back to the Future*

Back in the golden age of postwar rebellion, Beat and hippie youth considered home the antithesis of escape and adventure; but after the ambiguous messages about automobility made by the film auteurs in the 1970s, the road film takes us back to the family in the 1980s. Alienation no longer assumes the uncompromising stance of *Easy Rider,* with its implied attitude of "give me liberty or give me death"; in fact, this baby boomer philosophy is a bit like a hangover to the next generation, for whom just such grandiose gestures had lost impact. Rather, in the 1980s, alienation is occurring at the heart of our systems of meaning, for the steady pairing of signifier to signified—of a symbol to its meaning—seemed to implode. After all, grown-up hippies were working *in* the system by the 1980s, and their yuppie offspring were staying home, more interested in what is on television than what is on the road. For both young and not-so-old, the concept of rebellion desperately needed a remapping.

The dictums of modernism, upon which the rebellious postwar generations had relied thus far, no longer fit a nation moving far from the antiwar protests of the 1960s toward solidarity with American troops killed by suicide bombers in Beirut and Kuwait or responding to the kidnappings and hijackings of this troubled time. Stateside, adults wondered if they had sold out, irritating their children who saw them as timeworn radicals who couldn't even do something as important as program a VCR. The postmodern family made room for rebels and fostered individual autonomy, thereby robbing any inter-generational Oedipal conflicts of much of their fuel. No one knew where to settle down, ideologically, and irony became a self-protective defense system in the void. Given these cultural changes, it is no wonder that the road genre, just barely established as a genre by auteurs in the early 1970s, has nowhere to go later in that decade. Instead of stories about people on the road, cinematic travel in the 1980s goes backwards in time. The subliminal message in the 1980s was, if you don't like the present—don't rebel, rewind![1]

Postmodern theorists like Fredric Jameson called culture in this era "schizo-phrenic" (6), trying to characterize the loss of meaning that prevailed. Discussions of media in terms of ecstasy and schizophrenia helped intellectuals characterize the fact that news and entertainment were, indeed, becoming alarmingly con-solidated as multinational conglomerates bought up Hollywood studios, as we will see. Although Jameson's metaphor is uniquely characteristic of the 1980s, it is clear that the road genre *does* splinter into many different forms as various storytellers pondered whether to revive or reject rebellion and the aura that art once commanded. Hence this chapter splits between four different strands of road stories, and surveying these disparate directions will keep us moving here at quite a quick pace, but it is important to understand these myriad options in order to appreciate where the genre does go in the 1990s, as we will see in the next chapter, and what qualities return in the first decade of the new century, when we live under another Republican administration. The 1980s are a turning point in the maturation of this genre, a true test of its status as a genre to see whether the form can stand free of its content of anti-authoritarian social liberalism. Despite the irony and nostalgia of this decade, the road genre does ultimately survive the end of modernism (which is more than can be said for many of the heroes at the end of road films in the 1970s, many of whom die in the final scene). Learning to accommodate to change, rather than just rebel against the old, is a crucial move-ment forward accomplished in the 1980s as a whole new generation of storytellers remap the road genre.

In this new decade, media technology transformed an adolescent's experience of rebellion in ways unfathomable to older generations. Television, the Sony Walkman, video cassette recorders, and personal computers offered new ways to tune out family annoyances and responsibilities, yet also gave family members something in common, as when they decided together which video to rent for the Betamax, or whether to watch reruns of *The Honeymooners* or that brand-new genre of music videos. People became so immersed in media—so at home in the "mediascape"—that railing against a monolithic "media," as Allen Ginsberg had done in 1961, ceased to have much point. Instead, postmodernists accommodated to the "ecstasy of communication," with the "landscape unfolding like a televised screen" (Baudrillard, "Ecstasy" 130, 127). As with almost all postwar technological change, young people were the early adopters, but unlike any previous generation, they weren't eager to leave home.

Modernism had valued rebellion and authentic experience, but the postmodern age of digital reproduction undermined the very concept of authenticity; mod-ernist ideals seemed irrelevant when images could be endlessly manipulated and when rebellion could be co-opted so easily by corporations. The protest chant most heard during those years was one encouraged by the new cable network—"I want my MTV." A new national zeitgeist put faith in advanced technology, family bonds, and fierce battles between good and evil. Was it irony or genius that this return to traditional values was called a revolution—the "Reagan Revolution," to be precise, named after America's media-savvy president who was a former actor? Why bother to go on the road once the revolution is televised?

In Hollywood, the rebel auteurs of the 1970s were either dropping away from the spotlight or making blockbuster films, no longer remapping the road genre they had helped create.[2] Film production changed permanently in the 1980s after decades during which multinational conglomerates had been buying up the film studios and shifting production to films with simple plots, enormous budgets, sure-fire stars, and aggressive strategies for maximizing profits—an approach that film historians call "High Concept" filmmaking. This emphasis on entertainment trickled down—families were deemed progressive not by their politics or creativity, but by their technology purchases, by being the first on the block to own a camcorder or Apple's Lisa computer.

Despite the comforting reassurances of the Reagan Revolution and the optimistic focus on the family, the 1980s was a time of tremendous moral ambiguity. CIA operatives, it was alleged, sold cocaine to finance a war in Iran. Automobile executive John DeLorean, it was also alleged, sold cocaine to rescue his failing car company. Junk bonds provided new ways to buy and sell companies, transforming the corporate landscape and eventually weakening the economy, which suffered through a stock market crash in 1987 and a subsequent recession.

In the face of these changes, the dividing line between rebellion and traditional values blurred, and irony prevailed. The road story responded by moving in four different directions in the 1980s. First, there are the big-budget, High Concept productions influenced by Roger Corman's efforts in the 1970s. Robert Zemeckis's *Back to the Future* (1985) leads the way, followed by late 1980s films like *Midnight Run, Rain Man,* and *Driving Miss Daisy.* Second, we see a new generation of independent film studios—like Orion, Miramax, Geffen, New Line, Amblin—keeping auteurism alive for small audiences, through road films such as *Stranger Than Paradise* (1984), *Paris, Texas* (1984), *Lost in America* (1985), *The Sure Thing* (1985), *Something Wild* (1986), *Wild at Heart* (1990), and *Bright Angel* (1991). The indie studios, then, and the auteurs resisting MTV and High Concept filmmaking styles kept the rebel theme going, even though the road in their narratives also returns to the family, as it does in the High Concept road films.

For the other two trends in the postmodern road story, we will see that the road also becomes an important symbol for writers in the 1980s, particularly for intellectuals opposed to Reagan's cultural conservatism. In particular, European and American philosophers looked at the road and decided there was "nowhere to escape anymore" (Acker, *Don Quixote* 22), expounding their arguments in such books as Jean Baudrillard's *America* (1986), Umberto Eco's *Travels in Hyperreality* (1986), and fiction writer Kathy Acker's *Don Quixote* (1986). Finally, female mass-market novelists began creating young heroines who go on the road (heroines who were overlooked by feminists at the time), including *In Country* (1985) by Bobbie Ann Mason, *Anywhere But Here* (1986) by Mona Simpson, *The Bean Trees* (1988) and *Pigs in Heaven* (1991) by Barbara Kingsolver, and *The Floating World* (1989) by Cynthia Kadohata.

When we look back upon this decade, it is clear that these efforts updated the road genre and kept it alive. In each of these four categories, the genre's key questions about autonomy, mobility, and automobility were sustained, even if they often went without answers.

GOING BACK IN TIME
Remapping the Familyscape

Past, present, here, there—all become options in the electronic eighties, accessible via the replay button on a boom box or the rewind option on a VCR or by tuning in to one of the new cable channels providing vintage reruns, making the past accessible by remote control. Given the media choices, the location of one's home was not as fateful as it once had been, for a television that was "always on" (as the Talking Heads sang) brought home images of other people and places, broadening one's world view. People began to consider media experiences themselves as transformative, the way we used to find (or lose) ourselves on the road; in fact, the road books that celebrated more authentic experiences, such as William Least Heat Moon's *Blue Highways* (1982) and Robert M. Pirsig's *Zen and the Art of Motorcycle Maintenance* (1974) were popular precisely because people were accepting a mediated environment, and these books look back to a less complicated urban life in a fashion that is entirely consistent with the time travel of these years.

As part of this shift from immediate experience to mediated representations, 1980s road stories tend to travel through time rather than traverse geographic space. In these stories, it is the familiar that is sought—the family of the past—rather than some mysterious adventure outside our imagination. More families let go of the absolutism of older generations, rejecting at long last Archie Bunker's bigotry in CBS's familyscape, *All in the Family* (1971–79), which meant that rebels and misfits *could* go home once again without being called a meathead. Eighties pop culture thus fosters the idea that identity is relational, created in terms of position to others, rather than within rigid belief systems. Family identity evolved in different contexts rather than being fixed to one set of references or ideals.

Nostalgia for the past became part of this relational remapping of identity during the 1980s in ways unlike any other postwar decade, as the election of Reagan—himself an image from the past, as *Back to the Future* repeatedly jokes—demonstrates. In 1985, *Back to the Future* skillfully balanced between modernist rebellion and postmodernism's irony and self-consciousness, which is in no small measure one reason for the film's tremendous success. This big-budget, science-fiction comedy focuses on a car, but the plot is about time travel, not the road. Early in the film, Marty (Michael J. Fox) is videotaping Doc Brown (Christopher Lloyd) in an empty shopping mall when Marty comes under attack by Libyan terrorists, jumps in Doc's time-traveling De Lorean car (see fig. 13), speeds away and, at eighty-eight miles per hour, zooms back to the year 1955.[3] Landing in a farmer's barn, before the landscape had been paved over for the suburb in which he lived in the present, Marty emerges from the car looking very much like a science-fiction alien.

Fig. 13. Marty McFly (Michael J. Fox) taking the De Lorean time machine back to 1955 in *Back to the Future* (1985), directed by Robert Zemeckis. The 1980s road films rewind time to return to the "familyscape." Film copyright © Universal Pictures.

Like most road films of the 1980s, *Back to the Future* stages a return to origins with the goal of repairing some identity crisis left unresolved. Marty may be back in the fifties, when the Beats were roaring through the vast backyard of America, but his goal will be to make his father into a man. In this way, *Back to the Future* is the happily-ever-after revision of *Rebel Without a Cause,* the 1955 film about a mobile son and his weak father. In *Back to the Future,* Marty becomes the modern-day James Dean who succeeds this time in transforming his weak father. Success, it seems, is worth more in America's new emotional economy than freedom; in any case, the two became linked as basic American rights. A return to the past becomes reason enough for a road trip, if it helps one reclaim the good life.

The final frontier of rebellion and alienation in the 1980s is actually the "familyscape" of the 1950s—the return of the repressed in the form of television's fantasmatic fiction of family. The familyscape, echoing the term "mediascape" introduced at the beginning of this book, is an electronically generated archetype that has accumulated over the postwar years; it is an amalgam of all of TV's virtual families that holds significant sway over the real-time family by giving it standards of unity to achieve, even while the family recognizes it is emulating an impossible fiction (talk about schizophrenia!). In the 1950s, the Beats had needed to remap the cinemascape of the Depression they experienced growing up; now the generation raised watching *Father Knows Best* and *The Honeymooners* needed to reconcile with *this* familyscape, which had shaped its standards of family. More ironically, so did their children, who seemed equally invested in this 1950s familyscape thanks to reruns on the Nickelodeon channel. (Even old shows like *The Honeymooners* ended up influencing many 1980s road films—from *Back to the Future* to the low-budget independent road film *Stranger Than Paradise*.)[4] These kids also contended with the familyscapes of their own generation, especially *The Brady Bunch* (1969–74).

The familyscape is key to the 1980s backward-looking road stories, for even in accepting the fragility of family in contemporary America, everyone had to come to terms with its power as an image. Reagan tapped the American nostalgia for family and was willing to act like a father who did indeed know best, yet the masses had to reconcile his idealized portraits of family with the complex realities of divorce, drugs, homelessness, immigration, the aftermath of the Vietnam War, or whatever was making any particular family different from the Cleavers. TV gave a shared vocabulary of identity to hyper-literate spectators, especially those in middle-class white homes being overwhelmed by the vast freedoms of choice in postmodern society. Why leave home if mom or dad already had? The rebel in the 1980s is the one who works toward family unity rather than hitting the road in search of an elusive truth. As the postmodern time traveler, Marty learns in *Back to the Future* that there's no place like home.

Reagan embodied at one time or another all the subject positions that fuel the entertainment in *Back to the Future*.[5] The president's moral vision drew from film and television's golden years, his Strategic Defense Initiative provided a science-fiction fantasy of omnipotence, and yet he himself was planted in the 1980s. Even journalist George Wills called attention to how all these symbols intersect in the president, for Reagan represented "a time when movie imagery, broadcast immediacy, and highway mobility entered Americans' lives—or, rather, when Americans entered the new atmosphere created by those inventions. This was the past that most vividly created our future" (371). Reagan's ability to bridge generations lent continuity and comfort, and helped normalize the changes of the 1970s and 1980s. Reagan trusted that he had returned America to familiar values after the hostage turmoil of the Carter administration, stating in his final presidential address that his greatest accomplishment was "the recovery of our morale. America is respected again in the world and looked to for leadership" (Jeffords 3). *Back to the Future* aims at something similar, restoring the father's lost dignity, yet the film nuances the reassurances it offers, understanding that its young audience was so suspicious of its own vulnerable yearnings that it persistently deconstructed them (something the Reagan administration avoided).

At the same time, *Back to the Future* clumsily whitewashes the dark days in 1955 of racial segregation, getting an uneasy laugh by suggesting that Marty taught Chuck Berry how to rock and roll. *Back to the Future* rewinds to a uniquely white form of 1950s rebellion—back to the Oedipal power of the television family rather than to the black power of civil rights—turning a blind eye to social realities beyond the familyscape. What *Back to the Future* also makes clear with its portrayal of Libyan terrorists is that the new national chauvinism was built, in part, through anxiety about foreigners. In the 1980s, illegal immigrants and terrorists seem to be on everyone's mind, for Arabs had taken Americans hostage in Iran in 1979, Haitians were blamed as carriers of AIDS, and there was a growing number of immigrants living in the United States (especially after the Simpson-Rodino Amnesty Law of 1987 granted immunity to many illegal immigrants), but the film is only explicit in its battle against wimps, portrayed as a threat to the American family.

Back to the Future deals squarely with the loss of rebellion, joking about the reversal of roles that arises when we discover that our own mother as a teen liked to drink and neck. The children of former hippie rebels could no doubt relate to a teenage hero who is the one worrying about the future. What does it mean that a generation can remake the father in its own image, when the Oedipal turmoil of Peter Fonda in *The Wild Angels* can simply be zapped away—with the help of a Sony Walkman, as Marty does in *Back to the Future*? (In this humorous scene, Marty co-opts his father's fantasies about space aliens by assuming the identity of Darth Vadar, who, of course, is Luke Skywalker's father in *Star Wars*.) *Back to the Future* depicts the powerful, post-Oedipal son who can rewind time.

Back to the 1970s to Corman's Chase/Race Films

To understand how we got to High Concept films like *Back to the Future* and *Midnight Run,* we ourselves must rewind time and go back once again to Roger Corman. After he left American International Pictures (AIP), Corman's New World production company launched a trend of cross-country race films beginning in 1975.[6] We have already seen Corman's influence on the New Hollywood auteurs, and in this chapter, we will learn of his impact on a younger set of film directors. When he turned full-time to production in 1970, Corman became the quintessential "producer-auteur," a producer who earns more of a name and reputation than his director, whose own role is subordinated to the producer's vision.[7] By the time Corman closed New World Pictures in 1983, the major studios had also adopted a producer-driven system, having learned from exploitation studios like New World (as well as porn films and family films) how to market effectively in the changing global economics of the film industry (Wyatt, "Roadshowing" 70, 75). Corman's sales tactics of "saturation booking" and pre-selling rights to cable and video tremendously influenced High Concept filmmaking in mainstream Hollywood (Hillier and Lipstadt 48).

Corman shaped the road genre through the "crash-and-burn" films he produced. In mid-1976, an important transitional phase for Corman's studio, New World launched a new, car-themed film at the rate of almost one per month.[8] Even as early as 1975, New World released *Death Race 2000,* directed by Paul Bartel, a goofy cult film about four race teams (male-female pairs, of course) that gain points by killing bystanders en route across country. In April 1976, New World featured *Eat My Dust!,* starring ex-television child actor Ron Howard, which *Variety* called "a car chase comedy for the teenage market [that] win[s] its stripes as a clever money-making vehicle." Corman confirmed the profitability of this film: "The last couple of years I thought that a large proportion of the American public wanted to see blood or breasts. Now I think they want to see cars. Our biggest film to date, *Eat My Dust!,* just piles up one car after another" (Hillier and Lipstadt 47). In May 1976, New World released *Jackson County Jail,* introducing Tommy Lee Jones and starring Yvette Mimieux as Dinah Hunter, a successful businesswoman raped by a corrupt cop during her cross-country drive. In July of 1976, New World offered *Cannonball,* a pivotal film discussed below. Later, in June of 1977, New World handled *Grand Theft Auto,* Ron Howard's directorial debut. About this time, the major Hollywood studios began competing directly against the exploitation houses with their own chase/race films. They were following the money, and Twentieth Century Fox was literally following Corman, whom that studio hired to produce a film by Jonathan Demme (who will make *Something Wild* in a few years), as well as a few others.

Cannonball marks a significant transition between the auteurs' road films of 1970s New Hollywood and 1980s High Concept films, in part because *Cannonball* inspired so many cross-country race film knock-offs in the major studios for the next half-dozen years. Paul Bartel co-scripted the film with Don Simpson, an unknown producer whose name would shortly became synonymous with High Concept.[9] In *Cannonball,* which Bartel also directed, we can pinpoint a significant shift away from New World's titillating but somewhat sympathetic view of female automobility in *Jackson County Jail* to more conservative ideas about gender, for the hero Cannonball protects his girlfriend Linda when she decides to come along

167

on the cross-country race. Compared to Dinah Hunter of *Jackson County Jail,* who drives herself across country, *Cannonball*'s Linda (who has no last name in the credits) is a career woman but no woman's libber, just a compliant passenger in love with her man. *Cannonball* demonstrates that, even in 1976, Simpson had his finger on the cultural pulse of the "hard body" backlash long before his fingerprints were all over the High Concept films of the 1980s.[10]

The profitability of *Cannonball* and the other race/chase films meant that the "crash-and-burn" films overwhelmed the new road film genre established only a short while earlier by *Easy Rider.* Also in 1976, for instance, Warner Bros. and First Artists released a film about the same race, *The Gumball Rally,* then Universal introduced its liquor-running chase film, *Smokey and the Bandit* (dir. Hal Needham, 1977), which was so profitable that it spawned *Smokey and the Bandit II* (dir. Needham, 1980), and *Smokey and the Bandit 3* (dir. Dick Lowry, 1983). In 1980, Paramount released *Coast to Coast,* about a happy hooker and a truck driver. The Cannonball empire extended with *The Cannonball Run* (Twentieth Century Fox, produced in conjunction with Golden Harvest, a Hong-Kong company, 1981), directed by Hal Needham and written by Brock Yates, based on the experiences the two had in the famous cross-country race.[11] *The Cannonball Run* was "one of the five hottest movies of 1981," according to Bill Kaufman of *Newsday* (266). *Cannonball Run II* was released by Warner Bros., which also created another road film franchise—slapstick family travel films—under the National Lampoon banner, beginning with *Vacation* (1983), *European Vacation* (1985), and *Christmas Vacation* (1989).

These genre films are so predictable that a content analysis would only divert attention from their real significance, as backlash against the social rebellions of hippies and feminists. These silly, fast-paced films catered to the masses, as compared to auteurist New Hollywood road films like *Two-Lane Blacktop.* In the *New York Times,* Vincent Canby speculated on why *Smokey and the Bandit* made such a profit in 1977, second only to *Star Wars,* the record-breaking moneymaker. "*Smokey and the Bandit* . . . represents a dramatic change in mood from most of the post–*Easy Rider*" films ("Why" 146), Canby suggested, eliminating the violence and villainy of films like AIP's *Macon County Line,* Twentieth Century Fox's *Dirty Mary Crazy Larry* (1974), and New World's *Jackson County Jail.* Canby's comparison of *Smokey and the Bandit* with these other titles is significant, showing that critics recognized that *Smokey* was just a "high-budget versio[n] of New World's redneck comedies" (*Film Review Archive* 1982 155). Canby notes that the politics offered by these High Concept films is part of the reason for their success: "As politics they may be naïve, but as movies they are a welcome change from the movies of mayhem and murder of the post–*Easy Rider* years. Those films were just as naïve but, being gloomy, they tended to intimidate audiences into taking them seriously" (147). Put another way, big-budget race and chase films democratized rebellion, bringing it from the margins to the masses, that is, from the art houses and drive-in theaters to the new mall multiplexes where families went to see films.

But the politics of these films was less naïve than anti-authoritarian—*Smokey's* tag line proclaims, "What we have here is a total lack of respect for the law!"—without being anti-American. As does *Back to the Future,* these films "rewind" to the good ol' boys politics of 1950s white society, a politics that had become, in the conflicted multicultural world of the 1980s, wonderfully familiar and willfully straightforward.

To be sure, there is nothing challenging in the plot lines, philosophical stances, or gender politics of the "crash-and-burn" films, except for their uninspired acting. This subgenre recuperates predictable, sexist gender roles, although several of the exploitation road films are downright misogynist. The roles played by Susan George in *Dirty Mary Crazy Larry* and Sally Field[12] in the first two *Smokey* films are reactionary compared to the female automobility in New World's *Jackson County Jail.* Eventually, the male buddy story would be made with more subtlety, for in the late 1980s a rapid sequence of males partner up in road films. What's interesting to note, in anticipation of this upcoming discussion, is that a *Village Voice* reviewer linked *Midnight Run* back to the exploitation genre, saying, "it's a chance to see De Niro in a *Smokey and the Bandit*" (*Film Review Annual 1989* 949).

Back to the Bottom Line

Back in the 1960s, Hollywood studios began losing large sums of money,[13] which is one reason they experimented with the low-budget auteur films of New Hollywood, hoping to hit a jackpot like Columbia had with *Easy Rider* in 1969. The short-lived auteurism of the 1970s, however, did not pay off. New problems compounded old during the 1980s; due to the growth of suburban multi-screen theaters, especially in malls, there were more screens than ever, even though Hollywood was producing fewer films. Furthermore, there was a steep drop in film audiences (Hillier 13). This is why studios turned to aggressive marketing tactics like "saturation-release" strategies, pioneered by Corman and others in the exploitation film industry, using heavy national television advertising to build word-of-mouth quickly, rather than relying upon the traditional slow rollout style known as "roadshowing" (Wyatt 70).

Despite these efforts to improve profitability, the Hollywood studios were acquired, one by one, by foreign multinational companies or vast conglomerates.[14] These large, publicly traded corporations then sold off key studio assets to recoup their acquisition costs, in the process decimating studios' film libraries, real-estate holdings, and capital equipment. The new owners treated filmmaking as just one more industry in their diversified portfolios. Although many of these corporations had investments in other media, such as publishing or television, they had little experience in the film business. They attempted to run the studios just like their other businesses, which is how the High Concept production methods gained momentum.

In one sense, conglomerates like Gulf & Western and Sony did offer the film industry a degree of financial stability. They upped the ante for filmmaking because they helped studios to invest in new computer and laser technology as well as to option costly books as scripts. Only under such conditions could there emerge the High Concept characteristics, such as huge increases in salaries for stars that drew audiences, like Burt Reynolds's fee of $5 million in *Smokey and the Bandit* (Biskind 403). By 1980, "the average America film had to earn 40 million dollars simply to return its investment" (D. Cook 888). Furthermore, the conglomerates gave studios access to their media subsidiaries, thereby creating secondary markets in television, publishing, music, and even toy manufacturers willing to pay to license film characters and thus boost a film's long-term profits. The new market of video rental, in particular, gave the studios an opportunity to recoup production costs, as the VCR presence in American households jumped from 4 percent to 60 percent between 1982 and 1988 ("The 1980s" 86). Between 1980 and 1989, the number of households with VCRs increased over 3,200 percent ("The 1980s" 86), and the sale of pre-recorded video cassettes to U.S. dealers increased by over 6,400 percent ("The 1980s" 86–87). The market was changing, and the road genre changed concurrently.

HIGH CONCEPT HOLLYWOOD AND THE ROAD FILM
Buying into Reagan-Era Capitalist Patriarchy

We went back in time in order to consider in this analysis the influence of exploitation films like *Cannonball* and *Smokey and the Bandit* on the road films of the 1980s. Turning now to films that earned both profits and high critical praise—road films like *Midnight Run* and *Rain Man*—we can characterize these High Concept films from the auteurs' films we will also consider; the former focused on masculinity and male relationships, while the latter rely upon a woman to motivate the narrative action.

By the end of the 1980s, masculinity is the subject of the bigger-budget, saturation-release road films, most of which take the form of the buddy movie, namely *Planes, Trains and Automobiles* (dir. John Hughes, Paramount, 1987), *Midnight Run* (dir. Martin Brest, Universal, 1988), and *Rain Man* (dir. Barry Levinson, United Artists, 1988). These films feature men whose "neurotic" weaknesses in the realm of masculinity and money, argues film scholar Ina Rae Hark, must be balanced with the "high flyer" men who are "successfully inscribed into capitalist patriarchy" (208). Hark argues the late-eighties road films critique yuppie excess and are part of the ideological adjustments made after the 1987 stock market crash

(205). Noting that travel by airplane "embodies capitalistic success; [while] the road is for economic losers" (205), Hark continues, "buddy-road movies of the 1980s, therefore, almost reflexively explain both why the buddies didn't travel by plane and that they aren't gay" (206).

Yet these films also point out compulsively that their heroes are not rebels. Despite being aggressive men who recognize themselves as alienated from their labor, they work hard within the system. (De Niro's character in *Midnight Run* simply wants to feel like a cop again.) Hark suggests that these films function not to criticize capitalism or patriarchy but to "shift from culture critique to redemptive psychodrama," in which the overachiever becomes a better person, less selfish and more openhearted (205). With Hark's point in mind, it is true that Jack (Robert De Niro) isn't really mad at anyone, not even the gangster who cheated him out of his career or the justice system that tolerated that, and *Rain Man*'s Charlie Babbit (Tom Cruise) is mad only at his dead father. Furthermore, road films in the 1980s always end well, even if the protagonists end up back where they started—Marty at home with his transformed parents, David and Linda at their old employers, Hunter and Jane reunited as family, Raymond back at the institution in Cincinnati, Jonathan Mardukas safe from the mob. In each case, the automobile is a tool used to uncover some family problem that must be put right, and by the end of these films, profound changes have taken place in the hearts of the characters. Consequently, there is no need to criticize society or government.

The most provocative fact about these road films is that, instead of looking ahead, toward the genre's classic theme of transformation, these 1980s films look backward. The genre's dream of something better is harnessed instead to the past. To accomplish this, the major studios used veteran directors—not New Hollywood rebels. John Hughes, director of *Planes, Trains and Automobiles,* was famous for directing youth films (namely, *Sixteen Candles* in 1984 and *The Breakfast Club* in 1985), but he also put his signature on all the National Lampoon family road films, and his new production company worked with Warner Bros. to make the third, *Christmas Vacation* (1989). Unlike Hughes, who specialized in adolescent humor, Barry Levinson, the director of *Rain Man,* was famous for his focus on films about men. (His 1982 directorial debut, *Diner,* looks back in time to the 1950s.) In *Rain Man,* Levinson brilliantly pairs the graduate of youthful bourgeois mobility from the 1960s, Dustin Hoffman, with Mr. High Concept himself, Tom Cruise, who was once again playing a son preoccupied with his father's car (Cruise first portrayed a character in this situation in *Risky Business* in 1983). *Rain Man* is set in the present, but it is all about the past—the father's vintage car serves as a time travel machine that takes Cruise's character back into repressed family issues and a new role as protector of his brother. The road goes to the past in the 1980s more than in any other era.

Auteurism Moves from New Hollywood to New York

While Hollywood was using High Concept tactics to attract audiences into mall cineplexes, the cable television industry began "narrowcasting," targeting smaller and more specific audiences.[15] For instance, MTV began its music television channel in August 1981, effectively launching the new genre of music videos. Young auteurs working outside High Concept Hollywood found that directing music videos afforded them some financial support and artistic freedom.

These new cultural rebels followed in the wake of New Hollywood but were unquestionably part of the new decade's postmodern sensibility, which tilted toward New York's music and conceptual art scene rather than Hollywood's power lunches. The band Talking Heads, for instance, was one of the first to pioneer the new art of music videos, with the band members drawing from their art school backgrounds to create videos that generated an artsy image that was as important as the sales generated by the videos. Over the course of the band's career, its music videos were directed by many, including Toni Basil (the dancer who had a part in *Easy Rider*), filmmaker Jim Jarmusch, and the band's lead singer, David Byrne. Byrne directed the music video "Road to Nowhere," a postmodern road story in which the journey is, once again, through time as the familyscape from infancy to old age accelerates backwards. Byrne also directed the full-length feature film *True Stories* (1986), produced by Warner Bros., in which he, a mobile narrator, drives a vintage red convertible Cadillac around the fictional town of Virgil, Texas, observing the strange inhabitants of this obscure, rural community. (While not a road story, *True Stories* shares the irony of David Lynch's *Blue Velvet* and *Wild at Heart* in finding weirdness on the backroads of America's heartlands.) At the height of the band's popularity, Talking Heads released *Stop Making Sense* (1984), a concert film co-produced with MTV, directed by Jonathan Demme, another Corman protégé who, two years later, would direct one of the independent road films of the decade, *Something Wild*.[16] Linked to the New York post-punk music scene, independent directors like Byrne, Demme, and Jarmusch exemplify the faction of rebel auteurs working outside of High Concept Hollywood.

As these indie directors sought to distance themselves from High Concept dealmaking and aesthetics, they consistently gravitated to the road genre established by the earlier generation of auteurs. The road genre goes hand in hand with auteurism, whether because of the convenience of the genre's narrative arc, or the ease or low cost of shooting, or simply because of the time-honored role of this genre of rebellion to an auteur's sensibility. Perhaps this is the reason longtime film commentator J. Hoberman noted "the so-called independent cinema has [finally] become the third force in American narrative film," standing alongside Old Hollywood and New ("Review" 1282), when Jim Jarmusch directed his first feature, *Stranger Than Paradise* (1984). While still an NYU film student, Jarmusch had been encouraged by the established German director Wim Wenders (who was making his own auteurist road film, *Paris, Texas,* to which we will soon turn).[17] Jarmusch's student film, a short titled "The New World" (1982), became the first part of *Stranger Than Paradise,* a triptych, whose final two-thirds take place on the road (Hoberman, "Review" 1282–83). This first segment of *Stranger Than Paradise* focuses on the young woman Eva (Ezster Balint), newly arrived from Hungary and staying temporarily in New York with her cousin, Willie (John Lurie); it takes place almost entirely in Willie's small Manhattan apartment, in front of the television.[18] In part two, Willie and his friend Eddie (Richard Edson) drive to Cleveland to visit Eva and Aunt Lotte (Cecillia Stark), and in part three, the two men drive Eva to Florida for a disappointing vacation. With Eva, Jarmusch carries into the 1980s the auteurist fascination with female automobility, which we saw in the previous chapter as being characteristic of New Hollywood's road films.

Stranger Than Paradise might be considered the postmodern version of *Two-Lane Blacktop* since, in both films, one woman stimulates the imagination of her two male traveling companions before she abandons them in the end; but even *Two-Lane Blacktop* seemed clearer about how all the traveling companions had changed in response to the others. *Stranger Than Paradise* is strikingly noncommittal, even compared to the vague films of New Hollywood, showing thereby the depth of postmodernism's cynicism and retreat into obscurity.

The road genre usually revolves around a major transformation in the main character, but any metamorphosis in all these auteurs' films is enigmatic, as if the filmmakers wanted to retain the road as a symbol of hoped-for change even though they themselves were reluctant to direct a script about change. In this era of MTV and High Concept, the slow and ambiguous action on the road is itself a rebellion against the crash-and-burn excitement of High Concept films.[19] Furthermore, Jarmusch's filmic style was deliberately antithetical to MTV's slickness, despite the fact that Jarmusch had directed music videos. *Stranger Than Paradise* is famous for its stasis, the result of Jarmusch's long single takes and sparse editing that he used to resist intermingling the styles of advertising and filmmaking. The slow pace of *Stranger Than Paradise* led Sidney Gottlieb to call it "a road film in which the road leads nowhere" (455).[20] (This is apt, as many of the New York artists drawn toward road stories repeatedly emphasized that the road went nowhere.) Indie audiences loved the distinctive, defiantly anti-commercial filmmaking style of both Jarmusch and Wenders (whose *Paris, Texas* road film will be discussed in the next section). Both of their road films swept the Cannes Film Festival in 1984.

The independent road films of the mid-1980s were financed in two ways. On the one hand, Jarmusch and Wenders obtained private funding for their indie road films, as did Peter Masterson for *The Trip to Bountiful* (1986) and Robert Frank for *Candy Mountain* (1987). Small new studios like Orion, Miramax, Geffen Pictures, and Propaganda Films backed other road films of the decade. These alternative producers began in protest to the growing corporatization of Hollywood's major film studios, and quickly had great success with road films like *Lost in America* (1985), *Something Wild* (1986), and *Wild at Heart* (1990). In contrast, fast-edited stories about war and far-away galaxies attracted mainstream audiences in the late 1970s and 1980s, with *Rambo First Blood* and *Top Gun,* as well as the big-budget science-fiction blockbusters like *Star Wars, Close Encounters of the Third Kind, Alien, Star Trek: The Motion Picture,* and *E.T. the Extra-Terrestrial.* Compared to these exotic special-effects blockbusters, road films offered familiar and familial terrain to repair old social rifts.

Wild Women and Wall Street Men

The indie films of the 1980s give counter-evidence to the prevailing sentiment that road films tend to focus—"almost exclusively" (Corrigan 143)—on men; yet they do reinforce the idea that the woman is the alien or wild one. Despite freeing up the men from their rat race lives, the women also anchor them just a little bit more to daily life, as we will now see in some of the other indie films of the decade.

In both High Concept and indie road films, characters who would have been seen as rebels in an earlier decade are now cast as "aliens," weirdos who need to be reintegrated into the family unit. There's Lulu, the wild girl of *Something Wild,* a character who lets her passions rule—something also true of the gambling wife of *Lost in America* and the rambling father of *Paris, Texas.* Even the more sentimental High Concept films of the late 1980s, *Rain Man* and *Driving Miss Daisy,* focus on forging a family bond on the road with an "alien"—the autistic brother in the former and an African American in the latter. The most provocative image of this phase of filmmaking has to be Marietta Pace (Diane Ladd), the mother in *Wild at Heart,* who seduces a gangster so he will kill her daughter's boyfriend—in one shot, Ladd vomits in the toilet, then laughs and turns to the camera, her face covered entirely with shiny red lipstick.

In this decade's road films, contact with the alien is threatening at first, but the encounter typically resolves into a therapeutic outcome.[21] Rebellion is portrayed as "risky business," something that seduces the white yuppie male; but he returns to his proper place after sowing his wild oats. Rebellion might have been easy back in the past for hippies, but engaging in subversion now requires prophylactic irony. By the curtain's close, order is restored and the status quo is "new and improved," protected against the foreign bodies that threaten the family.

Whereas the High Concept films may feature a slick, business-savvy "high-flyer," the 1980s indie road films are more likely to feature a male protagonist who wishes he had been a rebel in the past. Now feeling alienated from his Id, he meets an out-of-control woman who helps him break free of his self-imposed rules. Typically, it is she who sets the wheels in motion—witness *Something Wild, Lost in America, Stranger Than Paradise,* and *Bright Angel* (along with other films of the 1980s in which a woman helps a young man explore his rebellions, like *Risky Business, Ferris Bueller's Day Off,* and *Blue Velvet*). Female mobility is a plot device in these films that is tied more to the male's need to be free than it is to the woman's own transformation.

The comedy *Lost in America* (1985) connects the man's fantasy of rebellion explicitly to *Easy Rider* from his wistful perch of yuppie responsibility. One of the first films produced by the new, independent studio, Geffen Pictures,[22] *Lost in America* centers on a road trip undertaken by a couple who had, until now, forsaken hippie social experiments in order to get ahead in business. Director/writer/star Albert Brooks pokes fun at his character's belated revival of this fantasy of rebellion. Brooks plays David Howard, a high-powered Los Angeles advertising executive who feels exploited when he fails to receive a promotion. Impulsively quitting his job, David also convinces his wife Linda (Julie Hagerty) to quit her managerial post. The couple take to the road, not on Harley-Davidsons, but in a Winnebago—they intend to live in their "nest egg" while searching for higher meaning.

The motor home signals from the start that this road rebellion is doomed. The conflict begins on the first travel day, when Linda gambles away their entire life savings in Las Vegas. The rest of the road trip is directed toward mending that loss, which leads the prodigal couple back to their old employers in a new city. *Lost in America* takes David through his past fantasies to his present regrets, ending in a metaphoric rewinding in which he is able to restore order as the grateful yuppie he should have been six months earlier.

The wild woman is used by many of these films to explore the threat of broken families. In *Something Wild,* Audrey, also called Lulu (Melanie Griffith), kidnaps a Wall Street executive, Charley (Jeff Daniels), who inwardly laments that his life has been so straight and narrow. Lulu takes Charlie home to her mother, of all places, and to her high school reunion, where her ex-husband lurks like some adolescent bully. The backwards glance that characterizes road films of this decade is part of the genre's recuperative work, reconciling the imaginary familyscape of vintage TV reruns with the changing realities of the family in the 1980s. The messy outcomes of some hippie freedoms must have made the rules and conformities of the 1950s familyscape seem like vintage fun.

The damaging excess left after a wild romance is depicted in *Paris, Texas,* made by German director Wim Wenders in 1984. Wenders had already made a trilogy of road films in Germany, as well as other films in English.[23] *Paris, Texas* has a spontaneous, slow-moving auteur's style, with an eye for desert scenes (developed most likely during Wenders's photographic explorations in his *Written in the West* [1987]). The film opens in the Texas desert, where a nomadic American man (Harry Dean Stanton) passes out from heat exhaustion. His brother Walt (Dean Stockwell)[24] comes out to pick up Travis and take him home—the film's first road trip—to Burbank, California, where Walt and his French wife, Anne

(Aurore Clément), have been raising Travis's son, Hunter. (Hunter is played by Hunter Carson, the son of Karen Black, a New Hollywood actress, and L. M. Kit Carson, the writer who adapted Sam Shepard's screenplay for *Paris, Texas.*) Years before, Travis and his wife Jane (Nastassja Kinski) had abandoned Hunter to this more stable home when their own family fell apart, and the film focuses on Travis reacquainting himself with his eight-year-old son. Once trust builds between the two of them, they set out on the road, traveling to Houston to find Jane.

Part of what makes a film postmodern is its focus on the construction of images, a focus evident in the scenes at the Keyhole Club, where women sell erotic performances in a booth-like room for men who can view them through a pane of glass and talk to them via telephone. In Texas, Travis discovers that Jane works at this club, and from one of these booths, he talks to her in a sort of apology for the past. As these double-sided scenes emphasize, Wenders deconstructs the images presented to audiences, going behind the surface to document their artifice, as if this in itself could mitigate the challenge posed by postmodernism. As he said in one interview, Wenders aims to "redefine a relationship between life and images made from life" (van Oostrum 19). *Paris, Texas* suggests that images move people and generate desire, yet people get lost in the vast cinemascape—much as Travis was lost in the desert in the opening scenes. Being adrift without bearings has become the postmodern form of autonomy and mobility.

In particular, *Paris, Texas* examines the multilayered image of family. Anticipating the dissection of appearances in the Keyhole Club, one early scene in Burbank shows Hunter sitting between his two fathers, watching a Super-8 home movie of his mother. "That's not her," he says. "That's only her in a movie . . . a long time ago . . . in a galaxy far, far away." Initially, Travis hopes to reunite his family, but as he comes to understand himself, he decides instead to bring together mother and son before taking off on his own again. Father may know best, yet he has decided to remain out of this image. For his part, Travis longs to return to Paris, Texas, the place where he believes he was conceived; but his birthplace is never actually seen in the film, aside from a Polaroid image of an empty lot. The film shows that while the idealized familyscape may be divorced from reality, both the image and the messy reality have significance.

Like Vladimir Nabokov, Robert Frank, and many other expatriates fascinated with the American road, Wenders portrays America as a bleak, stark, and enigmatic place. When Frank finally made a feature film in 1987, almost three decades after *Pull My Daisy,*[25] the road leaves the United States for the vast mountain reaches of the eastern Canadian coastline. Frank's *Candy Mountain* is a quirky, auteuristic film about a down-and-out musician who travels from New York to Nova Scotia to find a master guitar maker, living there in seclusion. Frank co-directed the film with Rudy Wurlitzer, who wrote the screenplay. Wurlitzer also scripted the road film *Two-Lane Blacktop* in 1971, and, in 1969, he published *Nog,* a novel about psychedelic experiences that occur on the road. *Candy Mountain* was one of several low-budget indie road films that got lost in the 1980s; it never had the impact of Frank's 1959 art film *Pull My Daisy,* made in collaboration with Jack Kerouac and other Beats.

In contrast, road films from Australian director George Miller became important in America during this time.[26] *Mad Max* (1979) and *The Road Warrior* (1982), distributed in the United States by Warner Bros., both paint a dystopic picture of the future in which post-apocalyptic survivors battle over gasoline, living in communal fortresses under constant siege. In some ways, the excessive violence of these films comes back a dozen years later in American road films, with over-the-top murder and mayhem in films like *Kalifornia, Doom Generation,* and *Natural Born Killers.*

To recap, the road genre's significant themes in the 1980s include an emphasis on past lives that must be made healthy once again and questions of autonomy and mobility posed as automobility. These themes are shared by the High Concept and independent films of the decade, connected to the larger postmodern reexamination of 1950s late modernism and the messages of rebellion, family, and autonomy that characterized the 1980s.

POSTMODERN PHILOSOPHY AND PUNK
Similarities Between Jean Baudrillard and Wim Wenders

After World War II, philosophers in France began to question the adequacy of modernist ideas in light of postwar global realities, especially as communications media dominated everyday life and eroded the dichotomy between the material world and mere representation. For instance, Jean Baudrillard wrote: "The territory no longer precedes the map, nor survives it. . . . But it is no longer a question of either maps or territory. Something has disappeared: the sovereign difference between them that was the abstraction's charm" ("Precession" 253). Feeling they had reached the end of the road with structuralist theory, some intellectuals turned to Sigmund Freud's turn-of-the-century concepts about family, gender, and sexuality. Eventually, these "postmodern" questions made their way into American universities of the late 1970s and 1980s, spilling out into popular culture soon thereafter. By the late 1980s, American intellectuals were intimately familiar with France's key postmodern theorists, and even some non-academics knew the authors as if they were brand names—"a Foucault, a Jacques Derrida, or a Roland Barthes"—as Hal Foster listed them in the influential book, *The Anti-Aesthetic* (1983).

In some respects, these European "auteurs" took the place of 1970s New Hollywood filmmakers as arbiters of rebellion. Two of these European authors even published American road stories—Jean Baudrillard, most famously, with his road memoir *America* (1986), and Umberto Eco, who said in his *Travels in Hyperreality* (1986): "This is the reason for this journey into hyperreality, in search of instances where the American imagination demands the real thing and, to attain it, must fabricate the absolute fake; where the boundaries between game and illusion are blurred" (8). At first, American intellectuals were confounded by the return to Freud, whom American feminists had revisited and largely rejected in the 1960s and 1970s, and also because these European writers—through purposefully difficult prose—were saying that rebellion, that great American pastime, was an illusion, a mere seduction. This last point was particularly grating on many in the university system who saw the academy as a last stronghold of rebellion, or if not rebellion, at least criticism—of capitalism, dominant culture, and gender relations.

Like many previous European visitors to America—such as Vladimir Nabokov, Simone de Beauvoir, and Theodor Adorno—the postmodern theorists were fascinated by American automobility.[27] These scholars treated cars as profound metaphors and equated their road trips through the American landscape with philosophical meditations. In an influential 1983 essay, Baudrillard used automobility to explicate the difficult concept that binaries of meaning had broken down, making the subject no longer distinguishable from the object:

> Little by little a logic of "driving" has replaced a very subjective logic of possession and projection. No more fantasies of power, speed and appropriation linked to the object itself, but instead a tactic of potentialities linked to usage: master, control and command, an optimalization of the play of possibilities offered by the car as vector and vehicle, and no longer as object of psychological sanctuary. ("Ecstasy" 127)

Alienation, Baudrillard explains, requires a split between the subject and the object, which has disappeared in the postmodern world:

> Something has changed, and the Faustian, Promethean (perhaps Oedipal) period of production and consumption gives way to the "proteinic" era of networks, to the narcissistic and protean era of connections, contact, contiguity, feedback and generalized interface that goes with the universe of communication. With the television image—the television being the ultimate and perfect object for this new era—our own body and the whole surrounding universe become a control screen. ("Ecstasy" 127)

Given Baudrillard's investment in symbols like automobility and television, it was perhaps inevitable that he would turn to the road story, as he did in 1986 with *America*. He used the desert to symbolize the vast wasteland of American culture: "I looked for [America] in . . . the indifferent reflex of television, in the film of days and nights projected across an empty space, in the marvelously affectless succession of signs, images, faces, and ritual acts on the road" (5).[28] With a condescending ennui, Baudrillard seemed intent on stripping the road (if not America) of its symbolic power. Interestingly, the main contribution Baudrillard's road book *America* seems to have made is as a source of short quotes for scholars who write about Wenders's road film *Paris, Texas*. Comparisons between Baudrillard and Wenders are easy to make, since they both took an arch attitude toward Americans. Take this quote from Baudrillard's *America*:

> It may be that the truth of America can only be seen by a European, since he alone will discover there the perfect simulacrum—that of the immanence and material transcription of all values. The Americans, for their part, have no sense of simulation. They are themselves simulation in its most developed state, but *they have no language in which to describe it,* since they themselves are the model. As a result, they are the ideal material for an analysis of all the possible variants of the modern world. No more and no less in fact than were primitive societies in their day. The same mythical and analytic excitement that made us look towards those earlier societies today impels us to look in the direction of America. (emphasis added, 28–29)

Wenders has also written about the advantages of being an alien observer:

> Americans themselves can't [write about the American dream]. They're confused. They don't know what's happening to them. First their dream is stolen from them, and then it's sold back to them day by day. Blunted by too many false images and sounds of their dream, by too many empty forms and soothing formulas, it now happens that they'd rather believe in these false images and let them become a new standard of their way of life than dare to doubt their state philosophy of "entertainment," a real "American Superpower." "American identity": a gaping wound. (149–50)

Underneath it all, however, the differences between Wenders and Baudrillard are more significant than their similarities. Wenders maintains a dialectic between the image and experience, but Baudrillard collapses the two as "simulacra." Baudrillard's travelogue is so subjective and ironic that it exhausts itself, offering up an imaginary America free of gender, free of identity—a backlash to America's insistence on body and autonomy. The portraits in *Paris, Texas,* on the other hand, are fraught with tension and questions of identity.[29] Rather than ignore subject position, Wenders focuses on it, seeing it as an image that can be occupied—as when Travis learns how to look like a father from the Latina housekeeper before he actually acts like a father to Hunter.

"Oedipal with a Vengeance"

Kathy Acker brings to avant-garde literature the angry gender politics that came to constitute one offshoot of postmodern aesthetics. In her novel *Don Quixote* (1986), Acker turns the postmodern "anxiety of influence" regarding one's intellectual predecessors into a source of inspiration rather than a debilitating onus. Cervantes, as "father" of the modern novel, is the Oedipal influence whom Acker flattens in order to use her own voice as a woman writer.[30] Acker has said that her *Don Quixote* "is about appropriating male texts and that the middle part of *Don Quixote* is very much about trying to find your voice as a woman" (Friedman 12). She demonstrates what Teresa de Lauretis refers to as the need for feminists to be "Oedipal with a vengeance," to exaggerate any inherently male structures of narrative as a feminist tactic of self-defense.[31] Acker's protagonist, a "FEMALE" knight named Don Quixote, notes: "BEING BORN INTO AND PART OF A MALE WORLD, SHE HAD NO SPEECH OF HER OWN. ALL SHE COULD DO WAS READ MALE TEXTS WHICH WEREN'T HERS" (39). With "nowhere to escape to anymore," Acker's Don Quixote must learn to fight off the passivity of suicide and despair in order to find a new world. Such survival, as it turns out, requires knowledge of both narrative and desire:

> In Our Bible or The Storehouse Of Language, we tried to tell women who they are: The-Loving-Mother-Who-Has-No-Sex-So-Her-Sex-Isn't-A-Crab or The-Woman-Who-Loves-That-Is-Needs Love So Much She Will Let Anything Be Done To Her. But women aren't either of these. (27)

Acker's novels sketch out the goal of female protagonists to find a voice that will "transport" them to new places, even if they must speak in a patriarchal language that benefits men: "For 2,000 years you've had the nerve to tell women who we are. We use your words; we eat your food. Every way we get money has to be a crime. We are plagiarists, liars, and criminals" (*Blood and Guts* 132). Although she begins by blaming "male texts," Acker charts the painful transition from the masochistic autism of girl readers to the furious narrative ruptures created by female writers like her. The wheelchair transporting Don Quixote to her abortion is the "k/night's" transportation: "It had once been a hack, the same as all the hacks on grub street" (9). But to emphasize Acker's overall point, the k/night's real mode of transportation is words, and Acker glorifies those words generated by the lowest level of commodity writers, the hacks who depend upon formulaic writing and cheap thrills. Acker continues the avant-garde tradition of rupture and shock, inflecting it with the hackneyed detritus of mass-market fiction. She destroys narrative pleasure by writing of incest, damning Oedipal desire in her pedagogy of cruelty, and confounds genre structure by rejecting the fantasy of escape that one expects to encounter in a road story. These techniques exemplify a point of view later articulated by her Don Quixote: "An alteration of language, rather than of material, usually changes material conditions" (27).

As an artist associated with the punk movement, Acker brought punk's interest in gender "performance" to the novel as a genre, and to the road story in particular.[32] Former postwar generations worried about authenticity and tradition, whereas punk attacked tradition and exalted the artificial. Although punk was a significant movement of cultural resistance in the late 1970s, even for these iconoclasts the road story continued to be seen as a viable genre, as a useful way to express feelings of rebellion, although punk road stories radically remap the genre in order to reject its romantic core. Neither feminist nor narrative theory takes much account of punk, but many women found a voice in its anger, especially in London, where Acker lived during those years, for London was home to several girl punk bands, including The Slits and X-Ray-Spex, who sang about the "acrylic road."

Acker's *Don Quixote* relentlessly problematizes the trope of escape, including the road as the place that leads to escape. The common refrain in *Don Quixote* is "there's nowhere to run anymore" (22). Don Quixote refuses to be intimidated by this, insisting, "I won't not be: I'll perceive and I'll speak" (28). She encounters God, who informs her: "There are no more new stories, no more tracks, no more memories: there is you, knight. Since I am no more, forget Me. Forget morality. Forget about saving the world. Make Me up" (207). The final sentence of *Don Quixote* ends optimistically, as Don Quixote describes awakening "to the world which lay before me" (207). This is a great departure from traditional narrative, in which women's escapes have too often ended in suicide or more subtle forms of self-destruction.

DIFFERENT FORMS OF FEMINISM IN MASS-MARKET NOVELS

Feminist film scholars in the 1980s balanced the era's keen interest in psychoanalytic and postmodern discourse with the identity politics of feminism. Much feminist film and narrative theory addressed the subject of the male gaze and the nature of desire. There was the sense that women had to "escape . . . male texts" (Gilbert and Gubar 13) if they were ever to be free to create or, as Adrienne Rich wrote, to "re-vision," which she defined as "the act of looking back, of seeing with fresh eyes, of entering an old text from a new critical direction . . . [Re-vision] is for women more than a chapter in cultural history; it is an act of survival" (35). The influential British film scholar Laura Mulvey suggested destroying the traditional pleasure derived from film spectatorship as a tactic to further a more progressive approach to female subjectivity; de Lauretis's solution, already mentioned, was for women to be "Oedipal with a vengeance." These debates might well have continued into the 1990s had not films like *Thelma and Louise* turned the rules of genre back on themselves with a vengeance, as we will see in the next chapter.

Concurrent with these feminist film and literature scholars—yet not in discourse with them—were several women novelists who took a different approach to the issues of the era. Their female protagonists went on the road and found peace with their fathers, not in any vengeful or Oedipal way, but simply as part of their transformation from adolescents to young women. These novels offer a counter position to the crisis in gender articulated by feminist film theorists, demonstrating that there is nothing inherently masculine in road stories—after all, escapist fantasies play a critical role in female subjectivity, too.

Beginning in the 1980s, several women writers aiming at the mass market published their first novels, using the road as a device to take a young female protagonist to someplace new and positive rather than reinforcing her gender's marginality or victim status. These novels—all of which approach female automobility without anger or strife—reveal that there is a tremendous divide between the academic feminists reading Freud and Foucault on campuses and the women authors writing popular fiction in their kitchens. In their novels, Barbara Kingsolver, Bobbie Ann Mason, Mona Simpson, and Cynthia Kadohata pay little attention to the literary tradition of male epics and heroic odysseys; in fact, they pay little attention to men at all. Their work is distinguished not only in its difference from academic thought at this time, but also in its notable difference from films of the era. Many of the male-oriented road films of this decade narrate a return to the past, but these road novels of the 1980s point optimistically toward the future.

Academic feminists were suspicious of narrative, but Barbara Kingsolver feels that narrative pleasure is something to appreciate. The author, who followed her first road novel *The Bean Trees* (1988) with another, *Pigs in Heaven* in 1993, says this on her web site:

> First, a novel has to entertain—that's the contract with the reader: you give me ten hours and I'll give you a reason to turn every page. I have a commitment to accessibility. I believe in plot. I want an English professor to understand the symbolism while at the same time I want the people I grew up with—who may not often read anything but the Sears catalogue—to read my books.

Kingsolver also considers writing to be political activism, but for her, education comes second to the goal of pleasure. Both of Kingsolver's road novels revolve around Taylor, a young independent woman who finds an abandoned infant on her first road trip, adopts it, and then, in *Pigs in Heaven,* learns that her daughter, Turtle, is a Cherokee whom the Cherokee nation declares must be held in joint custody by Taylor and the child's grandfather. Any potential crisis created by racial difference is averted by the fact that Taylor is related to this Cherokee clan by birth and, by the closing pages of the novel, by marriage, as her mother agrees to marry Turtle's grandfather, her new beau.

Similarly, Bobbie Ann Mason's novel, *In Country* (1985), is not vengeful of masculine traditions of adventure literature, but Mason does ponder her female protagonist's relationship to traditionally male-dominated genres. *In Country* follows Sam, the heroine recently graduated from high school, as she travels from Kentucky to Washington DC in her VW bug. Sam's description of the road uses the metaphors of aerobics (this passage was discussed earlier in chap. 1), inspired by the new space of women's aerobics classes that opened up in the 1980s. In fact, Sam's decidedly mass-market cultural models also include television and Bruce Springsteen's songs about the road. Mason seems to be celebrating purposefully the metaphors, genres, and identities used by someone with limited experience—a young woman's lack of worldliness, in other words—to express her innermost philosophies to others.

In one subplot of *In Country,* Sam's boyfriend Lonnie drives to a nearby lake with his high school pals for a long weekend bachelor party. His absence gives Sam time to think and to develop the desire to move beyond him. This section of *In Country* seems to rebut T. Coraghessan Boyle's early-1980's short story "Greasy Lake," which is also about high school boys who drive to a lake; in Boyle's story, the narrator imagines himself to be in a Norman Mailer war novel while he and his friends listen to Bruce Springsteen, fight with a stranger, and nearly rape the stranger's girlfriend. Mason's novel remixes the same ingredients—Springsteen, small town life, high school automobility—to offer an intelligent alternative without vengefully denouncing "male" genre altogether. Mason's lack of inhibition by the male canon serves as a welcome reminder that women may be affected by war narratives and male-oriented road stories, but they are not always victimized by them. *In Country* portrays a young woman capable of navigating mainstream masculine culture without losing hold of her own dreams. Sam spends a night in the swamp near her home, reenacting what she imagines her father's experiences "in country" in Vietnam might have been like. After taking her road trip to the Vietnam Memorial in Washington DC to forge a bond to the father who died in Vietnam before she was born, Sam decides to leave her small Kentucky hometown and her boyfriend to attend college in Lexington.

Sadly, feminists in the universities were far more welcoming of angry narrative politics of gender, as exemplified by Acker's *Don Quixote,* than the "genre bend-ing" of Mason or the unabashed autonomy of the female protagonists of other mass-market road stories. A case in point can be found in *The Remasculinization of America: Gender and the Vietnam War* (1989), where Susan Jeffords concludes that *In Country* falls victim to the "Vietnam narrative," which tends to reduce all female characters to roles that are "pitiable and contemptible," no matter how strong they seem at one point (64). Not surprisingly, Jeffords sees *In Country* as a failed feminist intervention, arguing that the plot "force[s]" Sam into a debased position "in order for the narrative to progress":

> Sam Hughes of *In Country* can only join the collectivity of Vietnam through her own father and her "own" name as a man appearing on the Vietnam Memorial [where she sees inscribed the name of some stranger, a fallen male soldier also named Sam Hughes]. In this way the feminine is denied power in Vietnam representation, its multiplicity being presented only as fragmented failure. (64)

Jeffords reads Sam's night in the swamps as a botched attempt to put herself in the Vietnam narrative, but we can also interpret Sam's simulated experience "in country" as her awareness about her own autonomy and mobility within a vast range of subject positions and narrative genres. Her uncle's admonishment that she could never truly experience what soldiers went through in Vietnam would have been just as true had Sam been a boy instead of a girl. For the offspring of veterans, war is always mediated, known through someone else's words, writing, and images. Sam has read her father's letters from the battlefield, and so she is more likely to have a visceral understanding of the war maneuvers she mimics than the narrator of Boyle's short story, who knows war only from Mailer's World War II epic: "I inched forward, elbows and knees, my belly pressed to the much, thinking of guerrillas and commandos and *The Naked and the Dead*" (8). The boy in "Greasy Lake" uses the war story to justify his brutality, whereas Sam uses both the "Vietnam narrative" *and* the road genre to gain freedom in her own life. She lets go of the past and moves into the future, refusing to fall victim to the gendered barriers of women in rural Kentucky—often characterized by unplanned pregnancies followed by poverty—and expanding instead as a university student.

Previous generations of women writers may have felt "penned in" by the masculine authority of high literature, but the 1980s opened up to women authors an alternative set of references in popular culture. Sam's understanding of gender relations is influenced by the television show *M*A*S*H* and her cross-dressing uncle. Sam is disconnected from the patriarchal past, and she is actually inspired by the fact that she doesn't know where to go next. Indeed, what is so interesting about *In Country* is Sam's curiosity about the war and her fearless confrontation of masculine landscapes—the swamps and the road—which she feels quite entitled to explore.[33] This might be said of all of these authors themselves, all of whom find the road story offers a new range of possibilities.

For instance, the women authors of the 1980s mass-market novels are not fighting to remap Kerouac's influence or surrendering to postmodern schizophrenia. Rather, the road is a place of family stability, and the car, a container of unity, as in

Mona Simpson's second novel, *Anywhere But Here* (1986). The title derives from an Emerson quotation that expresses the restless desire for mobility. Simpson portrays the confusions of a girl, Ann, just at the age of puberty, as she sorts out her identity within and without her family. After Ann's biological father leaves and before her mom remarries, Ann and her mother hear the "call" of the open road:

> The highway was barely visible but we heard the constant running noise of travel. . . . It seemed to me then, as we stood there, for a long time on the verge of leaving, that we shouldn't have really had to go. Something had gone wrong. My mother and I should have both been girls who stayed out on the porch a little longer than the rest, girls who strained to hear the long-distance trucks on the highway and who listened to them, not the nearer crickets . . . but who finally sighed and, calling the dog with a mixture of reluctance and relief, shut the door and went in home. (61)

Ann's mother Adele remarries in an attempt to settle down, but neither Ann nor Adele can relinquish the promise of the open road. For instance, one night Ann sneaks away from her mother to sleep in her stepdad's Cadillac:

> I closed my eyes and thought about driving all night on a dark road, the car moving smoothly, my mother and father in the front, my mother's arm falling down over the seat on my stomach, patting my hands under the blanket, telling me to Don't worry, go to sleep, it's still a long ways away. (72)

Inevitably, Adele becomes restless and leaves her new marriage, taking Ann (along with her new husband's car and credit cards) to drive across country to a new life in Los Angeles. En route, the car comforts Ann again: "We felt safe together in Ted's car, we could feel ourselves moving" (65).

It is racial heritage, rather than the Oedipal conflict, that burdens the characters of Cynthia Kadohata's *The Floating World* (1989). Olivia Ann, the girl narrating the story, explains:

> We were traveling then in what she [Obäsan, the grandmother] called ukiyo, the floating world. The floating world was the gas station attendants, restaurants, and jobs we depended on, the motel towns floating in the middle of fields and mountains. In old Japan, ukiyo meant the districts full of brothels, teahouses, and public baths, but it also referred to change and the pleasures and loneliness change brings. For a long time, I never exactly thought of us as part of any of that, though. *We* were stable, traveling through an unstable world while my father looked for jobs. (5)

As Olivia Ann's account reveals, these migrations were the result of bad luck, beginning with the overall difficulties experienced by Japanese Americans looking for decent jobs in the 1950s and 1960s, and encompassing the unhappiness of her parents' marriage. Travel comforts Olivia Ann: "I remember how fine it was to drive through the passage of light from morning to noon to night" (6–7). Like *In Country*'s Sam, Olivia Ann leaves a small southern town with the intention of attending college. Instead of going to school in Los Angeles, she ends up servicing vending machines in gas stations and restaurants along the road, a job she inherited from her estranged biological father after he died. (Because she did not know him, she does not suffer any Oedipal conflict in assuming his place, but she does mend the family wounds of the past.) Olivia Ann thus finds a place in the floating world, remaining comfortable with her gender, race, and independence—despite the fact that all of these place her outside the mainstream.

In 1980s mass-market road fiction written by women, female protagonists celebrate their autonomy and mobility. They don't feel trapped. Instead, for a variety of reasons, these characters are comfortable with themselves and their freedom. They embrace mass culture, racial difference, and gender as raw materials from which to build their own identities. While these girls recognize their difference from those who opt to "stay put," it is significant to note that they do not feel marginalized by or defensive about their differences, nor do they condemn those women who stay behind. The road brings these young women in contact with the future, not old patriarchs.

These stories offer a significant counter-voice to the feminist scholarship that suggested women could only escape the prison of patriarchy through the destruction of pleasure. Indeed, they contradict postmodern theory in general, standing against the passivity implicit in theories of ecstasy, schizophrenia, and even vengeance, which all reject the possibility of resistance by marginalized subcultures. But just as few foresaw the dismantling of the Berlin Wall in 1989, few could have predicted the coming revitalization of genre that would come in the 1990s.

When Michel de Certeau enthused, in 1984, that "every story is a travel story" (115), he was recognizing the active aspect of consumption—reading as a kind of travel through a "narrative space" in which autonomy can be practiced. De Certeau also made an important distinction between "the map" and "the tour"—a distinction that is central to the argument being developed here. According to de Certeau, the map presents a geographically stable place, an inert tableau based upon observation, while the tour offers a series of operations and movements—an empirical space full of actors and actions (121). The road story might be thought of as a kind of tour—that is, as a record of itineraries, travelers, and actions, all of which are fleshed out by means of an inherited system of representation that can be remapped, even in postmodernism. By contrast, theorists like Baudrillard insisted that the map precedes the territory, that all our experiences and actions are less important than the media technologies that depict them.

In the 1980s, an identity crisis did emerge in America, the nation that had always defined itself as mobile, restless, and free. Despite confusion over rebellion, despite the spread of commodities into our innermost desires, the road genre survives the challenges of the 1980s. Indeed, its splintering into the forms examined here attest, once again, to the maturation of the genre, which enables it to diversify in so many different directions. Its adaptability to outlive so many narrative variants and economic situations reveals it to be a genre growing ever more substantial with each postwar generation. In fact, this wide recognition of the genre is a precondition to the next phase of innovation. As we shall see, the road story in the 1990s introduces audiences to new concepts of community, shaking up social views of gender, sexuality, and race, bringing us back, at the start of the new millennium, to the road as a space of rebellion.

8
Rebels with a Cause
Genre and Identity Politics

In the postmodern 1980s, rebellion seemed to implode in on itself; yet inevitably, rebels began to reject postmodernism's amused contempt in order to reinvest in communal symbolic systems—particularly genre. As identity politics came to the forefront of cultural expression during the 1990s, storytellers began remapping genre to reveal in its traditions the tacit collusion in social inequities that can occur when we fail to examine the stories we tell ourselves. There was a rising awareness that the purportedly universal "family of man" must be explicitly opened up to include women and minorities and that, furthermore, as altruistically proclaimed in the road film, *To Wong Foo Thanks for Everything! Love Julie Newmar* (1995), "we are all drag queens!" Of course we're not all drag queens, but the point is that more and more of us linked in sympathy if not in fact with some minority community in the self-consciously multicultural 1990s. This is how, in the road films of this decade, faith in rebellion returned at the same time that Americans gained a more global sense of identity. Indeed, there was a new hope that narrative intervention, rather than politics' conventional tactics, might be a better way to engage vast numbers of people. As filmmakers used the road genre to focus on race, gender, and sexual orientation, rebellion returned to the road genre once again.

From *Easy Rider* to *Rain Man,* there were two busy decades in which film-makers used automobility in varying cultural and political environments. With *Easy Rider*'s facile critique of capitalism and *Rain Man*'s facile celebration of it, the road genre film runs all over the ideological map of rebellion, yet holds fast to the theme that being on the road is transformative. The road remains a space of metamorphosis, as it has been throughout the postwar decades, but in the nineties this evolution extended beyond those who travel on the road to those communities touched by the protagonist who travels. Alienation exists only as a conflict to be resolved through the community's transformation rather than the individual's rebellion. Walt Whitman once noted, "I am bigger than I thought myself," and the films of the nineties shift focus from the self to the interconnections of that self to a larger group of people.

By the mid-to-late 1990s, even the mainstream press recognized that the road film had become a genre for mapping racial autonomy as automobility. A *Time* magazine headline (29 June 1998) suggested that each minority would soon aim for a road film of its own: "what Spike Lee's film [*Get on the Bus*] did for African Americans, *Smoke Signals* aims to do for Native Americans" (Ressner 58). Myriad reasons exist for the new focus on race in road films, including the 1991 race riots in Los Angeles, just a few miles from Hollywood, where most of the nation's films—indie and High Concept—are produced. These riots erupted when an all-white jury acquitted the white LAPD officers who had beaten Rodney King (indeed, the beating and arrest of this African American driver, thought to be on drugs, taped on video and played endlessly on TV news, is a reality "road story" itself). More than anything, the riots served as a wake-up call to the nation that a colorblind society was a fiction in which we could no longer afford to indulge. (They also brought attention to the larger problem of racial profiling, a phenomenon so commonplace among law enforcement officers in certain areas of the United States that the provocation came to be called "driving while black.") No longer could the nation smugly assume that the civil rights movement had completed the task of integration. This is, no doubt, one reason why some of the films of the early nineties are set in the Jim Crow south, as we will soon see.

Another part of the explicit attention to race, sexual orientation, class, and age in road films of the 1990s came with the swing back, politically, to the Democrats when Bill Clinton took over the presidency for an eight-year run. As we have seen throughout this study and will confirm again in the next chapter, the road film's sympathies shift with each party in power. What's more, we will continue to find that the road film cycles persistently between commodification and innovation—and conditions in the film industry are such that the nineties became a time of grand invention and full flowering of the genre.

During the 1980s, as the indie studios gained viability in the marketplace, we saw that the narrative trajectory of road films could be predicted by the source of production funds—a High Concept, high-budget film featured financially successful characters, whereas the indie films of the eighties focused on more quirky characters who rebel because of a woman. In the nineties, the rise in importance of the indie market is reflected in the growth of film festivals like Sundance and Toronto; there was also some consolidation of indie houses, as when Miramax merged with Disney and Dreamworks was started in 1994 by Steven Spielberg, Jeffrey Katzenberg, and David Geffen. In the nineties, then, even the High Concept films are revitalizing stories of automobility for people in the margins of society rather than simply those driving the engines of the American economy.

Most likely, the biggest reason for the growing presence of people of color in road films is the fact that minority filmmakers were finally given funding—and directors like Carl Franklin and John Singleton chose to make fiction films about black female automobility. As women gained opportunities in Hollywood, a screenwriter like Callie Khouri could finally sell a script like *Thelma and Louise* to MGM—and the marketplace confirmed the timeliness of the film's focus on white women's rebellion against the patriarchal norm. For the first time in the history of postwar American road films, minority identity became the fuel of the genre's celebration of autonomy and mobility.

"DOUBLE CONSCIOUSNESS" AND GENRE

Two road films from 1989, *Driving Miss Daisy* and *Powwow Highway*, anticipate the rise of identity politics within narratives of autonomy and mobility that characterize road films in the 1990s.[1] Other than their emphasis on race, however, these films could not be more different in terms of budget, acclaim, and impact—*Driving Miss Daisy* is a High Concept film, bankrolled by a major studio, which won four Oscars, whereas *Powwow Highway* is an indie film; it earned fifty times less than *Miss Daisy* and was seen by only small fraction of the other film's audience. Yet these films share a mission to show the "double consciousness" of people in the margins and, thus, to deconstruct the "genre" of identity constituted by one's skin color.

By extending genre theory to identity, we can begin to investigate how remapping the road genre becomes an eloquent yet politicized innovation in how we "read" each other. As rhetorician Amy Devitt notes, "Part of what all readers and writers recognize when they recognize genres are the roles they are to play, the roles being played by other people, what they can gain from the discourse, and what the discourses are about" (12). The intervention of genre films comes from the eventual overturning of restrictive roles and the dismantling of discourses in order to reveal their presumptions about social relations. The road genre in the 1990s thus brings the tropes of autonomy and mobility into the narrative conflict about who, in practical terms rather than metaphoric ones, is mobile and free.

In *Powwow Highway,* genre is the source of the film's deft reversal of authority that leads to the triumph of the rebel, for the film intelligently deconstructs identity as a genre in tandem with its use of narrative genre. The film's road trip begins at the Cheyenne reservation in Montana and relies upon Indian tropes, like tricksters and war ponies, to enhance the road genre's preoccupation with transformation. The mismatched travelers, Philbert (Gary Farmer) and Red Bow (A Martinez), are among the first of the new wave of rebels with a cause.

Given the low budget of the film, its trickster intervention comes by way of genre—only by remapping stereotypes and familiar narrative structure could the film do so much with so little. The plot emphasizes that even though the Cheyenne of *Powwow Highway* constitute a sovereign nation, land developers prey upon them, for Wall Street types invade the tribe's privacy with their sales pitches. By putting American Indians in the comedic road genre, *Powwow Highway* turns the tables on who the outlaws are—land developers and white police who plant evidence—not the mobile, ethnic men. They go on the road to buy cattle for the tribe but end up on a spiritual journey that culminates in a comedic prison escape inspired by a television program, and they finish by saving the tribe from unscrupulous business people.

In many ways, *Powwow Highway* offers a refreshing indie alternative to the auteurs who had, thus far in the 1980s, featured white, middle-class people on the road. *Powwow Highway* and *Driving Miss Daisy* look instead at characters who never left the heartland, because their racial heritage tied them to their home geography through a lack of mobility and autonomy. *Powwow Highway*'s director Jonathan Wacks was part of the "next generation" of indie filmmakers after the New York auteurs of the 1980s; as with previous generations of independent-minded new directors, a closeknit network evolved of people contributing to the road genre.[2] For instance, *Powwow Highway* was nurtured by Beatle bassist George Harrison, executive producer of the film, and financed by his company, Handmade Films Ltd., rather than by one of the new indie studios like Miramax, Orion, New Line, or Geffen Pictures.

Alongside *Powwow Highway*, *Driving Miss Daisy* confirms in 1989 that the transformation theme of the road genre will move from a focus on personal accomplishment to a wider message about social desegregation as people move away from "generic" relations between the races. Bruce Beresford's movie about Miss Daisy (Jessica Tandy) and her chauffeur, Hoke Colburn (Morgan Freeman), looks genteelly at a strictly hierarchical, interracial relationship that slowly turns into a friendship over the fifteen years of the South's molasses-paced desegregation. Miss Daisy is a tough old bird who likes things just so, yet the movie patiently and carefully builds the emotional ties and even dependence each character develops for the other. The attachment between Hoke and Miss Daisy can never be said in so many words, merely in the rituals of a long-term working partnership. In its moments of criticism, as when Miss Daisy stubbornly refuses to invite Hoke to accompany her to a dinner speech by Martin Luther King Jr., the film indicts all who have relied on generic rules of interracial engagement rather than their inner compass.

The road film, with its emphasis on autonomy and mobility as automobility, has long provided pop cultural insight into how identity is actively *constructed* rather than *expressed* as part of some essential being. Minorities living in "double consciousness" of their similarities to and differences from mainstream whites might understandably emphasize a sophisticated understanding of identity in films, yet so do films about white automobility, especially in classic films about white women as outlaws. For instance, *Bonnie and Clyde* (1967) explicitly displays how the two bank robbers manipulated their image with both individuals and the press. Made just a few years later, *Badlands* (1973) looks at two kids on the lam, the young man self-consciously molding himself after the rebel James Dean and his girlfriend experimenting with various roles of femininity, from cheerleader to a curler-wearing fugitive to retrospective narrator giving a voice-over of her story on the road. Outlaws frequently take on false identities, working disguised in offices they intend to rob, as in *Gun Crazy* (1949), or they keep their cool with cops in tense situations, as with *The Getaway* (1972). The subgenre of outlaw road films presents to the masses an exciting, entertaining lesson in the mobility of identity, the power in posing as someone else, *and* the ease with which one can do that as long as one is well-armed.

Even though these road films dismantle notions of identity as fixed, we have seen that high budget entertainments are likely to focus—up until the nineties—on white protagonists. Female automobility is a stable subtheme of the road genre, but until *Thelma and Louise* in 1991, women road travelers function somewhat like catalytic converters—they get the men of the narrative into action, but their automobility does not represent social change. Beginning with *Thelma and Louise,* road films focus on everyday people who suddenly find themselves in the wrong genre, as do Thelma and Louise when they get sucked deeper and deeper into a Kafka-esque metamorphosis that turns smartly on the outlaw road genre. Then follows a decade in which minority directors exert their power over genre by remapping its presumptions of privilege to show new ways to recognize race, sexuality, and gender.

Powwow Highway, Driving Miss Daisy, and *Thelma and Louise* meld the lessons of identity politics with the pleasures of pop culture. For instance, *Thelma and Louise* successfully awoke the nation to the topic of women's desires in an age called post-feminist and even stimulated disputes about what feminism is (since many reviewers expended considerable energy pronouncing the film as feminist or not). Yet it is unlikely anyone would have bothered to discuss feminism had the script not used genre to expose social expectations regarding gender—in other words, had *Thelma and Louise* been a "chick flick" instead of an outlaw road film starring women. (It helped that the big-name cast and crew possessed enough talent to bring to life the frustrations of women who aren't listened to unless they're holding a gun, unlike the inferior road film, *Bound and Gagged: A Love Story* [1992].) Similarly, had *Powwow Highway* not taken Philbert and Red Bow off "the Res" and put them into the comedy genre, with its light-hearted reversals of fortune, the film's social critiques would have been didactic rather than charming.

It is the road film in the 1990s that launches much of the play with genre that would soon become characteristic of the film revisionism of this decade. As minority characters take center stage in the nineties genre films, they bring to vast audiences a widening range of identificatory possibilities. Not only did members of subcultures have more chances to see themselves represented on the big screen, but also genre became the common ground for viewers eagerly attending films that required cross-identification with characters unlike them.

THELMA AND LOUISE'S GENRE-BENDING REVOLUTION

By something as simple as putting women in the driver's seat of the outlaw film, *Thelma and Louise* solidified the genre renaissance of the 1990s and inspired a national debate on gender. Screenwriter Callie Khouri simply used common sense when she wrote *Thelma and Louise:* "I just got fed up with the passive role of women. They were never driving the story, because they were never driving the car" (Willis 125). Both a metaphor of power and a plot device, the depiction of women drivers, as seen in figure 14, celebrated a genre film revolution, for Khouri's "just do it" attitude might not have had so much impact had she not turned to genre, reinvesting this shared semiotic system with the specifics of gender identity. That this remapping of the outlaw road genre shocked viewers in 1991 gives evidence of just how unconsciously audiences followed the unspoken rules of genre until this time.

Fig. 14. Geena Davis (Thelma) and Susan Sarandon (Louise) in *Thelma and Louise* (1991), which depicted the shortcomings of patriarchy for its titular rebels and led the genre revitalization of the 1990s. Directed by Ridley Scott; film copyright © Metro-Goldwyn-Mayer.

Sharon Willis argues that *Thelma and Louise* "plugged into ambient anxieties about sexual difference" (120) but, by the late 1980s, sexual difference was less the problem than the gender indifference characterized by the High Concept directors' omission of women from their road films—especially the late-1980s, male-buddy films like *Midnight Run* and *Rain Man*. *Thelma and Louise* brings into the big leagues a film about the mobility of types not representable by Tom Cruise, Dustin Hoffman, Robert de Niro, or Steve Martin, all of whom had starred in the High Concept road films of the late 1980s. Even *Thelma and Louise*'s theme of female automobility was not new, for we know by now that most of the auteurs of 1970s New Hollywood crafted the road genre from the timely trope of women's movement, and most of the independent directors of the 1980s continued with this theme of female automobility. Hence, what was new was female automobility in a mainstream production—with a hefty marketing campaign, a famous director, and glamorous stars who unambiguously rejected patriarchy's compromises. In 1988, the road film had commanded Hollywood's attention when *Rain Man* grossed $413 million worldwide and was nominated for eight Academy Awards—excellent return on the initial budget of $25 million. Although it cost less, *Thelma and Louise* was still one of the larger budget road films of its time, for MGM spent $17.5 million (Sturken 8), quite a good sum for a genre film with two female leads and no romantic, happy ending. When *Thelma and Louise* appeared on the cover of *Time, Newsweek,* and *U.S. News and Report,* and won an Oscar, it became clear that, once again, a road film was hitting a national nerve, as *Easy Rider* had back in 1969. Both catalyzed discussion about the power of film but, unlike *Easy Rider, Thelma and Louise* got people talking about women's fantasies of violence and rebellion, rather than about rednecks in the south with shotguns.

Thelma and Louise was the first High Concept road film to focus exclusively on mobile women as friends, who in this case, grow closer even as they grow wilder with each mile traveled. Even more significantly, the film was neither afraid of nor apologetic about the women's ability to take charge—in fact, the entire conflict stems from Louise killing Harlan after she had rescued Thelma from harm. These characters thus differ in every way from most road genre women, except for Bonnie in *Bonnie and Clyde*. *Thelma and Louise* rejects the ambiguity in earlier road films about female automobility that fail to explore a woman's autonomy, films like *Something Wild,* which seemed to want to appear political without in fact being so. With as simple a premise as this short-circuiting of gender and genre expectations, *Thelma and Louise* brought national attention to female automobility as the desire for autonomy from patriarchal structure and rebellion against male privilege. Rarely had genre ever been used to such smart effect, yet *Thelma and Louise* is merely the most visible of many road films of the 1990s that made significant social comment by bending genre expectations.

We can see *Thelma and Louise* as turning the inevitable cycle of commodification of the road film one more rotation, bringing it back to innovation by means of gender. Even more important is the fact that discussions about film genre and identity politics were not confined to the ivory towers, where people use terms like "sexual difference" and "male gaze." Feminists in the academy were still contending with Laura Mulvey's strict ideas about the gaze of film spectators being necessarily and only male. Along comes *Thelma and Louise* to suggest that through as basic a gesture as deconstructing the male outlaw role by casting women—women who literally appropriate the discourse of male outlaws, as Thelma did by using J.D.'s robbery speech—we can liberate women from their narrative prisons and imagine new identificatory pleasures for film audiences. Even if the popular press hosted superficial debates about feminism, post-feminism, and the femininity of the stars Geena Davis and Susan Sarandon, the widespread conversations succeeded in articulating new ideas about spectator difference in film—particularly the intersections of genre and gender that few, amazingly, had yet begun to question.

Thelma and Louise helped feminist scholars soften their views about the male gaze and narrative pleasure, leading to new, more useful theories of identification and fantasy. Many feminist critics were deeply touched by *Thelma and Louise;* for example, Willis wrote:

> identification is not a state, but a process, and that as such, it is likely to be *mobile* and intermittent, rather than consistent [or based on consciously perceived or desired resemblances]. We will do better to think of viewer identifications as scenarios, rather than *fixations* . . . confined to identifications with characters. (emphasis added, 121)

As Willis recounts her childhood fascination with the television series *Route 66,* she dispels the myth, which lingered for too long in feminist film scholarship, that girls/women do not respond to stories about men, except as a "transvestite" who have adopted the tomboy pleasures of the male gaze (Mulvey 129). Yet, by seeing Thelma and Louise occupy that subject position on the screen, many feminist scholars could suddenly pinpoint what had been missing from their theories. In other words, by watching powerful women act out their mobility and what limited autonomy is available to them as criminals, scholars could recognize the crossgendered identificatory positions that had been there all along. Of course, the women's novels in the 1980s about female automobility worked with this mobility of identificatory possibilities inherent in narrative, but feminists in the academy were more likely immersed in Mulvey's and Teresa de Lauretis's suspicions of patriarchal forms than in subversive pleasures.

Thelma and Louise serve as foils to each other's type. Louise (Susan Sarandon) is tough and pragmatic, awakening somewhat belatedly to her station in life—old enough to realize she's stuck being a waitress as well as to recognize that marriage may not be in her future. Yet she's not yet ossified into bitterness, for she still holds out a weak hope for the American dream of middle-class white women. Yet the film indicts those dreams as a gilded cage for women, as evidenced by Thelma's (Geena Davis) stultification in her suburban marriage. These women are damned in and out of marriage, for the film blames the shortcomings on all the men and thus patriarchy rather than any individual character per se. The men are all generic types—the self-absorbed salesman, the beaten down musician, the two-bit hustler, even the compassionate FBI agent—and this erasure of the conventional realism of the male characters was judged to be a flaw of the film rather than a smart play on genre.

Both *Thelma and Louise* and the independent film that came out the next year, Gregg Araki's *The Living End,* are unusually smart about genre, revealing to viewers the mechanisms by which genre shapes what we take for granted about gender or heterosexuality. *Thelma and Louise* shocks with its ending, when the Thunderbird flies off the cliff into the Grand Canyon, even though the genre of outlaw films dictates just such a demise. In taking Thelma and Louise toward an inevitable death, like that faced by Butch Cassidy and the Sundance Kid, the end helps audiences recall the patterns of earlier films while also calling attention to the differences, like the fact that women rarely face certain death at the end of a road film. This dramatic ending can be read as a rejection of the 1980s "happy face" endings, that magical resolution in the McFly or Babbit family that made audiences feel satisfied with closure. In *Thelma and Louise,* the final scene takes advantage of the fiction of film to use their leap into the unknown as a wake-up call to the audience not to settle for what one is given—as Louise repeatedly advises—but to actively construct a life worth living.

Similarly, *The Living End* twists the buddy film genre in making its fugitives not only male lovers, but HIV-infected men who overturn the conventions of the outlaw road genre and the HIV-narratives of the early 1990s, both of which end consistently in death. By offering a *living* end rather than the inevitable death, Araki's film is as canny as *Thelma and Louise*'s dead end. Each film uses its finale to underscore its metaphoric message about the life-and-death significance of identity politics.

This return to genre and use of popular narrative to raise political consciousness reveals a new strategy for constructing a rebel viewing position compared to what was seen in the 1980s. No longer do minority scriptwriters like *Thelma and Louise*'s Khouri and *Smoke Signal*'s Alexie or gay directors like Araki need to *settle for* the genres traditionally available to various subcultures, nor do these rebels need to rely upon the ahedonic strategies of avant-garde filmmaking, which only limit the distribution and impact of their films. What *Thelma and Louise, The Living End, Smoke Signals,* and the others utilize is the ready narratological structure of the road genre to represent rebellion as well as the collective longing for transformation of a minority community. Genre is a structure that can be twisted to expose the unvoiced expectations about gender, sexuality, or race that previous genre films left unquestioned. Leading the way for many of the genre revision films to follow in the 1990s, *The Living End* breaks the unspoken taboos against homosexuality in male buddy films (like *Easy Rider*) or the heterosexual tradition of lovers on the lam, while *Thelma and Louise* erases the ambiguous silences of female travelers so characteristic of auteurs' films, as seen earlier in *Two-Lane Blacktop* or *Badlands,* for instance. By remapping the road genre as a repository for images of mobility and autonomy—thus using the mediascape history of road stories in order to foreground differences in identity—the 1990s road films call attention to popular genre as a performative space for imaginative revisions of individual identity and collective society.

Even while *The Living End* uses strategies of popular narrative, as an art film it also offers meta-critical commentary on the future of film in the age of AIDS. Merged with the film's questions about mortality is an equally fervent revival of the inquiry raised by avant-garde filmmaker Jean-Luc Godard about the "End of Cinema" in his road film *Weekend* (1967). Araki's characters, Jon and Luke, do more than flesh out the concerns about the future of film, for they "marry" the two modes of filmmaking by uniting Jon's avant-garde intellectualism (he's writing an article on "The Death of Cinema") and Luke's unabashed pleasures (he's a hustler, a generic character of gay porn). Through witty, educated citations of genre and auteurism, Araki transforms Godard's anxiety that narrative is ideology into an ideological narrative about survival and pleasure. Rather than destroy narrative or mistrust entertainment, he constructs a different frame of reference in order to recharge the libidinal battery of film and build the postmodern corpus of "queer cinema."

In Jon and Luke, furthermore, Araki creates two antithetical responses to being diagnosed as HIV-positive, which find dialectical resolution by the end of the film. The first scene with Luke shows him spray-painting "I Blame Society" on urban walls, and his anger and nihilism represent one perspective on AIDS. Jon, however, blames himself for contracting the disease and implodes. A loner even prior to the diagnosis, Jon isolates into his world of movies until Luke seduces him into a different subject position. Jon abandons his incomplete essay on the death of cinema and leaves his movie-postered home to go on the run with Luke. What's at stake, as the film makes clear, is that Jon learns to leave his responsible rut and shed his self-incriminating response to testing HIV-positive. Jon is swept up in the fantasy of being a fugitive in a road film, as if he forced himself to leap from his lonely cinematic voyeurism into a leading role in his own life, reluctant all the while with playing the rebel he admires. His "play-acting" is heroic, for through it he escapes the fixity of self-blame, seen here as deadly.

REMAPPING THE JIM CROW SOUTHERN ROAD

In addition to *Driving Miss Daisy,* several road films from the 1990s deliberately return to the incendiary Jim Crow geography of the United States to remap racial relations within the genre's transformative themes. Revisionary road films like *Love Field* and *One False Move* peel the scab off race relations and interracial romance and suggest that family extends further than one's nuclear center—showing that we are one vast, if malleable, collective with a stake in each other's welfare. Two road films written by Billy Bob Thornton early in his career expose secret interracial family connections in Arkansas: first, in the powerful *One False Move* (1992, dir. Carl Franklin), about a sheriff's secrets and a young woman's lost identity, and in the lesser film with a bigger cast, *A Family Thing* (1996), in which Robert Duvall's character realizes he's related to James Earl Jones's character. The metaphoric message of these films is that we are all related somehow and cannot afford to ignore this truth.

Love Field (1992) looks at interracial relationships that move away from socially sanctioned stereotypes to show the perspective of racial difference and to propose that trust might be developed between the races. By looking back to 1963, to the day when Kennedy flew into Dallas's Love Field and later was shot in his motorcade, *Love Field* crosses the Jim Crow line in the back of a Scenic Trailways bus bound for DC. The news of Kennedy's assassination mobilizes the high-strung Lurene (Michelle Pfeiffer) onto the road to attend the public funeral. What's interesting about this road trip, however, is that she's a young housewife who defies her husband Ray (Brian Kerwin) by sneaking off in the middle of the night. Devoted to the Kennedys, dressed like Jackie, she's simply not the type to disobey her husband, yet the fact that she does gives this period piece a taste of the feminism about to come to American women—because we're looking back from the other side of the women's movement, we're willing to accept Lurene's unusual move and all that happens between her and Paul (Dennis Haysbert).

But *Love Field* does not look back in order to fix the past, as did the films of the 1980s; instead, it calls attention to the barriers sanctioned in the past that stubbornly persist today in society despite the fact that they have long been deemed illegal by the U.S. Supreme Court. For this reason, reviewer John Anderson couldn't be more wrong when he writes, "A road movie about a black man and a white woman set during the weekend of the Kennedy assassination might have been provocative 20 years ago. But road movies have been done, the assassination's been done and miscegenation just doesn't pack the same punch anymore" (840). While this is all well and good, the point is that films about blacks and whites together on the road simply did not exist "twenty years ago," in the 1970s. In fact, Hollywood films are remarkably slow to remap the past—even the dissatisfactions of *Thelma and Louise* were old news by 1991, but as these concerns about identity come belatedly to the big screen in the 1990s, it is important to note that they do so within the road genre.

Love Field uses the Jim Crow line in the bus to show just how porous and flimsy such a demarcation really was. Very few films ever show the race line in buses—more often, as in *It Happened One Night* (1934), a film simply excludes African Americans from the bus altogether so as to keep the ugly reality of segregation from marring the light-hearted storyline. But by seeing the power of this imaginary line from the past, a line in which we no longer place stock, film viewers in the 1990s might have been reminded of the generic roles we dutifully fulfill, which we need to question. Directed by a former Roger Corman protégé, Jonathan Kaplan, *Love Field* was written by Don Roos, who also wrote the road film *Boys on the Side* (1995). The fact that Roos later came out as gay might explain the depth to this "tabooed" love affair between a white and a black. The film was bankrolled by Orion Studios, one of the new indie boutique houses, which shelved the film for a year due to lack of funds to promote it (a problem that plagued Orion and other small studios).

Of all the ways the road genre can unfold, the story of two unlikely mates falling in love on the road is probably one of the most formulaic. Time spent together on the road helps mortal enemies come to know each other's humanity and endearing qualities. *Love Field* used this conceit not only for the leads to fall in love but also so white viewers would see through Paul's eyes that Kennedy was no hero of the blacks. Likewise, John Singleton's use of the screwball road story in *Poetic Justice* (1993) serves the purpose of humanizing a rapper with a dream. The film's big-name stars—Janet Jackson and Tupac Shakur—are working-class characters who drive together from Los Angeles to Oakland. Although named Justice and Lucky, there is neither luck nor justice in this narrative, as might be expected from a rather heavy-handed director like Singleton; even the poems by Maya Angelou don't translate to Justice's character. But Justice realizes that she has misjudged Lucky's type; as she learns enough about him to remap her impression of the man behind the stereotypes of a rapper and a "playa," she falls in love.

Avoiding the screwball romance by any means necessary is veteran director Spike Lee's *Get on the Bus,* from 1996 (see again fig. 3). Lee is certainly aware of this cinematic tradition but turns his focus to the symbolically weighted imagery of blacks on buses and the narrative potential offered when a group of fifteen or so strangers join each other on a bus for a three-day trip across country to attend the Million Man March in 1995 in Washington DC. As Jeremiah (Ossie Davis) says, this march was a way for all who missed the 1963 March on Washington to be part of history—even for Spike Lee or anyone who had been too young or not yet born at that time. Of all those men who climb aboard the bus at South Central's AME Church, Jeremiah is the ancestor figure who anchors the hearts and minds of these men, especially by the end of the film. There is a former gang-banger turned Muslim (Gabriel Casseus), a biracial LAPD officer (Roger Guenveur Smith), an up-and-coming film director called Spike Jr. (Hill Harper), and many others all called to comment on the state of affairs for black men at the approach of the millennium, on the eve of a historic event. Lee begins with these stereotyped black male identities and brings depth and transformation through the road trip.

Emphasizing the power of people to make stories (or finance a film), *Get on the Bus* was shot in three weeks for $2.4 million and released on the first anniversary of the march. Fifteen investors put up the funds for Lee to make the film as quickly and ingeniously as he did. (They were paid back in seven months with an 8 percent profit [Grover 6].) Columbia Pictures kicked in over $10 million to market the film (Brennan F6). By shooting in the limited location of the bus and using documentary television coverage to supplement the live-action sequences, Lee created a low-budget, highly effective movie about the complexities of identity even within the self-selected community of black men on the bus.

Self-financed projects by minority filmmakers gained audiences in the eighties and nineties with the rise of film festivals, not only at Sundance but those organized around the identity of the audience or the location of the host city. For instance, gay and queer cinema became a movement during the 1990s, in large part because gay film festivals created a market for the low-budget, independently produced films that would never have otherwise been made. Gus van Sant's road film *My Own Private Idaho* (1991) was one of the early gay films with crossover appeal to straight audiences, blending its art film sensibilities with Shakespeare and cinema vérité.

NICHE MARKETING

Some upstart indie production houses began to find the right combination of promotion and distribution techniques, and some films from festivals had crossover success with the public. As a consequence, Hollywood helped propagate identity politics—as a form of niche marketing rather than social liberalism. Thus even long-established studios like Warner Bros. and newcomers like Miramax backed road genre films that capitalized on the "women's market," like *Boys on the Side* (1995), *Leaving Normal* (1992), and *Camilla* (1994). Other road films in this category include Touchstone's *Nothing to Lose* (1997), about the unlikely alliance reached on the road by a white businessman and his African American carjacker, and *Ride* (1998), for the MTV generation of blacks. It's rather amazing how few road films were made for adolescent men, given the size and profitability of this market, although the strength of this market is clear from road films like *Dumb and Dumber* (1994), *Tommy Boy* (1995), *Beavis and Butt-head Do America* (1996), and *Road Trip* (2000). Worth mentioning, too, is Clint Eastwood's touching *A Perfect World* (1993), in which a fugitive played by Kevin Costner mentors a young, fatherless boy.

The curious evolution of audiences for road genre films is evident in the example of *To Wong Foo Thanks for Everything! Julie Newmar* (1995), an American remake of the wildly popular film about drag queens in Australia, *The Adventures of Priscilla, Queen of the Desert* (1994). Mainstream audiences and even families found themselves going to see this film produced by the indie studio Amblin Entertainment, Steven Spielberg's earliest company. Universal Pictures distributed to multiplexes all over America this film that proclaimed the universal sisterhood of drag queens. (This was after the import film *The Crying Game* [1992] seemed to open up the nation to a liberal empathy with transvestites.) The gay community and actors looking for work objected to the fact that the actors were straight rather than gay—and that they went out of their way to flaunt their heterosexuality at any opportunity with the press. Even in these complaints, we can measure how fluidly identity has come to be imagined in film compared to the fixities portrayed back in the 1950s and 1960s.

Old White Men on the Road

As the baby boomers age, it is understandable that we are seeing the return of the *Easy Rider* generation to the road. Alexander Payne's *About Schmidt* (2002) gives this demographic the opportunity to see Jack Nicholson back on the road again. This time, he's not a crazy rebel like his character George in *Easy Rider* but a pillar of the establishment, a "sad, sad man" with a motor-home and few places to go, as seen in figure 15, who finds himself falling down the rabbit hole of retirement, widowhood, and the utter disdain of his only child. In 1970, in *Five Easy Pieces*, Nicholson's character unleashed such rage at a waitress that his "chicken salad" scene is a classic in film history; in contrast, his character Warren Schmidt dutifully sits on the toilet to urinate at the command of his wife and only realizes his anger while writing to Ndugu, the Nigerian orphan he has adopted through prompting by a television ad.

Payne's more recent road film, *Sideways* (2004), won the Academy Award that *About Schmidt* narrowly missed. This film about the male search for love is also about aging, even though the two male leads are only on the spring side of middle age. Like *Thelma and Louise*, however, they are nonetheless facing the closing down of opportunities. *Sideways* reveals the inner workings of men who have a little too much autonomy and mobility in their unhappy lives. Payne's films return rebellion to the average white-collar man, using the genre to comment on the unmooring of identity in a mass-mediated world for people negotiating (or failing to negotiate) the gap between the image and the reality. Similarly, Jim Jarmusch's most recent

Fig. 15. Jack Nicholson as Warren Schmidt in Alexander Payne's first road film, *About Schmidt* (2002). The Winnebago becomes a character in this movie and, later, in the Generation X reality TV shows. Film copyright © New Line Cinema.

film, *Broken Flowers* (2005), puts Bill Murray on the road as an aging Don Juan to review his past loves and search for a possible son. In contrast, *Transamerica* (2005) is yet another road film about a man seeking out his son, yet this protagonist is a male-to-female transsexual awaiting his transformative surgery.

When director David Lynch returns to the road film with *The Straight Story* in 1999, part of what intrigues is how Lynch offers a relatively straight story about a real person instead of his typical trick of hijacking us to the weirdness depicted in his two other road stories, *Wild at Heart* (1990) and *Lost Highway* (1997). The journey by tractor undertaken by Alvin Straight (Richard Farnsworth) is unlikely enough, despite being a true story, and Straight's ability to overcome these odds makes him kin to all the lost animals in films like *The Incredible Journey*—for Straight is largely a mute being who travels by instinct. After months on the road traveling to visit his aged brother, he says nearly nothing when they finally reunite. Both Lynch and Payne explore in these films the drama of quiet revelations rather than the dramatic gestures of rebellion that characterized the 1960s and 1970s.

When the white man comes back to the road story—especially the aging white man—the road genre is still being used to explore identity. Senior citizens are perhaps even more preoccupied with issues of autonomy and mobility and the status of their driver's license than teens (if that is possible). The poignancy of this fact contributes to the appeal of road films featuring seniors out for their last fling, as was also true with *Harry and Tonto* (1984), *The Trip to Bountiful* (1985), and *Camilla* (1994).

The road story came full circle in the 1990s, relighting the same torch once burned by the Beats for passion, mystery, and love, but featuring a far more diverse group of people, suggesting that the social sympathies for the *"Fellaheen"* voiced by the postwar's avant-garde artists have finally become part of postmodernism's civic discourses. Groups marginalized by the power elite let go of the rhetoric of victimization used in the eighties and turned instead toward genre to re-organize the social expectations implied therein, acting with agency and authority to subvert those expectations and thus loosen the binds of the past.

9
First-Person Players
The Digital, "Transmedia" Road Story

> When you watch TV it's just boring. . . . I like the games better
> because you can do what you want to do. Like, I can make the
> player pass it or shoot it. But when you see it on TV, you're just
> watching.
>
> —A twelve-year-old fan of the video game *NBA: Live*

You play the game by controlling "CJ," a black man who is returning to gang-ridden Los Santos five years after he dropped out of the Grove St. OG gang. CJ hijacks cars and drives them throughout the San Andreas region, all the while profiting from violence, drug sales, and corrupt police. This video game, *Grand Theft Auto: San Andreas* (see fig. 16), is not a road story—it's called a "driving-and-killing game" by the *New York Times* (Herold E7)—but it does point toward one possible future of road stories in our electronic age. Because today's kids grew up as the stars of their family videos, today's road stories must speak to a generation accustomed to being in the picture or being the "first-person shooter," the character one becomes when playing a video game.

Games for Sony's PlayStation and Microsoft's XBox afford tremendous control over movement and narrative in their virtual environments. Fictional movement is possible in these games via a proxy controlled by a player (as opposed to the hands-off, "old fashioned" kind of mobility bestowed upon a character in a "non-interactive" novel or film), and as a result, psychological investment and identificatory possibility are now quite complex—evolving, just as when television was a new medium, and thus worth paying heed. The sense of movement is so real that some players require motion sickness medication to play. Each video game presents detailed and unique areas, such as CJ's Los Santos or Death City in *Need for Speed*—the better you know the geography of these virtual areas, the better you will be at surviving assaults, killing people, and escaping the police. The high-speed car chases found in these games require skill with the joystick and familiarity with the roads coded into the game. In the words of one player, *Grand Theft Auto* (*GTA*) offers

> a simulated "realistic" sense of space and time, conveys an expansive
> sense of "place" . . . a compelling human-computer encounter between

Fig. 16. Billboard advertisement for *Grand Theft Auto: San Andreas* (2004), an example of interactive, transmedia video games that put anyone in the picture.

> informational space and lived space . . . one in which a player performs actions with a tremendous degree of freedom and unscripted spontaneity. (Murray 91, 92)

Video games have the largest market share of entertainment—at annual sales of $7.3 billion, gaming is already a larger industry than film—and as a result of this impact, games are already altering the processes of commodification and innovation we have seen in the road story since the end of World War II.

The fantasy of projecting oneself into the road story is not new—after all, Sal Paradise in *On the Road* (1957) imagined himself on the red lines of the map. But as technology improves with each generation, so we consider—at the end of this study of sixty years of multimedia road stories—the new ways digital technology enables some people to construct their own stories, to do their own remapping of the road genre. Young people now expect to see themselves represented somehow in a story, and corporations are willing to sponsor people to make a road story that can then be used to help sell their products or their image.

There is a substantial difference between subverting a pre-existing narrative and starring in one that you yourself have created. In 2004, while baby boomers were in movie theaters watching the Oscar-winning road film *Sideways,* their kids and grandkids were most likely home, plugged in, putting themselves into stories created via game code, digital video cameras, or blog software, perhaps as part of a massive multi-player "immersive interactive entertainment" created by a corporation with an equally massive budget.[1]

It is a whole new form of automobility for the generation that grew up with Nintendo and MTV vying for their attention. Road stories written by the Beat generation valued mystery and celestial yearnings, but this generation's stories seem to revolve around the sure-fire excitement of money in reality shows and mastery in video games. Hoping to capture the vast spending power of young adults, gaming companies like Electronic Arts, Take-Two Entertainment, and Warner Online invest heavily—the budget for a game like *GTA/San Andreas* surpasses many mainstream film budgets. In this high-sensation generation of first-person players, collaboration around rules and code cheats replaces the autonomy the Beats and hippies expected to find on the road.

MTV fostered the expectation of these viewers that they would have the power to shape a story. Cable networks have long encouraged audiences to vote online for or against key characters, or to actually be in a reality show. The practice of open auditions, in which anyone of a certain age is invited to send in an audition tape, was popularized by Mary-Ellis Bunim and Jonathan Murray for their show *The Real World,* which they launched in 1992 and is still produced today, and then used again for its spin-off, *Road Rules* (1995–2004). The odds of being cast are ridiculously low, but the mere possibility sends out a powerful message. By exploiting this generation's desire to be in the picture *and* behind the wheel, MTV powerfully influenced youth culture's expectations about automobility, first through the linear yet open-ended structure of *Road Rules* and, next, with the car improvement show, *Pimp My Ride,* begun in 2004, in addition to the commercials and music videos that also sell automobility to this highly desirable demographic.[2]

Carmakers now contract with producers of video games, reality shows, and films to place their vehicles into the narratives, hoping to engage buyers in new ways through multiple media platforms. "Transmedia storytelling," as it is called, extends the same narrative on TV, video game, and film, for instance.[3] Elaborate transmedia road stories have been created by BMW that crossover from its web site to BMW comic books and films, and Audi has concocted its own multifaceted (fictional) Internet mystery around a stolen A3 hatchback. Other automakers have collaborated on projects that feature their cars, such as the comedy road film *Are We There Yet?* (2005), featuring a Lincoln Navigator, and the video game *Midnight Club 3: DUB Edition,* which prominently displays a Chrysler 300C sedan and Cadillac Escalade SUV. This crossover between product and story is not all that unusual—we saw it when Chevrolet sponsored the 1960s TV series *Route 66,* which practically starred the Corvette. But what is unprecedented is the extent to which product, narrative, and media work together in transmedia.

Now that cash is used to reward teens who follow the "rules" of the road or virtual thugs who get rich by selling drugs, as we will see in this chapter, there is perhaps little surprise that the drama of these road stories revolves around the acquisition of money and points. These game-focused road stories can foster a zero-sum ethos—the fact that one person is in the picture often means that someone else has lost out, thus reasserting a divide between the "haves" and the "have nots." In fact, these road games blatantly celebrate class differences rather than foster inner transformation: the more people you kill, the more drugs you sell, and the more police you escape, the richer you become in San Andreas, Vice City, and many other cyberspaces. Increasingly, class difference becomes the focus, as we will see with sexy heiress Paris Hilton and her sidekick (and ex-best friend), Nicole Richie, of *The Simple Life 2,* whose presence on the road (or on a farm, as in the show's first season, or on a bus in the third season) devastates the hopeful metaphors of social mobility that often ground the road genre.

But these "hypermarketed" road stories have not entirely crowded out alternatives produced by underdogs, independent filmmakers, and students. For instance, Ken Burns created the historical documentary, *Horatio's Drive: America's First Road Trip* (2003), about Horatio Nelson Jackson's cross-country drive in 1903. The nonprofit road stories still exist—in the margins, on public television channels like PBS, or on the Web, showing that the liberal, bohemian perspective is still in the running, even if its audience is woefully small in contrast to *Road Rules* at its peak. Even colleges encourage road trips. Professor Douglas Brinkley taught his history class from a bus, as described in his *The Majik Bus: An American Odyssey* (1993). Two students launched the "Roadtrip Scholars" program at Pepperdine University; as alumni, Mike Marriner and Nathan Gebhard went on to form Roadtrip Nation, creating documentaries for PBS and collateral materials sold on Amazon.com. Harvard University's Sheldon Traveling Fellowship financed law student Michael Lee Cohen's road trip, which became the basis of his book, *The Twenty-Something American Dream: A Cross-Country Quest for a Generation* (1993). After Chelsea Cain graduated from UC Irvine, she published *Dharma Girl: A Road Trip Across the American Generations* (1996), a memoir about being raised on a commune by hippie parents.

Now that low-cost, high-reach digital technologies are available, like hand-held video cameras, Final Cut Pro, and the Internet, those college students who do go on the road usually do so with the intention of making a documentary rather than writing a book. If it's an uplifting road document, corporate sponsors often step in to help defray costs (as long as they get some marketing advantage). For instance, a Coke TV commercial shows four young men on the road—who really *are* making a documentary—drinking Coke as they travel around interviewing cool, creative people. Similarly, non-profit Roadtrip Nation (RTN) offers grants underwritten by sponsors like State Farm Insurance, Starbucks, and Xbox to college students who will work within RTN's format of traveling around the country interviewing people about their career paths.[4] (The RTN web site encourages undergraduates to add their photos, films, and blogs from the road.) RTN itself was launched with a grant from the online jobs web site, Monster.com. Even as an intelligent alternative to a decade's worth of MTV's *Road Rules* foolishness, RTN lives only through the support of its sponsors. One of the companion books for the series, *Roadtrip Nation: A Guide to Discovering Your Path in Life* (2003), is notable for what it *does not* say—it never delves into the unemployment rates of inner city residents (like CJ), nor does it explore whether filmmakers and other creative people who rely on the patronage of the marketplace are more likely to create work that is congratulatory instead of analytical. These corporate-sponsored road stories exalt mobility, but it is the mobility of capital and labor that they celebrate.

INDEPENDENT SOULS WHO AVOID SELLING OUT
Escaping Entrapment

To understand how we ended up in San Andreas or on *The Open Road,* let's take one last glance back to 1991, when Douglas Coupland's novel *Generation X* united the Beats' romantic urge for transformation with postmodernism's ironic sentimentalism shaped by MTV and *The Brady Bunch.* Coupland's book investigates the identity struggles of those who grew up watching cable television. Beneath its mocking voice and metaphors drawn from Nickelodeon reruns, *Generation X* promises escape and redemption. As a mirror of the mediascape (and an attitude that anticipates the "sampling" and file-sharing practices of the netscape), this novel relies on the road genre in a small but significant section.

Soon after *Generation X* was published, the theme of road stories shifts from miracles to daredevil missions, so Coupland's is one of the last road stories we can compare to Kerouac's *On the Road.* Both Kerouac and Coupland offer a vision of the road to Mexico to their respective generations—Mexico as a place of mystery and long-sought dreams. "We had finally found the magic land at the end of the road and we never dreamed the extent of the magic," reported Sal upon their arrival in this land (*On the Road* 276). Headed down to Mexico in *Generation X,* narrator Andy is surrounded by a group whose "crush of love was unlike anything I had ever known" (Coupland 179). In both novels, the road is the place for desire, and young adulthood is the time for chasing those dreams. (The exotic reputation of Mexico and other southern countries perhaps explains why road films like *Y Tu Mamá También* [2001] and the South American odyssey of *The Motorcycle Diaries* [2004] met with success in the United States.) During Andy's drive to Mexico, he fantasizes about his yet-unwritten fiction, "Await Lightning," which will be centered on a young man who drives away from his job and girlfriend. Coupland's characters worry about selling out even though they expect nothing more from themselves, and much like Kerouac's idea in *The Dharma Bums* (1958), Coupland suggests one can escape entrapments by going on the road.

In updating the road story to the age of what Coupland calls "hypermarketing," *Generation X* reassures us that one can escape family fate by joining the classless group of creative people who refuse the ruts carved by socioeconomic status. Coupland borrowed the designation "X" from Paul Fussell's *Class: A Guide Through the American Status System* (1983). Fussell defined X people as those who separate from the mainstream and reject its restraints or status markers: "What class are we in, and what do we think about our *entrapment* there? . . . In discovering that you can become an X person you find the only *escape* from class" (emphasis added, Fussell 179). Fussell adds, "Impelled by insolence, intelligence, irony, and spirit, X people have *escaped* out the back doors of those theaters of class which *enclose* others" (emphasis added, 186). Entrapment is a feeling as old as rebellion, of course, and taking to the road as a form of escape is, as we know, a venerable plot device. Consciously or not, Coupland blends this solution with Fussell's 1980s observations about class, trying thus to discover autonomy and mobility for his own accelerated generation. In revisiting these generic desires, Coupland accomplished his own magic by articulating a sensibility so uniquely evocative of this generation that the novel's title soon came to characterize adults born between 1965 and 1979.

Gay and Lesbian Road Documentaries

These days, free spirits who leave home to search for kindred souls can create culture on the move, thanks to laptop computers and digital cameras. Gays and lesbians have been among the creative gypsies in recent times, and they have both political and personal reasons for putting themselves on the road. Between 1986 and 1997 (long before blogs), the famed "Mad Monks"—the self-proclaimed "fagabond" couple, Michael Lane and Jim Crotty—published their road chronicles, made with an early Mac computer and what we would now think of as primitive publishing software. Their mobile magazine, called *Monk,* attracted a cult-like following throughout the dozen years of their travels. Lane and Crotty owed something to Edmund White's 1983 *States of Desire: Travels in Gay America,* a book that chronicled how life in America, gay and straight, looks from the road. As did White's book, *Monk: The Mobile Magazine* aimed at enhancing the visibility and mobility of gays, many of whom were inspired by stories about men who had already come out, particularly during a time when AIDS was ravaging gay communities. Lane and Crotty produced nineteen issues on their own, and then their work began to be supported by publishers like Playboy Online and Simon & Schuster, the latter publishing their book *Mad Monks on the Road: A 47,000-Hour Dashboard Adventure from Paradise* in 1993 (Goodridge). Although they stopped traveling in 1997, their work lives on at Monk.com, a web site offering short video clips from the Monkmobile, interviews with performers and film directors, mail-order t-shirts, and advice for travelers.

Digital video cameras, audio recorders, and editing software all made documentary work easier and more affordable in the 1990s, even from the road. Close behind the Mad Monks came stories from other gays and lesbians—some inspired by *Monk: The Mobile Magazine.* For instance, director Ellen Spiro made her videos in her home, a fifteen-foot vintage Airstream, outfitted with Internet connection and the planned addition of "a full-scale, small-sized production studio on wheels," according to the web site at Independent Television Service (ITVS). Spiro's first film, *Greetings from Out Here* (1993), documented her travels through the south to explore gay and lesbian identity; her second, *Road Sweet Home* (1997), examined the life of senior citizens who spend their retirement years on the road. Both these documentaries were produced with the help of ITVS and shown on PBS.

Documentary video work by gays and lesbians was especially vital during the first decade of the AIDS crisis. In *Where Are We? Our Trip Through America* (1992), filmmakers Rob Epstein and Jeff Friedman videotaped their roadside interactions with gay Americans, offering a patchwork of perspectives about living with AIDS, and more broadly, about living as a queer person in a straight nation. (The HIV Quilt that memorializes those lost to AIDS was the subject of Epstein and Friedman's first documentary.) More recently, Dustin Lance Black created a documentary, *On the Bus,* about the road trip of several young gay men from Los Angeles to the Burning Man festival in Nevada. His film began as an Internet reality show commissioned by the now-defunct Digital Entertainment Network.

People Escaping MTV

People who make independent documentaries are typically rebels of one sort or another. This kind of work, done for creative satisfaction rather than money, is often supported by the Independent Television Service (ITVS) and shown on PBS. Funded by the Corporation for Public Broadcasting, ITVS utilizes technological innovations to "forg[e] alliances and . . . cultivate new audiences for independent media," according to its web site. Its mission is to give voice to underrepresented communities and address the needs of "underserved audiences, particularly minorities and children," criteria that fit many of the wonderful road documentaries it has sponsored, including Renee Tajima-Peña's *My America—Or, Honk If You Love Buddha* (1996).

ITVS helped nurture the road films of several producers who once worked at MTV but left the network in order to produce shows that give young adults greater control over their own representations.[5] Although there are plenty of documentaries in this category, we will focus first on *The Ride* (1994), because it precedes MTV's *Road Rules* and offers a contrast to that show, by giving creative control to young travelers rather than exploiting them as MTV did. *The Ride* is an eight-part road documentary created when thirty-year-old Shauna Garr left MTV because she "wanted something not made by and not manipulated by adults, but *real* teen videos that adults may not even want to watch" (emphasis added, Rosenberg, "To Learn" F9).

This vérité series thus stands as an early marker in the changing relationship between video documentary and the experience of younger people, with the road serving as a "real" space in contrast to the static homes found in *The Real World*. This series promised that its teen documentarians would discover the "real 'real world'" (according to itvs.com), for the crew of teen travelers work as participant-observers armed with the directorial authority to shape their vérité footage. Producer Garr traveled with the teens in the motor home, choose the locations, and had final edit, yet she gave the crew sweeping expressive freedom. The racially diverse teen "travelers" of *The Ride* produced segments that featured "guides"—other teens living in the cities visited in the Southwest and Midwest. In each location, half the travelers aligned themselves with one guide, who spoke openly about her or his town, life, hopes, fears and dreams. The other half of the crew went off with another local guide, who also offered a confessional tour of the same city, from a contrasting point-of-view. The two perspectives were interwoven throughout each of the half-hour segments. This format allowed participants to speak frankly about such subjects as bulimia, homosexuality, promiscuity, arrests, drugs, violence, and other problems that can plague teens. At a time when *The Real World* and *Beverly Hills, 90210* dominated teen programming, *The Ride* offered an alternative, full of candor, void of titillation. *The Ride* self-consciously used the road as a metaphor for a young person's path in life.

As our eyewitnesses, these travelers demonstrate how ordinary people holding video cameras can construct social meaning. This award-winning documentary encouraged further viewer investment by including the filmmakers' mistakes and their articulate discussions about the representational choices they were making. For instance, episode 3 focuses on a fourteen-year-old guide, Maria, who flirts with joining a gang in Chicago. Discussing the aesthetic and political aspects of their work with Maria, traveler Romona Catalanello says, "I'll have to say, Maria's like one of the realest people. I mean, she doesn't seem like she's putting on airs, or like putting on a show or anything." Her colleague Paula Patton responds: "I'm so glad we came here 'cause when they talk about cinema vérité, now I know what they're talking about." Paula's pleasure at transforming the textbook formalism of cinema vérité into lived experience draws in the show's viewers, who learn from both the travelers and the guides. With their motor home as a setting for conversations and relationships that evolve over time and distance, these voices from the road reveal far more cognitive process than the confessions of teens encouraged to spout off for *Road Rules'* cameras.

Mention should also be made of the written memoir *Dharma Girl,* in which twenty-one-year-old Chelsea Cain, part of Generation X, learns to situate herself with respect to her hippie parents. Cain travels with her mother, recently diagnosed with melanoma, and she searches for an identity that is distinct from her family and yet linked to her past: "There we were, my mother and me, out in the middle of nowhere . . . we had driven into the dark, trusting in the experience . . . I feel I am moving forward. I am learning" (170). If there is anything that distinguishes the members of Generation X from the generation that follows, it is this willingness to confront their yearnings for something more, rather than simplify them for the sound bite quips that characterize reality TV.

WHO'S YOUR DADDY? PROFITING FROM THE ROAD STORY
From the Real to the Rules: Rebels Without a Clue

While ITVS aims at the more self-aware audiences, MTV encourages the short attention spans of the reality generation. MTV shows created by Bunim-Murray Productions have single-handedly reinvented the road story for people born into this generation, much as Roger Corman and his protégés did for earlier generations. In 1987, soap opera producer Mary-Ellis Bunim began collaborating with Jonathan Murray, a producer of documentary and news programming. Using the open audition format to cast their programs, they launched *The Real World* in 1992, the first "reality genre" television show aimed at young adults. In each edition of the program, seven participants are selected to live in lavish pads (in New York, Los Angeles, San Francisco, and such) in exchange for having their every movement recorded. In July 1995, Bunim and Murray crossed their "docu-drama" format with the road story to create *Road Rules,* a hybrid referred to by MTV's press release as the "first docu-adventure series" (17 July 1995), and which Murray now calls a "game show." Murray has noted:

> MTV came to us and asked for a spin-off of *The Real World.* . . . We had some experience doing a show on the road during *The Real World, LA,* when we followed Tami, Dominic, and Jon across the country in a Winnebago. . . . [We added the missions to] assure us a beginning, middle, and end to each episode as well as give us something on which to hang the inevitable personal drama. (Field 66)

In other words, the producers created a structure in which they could manipulate and even predict the end of the story, even while the cast experienced its own reactions as spontaneous.

The difference between the passengers of ITVS's *The Ride* and those in MTV's *Road Rules* lies in the authority of the former to shape their stories. The participants on *Road Rules* are referred to as "cast" and treated as "talent," placed into situations guaranteed to erupt in conflict or explode with sexual tension. In contrast, the travelers in *The Ride* produce their narrative proactively. The difference between these two television shows is as distinct as that between a college-credited internship and a wild Spring Break. All the contradictions packed into the name "Road Rules"—the double entendre of "rules" as both a verb and a noun—reflect the producers' exploitation of these young adults' weaknesses and strengths. The producers purposefully underfunded the road trips, which forced the Road Rulers to work at unlikely jobs in order to earn enough to eat or stay in a hotel, with inevitably wacky results. The show mirrors a dysfunctional family, one in which the producers have the authority to punish and reward. With each successive season of *Road Rules* (as with all the reality game shows), the participants became increasingly savvy and manipulative, using their time on camera to lay the groundwork for their post-show media careers. Bunim-Murray Productions tried to keep the show exciting by sending its cast abroad on increasingly extreme missions, but in 2003 Bunim-Murray Productions turned its attention to *The Simple Life,* a new reality show produced for Fox TV.

While automobility is supposedly the purpose of *Road Rules,* the cast exchanged autonomy for celebrity, for its members were rarely free of the seventeen-hour-day camera crews. During the first season of *Road Rules,* Kit and Mark, unable to sneak a first kiss in privacy, hook up in front of the camera. Even off-camera events, such as the time Allison spends the night with the mayor of Nogales (also in the first season), live on in endless interviews in which she chronicles her regrets about having had too much to drink that night. Drinking and kissing may seem rebellious to most teens, but the producers who put the cast into these situations could pretty well predict such outcomes—and they could also predict that many other teens would want to put themselves in that picture. Each book accompanying *Road Rules* came with an application to be on the next season, and the pages inside feature the casts' applications and auditions, encouraging the reality generation to imagine themselves as part of MTV's vast mediascape.

Clearly, an important determinant of the shape of the road genre in the 1990s is who has control over the narrative. Sometimes it is the filmmaker, and sometimes the participant has control. New technology even raises the possibility of the *audience* controlling the narrative, by using a game console or voting on the outcome of a television show. Entertainment corporations strive to create "immersive interactive environments" that seem to put the audience in charge. Paradoxically, these environments may actually foreclose spontaneity and independence, but it remains to be seen whether a player tethered to a virtual character like CJ and his crimes is affected differently than a reader immersed in the novel featuring Don Quixote and his mishaps.

No One Knows the End of Easy Rider

Despite all this new technology, the road stories of the reality generation seem to return compulsively to old territory. One January 1995 episode of *Beverly Hills, 90210* helps us mark the curious role of *Easy Rider* for teens in the past decade. In this episode, the college-aged characters Dylan and Brandon are about to hit the road on their motorcycles. Gushing excitedly to his anxious parents, Brandon explains, "It's an American tradition—two old buds hitting the road. It's *Easy Rider.*"

His businessman father looks at him quizzically and patiently replies, "Brandon, that movie ended with both riders being blown to bits." Brandon retorts: "Guess that means it didn't have a happy ending, huh?" Needless to say, Brandon and Dylan end their road trip happily, after the obligatory arc of conflicts and mild rebellion against authority, punctuated by commercials.

Because he is at home in what Baudrillard calls the "simulacrum," Brandon picks and chooses among various road genre images and symbols, revealing his distance from the older generations' hope that revolutionary social change might be found on the road. Quoting Kerouac as he tries to pick up a waitress in a roadside diner, Dylan knows his act is hype, but he sports it like a vintage shirt.[6] Dylan flirts with the waitress by discussing his reading preferences: "I read *On the Road*—I hated it. I read *The Dharma Bums;* I hated that too." Kerouac, *Easy Rider,* and the road are atavistic desires to Dylan; they belong to an older generation and can no longer keep the attention of young adults. These books and films about the road are simply signifiers for this generation, not full narratives.

When MTV Productions started working on theatrical films, it made a road story as its first full-length film, namely *Beavis and Butt-Head Do America* (1996), based on its rebellious, animated adolescents who managed to survive on MTV for years (from 1993 to 1997) with almost no parental intervention whatsoever. (MTV also co-produced the road film *Crossroads* [2002], starring Britney Spears.) *Easy Rider* recurs as a motif in *Beavis and Butt-Head Do America,* as is obvious in a poster for the film (see fig. 17). In a clear homage to *Easy Rider*'s Wyatt and Billy, Beavis and Butt-Head are pictured on motorcycles in Monument Valley, even though the film narrative never actually puts them on motorcycles. In the film, the two *do* meet a pair of old bikers and camp out with them for the night; it is obvious from the bikers' conversation that they are the fathers of these two boys, but all four are too stupid to realize their genetic links. Just as Beavis and Butt-Head fail to recognize their fathers, so the link between *Easy Rider* and this generation is also obscure. *Easy Rider* seems to be a symbol of automobility from their parents' generation with which they must reckon (even though they don't know about its unhappy ending). It is no accident that Beavis and Butt-Head never miss their fathers, only their stolen television, for the familyscape of the 1980s has already given way to the MTV rebellions (and rules) of the 1990s.

Beavis and Butt-Head are not the only comic book characters to go on the road. Stan Lee's classic Marvel comics include the famous X-Men, a franchise that began in 1963, but here we will focus on the *Generation X* offshoot (1994–2001), in which mutant teens learn to control their superpowers. Living in a time when the nation detests and distrusts mutants, these teens remain good people under the tutelage of Banshee and Emma Frost at Massachusetts Academy in Boston. Like their X-Men and New Mutant relatives, they save the world from evil even as they struggle to convince the masses not to turn them into the outcasts and "Others" of society.

Fig. 17. Publicity for *Beavis and Butt-Head Do America* (1996) depicting the characters in an *Easy Rider* pose, even though they never ride motorcycles in the film. Directed by Mike Judge and Yvette Kaplan; film copyright © Paramount Pictures.

The *Generation X* franchise was designed to capture the teen market of GenX-ers, a goal aided by extending Marvel's characters to television and graphic novels. The animated program *X-Men* began on Fox TV in 1992, when the then-new cable channel was trying to build an audience by carving out an "edgy" reputation. In 1996, the same year Beavis and Butt-Head made their road film, Fox aired a *Generation X* film made by Marvel Entertainment as a possible pilot for a syndicated series. According to Wikipedia.com, "the extremely low-budget film was scoffed at by fans," as were some of the graphic novels made in the 1990s. One of those novels is *Crossroads (Generation X)* (1998) by J. Steven York.[7]

Whether or not Marvel's die-hard fans feel *Crossroads* is authentic, it *is* a good example of the road genre, using all the genre's dominant themes of identity, transformation, mobility, and autonomy—celebrating the cultish tradition of the road trip:

> "We'll be purchasing a pair of recreational vehicles and making the rest of the trip home by highway."
> Jubilee perked up. "Road trip?"
> Paige smiled broadly. "Road trip!"
> It wasn't clear who started it, but they began to chant softly, "Road trip, road trip, road trip." (York 9)

The road trip in *Crossroads* reveals the nation as one vast mediascape—an environment linked, in this case, by hate radio. The key narrative conflict in *Crossroads* is over the power of self-representation, as Paige (who is Husk when in fighting mode) valiantly argues on the air with the syndicated daily radio host Walt Norman, who raises his ratings by fomenting hysteria about mutants. Paige's difficulties dealing with Norman while on the radio are due less to the fact that she is a mutant than that she is a teenager, and as such, does not have enough authority or experience to voice her views expertly on a public medium like radio. Paige inadvertently becomes a hapless teen sacrificed to bloodthirsty listeners. Eventually, she learns to deal with Norman's media maneuverings, and she and the rest of the *Generation X* heroes also manage to save the world by the end of the story.

The graphic novel has also been a source for new perspectives on the road story, in this case, for teens with cell phones, as found in Bryan Lee O'Malley's *Lost at Sea* (2005). Raleigh, the main character of the story (pictured in fig. 18), is the angst-filled teen of every generation—no superhero, just a young traveler who faces her fears and learns to trust her friends while on the road.

The Transmediascape

In previous chapters, we have emphasized *intermediary* methods, which follow the genre (rather than a specific story) across different media platforms; this methodology has enabled us to trace cycles of innovation and commodification in the road

Fig. 18. Raleigh, who expresses the angst of every shy adolescent—no matter which generation, in Bryan Lee O'Malley's graphic novel *Lost at Sea* (2005), published by Oni Press. Reprinted with permission from Bryan Lee O'Malley.

story. In this chapter, however, we are focusing on *transmedia narratives,* when a specific story or character is extended across multiple platforms—such as comic books, graphic novels, television shows, movies, and/or video games. This approach to storytelling has also been incorporated into the marketing strategies of major corporations, some of which use the road and automobility to attract their audiences' attention, then keep it by entertaining them in the "transmediascape."

BMW is one such innovator of transmedia marketing, achieving its hip cachet by hiring top directors to make high-budget, fifteen-minute films featuring BMW automobiles. The series features a character called "The Hire," played by Clive Owens. These are not road films, exactly—they do not attempt to remap the road genre, but they expertly exploit the adrenaline of automobility. The first series showcased the work of directors like John Frankenheimer, Ang Lee, and Guy Ritchie (who included his wife, Madonna, in an uncredited role).[8] The second series, created under the eye of executive producer Ridley Scott (director of *Thelma and Louise,* among many other films) and associates, features the BMW Z4 roadster in three short films, including *Hostage,* directed by John Woo. At BMWfilms.com, one used to be able to watch the films, or click through to buy comic books featuring the cars, including Matt Wagner's *Scandal,* about a rich heiress (modeled on Paris Hilton) safely delivered by The Hire to her destination, and *Precious Cargo,* about a pregnant woman who needs rescuing by The Hire, written by Bruce Campbell and illustrated by Kilian Plunkett. The plots in both film and comic book form, in sum, center on white women who need to be rescued by The Hire, who escapes bullets and certain death thanks to the BMW he drives. Apparently, these chivalric stories drive the American consumer.

BMW has just scratched the surface, however. We are moving into an era when companies will take full advantage of the phenomenon called "Alternate Reality Gaming," in which a community of users becomes a part of the story, interacting with the characters of the story and helping each other unravel the mysteries of the story as in-game and out-of-game experiences blend. One of the more complex transmedia marketing strategies comes from Audi, which began a viral marketing campaign in spring 2005 for the release of its new A3 hatchback. Audi's web site alerted viewers to a "stolen" A3, which linked to a web site called "The Art of the Heist"; this micro-site featured a faux-documentary about the fictional robbery, tying it to a global ring of art thieves. There are elaborate character summaries, (fictional) videocam surveillance footage, and links to companion web sites, including StolenA3.com, which offers a blog-like backstory called "The Nisha Chronicles." The complexity of detail is impressive, drawing potential buyers into a hypermarketed hypertextual universe.[9] And Audi offers a separate marketing campaign, presumably for creative types rather than thrill seekers, consisting of road-trip documentaries. Three up-and-coming filmmakers traveled across America in their A3s, blogging about their experiences and posting electronic "dailies" of their road footage. Ads for this commercial film series featured prominently on page one of *Variety,* as Audi hustled to establish firm footing among filmmakers.

Not only can road story audiences choose certain aspects of a story, they can also play out the identity politics within the story as if it were an extreme sport. *Grand Theft Auto's* character CJ is a black man in the ghetto, ranking him among America's most disenfranchised populations, yet millions of players willfully become CJ in the game. In the words of one fan, "San Andreas . . . allow[s] foolish white boys the world over to indulge their 'playa' fantasies and inhabit the role of an African-American character" ("San Andreas Game"). Electronic technology offers a hypermobility of identity, for with the Internet and video games, anyone can create and perform a provisional identity. The impact of such identity play remains to be seen. However, it should be noted that there are now cheat codes available that allow players to turn CJ into a white person, which suggests some players will always want greater control over their virtual identity. This cheat code might also suggest that identity play does not foster new social sympathies, but may eventually fuel a familiarity with difference that breeds contempt.

From Screwball Comedy to Screw You

These days, the television medium attracts viewers by showing people doing shocking things, things that people do not do everyday, like working in a nudist camp or eating worms. Reality shows have fostered the Horatio Algier myth that anyone can succeed on reality TV (well, anyone who is good looking and garrulous, or conniving and bad, or willing to eat worms). For most of the participants of these shows, money and fame seem to be the driving forces. Once heiress Paris Hilton and wealthy Nicole Richie entered into the reality TV road genre, however, an entirely new class discourse could be seen—the dream of social mobility is flattened somewhat when the very rich are the stars of a reality road series. Bunim-Murray Productions, which mastered the "open audition" fantasy of *The Real World* and *Road Rules,* switched premises entirely when creating *The Simple Life* franchise for Fox TV in 2003.[10] (It is worth keeping in mind that Paris Hilton is the age of viewers who started watching *Road Rules* back in 1995 as adolescents. In that sense, *The Simple Life 2* is already next-generation reality road TV.)

Role reversal is the essence of comedy. *The Simple Life 2* plays on the "fish out of water" premise of rich girls in low-brow situations. *The Simple Life 2* is similar to *Road Rules* in that it leaves the contestants penniless, forcing them to travel to whatever city the producers dictate (in a top-of-the-line $47,000 Airstream, of course), to work at whatever job is assigned to them so that they can earn enough money to eat. This reversal theme was also the source of humor in *It Happened One Night,* directed by Frank Capra, the classic 1934 screwball comedy of an heiress on the road. Like Capra's Ellie (played by Claudette Colbert), Hilton and Richie are penniless during their travels, but rather than pretending to be a plumber's daughter, as Ellie did to escape her father's detectives, these twenty-first-century heiresses parade like haughty princesses in the face of the people who help them along their way.

The Simple Life 2 offers a measure of the changes in moral values between the Depression era of *It Happened One Night* and the George W. Bush administration, which has been working to dismantle the social security system set up during the economic crisis of the 1930s. In Capra's film, Ellie learns that the honest goodness of her traveling companion, Peter (Clark Gable), is far superior to that of his rival, King Wesley, a rich opportunist who seeks to add to his wealth by marrying Ellie. In contrast, Paris Hilton's penniless charade demonstrates her to be a good businesswoman, on a par with Donald Trump and other millionaires now picking up extra cash on reality TV shows. When Peter and Ellie finally marry in *It Happened One Night,* their union is seen as the symbolic reconciliation of the rich and the common folk—the "green-backers and piggy backers" joked about in the film. But all consideration of the common folk is gone in *The Simple Life 2.* The two girls personify the selfishness of wealthy King Wesley—in fact, the polite hosts of one episode cannot get Richie to stop cursing, no matter how much they plead. Richie and Hilton live up to their reputation as spoiled rich girls, and in the process, they provide some public catharsis of contempt at these wealthy characters who offer so little.

Strangely enough, *The Simple Life 2* compares itself to *Easy Rider,* again confirming the lasting power of this landmark road film to a generation that doesn't know how that film ends—or the critique of wealth it ambivalently makes. The DVD cover of *The Simple Life 2* speaks volumes—these two young women are putting themselves into the picture of rebellion, but the posture might be backfiring somewhat. Hilton and Richie adopt the very same pose as Fonda and Hopper (seen in fig. 19), with the big star in the foreground and the sidekick smaller but slightly ahead in the background. And, just to make sure the reference is clear, Hilton rides a bike with a star spangled gas tank—the same as Fonda—its proximity to her bare thighs emphasized even though her crotch is masked by the upwardly slanting title "Road Trip."

At first glance, the DVD cover to *The Simple Life 2* could seem like a feminist remapping, with a vengeance. Hilton and Richie assert their sexual power and authority to assume the iconic identity of easy riders. But more than their sexuality, Hilton and Richie flaunt their wealth and privilege—it is unlikely that they are aware of the (admittedly vague) criticism about easy wealth in *Easy Rider,* explained by Peter Fonda in the 1969 *Rolling Stone* interview mentioned in chapter 5: "Liberty's become a whore, and we're all taking an easy ride" (Campbell 26). This celebration of wealth is an "easy ride"—viewers can simultaneously resent and envy Hilton and Richie, while sponsors and Fox TV rack up the profits. After

Fig. 19. The classic *Easy Rider* (1969) image, with Peter Fonda as Wyatt *(right)* and Dennis Hopper as Billy *(left)*. Directed by Hopper; film copyright © Columbia Pictures.

a decade of paying the common folk to act out for their cameras, Bunim-Murray Productions began peddling elitism and privilege, remapping its previous work through the incorporation of "celebutantes" who sell themselves as "Rich Girls Gone Wild."[11]

MTV's reality show, *Pimp My Ride,* began airing in 2004, and perpetuates the "audition" fantasy that a young viewer will be selected to be put in the picture while his or her car is fully "pimped" by the MTV car artists, 2Shae and Mad Mike. In episode 207, for example, contestant Quoc-Viet's Nissan 240SX was made over to look exactly like the Nissan in the video game *Need for Speed Underground 2,* with an Xbox installed in the car and hooked up to link twelve players. "When he isn't on the road cruising around in his new ride," states MTV.com, "he can race the same car with up to 12 players on the brand new gaming center in his trunk." Now that we have the technology to put ourselves in the road story, how is it that pimps and easy riders are the recurring images of the current cycle of commodification and innovation?

The Winnebagos and Airstreams that house our last decade's road travelers, from *About Schmidt* to *The Simple Life 2,* use an awful lot of gas. We live now in a global economy and a time of global warming, both of which tie centrally to our use of oil. While the road story rests upon an ethos of rebellion and transformation, our current dependence on imported oil extracted from the Middle East makes the American road genre into something far more self-serving and wish fulfilling than ever before. Relying on foreign oil from nations we are at war with is about as foolish as encouraging sales of SUVs, Hummers, and oversize trucks.

Whereas the Beats celebrated creativity and freedom, this latest generation of corporate-sponsored road stories celebrate wealth and danger. With Paris Hilton and Nicole Richie guzzling gas and flaunting class on the road, and white men pretending to be CJ in the ghetto, it is clear that the genre of autonomy and mobility continues to negotiate identity—but now characters seek privilege and mastery rather than autonomy and subversion. Even conservatives want to rebel now—rebel against rebellion.

Katherine Marsh said this about identity in *Rolling Stone:*

> We are a generation that lets ourselves be defined by the corporate world—by shows like *The Real World,* which claim to tell us who we are—in exchange for a pat on the head, for a little approval, for the illusion of success. And it is these things, rather than truth, that so many of us are looking for . . . we are sucking up and selling out instead of saying, clearly and quietly, in the sanctity of our anonymous but still very valuable selves, who we really are.

Certainly compared to the Beats and hippies, it seems that young adults today do search for their identity in the opinions of others rather than in themselves. A young woman recently explained her reason for auditioning for MTV Desi, a new MTV channel aimed at second-generation immigrants to America from the Indian subcontinent—she wanted to see "what corporate America thinks of me" (D. Sontag 29). The reality generation might need to see itself in the picture, but sixty years of autonomy and mobility in the road story suggest that there will be a different outcome to this phase of road-themed storytelling.

If the history traced in this book teaches us anything, it is that this cycle of commodification will be followed by a period of innovation. After Ronald Reagan's presidency, road films went from High Concept fantasies about bringing rebels back into the family to the edgy, indie road films of the nineties, which celebrated communities trying to gain rights and recognition—women, blacks, gays, lesbians, Asian Americans, documentarians, and creative people. Today, road stories favor material desires, so we have the right to hope that the road genre will swing back toward values like transformation and rebellion as states in themselves, rather than brand attributes.

We opened this inquiry with an image from the film *Sunset Blvd.*—a picture of Norma Desmond, who rejected the "chromium and spit" of post–World War

II cars (see again fig. 1). There was no mistaking her disdain of new American automobiles, which symbolized social mobility and the growing autonomy of people of lower class and lesser taste. Although Norma had become accustomed to being *in* the picture, her privileges were no longer viable in a world shaped by war and evolving media technologies.

Norma also serves as a cautionary closing figure, lest we too forget that the world moves on, even if we stay behind stuck in our old roles. It is clear from this study that each generation remaps its own definitions of autonomy and mobility. Identity and change are potent themes for any genre, but in a time of hybrid cars and search engines, after the cold war and in the midst of global warming, the road genre faces an entirely new set of imperatives than it did with the Beats. And so do we—we are in the picture of an unfolding worldwide narrative about autonomy and mobility. The attacks on 9/11 and the war on terror we staged in response have indeed changed everything for Americans, although we drive as if that were not so. In this new reality, however, the roads in Iraq are more dangerous than those in Los Santos, the drugs of Afghanistan support a far greater economy than that of San Andreas, and the unpimped "rides" of our troops are woefully inadequate for enemy assaults.

Still, we aim for happy endings. We have seen in this history how the resilient road genre survives war, gas shortages, High Concept commodification, corporate sponsorship, conservative administrations, and changing media. Optimism, subversion, opportunity, and innovation—these are the recurring themes of the road genre, and they should be ours as well. Over the past sixty years, the road story has served as a kind of declaration of independence, offering a vision of how we might break free of unwanted loyalties and obligations to create new identities for ourselves. We can put ourselves back in the picture, and take the discussion of autonomy and mobility away from the corporate sponsors in order to ponder our own sense of power in this complex global village, all fueled by the same energy sources.

The road story will continue to be remapped by each new generation of storytellers as they grapple with the nature of rebellion, the mobility of identity, and life in a global economy during a time of media convergence. If the history provided here is any indication, the next generation of road stories will find a way to break from corporate space, to provide us with stories that go beyond our identities as consumers, to remind us—once again—that we are citizens (and immigrants) guaranteed the right to rebel and entrusted with the responsibility of upholding our foundational values of liberty and justice for all.

Notes

Works Cited

Index

Notes

INTRODUCTION: WHAT AUTOMOBILITY OFFERS CULTURAL STUDIES

1. Dettlebach quotes the 1950 novel *Hot Rod* by Henry Gregor Felsen, which describes automobility thus: "Once removed from bodily contact with the ground, once in motion, once in a world of his own making, he escaped his troubles and sorrows in speed" (17).

2. Lackey notes:

> Any taxonomy of twentieth-century highway books about America will be troubled by a surfeit of grounds for comparing them. I have mentioned a number of possible rubrics under which they could be grouped: literary mode (naturalism, pastoral, picaresque, satire); theme (self-discovery, escape from bourgeois confinement, racial identity); literary genre (autobiography, fiction, nonfiction, travelogue); persona (picaro, curmudgeon, social critic, troubadour); and tone (nostalgic, bitter, beat, euphoric). (24)

3. "Intermediation" thus stands apart from other useful terms, like Carroll's "hypermediation," which is "the process by which one medium directs the representation of another" (12), as when the Internet became known as the "information Superhighway," for instance. Yet intermedia is not the same as multimedia, for it stems from the desire of an artist in one medium to be inspired by another medium, as when Kerouac wishes to write a photo in *The Americans* (5); Dick Higgins used the term in 1965.

4. Film scholar Schatz addresses the problem of genre studies based only in film:

> Genre study has tended to disengage the genre from the conditions of its production to treat it as an isolated, autonomous system of conventions. As a result, genre study tends to give only marginal attention to the role of the audience and the production system in formulating conventions and participating in their evolutionary development. (15)

Rhetorical theories of genre help overcome this tendency.

5. I have added the notes about difference and rebellion since the tendency of storytellers using the road genres is to foreground differences rather than similarities.

6. Cohen only hints at "generic variations" of a single narrative, looking briefly at how a ballad might be rewritten as "a prose fiction, a tragedy, a memoir," and so on, as a way of "reshifting . . . the hierarchy of generic kinds" ("History" 215). Perloff notes that postmodern genres can be characterized by terms such as "*violation, disruption, dislocation, contradiction, confrontation, multiplicity,* and *indeterminacy.* Postmodern texts are regularly seen as *problematizing* prior forms, as installing one mode only to contest it . . . *transgression* and *contamination,* of what Derrida calls the play of representations" (emphasis in original, 7–8).

7. Morley creates interdisciplinary methods for "making links between questions of residence, mobility, communications and cultural consumption in the constructions of identities" (3). His idea of the "conceptual space" of home, through which different discourses pass, can also be applied to the road (6).

8. E. L. Widmer argues that both automobiles and rock music provided "an important voice for a rising [postwar] generation of Americans eager to leave their impress on the national culture" (82).

9. For instance, Rascaroli notes the way European road films respond to American road films and differ from them.

10. Fowler reports on the Ford Motor company's game show on Chinese television.

11. To achieve the latter goal, I do refer to films or books now out of print, including the novel *Come and Join the Dance* by Joyce Johnson (now Joyce Glassman) and *The System of Dante's Hell* by LeRoi Jones (now Amiri Baraka). The road film *Wanda* by Barbara Loden has been re-released in Europe.

12. Road stories from the 1940s often link unwitting common citizens with criminals; these works were, by and large, still being created by people who had been adults during World War II, rather than by the new generation embodied in Kerouac or Updike.

13. Etymologically from an Arabic root, "Fellaheen" means peasant (usually defined as an Egyptian peasant) and precedes Spengler. In *The Decline of the West* (1922), Spengler uses "Fellaheen" to describe people in old and exhausted cultures who are unable to reconstruct political agency.

14. As Corrigan acknowledges when he lists his influences for using hysteria "as metaphor" (137, 142–43), many scholars turned to this psychoanalytic concept in the seventies and eighties.

15. In texts like Cixous' *Portrait de Dora* (1979) and Bernheimer and Kahane's *In Dora's Case: Freud, Hysteria, Feminism* (1985), scholars remapped hysteria as a feminist concept by revealing Freud's will to power as well as his own counter-transference with his hysterical patient, Dora.

16. C. Kaplan echoes this approach in her studies of the metaphors of displacement and travel in the global context: "We need to know how to account for agency, resistance, subjectivity, and movement or event in the face of totalizing fixities or hegemonic structures without constructing narratives of oppositional binaries" (19).

17. For instance, evidence to the contrary can be found in works by Scharff: *Twenty Thousand Roads: Women, Movement, and the West* (2003) and *Taking the Wheel: Women and the Coming of the Motor Age* (1991).

18. We see this resistance mirrored even in Tehran during the mid-nineties, when Azar Nafisi led her group of defiant female students through novels like the road story *Lolita*. She notes "we did hope to find a link between the open spaces the novels provided and the closed ones we were confined to" (19), for they found in Vladimir Nabokov's fiction and life "the possibility of a boundless freedom when all options are taken away" (24). Eventually, many of these women did leave their environment, but their early rebellions via literature are equally important.

19. It is crucial to consider, as Wolff does, the ways in which critical theory might repress groups by virtue of their gender, race, and class; but Wolff's argument makes its point by taking Said's metaphor of traveling too literally. For instance, her critique of Said's phrase "traveling theory" focuses on the adjective "traveling" and drops the second term, "theory," as if the need to describe the diachronic changes in theory were irrelevant in light of the egregious nature of the metaphor "traveling." Thus, Wolff's quarrel with Said's theory ignores his emphasis that any theory inevitably fails, and that the critic's job is to offer the *necessary* resistances to theory that help it change in new circumstances—the very sort of "critical consciousness" that Wolff herself exercises.

20. See Corrigan 152 and Laderman 3.

I. REWRITING PROHIBITIONS WITH NARRATIVES OF POSSIBILITY

1. For excellent studies of pre–World War II automobility, see Belasco for an overview of car vacationing and Scharff's *Taking the Wheel* on early female automobility.

2. Musser calls this earliest era the "cinema of attractions" (127–32).

3. Heath speaks thus of the spectator:

> What moves in film, finally, is the spectator, immobile in front of the screen. Film is the regulation of that movement, the individual as subject held in a shifting and placing of desire, energy, contradiction, in a perpetual retotalization of the imaginary (the set scene of image and subject). This is the investment of film in narrativization; and crucially for a coherent space, the unity of place for vision. (53)

A critique of this concept can be found in Cooper.

4. This is an extension of what Schivelbusch noted in nineteenth-century train travel as "panoramic perception"; he explains,

> as speed [from trains] causes the *foreground* to disappear, it detaches the subject from the space that immediately surrounds him. . . . The landscape that is seen in this way is no longer experienced intensively, auratically . . . but evanescently, impressionistically—panoramically . . . by contrast with the traditional one that involves a static, intensive relationship with the objects observed. (183)

5. McLuhan noted, "Western man acquired from the technology of literacy the power to act without reacting" (20).

6. McLuhan does, in fact, explain how media function in representing minority communities:

> Electric speed in bringing all social and political functions together in a sudden implosion has heightened human awareness of responsibility to an intense degree. It is this implosive factor that alters the position of the Negro, the teen-ager, and some other groups. They can no longer be *contained,* in the political sense of limited association. They are now *involved* in our lives, as we in theirs, thanks to the electric media. (20)

He continues, "Especially the child, the cripple, the woman, and the colored person appear in a world of visual and typographic technology as victims of injustice" (31).

7. "Messenger" works here as a rhetorical device rather than a precise term, signaling our focus on the identity politics of the protagonist and the storyteller.

8. This movement across media is distinct from adaptation, such as how *Lolita* by Vladimir Nabokov compares to Stanley Kubrick's film version of the novel. We will be looking at the ways in which a broad genre, rather than a particular narrative, travels between media platforms in the hands of cultural rebels.

9. Indeed, the phenomenological crisis in this novel is how Sam can comprehend the war in Vietnam despite not having been there; she knows of it primarily through representation, that is, through the letters written from the war by her father before he was killed, back before she was born. Even so, the war has affected her in as much of a real fashion as it did the veterans she knows.

2. BEFORE THE ROAD GENRE: THE BEATS AND *ON THE ROAD*

1. Holmes described it thus: "There was a feeling in the first years after World War Two that is difficult to evoke now. It was a feeling of expectation without reasonable hope, of recklessness without motivation, of uniqueness seeking an image" ("Name of the Game" 627).

2. Note that both authors now go by different names than those under which they published the works I am discussing; for simplicity's sake, I will use the names they published under.

3. In 1931, nine black teens were arrested for raping two white women, then sentenced to death in Scottsboro, Alabama. The famous appeals and dramatic retraction of the charge by one of the accusers made the Scottsboro Boys a lasting symbol of the travesty of justice in racist America.

4. My use of the term avant-garde coincides with the definition offered by Suarèz: "a type of subcultural practice that deconstructs 'bourgeois' ideas of art while appropriating, at the same time, certain images and strategies from the culture industry" (xiii). This definition focuses on the "contextual matrix" (Suarèz xiv) in which the work circulated, rather than details of lineage or timelines.

5. Jones writes about the postwar poetic renaissance that

> continu[ed] the tradition of twentieth century modernism that had been initiated in the early part of this century. William Carlos Williams, Ezra Pound, The Imagists, and the French symbolist poets were restored to importance as beginners of a still vital tradition of Western poetry. It was an attempt to restore American poetry to the mainstream of modern poetry after it had been cut off from that tradition by the Anglo-Eliotic domination of the academies. (*The Moderns* x–xi)

6. Ellison notes, "only the rear [of the bus] was reserved for us and there was nothing to do but move back" (155).

7. Tom Joad's emotional speech before he runs from the police epitomizes the Depression-era populist ethos:

> "I'll be all aroun' in the dark. I'll be ever'where—wherever you look. Wherever they's a fight so hungry people can eat, I'll be there. Wherever they's a cop beatin' up a guy, I'll be there. I'll be in the way guys yell when they're mad an'—I'll be in the way kids laugh when they're hungry an' they know supper's ready. An' when the people are eating the stuff they raise an' live in the houses they build—why, I'll be there."

8. Lhamon notes that Ginsberg read *Invisible Man* in 1954, adding: "The oscillations between withdrawal and engagement that mark most of Ginsberg's mid-fifties poems, their struggle against the affectlessness and victimization common in the previous generation, their allusions to jazz—all these were lessons garnered from black culture" (69).

9. In *Invisible Man,* the narrator readies to conclude the novel: "too much of your life will be lost, its meaning lost, unless you approach it as much through love

as through hate. So I approach it through division. So I denounce and I defend and I hate and I love" (579–80).

10. The Beats were not the only ones to be so presumptuous. John Howard Griffin wrote a documentary "road story" about his travels through the South as a white man disguised as an African American, *Black Like Me* (1961).

11. Sterritt points to Kerouac's focus on the "moral category of sin [rather] than the political category of social analysis when it comes to assessing and dealing with societal ills" (2).

12. Kerouac's novel, *Pic* (1971), which was published posthumously, narrates a road story from the perspective of an African American boy.

13. In retrospect nearly thirty years later, Baraka said: "I suppose the most politically sensitive of us [black men living in Greenwich Village] began to pull away from the bourgeois rubric that art and politics were separate and exclusive entities" (*Black Arts Movement* 1).

14. In his 1959 letter to *Evergreen Review,* Jones concludes: "All legitimate spontaneous prose is full of nouns since these are the simplest and most uncomplex parts of speech, i.e., unfettered by the need of complex definitions to explain them" (Letter 351). Jones celebrates Kerouac's string of nouns in describing the characters' itinerary, citing this quote from Kerouac's novel: "Memphis, Greenville, Eudora, Vicksburg, Natchez, Port Allen, and Port Orleans, and Port of the Deltas, by Potash, Venice, and the Night's Great Gulf" (Letter 254). He argues that this passage is "honest" because the itinerary "exists in a definite geographical location" and because nouns "ha[ve] not the necessary semantic dichotomy and complexity that is encountered in, say, adjectives, adverbs, etc." (Letter 254). Unsurprisingly, large sections of the prose in *The System of Dante's Hell* display Jones's lists of nouns, as in this passage that describes the healing Roi experiences with Peaches:

> All lies before, I thought. All fraud and sickness. This was the world. . . .
> A real world . . . of flesh, of smells, of soft black harmonies and color.
> The dead maelstrom of my head, a sickness. (ellipses in original, 148)

But Jones's system of values regarding verbs and nouns turns upside down when he fully moves from Beat effete to a politicized black voice, from his letter to *Evergreen Review* (1959) to his tactics in *Home: Social Essays* (1963). These turf battles between nouns and verbs demonstrate the "politics of semantics" at work in the transition from Jones to Baraka, and show how the author's shift from one aesthetic community, the Beats, to a very different one, the Black Arts Movement, can be traced in *The System of Dante's Hell.*

15. *More* (1969) by Barbet Schroeder is a darker version of this fantasy. In another example, American writer Katherine Dunn was living in Greece when she published her novel *Truck* (1971), about a girl who runs away from home on the bus and lives by the side of the road.

16. Glassman's novel has long been out of print. As one of Jack Kerouac's former girlfriends, she became far more famous for writing her memoirs, *Minor Characters* in 1983 and *Missing Men: A Memoir* in 2004.

17. Note that "mysteries" appears in her passage, as in Kerouac's work.

18. They met in 1957, when Frank told Kerouac his wish to film one of Kerouac's stories and asked him to write the introduction to *The Americans* (Nicosia 559). Grove Press was simultaneously publishing *The Americans* and Kerouac's third novel, *The Subterraneans,* and soon promoted their project, *Pull My Daisy,* in its literary journal, *Evergreen Review.* Grove also published the text of *Pull My Daisy,* complete with stills from the film in 1959.

19. The first edition, by Grove Press, has a slightly different format.

20. Although photographers of each generation are drawn to photograph the road, Frank's *The Americans* set a precedent that legitimated the photo road book. Another important text is Ed Ruscha's *Twenty-Six Gasoline Stations* (1962), a self-published, small-run book of casual snapshots of gas stations taken between Los Angeles and Oklahoma City along Route 66. As a painter, Ruscha used photography as a form of spontaneous "sketching," which thus makes it an adventure in "intermedia."

21. Wartime inventions led to new postwar consumer products, like the pocket-sized 35 mm Leica, which encouraged Frank's legendary "snapshot" aesthetic, and affordable movie cameras (along with inexpensive film stock left over from the war). In turn, these developments extended the medium of film to artists who had never worked in Hollywood, which thus fostered the "intermedia" experiments in which an artist found inspiration by working outside of his or her primary medium.

22. Warner Bros. actually offered him $110,000, but Kerouac's agent, Sterling Lord, held out at the request of Marlon Brando, hoping that Paramount would pick it up for $150,000 (Nicosia 567, 559). Twentieth Century's Jerry Wald offered to consult on a script—he wanted to have Dean die at the end in a car crash so as "to exploit the sensational publicity over the death of James Dean" (Nicosia 567).

23. Hunt links Kerouac's "wild form" to sketching and film, reflecting "Kerouac's interest in film as a medium" (155).

24. This Summer 1958 issue covers wide-ranging topics of interest to intellectuals, including film (a feature on James Dean, pictured on the cover), abstract expressionism (by Clement Greenberg), literary analysis (by Roland Barthes), poems (by Charles Olson, Denise Levertov, HD, Robert Creely, and Philip Whalen). The issue also featured work by John Rechy, Amos Tutuola, and Samuel Beckett. Many of the same writers dominate the early years of *Evergreen Review.*

25. This Spring 1959 issue of *Evergreen Review* contains Jones's letter that compliments and critiques Kerouac's methods.

26. Nicosia offers details (582–85).

3. TV GETS HIP ON *ROUTE 66*

1. Holmes speaks of the Beats' relationship to high modernism:

> T. S. Eliot's *The Wasteland* was more than the dead-end statement of
> a perceptive poet. The pervading atmosphere of that poem was an
> almost objectless sense of loss. . . . But the wild boys of today [i.e., the
> Beats] are not lost. . . . For this generation conspicuously lacks that
> eloquent air of bereavement which made so many of the exploits of
> the Lost Generation symbolic actions. ("Beat Generation" 630)

In *Beyond the Waste Land* (1972), Olderman also uses Eliot's metaphor to analyze
the 1960s novel, in ways that match the gender characteristics of the 1960s discussed later in my chapter:

> When I say that the image of the waste land dominates the novel of the
> sixties, I do not necessarily intend a statement of T. S. Eliot's influence
> on the contemporary novelist. . . . Wastelanders are characterized by
> enervating and neurotic pettiness, physical and spiritual sterility and
> debilitation, an inability to love, yearning and fear-ridden desires.
> They are sexually inadequate, divided by guilt, alienated, aimless,
> bored, and rootless; they long for escape and for death. (10–11)

2. Rexroth indicts authors caught up in success, such as the unnamed "popular
novelist [who] is always driving other people's Cadillacs . . . across the country at
two hundred and five miles an hour and wrecking them in small Iowa towns and
so forth" ("Commercialization" 649). Rexroth presumably is critiquing Kerouac,
since *On the Road* includes a story of Sal and Dean's trip East in a Cadillac, which
Dean destroyed in the course of the journey. A memorable passage comes when
the pair is in Iowa: "I could feel the road some twenty inches below me, unfurling
and flying and hissing at incredible speeds across the groaning continent with that
mad Ahab at the wheel" (*On the Road* 234).

3. In 1962, Evans wrote a fascinating analysis titled "Modern Man and the
Cowboy," exploring the appeal of Westerns. He notes that entertainment critics
put down Westerns "more often than even the soap serial or the quiz show, [the
Western] is held up as the symbol of television's cultural bankruptcy" (31). Evans
contrasts "the 'cool' behavior and the nihilist ideology of the beatnik [who] bel-
ligerently insists (mostly in order to convince himself) that positive effort is futile
since events are meaningless and social forces uncontrollable" (39–40).

4. Modleski notes how "our ways of thinking and feeling about mass culture are
so intricately bound up with notions of the feminine" (23). She points to the work
of Huyssen, who argues that media theory in the fifties tended to "eras[e] a whole
web of gender connotations . . . of mass culture as essentially feminine" (192).

234

5. Jeffries and Baughman each discuss this quest in detail.

6. Leonard claims he had "never heard" of *On the Road* when he got the idea for *Route 66* (Gehman 17), yet the kinship between Kerouac and Maharis was obvious. Instead, Leonard says he and Silliphant "were trying to show two young guys searching for values in the modern world" (19). Revealing the media rivalry between TV and cinema in the early 1960s, Gehman adds: "Since Kerouac's characters are searching mainly for kicks and hub caps to steal, this is at least one instance in which TV's aims are loftier than those of the modern novel" (19).

7. In contrast to the Beat-inspired attempt of *Route 66* to address larger social issues than romance, the main Beatnik character of television in this era is Maynerd Krebs on *The Many Loves of Doby Gillis,* a situation comedy whose title conveys its light humor.

8. Many episodes of *Route 66* center on Buz's secret vulnerability about his family, including: his serendipitous search for the mother who abandoned him ("The Mud Nest"); reemerging reminders of surrogate father-figures ("The Opponent," "Birdcage on My Foot"); or his willingness to help young, attractive women who are themselves orphaned or estranged from their families ("Welcome to Amity," "Love is a Skinny Kid," "The Clover Throne," "Incident on a Bridge," and "How Much a Pound is Albatross?"). Although Tod clearly takes a back seat to Buz in the series, he anxiously protects sons of widowed men because he himself was raised under such circumstances ("Hey Moth, Come Eat the Flame"). The narrative potential for the hip buddies to be troublesome drifters like Kerouac's characters never materializes because Buz and Tod anticipate the "New Frontier television dramas" of 1962–64, a term coined by Mary Ann Watson (36), which were populated by benevolent young adults whose occupations aimed at reforming society.

9. Television director Philip Leacock is the brother of Richard Leacock, famed cinematographer who worked during the Depression for Paul Strand films, creating some of the classic Depression-era iconography that his brother Philip seems to be simultaneously using and working against, especially evident in his *Route 66* episodes "Black November" and "Ten Drops of Water."

10. Episodes such as "Black November," "Incident on a Bridge," and "Play It Glissando" created story fragments to build complex revisions of first impressions in ways that were more intriguing and sophisticated than live broadcast scripts could ever be.

11. Watson reports that the Dodd committee began reviewing testimony in 1961 after FCC Chairman Newton Minow's "Wasteland" speech. This review coincided with an FCC formal inquiry into the demise of live programming and original drama.

12. Minow delivered the speech, "Never Have So Few Owed So Much to So Many," to the Thirty-ninth Annual Convention of the National Broadcasters, Washington DC, 9 May 1961.

13. Thanks to Peter Manning for informing me that Eliot himself disparaged television and urged the BBC not to embrace the new medium of television.

14. Seldes managed the *Dial,* which first published *The Waste Land* in 1922. He also wrote a favorable review of the poem for the *Nation* that same year.

15. Friedan makes many apt observations in her two-part essay, "Television and the Feminine Mystique," and includes this quote from an MGM executive producer:

> "For drama, there has to be action, conflict. If the action is led by a woman. . . . she has to triumph over opposition. [But] for a woman to make decisions, to triumph over anything, would be unpleasant [to viewers], dominant, masculine. After all, most women [viewers] are housewives, at home with children; most women are dominated by men, and they would react against a woman who succeeded at anything." (96)

Friedan concluded: "Television's image of women is *creating* millions of unnecessarily mindless, martyred housewives" (97).

16. In response to CBS's demand that *Route 66* include more "broads, bosoms, and fun," the series did in fact begin to feature a large array of female guest stars, including Anne Francis, Julie Newmar, Zina Bethune, Suzanne Pleshette, Joey Heatherton, Inger Stevens, Lois Smith, and Tuesday Weld. Many of these guests became known for their roles on TV and independent film. For instance, Newmar became Catwoman on *Batman* (1966–68), while Weld exemplifies the veteran female TV star who makes the transition to film star in the 1970s. She had been an actress since the age of three, and appeared in second-rate films and on TV for *Naked City, The Fugitive,* plus her long-running stint on *The Many Loves of Doby Gillis,* when she crossed over into more prestigious films with her leading role in BBS's *A Safe Place* (1971) and *Play It as It Lays* (1972).

17. Maharis's Method Acting machismo may have helped remove the taint of his having appeared on the soap opera *Search for Tomorrow* (Gehman 6), although Leonard and Silliphant had partially been inspired by the "smart-ass young actor" when Maharis had appeared in their earlier co-production *Naked City* (Maynard 44). They had incorporated their *Route 66* concept into one of the last episodes of *Naked City* and cast Maharis (Maynard 44). Later, it is rumored that Maharis became "blacklisted" because of his lifestyle choices.

4. KESEY'S QUIXOTIC ACID ROAD FILM

1. Wolfe uses this title, *The Merry Pranksters Search for the Kool Place,* throughout *The Electric Kool-Aid Acid Test.* In contrast, the video sold by Key-Z Productions is titled *Intrepid Traveler and His Merry Band of Pranksters Look for a Kool Place.* For simplicity, I will use the former.

2. Phone conversation with Zane Kesey, 20 May 2004.

3. However, Ken Babbs "had been giving an 'On the Road' audio-visual performance since 1981" while also trying to find a publisher for *On the Bus* via an agent (Goodrich and Feldman 34).

4. Phone conversation with Zane Kesey, 20 May 2004.

5. Some more recent examples are included in McClanahan's *Spit in the Ocean;* also, see Stone's essay commemorating the anniversary of the Pranksters' trip.

6. These videos are available at http://www.key-z.com.

7. For a fuller account of the editing in 1998, see David Stanford's piece in McClanahan (213–14).

8. This analysis of the Prankster road stories—those of the nineties and the sixties—benefits from conversations I had with surviving Pranksters and Kesey scholars at the 2003 Kesey Symposium at the University of Oregon.

9. Even as early as 1962, the Beats were just a memory in San Francisco's North Beach, yet North Beach was where the future Pranksters met one another (Faggen). Gordon Lish recalls how he went "to North Beach to see Dean Moriarity," and actually asked people if they could help him find Dean: "People would look at me like I was a lunatic. I didn't actually meet 'Dean Moriarity,' or Neal Cassady, until a couple of years later when I met Ken Kesey" (Perry and Babbs 34). In his interview with Faggen, Kesey recalls his conscious decision to follow the Beats: "I realized then that there was a choice. Cassady had gone down one road. I thought to myself, are you going to go down that road with Burroughs, Ginsberg and Kerouac—at that time still unproven crazies—or are you going to take the safer road that leads to John Updike."

10. Just a few years earlier, Malcolm Cowley had been Kerouac's editor at Viking Press for *On the Road* and *The Dharma Bums.*

11. Conversation at Kesey Symposium, November 2003.

12. Conversations at Kesey Symposium, November 2003.

13. As discussed at the Kesey Symposium and confirmed by Zane Kesey during conversation, May 2004, John Teton was one of these editors.

14. Wolfe's insider voice developed over time, for his newspaper articles published on the Pranksters' bus trip in early 1967 did not have the immediacy or style of the final book, which came out sixteen months later in August 1968. Wolfe published these two previews of the book in the short-lived newspaper *World Journal Tribune* in the Sunday magazine *New York* on 29 January 1967, and again the following Sunday, 5 February 1967. The first installment is a near-identical reprint of Wolfe's first chapter of his full-length book, with the Milton Glaser illustration from the original book cover appearing on the cover of *New York,* in an issue devoted to "the LSD life style." The issue brags that "Reporter Wolfe tells all about it in the first of a series on the LSD world." Kesey's article, "The Chief and His Merry Pranksters Take a Trip with Electric Kool Aid," was the lead story, followed by an article on Timothy Leary ("Saint Timothy: Messiah of Millbrook"

by Peter Dunn) and other LSD-related articles. There are a dozen photos by Ted Streshinsky accompanying the article with silly captions like "Kesey wearing red boots" and "One of the LSD arts: Face Painting." One caption educates readers: "Ecstatic dancing. Dancing on the acid scene is rock and roll but features much more leaping, turning and upward flinging of the arms than standard discotheque dancing" (Wolfe, "The Chief" 27). The bus is photographed, as is Neal Cassady. The follow-up article the next week, in contrast, is bookended by Jimmy Breslin's piece on Marines near Chu Lai and Jane Fisher's article "Pat Boone is Loyal, Brave, and Stout." And unlike his first article, Wolfe's second, "Super-Hud Plays the Game of Power," only vaguely resembles parts of *The Electric Kool-Aid Test*, suggesting that Wolfe took some time between these 1967 writings and the 1968 publication of his book to find the voice and techniques that would distinguish him as a ground-breaking journalist.

15. Kesey wrote in 1983:

> *On the Road* was . . . stance-changing. We all tried to imitate it. Yet, even then, no one considered it the work of a Truly Great Writer. I recall my initial interpretation of the phenomenon, that, yeah, it was a pretty groovy book, but not because this guy Ker-oh-wak was such hot potatoes; that what it was actually was one of those little serendipitous accidents of fate, that's all. ("Is There Any End" 60)

16. For instance, in "The Unspoken Thing," Wolfe quotes philosophers like Joachim Wach, Carl Jung, and Max Weber to give structure to the ineffable experiences of the Prankster collective: "I remember puzzling over this," writes Wolfe, "I remember I never truly understood what they were talking about when I first read of such things. I just took their weighty German word for it" (113). Thus Wolfe, the Ph.D. in American Studies from Yale, is transformed into a New Journalist by the Pranksters, who make the (German) word flesh. Wolfe thus gives form to the Pranksters' *terra incognita:* "after I got to know the Pranksters, I went back and read Joachim Wach's paradigm of the way religions are founded, written in 1944, and it was almost like a piece of occult precognition for me if I played it off against what I knew about the Pranksters" (114). Wolfe's illumination comes nine pages before he describes the Pranksters finding a similar "synch" between the *Ed Sullivan* show on television while "they turn down the sound to play a tape of, say, Babbs and somebody rapping off each other's words" (125). Whereas Wolfe's connection of the Pranksters to the philosophers seems quite insightful, he notes the reaction of outsiders to the Pranksters' TV experiences: "this kind of weird synchronization usually struck outsiders as mere coincidence or just whimsical, meaningless in any case" (125). This oblique comparison of the outcome of the Pranksters' "synch" with his own suggests once again that Wolfe portrays himself as successful in the very goals in which the Pranksters find themselves muddled.

17. Not surprisingly, the writer who does win approbation is fellow "New Journalist" Hunter Thompson, author of *Hell's Angels, a Strange and Terrible Saga* (1966), "a remarkable book, as a matter of fact" (Wolfe, *Electric* 150).

18. The difference between film and fiction, according to Wolfe, was perspective:

> one thing, however, that no electric medium can do so far—somebody may find a way to do it—is the interior monologue, or just simply "point of view." You don't have to give it such a name. But the real point of view, in which the audience feels that it is inside the mind, or the central nervous system, of a character—movies have *never* been able to do this. (Bellamy 51)

19. The term "intermedia" is used by Dick Higgins, a Fluxus artist of the 1960s who used the term to title an essay he wrote in 1965. The Happenings in which Fluxus took part during the 1960s were built upon an intermediary aesthetic.

20. "Hopper believed the film would be written in the process of filming the road trip" (Hill 171), as befits the aesthetic of the time, but Southern carefully crafted key parts of *Easy Rider.*

21. Fonda explained the critique made by his character Captain America in 1969 in a *Rolling Stone* interview: "'Easy Rider' is a Southern term for a whore's old man, not a pimp, but the dude who lives with the chick. Well, that's what's happened to America, man. . . . we're all taking an easy ride" (Campbell 28).

22. The blurb on the back cover of *Thumb Tripping* describes the novel: "The song of the open road—blue, bitter, and mostly a bummer. Gary and Chay met on an acid trip—her last, his first. They decided to spend the summer on the road—no hurry, no special destination. The trip was in the people they made it with."

23. For instance, Woody Harrelson sponsored a bus tour advocating the legalization of marijuana; upon visiting Kesey, the elder author nicknamed the entourage the "Merry Hempsters" ("Go Further"). Also, professor Douglas Brinkley brought his students on the "Majik Bus" to visit Kesey in 1992 (McClanahan 22–31).

5. ROAD FILM RISING: HELLS ANGELS, MERRY PRANKSTERS, AND EASY RIDERS

1. *Scorpio Rising,* one of the most widely distributed of all underground films (D. James 155), gained even greater notoriety when the courts judged it in 1964 to be a violation against "community standards" (Mekas 141).

2. Some gay filmmakers, like Ron Rice and James Broughton for instance, have quite direct ties to the Beats, but there is no overarching genealogy from the Beat to the underground because all these artisanal directors took the Beat

experiments in myriad directions. Hoberman called filmmaker Ron Rice "the most explicitly 'beat'" of the Baudelairean filmmakers, and describes his film *The Flower Thief* as "the beatnik film *par excellence* (*"Pull"* 38). And Frank himself spoke of his strong connection to *Flaming Creatures:* "although it's not my world and I didn't particularly like it. . . . I could really see that [Jack Smith] was an important artist" (Sargeant 45).

3. Staiger says: "[The underground cinema] posed sexual Otherness as even a popular culture . . . set in a complicated difference against serious bourgeois art culture" (125).

4. In 1955, Andy Warhol made the drawing titled "James Dean" as an homage to Dean after his death in a car accident.

5. For instance, Thompson writes about a biker named Loser and Bruce Dern's character in *The Wild Angels* has the same name. A 1968 film *The Losers* (dir. Edward L. Montoro and James Somich) is a proto-Rambo biker film. This generic, collective nature of bikers lends itself to appropriation in exploitation films.

6. "Gonzo" journalism has many affinities with Kerouac's values regarding spontaneous prose: "one of the basic tenets of gonzo: no revision. Gonzo was to be first-draft, written-at-the-moment [Thompson's *Fear and Loathing in Las Vegas*] has a genuinely spontaneous feel" (McKeen 49).

7. Fittingly, this event is memorialized in the documentary, *Gimmie Shelter* (1970), directed by David and Albert Maysles.

8. Corman discusses the motorcycle gang member as part of the social margins: "I thought of the Hells Angels as essentially people who were dropping out of the lowest level of American society and attempting to form a society of their own " (J. Mason 307).

9. With a similar lack of clarity, Fonda as Wyatt in *Easy Rider* cannot say why he thinks he and Billy "blew it." In the previous chapter, we saw how Wyatt's line links to Tom Wolfe's final portrait of Ken Kesey in *The Electric Kool-Aid Acid Test.*

10. Telephone interview, March 1998.

11. Arthur elaborates on what options were closed to the wanderer in 1964:

> to sing the Modern Man, to, with Whitman, "confer on equal terms with each of the States." . . . Even Kerouac's Sal Paradise celebrating poverty, the lumpen exemption, must have seemed a diluted myth. The losses of John Ford's searchers, Woody Guthrie's bevelled optimism. It was tough out there among all the ghosts. (33)

12. For Screen Gems, which Columbia Pictures set up in 1949, Bert Leonard and Stirling Silliphant were simultaneously producing *Naked City* and *Route 66* in 1960. Just a few years later, another powerful production team working for Screen Gems—producer Bert Schneider and director Bob Rafelson—also opened up new

markets by using hip innovations in styles and stories in a highly successful show targeted at teens, *The Monkees*.

13. Fonda comments on this process (and the resulting product) in regard to *Easy Rider:* "The Tape. God, these days it's almost like the Shroud. The Tape was the selling point. Bert Schneider bought the Tape, and we were under way again" (252). Similarly, Jack Kerouac and Neal Cassady had "rapped" onto a tape recorder, which was transcribed in one section of *Visions of Cody;* and a similar process would recur in 1973 with *Alice Doesn't Live Here Anymore* (Keyser 60).

14. With Terry Southern, a golden "post-Beat" writer, writing a script from the rapping story sessions, *Easy Rider* took on another key figure in the rebel pedigree. Southern wrote *Dr. Strangelove* for director Stanley Kubrick in 1964, *Barbarella* starring Jane Fonda in 1966, and protested against the war in Vietnam with Allen Ginsberg and William S. Burroughs.

15. Kesey's experiment did generate some of the earliest discussions about postmodernism, as in Kingsley Widmer's 1975 essay in the *Centennial Review,* where he said:

> With implicit cultural desperation, [Kesey and Norman Mailer] seek to go beyond the "waste land" despair of modernism over the fragmentation of traditional culture. They want to fuse with current popular mythology as found in exploitative media and on the streets, searching for a web of common symbology and social communion in technocracy's refuse. (122)

In literature, the novels of Tom Robbins took up these questions while using the road story format, as in *Another Roadside Attraction* (1971) and *Even Cowgirls Get the Blues* (1976).

16. As Grimes argues in discussing the films made in the 1970s by Raybert (which became BBS): "Although their endings are generally inconclusive, with nothing fully resolved, it is as if this move away from commitment is itself a positive act" (62).

17. *Easy Rider* disappoints, writes David James, because "Hopper fails to assimilate the film practices of various dissenting and countercultural groups into a coherent style," leaving the film a "pastiche" using "gestures of dissent" but leaving intact the standard Hollywood commodity form of film (16). James criticizes the derivative nature of the film, seeing in it the innovations of Stan Brakhage and Kenneth Anger, criticizing *Easy Rider*'s hand-held camera and anamorphic lenses that "are the staple motifs of countless underground films" (16). Similarly, Chris Hugo notes Hopper's trendy use of the 360 degree pan as being what "everyone uses . . . in their first film, even Roger Corman" (71), which turns *Easy Rider* into a "cinema of effects" (71), making the film "fashionable, striving always for effect but devoid of any intellectual rigour or political analysis" (70).

6. GENRE AND GENDER IN 1970S NEW HOLLYWOOD

1. Didion notes that Carter's film *Angel Beach* was made for $340,000 and grossed just under $8 million dollars (*Play It as It Lays* 18). In Hollywood, Corman's *The Wild Angels* (1966) was made for $360,000 and grossed $5 million during the 1960s; thus, the figures stated in Didion's fiction would have made Carter's *Angel Beach* more profitable than Corman's record-breaking *The Wild Angels*.

2. Didion was quite familiar with the biker genre, having written about her experience watching biker films in her column in *Life,* "Nine Bike Movies in Seven *Vroom!* Days." She thus knowingly alters the reality of AIP biker films, in which the male leads dominate, by making Maria the "hero" of *Angel Beach*. (In the novel, Didion credits the studio, not Carter, for this innovation.)

3. In the days prior to revival movie theaters and VCRs, few American fans in the 1950s could re-view classic films, since universities were only just beginning to create film departments and establish film archives. In contrast, France's Cinémathèque was one of the first centers to collect and screen films from around the world. Consequently, postwar film theory was highly developed in France, circulating during the 1950s in the journal *Cahiers du Cinéma,* where impassioned analyses were offered by the men who eventually became famous New Wave directors.

4. As Lawrence Murray argues in an excellent review of the literature on *Bonnie and Clyde:* "The theme of the 1930s 'underworld' inhabited by heroes was quite comparable to the 'underground' of the youth culture of the 1960s'" (249). The civil disobedience of the sixties, including occasional terrorist activity, explains mass culture's celebration of outlaws or criminals. The gangster genre of film focuses on people with no "legitimate" claim to power who gain their positions or authority by violence. Whereas Beats and other non-conformers prefer to attack culture via its literary canon, the gangster films depict outlaws motivated by power and financial gain.

5. Hellman referred to Siegfried Kracauer's *Theory of Film* during a question and answer period after a screening of *Two-Lane Blacktop* at the American Cinémathèque in Los Angeles on 25 July 1998. Kracauer notes that Sergei Eisenstein "equates life with the street. The street in the extended sense of the word is not only the arena of fleeting impressions and chance encounters but a place where the flow of life is bound to assert itself" (72). Kracauer concludes: "The medium's affinity for the flow of life would be enough to explain the attraction which the street has ever since exerted on the screen" (72).

6. During the 1960s, multinational corporations began accumulating film studios, thereby raising pressure on the studios to turn a profit (Corrigan 19).

7. These films included: *Five Easy Pieces,* directed by Rafelson in 1970, *The Last Picture Show* (dir. Bogdanovich, 1971), *A Safe Place* (dir. Jaglom, 1971), *Drive, He*

Said (dir. Nicholson, 1972), and *The King of Marvin Gardens* (dir. Rafelson, 1972). Hill notes, "The BBS films were almost all road movies of a kind" (67).

8. Many of the same actors appear in several road movies, as we can see with Peter Fonda, Dennis Hopper, Jack Nicholson, Michael J. Pollard, and Adam Roarke. For instance, Alan Vint was a veteran of AIP biker films when he appeared at the end of *Badlands* and starred in *Macon County Line* the next year; Ellen Burstyn briefly appears in *Harry and Tonto* the same year that *Alice* is released. The BBS productions utilized the people who had come to prominence in *Easy Rider:* Karen Black appeared in *Five Easy Pieces* and *Drive, He Said,* both of which depended on Nicholson as, first, actor and, next, director. Nicholson also appeared in Jaglom's *A Safe Place,* with Orson Welles, who befriended the BBS crowd (and put them in his work-in-progress *The Other Side of the Wind,* according to Hill), as well as Tuesday Weld, who starred in the film version of *Play It As It Lays* (1972).

The affiliations of producers is also noteworthy in New Hollywood's road films. For instance, Paul Lewis, the production manager and assistant director of *Easy Rider,* had worked with director Monte Hellman while he was making *The Shooting* and *Ride in the Whirlwind,* scripted by Nicholson (Hill 23, 25), and he had also worked for Corman. Scorsese hired him to work on *Alice.* After producing *Easy Rider* and all the BBS films, Bert Schneider eventually worked on Nicholson's *Going South* (1978), Terrence Malick's *Days of Heaven* (1978), and Nicholson's *Two Jakes* (1990).

Regarding the network of cinematographers, László Kovács filmed *Hells Angels on Wheels, Targets, Easy Rider, Paper Moon, Slither, Five Easy Pieces, The King of Marvin Gardens, The Sugarland Express* (plus many other films, such as *Shampoo,* that have nothing to do with the road). Kovács came from Hungary with cinematographer Vilmos Zsigmond in 1957, and eventually worked for AIP director Richard Rush on two biker films. Together, they experimented with shallow-rack-focus techniques, which focused between planes of action all staged within the frame, in the AIP films about drugs and motorcycles, *Psych-Out* and *The Savage Seven* (Hill 23).

9. Coppola's concept came from a story he wrote in 1960, "Echoes," about three housewives who leave home in a station wagon (R. Johnson 71).

10. Caan also starred in the road films *Rabbit, Run* (1970) and *Slither* (1972).

11. Kazan and Loden married in 1967, and although they separated, they remained legally married and fairly friendly until Loden's death from breast cancer in 1980.

12. Consider Nicholson's characters in *Easy Rider, Five Easy Pieces, King of Marvin Gardens,* and *One Flew Over the Cuckoo's Nest.*

13. For Corman as producer, Hellman had directed *The Shooting* (1967) and *Ride in the Whirlwind* (1965), both written by Jack Nicholson. Hellman edited Bogdanovich's first feature film, produced by Corman, *Targets* (1968); while not a

road film, the driving sequences and centrality of the drive-in movie theater attest to the importance of car culture to the up-and-coming auteurs.

14. Trumbo complains: "She [the Girl in *Two-Lane Blacktop*] is not permitted to express a single desire, thought or feeling" (149). While I certainly sympathize with feminist frustration with such moribund heroines, we cannot overlook what Trumbo also concedes: "In all fairness, it should be noted that *no one* in the movie is alive" (149).

15. Albert S. Ruddy produced *Little Fauss and Big Halsy* for Paramount, and he is a forerunner of the High Concept producers that wrestled Hollywood back from the auteurs in the late 1970s.

16. I take the term "folk resentments" from Didion's essay on watching biker films, "Nine Bike Movies in Seven *Vroom!* Days."

17. *Breakdown* is a similar road thriller about a threatening but elusive truck driver, but this 1997 film turns the male-male duel of Spielberg's better film into a chivalric quest, as the husband tries to rescue his wife from the kidnapping truck driver.

18. In 1975, *Rafferty and the Gold Dust Twins* features a teenage girl Frisbee (MacKenzie Phillips) and her older companion Mac (Sally Kellerman), who kidnap Gunner Rafferty (Alan Arkin), an ex-Marine, at gunpoint. The two women had met in jail in the "danny tank, where they put the lesbians" (although lesbianism never comes up again as a topic or even a subtext). Both Mac and Frisbee are similar to the *picaras* of the road in the Spanish tradition of literature, using their sexuality to get what they need along the road—not as prostitutes, but cunning women in full control of the seductions they initiate with men. Although Mac and Rafferty become lovers, and Rafferty decides he wants to stay with Mac, she amicably leaves him to travel with a country western band. (Unlike Alice in *Alice Doesn't Live Here Anymore,* Mac loves, sings, and leaves without turmoil.) When Frisbee and Gunner wind up together like daughter and father at the end, the film stresses the creation of a new family not based on biological ties, but on true concern for one another.

19. Didion and Dunne also co-scripted *The Panic in Needle Park* (1971), *Such Good Friends* (1971), and *Up Close and Personal* (1996).

20. According to Abramowitz, Perry was an activist for women's rights in the early seventies (65).

21. Perry's *Diary of a Mad Housewife* was one of the first post–*Easy Rider* deals made at Universal, given the go-ahead by Ned Tanen, who financed auteurs like Milos Forman, Hellman, and Fonda (Biskind 126).

22. In contrast, *Play It as It Lays* and *Alice* were championed by *Ms.* magazine, but several reviewers noted that "the National Kinney Corporation, which owns Warners, has 25 percent controlling interest in *Ms.*" (F. Kaplan 32). Indeed, Warner Bros. released both films (and *The Rain People*), and *Ms.* ran film reviews in each issue, hailing films with a leading female role.

23. In 1972, Corman hired Scorsese to direct the exploitation film *Box Car Bertha,* about the sexual exploits of a woman hobo during the Depression, and permitted Scorsese to innovate within the low-budget format with an homage to *Bonnie and Clyde.*

24. Sandy Weintraub is daughter of producer Fred Weintraub, who first gave Scorsese a break by making him a cameraman on *Woodstock* (Biskind 230).

25. Biskind claims that Robert Evans, head of production at Paramount, was tired of his wife, Ali McGraw, and pushed her into *The Getaway* to get rid of her (159–60). If true, this anecdote suggests that *this* road film was also influenced by a female significant other.

26. Although Cimino proved himself a talented auteur with his next film, *The Deer Hunter* (1978), which won five Oscars, he also symbolizes the breakdown of auteurism that would occur in the "High Concept" phase of Hollywood in the later 1970s and 1980s with his failed film, *Heaven's Gate* (1980), whose "very title became synonymous with failure" (Katz 254).

7. BACK TO THE FAMILY, OR REWINDING THE POSTMODERN ROAD STORY

1. Being elected at a moment in which America seemed to be *"reversing* its history," as Rupert Wilkinson described it in 1984 (emphasis added, Jeffords 3), Ronald Reagan was the nation's leader in that reversal, "intimately confus[ing] Hollywood plot lines and presidential politics" as America searched for a father-figure (Jeffords 6).

2. While Lucas, Spielberg, Scorsese, and Coppola were still major players in the 1980s—and are as well today—some directors including Rafelson, Cimino, Hellman, Bogdanovich, and Malick did not burn as brightly in the 1980s.

3. Doc's car is a handmade DeLorean, an apt symbol of the American dream in a nation newly invested in such symbols. In 1981, the noted General Motors car designer John Z. DeLorean began selling his custom cars. The new *People* magazine tracked DeLorean and his fashion-model wife, as this couple provided the real-life equivalent to prime-time soap operas *Dynasty* and *Dallas,* introduced to television that same year. In 1982, his company went bankrupt, and in 1983, DeLorean was caught in an FBI sting operation trying to buy cocaine, which he had planned to sell to raise money he needed to rescue his failing business.

4. The film's producer, auteur Stephen Spielberg, called *Back to the Future* "the greatest *Leave It to Beaver* episode ever produced" (Hoberman 70). Jameson called some of the films of the 1980s "nostalgia films" (287), recognizing these films' images of the 1950s as "derive[d] from its own television programs; in other words, [the boomer generation's] own representation of itself" (281).

5. Reagan is very much a part of *Back to the Future,* but Eisenhower, the actual president of 1955, is not. The film makes many references to Reagan; conversely,

the president's 1986 State of the Union address, refers to *Back to the Future*. Reagan is frequently discussed in terms of this film by historians like Garry Wills and Rogin or film scholars like Jeffords and Nadel.

6. As discussed in chapter 5, during the 1950s and 1960s, Corman had directed and produced at American International Pictures (AIP), the independent studio that provided exploitation films to drive-in theaters. In 1970, Corman left AIP to open his own film production company, New World Pictures. In fact, New World continued to collaborate with AIP films, as Corman produced Martin Scorsese's *Boxcar Bertha* for AIP in 1972 (then Scorsese went on to make the Oscar-winning road film *Alice Doesn't Live Here Anymore* in 1974). Corman also helped launch the careers of directors of other AIP road films, including Jonathan Kaplan (who later directed the road film *Love Field*) and Richard Compton of *Macon County Line* (both films were produced by AIP in 1974), as well as Jonathan Demme, who later directed the road film *Something Wild* (1986) and other major films.

7. Speaking of the aggressive producers like Don Simpson who followed Corman's example, Biskind notes: "The producers were the auteurs—of crash-and-burn action pictures—but their medium was not so much film as money" (414).

8. Hillier and Lipstadt note that New World was experiencing a transitional period between 1974 and 1977, which is when these films were made. New World slowed production in this phase, increasing budgets considerably (although they still were low, approaching $250,000–$500,000) and began distributing foreign films to art houses.

9. In the 1980s, Simpson went on, along with his partner Jerry Bruckheimer, to become a kingpin of High Concept's high-powered film production, responsible for *Flashdance* (1983), *Beverly Hills Cop* (1984), *Thief of Hearts* (1984), *Top Gun* (1986), *Beverly Hills Cop II* (1987), and *Days of Thunder* (1990). Fleming's book details Simpson's considerable drug problems, which led to his early death.

10. The term "hard body" is Jeffords's, meaning "the normative body that enveloped strength, labor, determination, loyalty and courage . . . the body that was to come to stand as the emblem of the Reagan philosophies, politics, and economies" (24–25).

11. Yates wrote *Cannonball Run* and numerous books on cars and motorcycles, including *Outlaw Machine*.

12. Field actually played a hooker on the road in the 1981 bomb, *Back Roads,* made as CBS Theatrical Films' first project.

13. Hillier notes that Fox lost $27 million in 1969 and $77 million in 1970; United Artists lost $85 million in 1969, the same year that MGM lost $72 million (10).

14. For instance, MCA, Inc. bought Universal in 1962, Gulf & Western purchased Paramount in 1966, Transamerica Corporation bought United Artists in

1967, Kinney Services bought Warner Bros. in 1969, and Kirk Kerkorian bought MGM in 1970 (and later bought United Artists to create MGM/UA, which Turner Broadcasting bought in 1985 in order to screen the archive's films on cable, then sold back to Kerkorian in 1986). In 1982, Coca Cola bought Columbia. The biggest merger came when Time, Inc., owner of HBO and Cinemax cable networks in addition to other media holdings, bought Warner Communications to form Time Warner, Inc. (D. Cook 889–90). The acquisitions and trades continued in the 1980s, with some hostile takeovers and some foreign conglomerates: that is, Rupert Murdoch's Australian News Corporation bought Twentieth Century Fox in 1986, Japan's Sony purchased Columbia in 1989, and Matushita took-over MCA and Universal in 1990–91, and Pathé Communications bought MGM/UA in 1990 (Corrigan 5). No wonder there were so many subtexts involving alien invasion in the Hollywood films of this era.

15. See Feuer on the "yuppie spectator" (43–59). HBO began service in 1972, Showtime in 1976, Nickelodeon in 1979, CNN in 1980, and Cinemax in 1980. Even when one conglomerate, like MTV, owns several networks—MTV, VH-1, and the Nickelodeon channels—the multiplicity of markets fosters a range of tastes. Pay cable subscriptions grew by nearly 70 percent between 1980 and 1981 alone, and grew by 365 percent through the decade ("The 1980s" 87). Thanks to premium channels like HBO or Cinemax, there opened up a huge secondary market for big-budget Hollywood films.

16. Demme scripted a biker film and directed two features for Corman's New World Pictures in the 1970s. He then moved into directing for major studios, including *Swing Shift* (1984) at Warner's, where he teamed up with the Talking Heads to make *Stop Making Sense* (1984) and then used their music on the soundtrack of *Something Wild*.

17. Jarmusch met Wenders when they worked on the documentary, *Lightning over Water,* about Nicholas Ray, director of *Rebel Without a Cause* and many other films. In turn, one of Jarmusch's protégées, Lisa Kreuger, went on to direct her own 1996 independent road film, *Manny and Lo.* Likewise, Tom DiCillo, Jarmusch's earliest director of photography, went on to direct films, including the road film *Box of Moonlight* (1996).

18. Jarmusch's entire cast was culled from New York's hip scene: Balint was a performance artist, Lurie was a saxophonist and leader of the band The Lounge Lizards as well as a filmmaker who made Super-8 art films, and Edson was the original drummer of the influential band Sonic Youth (Hoberman, "Review" 1283).

19. Jameson also suggests that the aimlessness of the 1980s "follows upon a strongly generational self-consciousness, such as what the 'people of the sixties' felt" (296).

20. Jarmusch went on to make several road-oriented films, including *Down By Law* (1986), about escaped prison inmates, *Mystery Train* (1989), not a road

247

film but a story about travelers, and *Night on Earth* (1991), which tells of people traveling in taxis.

21. There are films in which the alien cannot be integrated but must be killed, such as *Alien* and *Terminator* (and even *Fatal Attraction*). Eighties films also focus on how fictional characters inhabit our world; for example, in *The Purple Rose of Cairo,* the film star leaves the screen to fall in love with the most faithful member of the audience. Sometimes, people trade places temporarily with someone else, as in *Overboard, Working Girl,* and *9 to 5.*

22. David Geffen also formed DreamWorks SKG in 1994 with Steven Spielberg and Jeffrey Katzenberg.

23. The American titles of Wenders's German road films: *Wrong Move* (1975), *Alice in the Cities* (1974), and *King of the Road* (1976).

24. In 1982, Stockwell co-directed *Human Highway,* along with musician Neil Young as co-director, about a roadside diner near a leaking nuclear power plant.

25. See chapter 2 for more on Frank. Not only was *Candy Mountain* backed by financiers from several different countries, but Wurlitzer directed the actors in English while Frank handled the film crew in German (C. James 5). *Candy Mountain* contains cameo appearances by Jim Jarmusch and the musicians Leon Redbone, Dr. John, and Tom Waits. Waits appeared in several films by Jarmusch and Coppola, and he wrote the musical and recorded the album, *Frank's Wild Years* (1986), inspired by Frank's time with the Beats.

26. The 1980s is also important for other Australian directors, especially Bruce Beresford, who moved to America, where he directed *Driving Miss Daisy* in 1989 and many other films.

27. Keller offers a good overview (10–12).

28. Hughes accuses Baudrillard of being "the star of his own road movie" (31), searching for "the old comic-book version of America from the France of the Sixties" (31).

29. Unlike the auteuristic road films of the 1970s and 1980s, *Paris, Texas* is not interested in female automobility. This is not a film about Jane or her autonomy, for the film clearly portrays Travis's insanity when he relays how he tied her up to keep her home. *Paris, Texas* portrays the woman only as an image of motherhood, to better reveal Travis's need to master that image.

30. Monique Wittig, the French author and theorist of lesbian and avant-garde fiction, also revised *Don Quixote* as a play called "The Constant Journey," which was first staged in Paris in 1985 and played in New York.

31. De Lauretis coined this term in *Alice Doesn't* (1984), as part of her discussion of Roland Barthes and Laura Mulvey on desire in narrative and where men and women stand in relation to its Oedipal nature.

32. McCaffery discusses Acker's ties to punk.

33. At one point, Mason suggests a link between the road and the Vietnamese

war, when a veteran who misses battle muses: "'We should have paved the Ho Chi Minh Trail and made a four-lane interstate out of it. We could have seen where Charlie was hiding and we would have been ready for him. With an interstate, you always know where you're going'" (134).

8. REBELS WITH A CAUSE: GENRE AND IDENTITY POLITICS

1. Norman Jewison's 1989 film *In Country,* adpated from Mason's novel, turns the road trip from the novel into a minor part of the film.

2. Wack's UCLA classmate, Alex Cox, who became known for directing *Sid and Nancy* (1986), also made subsequent films that skirted the road genre: *Straight to Hell* (1987) features bank robbers on the run in the desert, and *Highway Patrolman* (1992) is about a Mexican highway patrol agent. Cox was connected to people, however, who were building the road genre in the late 1980s: Harry Dean Stanton (from *Paris, Texas*) was in Cox's *Repo Man* and had introduced Cox to Rudy Wurlitzer, who was at the time co-directing the road film *Candy Mountain* with Robert Frank (Wurlitzer had also written *Two-Lane Blacktop*). Cox also assisted on two films by Abbe Wool, who went on to direct her own road film *Roadside Prophets* (1992).

And in the late 1980s and early 1990s, another group of young independent filmmakers came, once again, to the road film genre, including Kathryn Bigelow, Jonathan Wacks, Jonathan Kaplan, Abbe Wool, Tom de Cillo, Lisa Kreuger, Bruce McDonald, and Beeban Kidron.

9. FIRST-PERSON PLAYERS: THE DIGITAL, "TRANSMEDIA" ROAD STORY

1. These technologies can even motivate a road story. The film *Road Trip* (2000) shows college students who travel because a homemade sex video accidentally winds up in the wrong place—an implausible premise that nonetheless reflects precisely what happened to Paris Hilton, right before she became star of the reality road show *The Simple Life 2.*

2. The reality shows have succeeded over attempts to create an ongoing road series, as evidenced by the short-lived remake of *Route 66* (1993) and Showtime's *Goin' to California* (2000–2001).

3. Media scholar Henry Jenkins defines "transmedia storytelling" as enhanced storytelling intended for multiple electronic platforms. He realizes we live in an

> era of media convergence that makes the flow of content across multiple media channels almost inevitable. The move toward digital effects in film and the improved quality of video game graphics means that it is becoming much more realistic to lower production costs by sharing assets across media . . . we need a new model for

> co-creation—rather than adaptation—of content that crosses media. ("Transmedia")

Thus *transmedia* narrative is considerably different from what we have been calling the *intermediary* nature of the road genre. Intermedia innovators, it will be recalled, use the qualities of one medium to inspire creativity in another. For instance, Kerouac tried to "write" a photo in words; transmedia, in contrast, describes the BMW campaign and others we will examine in this chapter.

4. By interviewing business leaders from Starbucks, Nike, and Dell, Roadtrip Nation (RTN) seems to embrace mass production and the businesses that some college students like to boycott. But RTN does offer young people an opportunity to be in a road story, traveling to interview adults in various careers.

In this way, RTN is similar to a documentary *The Journey* (1997) by Eric Saperston, who traveled across country with some friends and interviewed people "who positively affect the lives of those around them," from creative types like Ken Kesey and Jerry Garcia to the CEOs of Coke, Home Depot, and UPS, plus politicians like former President Carter. A short version is available online at http://www.atomfilms.com/af/content/atom_1014.

5. ITVS has provided support to other road documentaries by and for young adults, including *The United States of Poetry* (1996), made by co-creators Joshua Blum and Bob Homan, artistic director for Nuyorican Poets Café in New York, and directed by Mark Pellington, a music video director who had also worked at MTV. The crew traveled for three months, driving across thirty-six states to film eighty-two poets (Rosenberg, "Poetry" F1).

6. In *Generation X*, Coupland calls this type of phenomenon "O'Propriation": "The inclusion of advertising, packaging, and entertainment jargon from earlier eras in everyday speech for ironic and or comic effect" (107).

7. *Crossroads* appeared immediately after the departure of the series's creators, writer Scott Lobdell and artist Chris Bachalo, in 1997.

8. Wong Kar-wai and Alejandro González Iñárritu complete the roster for the first series' films, which were shown in movie theaters. The second series' directors included Joe Carnahan and Tony Scott.

9. Gosney writes about the Audi ad campaign (35–54) and an Alternate Reality Game called *Route 66* (105–80). Other companies have also established elaborate transmedia road stories, including DKNY's campaign in 2003 and Perrier's road film contest in 2002.

10. Bunim died in 2004.

11. Shaw's article had this title.

Works Cited

Abramowitz, Rachel. *Is That a Gun in Your Pocket? Women's Experience of Power in Hollywood.* New York: Random, 2000.

Acker, Kathy. *Blood and Guts in High School.* New York: Grove, 1978.

———. *Don Quixote.* New York: Grove, 1986.

Agee, James, and Walker Evans. *Let Us Now Praise Famous Men.* 1941. Boston: Houghton, 1988.

Anderson, Christopher. *Hollywood TV: The Studio System in the Fifties.* Austin: U of Texas P, 1994.

Anderson, John. "Rev. of *Love Field* in *Newsday*." *Film Review Annual* 11 Dec. 1992: 840.

Arthur, Paul. "'Quixote' and its Contexts." *Film Culture* 67–68–69 (1979): 32–55.

"As We See It." Editorial. *TV Guide* 22–28 Oct. 1960: 4.

Baillie, Bruce. Telephone interview. 20 March 1998.

Baraka, Amiri [see also LeRoi Jones]. *The Black Arts Movement.* Author's self-printed mimeograph, 1994.

Barnouw, Erik. *The Sponsor: Notes on a Modern Potentate.* Oxford: Oxford UP, 1978.

Baudrillard, Jean. *America.* 1986. Trans. Chris Turner. New York: Verso, 1988.

———. "The Ecstasy of Communication." *The Anti-Aesthetic.* Ed. Hal Foster. Seattle: Bay, 1983. 126–34.

———. "The Precession of Simulacra." *Art After Modernism: Rethinking Representation.* Ed. Brian Wallis. New York: New Museum of Contemporary Art (with David R. Godine), 1984. 253–82.

Baughman, James L. "The National Purpose and the Newest Medium: Liberal Critics of Television, 1958–1960." *Mid-American Historical Review* 64 (1982): 41–55.

Beauvoir, Simone de. *America Day by Day.* New York: Grove, 1953.

Belasco, Warren. *Americans on the Road: From Autocamp to Motel, 1910–1945.* Cambridge: MIT Press, 1979.

Bellamy, Joe David. "Tom Wolfe." *Conversations with Tom Wolfe.* Ed. Dorothy M. Scura. Jackson: UP of Mississippi, 1990. 36–55.

Biskind, Peter. *Easy Riders, Raging Bulls: How the Sex-Drugs-and-Rock 'n' Roll Generation Saved Hollywood.* New York: Simon, 1998.

"Black November." Rev. of *Route 66* episode. *Variety* 12 Oct. 1960: 34.

Boddy, William. *Fifties Television: The Industry and Its Critics.* 1990. Urbana: U of Illinois P, 1993.

Booth, Philip. "*Route 66*—Television on the Road Toward People." *Television Quarterly* 2 (Winter 1963): 5–12.

Boyle, Kevin Jon. *RearView Mirror: Automobile Images and American Identities.* Riverside: UCR/California Museum of Photography, U of C, 2000.

Boyle, T. Coraghessan. "Greasy Lake." *Greasy Lake and Other Stories.* New York: Viking, 1985. 1–11.

Brennan, Judy. "The Bus Stopped Here." *LA Times* 16 Oct. 1996: F1+.

Cain, Chelsea. *Dharma Girl: A Road Trip Across the American Generations.* Seattle: Seal, 1996.

Campbell, Elizabeth. "Rolling Stone Raps with Peter Fonda." *Easy Rider.* Ed. Nancy Hardin and Marilyn Schlossberg. 26–35.

Canby, Vincent. "Rev. of *Play It as It Lays,* dir. Frank Perry." *New York Times* 30 Oct. 1972: 36.

———. "Terrific, Tough-Talking 'Alice.'" Rev. of *Alice Doesn't Live Here Anymore,* dir. Martin Scorsese. *New York Times* 2 Feb. 1975: 13.

———. "Why 'Smokey and the Bandit' is Making a Killing." *New York Times* 18 Dec. 1977, sec. 2: 13.

Carroll, Michael Thomas. *Popular Modernity in America: Experience, Technology, Mythohistory.* New York: SUNY P, 2000.

Castleman, Harry, and Walter J. Podrazik. *Watching TV: Four Decades of American Television.* New York: McGraw, 1982.

Cervantes, Miguel Saavedra de. *The Ingenious Gentleman Don Quixote of La Mancha.* Ed. Joseph R. Jones and Kenneth Douglas. New York: Norton, 1981.

Charters, Ann, ed. *The Beats: Literary Bohemians in Postwar America, Part 2.* Dictionary of Literary Biography. Detroit: Gale Publishing Group, 1983.

———, ed. *Jack Kerouac: Selected Letters 1940–1956.* New York: Viking, 1995.

———, ed. *Jack Kerouac: Selected Letters 1957–1969.* New York: Viking, 1999.

———, ed. *The Portable Beat Reader.* New York: Penguin, 1992.

———, ed. *The Portable Jack Kerouac.* New York: Viking, 1995.

Cisneros, Sandra. *Caramelo, or Puro Cuento.* New York: Knopf, 2002.

Cixous, Hélène. "Sorties." 1975. *Modern Criticism and Theory.* Ed. David Lodge. New York: Longman, 1988. 287–93.

Cohan, Steven, and Ina Rae Hark. *The Road Movie Book.* New York: Routledge, 1997.

Cohen, Ralph. "Do Postmodern Genres Exist?" *Postmodern Genres.* Ed. Marjorie Perloff. Norman: U of Oklahoma P, 1989. 11–27.

———. "History and Genre." *New Literary History* 17.2 (Winter 1986): 203–18.

Cook, David A. *A History of Narrative Film.* 1981. 2nd ed. New York: Norton, 1990.

Cook, Roger F., and Gerd Gemünden. *The Cinema of Wim Wenders: Image, Narrative, and the Postmodern Condition.* Detroit: Wayne State UP, 1997.

Cooper, Mark Garrett. "Narrative Spaces." *Screen* 43 (Summer 2002): 139–57.

Corman, Roger, with Jim Jerome. *Maverick: How I Made a Hundred Movies in Hollywood and Never Lost a Dime.* New York: Random, 1990.

Corrigan, Timothy. *A Cinema Without Walls: Movies and Culture after Vietnam.* New Brunswick, NJ: Rutgers UP, 1991.

Corso, Gregory. "Marriage." Ed. Ann Charters. *Portable Beat Reader.* 179–82.

Coupland, Douglas. *Generation X: Tales for an Accelerated Culture*. New York: St. Martin's, 1991.

Crane, Robert David, and Christopher Fryer. *Jack Nicholson, Face to Face*. New York: M. Evans, 1975.

Debord, Guy. *The Society of the Spectacle*. 1967. Trans. Donald Nicholson-Smith. New York: Zone, 1995.

DeCerteau, Michel. *The Practice of Everyday Life*. 1984. Trans. Steven Rendall. Berkeley: U of California P, 1988.

De Lauretis, Teresa. *Alice Doesn't: Feminism, Semiotics, Cinema*. Bloomington: Indiana UP, 1984.

DeLillo, Don. *Americana*. New York: Penguin, 1971.

Dettelbach, Cynthia Golomb. *In the Driver's Seat: The Automobile in American Literature and Popular Culture*. Westport, CT: Greenwood, 1976.

Devitt, Amy J. *Writing Genres*. Carbondale: Southern Illinois UP, 2004.

Didion, Joan. "Nine Bike Movies in Seven *Vroom!* Days." *Life* 8 May 1970: 4.

———. *Play It as It Lays*. New York: Farrar, 1970.

Dyer, Richard. *Now You See It: Studies on Lesbian and Gay Film*. New York: Routledge, 1990.

Eco, Umberto. *Travels in Hyperreality*. Trans. William Weaver. San Diego: Harcourt, 1986.

Eliot, T. S. "Frontiers of Criticism." *Telefilm Magazine* 5 (Jan. 1961): 16.

Ellison, Ralph. *Invisible Man*. 1947. New York: Vintage, 1990.

Evans, John W. "Modern Man and the Cowboy." *Television Quarterly* 1 (May 1962): 31–41.

Faggen, Robert. "Ken Kesey: The Art of Fiction CXXVI." *The Paris Review* 36 (Spring 1994): 58+. *Proquest*. 25 Mar. 2004.

Farber, Stephen. "Something Sour." Rev. of *The Sugarland Express,* dir. Stephen Spielberg. *New York Times* 28 Apr. 1974, sec. 2: 11.

Feldman, Paula R. "Joan Didion." *American Novelists since World War II*. 2. Ed. Jeffrey Helterman and Richard Layman. Dictionary of Literary Biography. Detroit: Gale, 1978. 121–27.

Ferlinghetti, Lawrence. *A Coney Island of the Mind*. New York: New Directions, 1958.

Feuer, Jane. *Seeing Through the Eighties: Television and Reaganism*. Durham: Duke UP, 1995.

Field, Genevieve. *Road Rules*. Produced by Melcher Media. New York: Pocket Books, 1996.

Fleming, Charles. *High Concept: Don Simpson and the Hollywood Culture of Excess*. New York: Doubleday, 1998.

Fonda, Peter. *Don't Tell Dad: A Memoir*. New York: Hyperion, 1998.

Foster, Hal. *The Anti-Aesthetic: Essays on Postmodern Culture*. Seattle: Bay, 1983.

Fowler, Geoffrey A. "Product Placements Now Star on Chinese TV." *Wall Street Journal* 2 June 2004: B1.

Frank, Robert. *The Americans*. 1959. New York: Aperture, 1978.

———. *Robert Frank: From New York to Nova Scotia.* Ed. Anne Wilkes Tucker. Boston: Little, 1986.

Friedan, Betty. "Television and the Feminine Mystique." 1964. *TV Guide: The First 25 Years.* Ed. Jay S. Harris. New York: Simon, 1978. 93–98.

———. "Unmasking the Rage in the American Dream House." *New York Times* 31 Jan. 1971, sec. 2: 15.

Friedman, Ellen. "A Conversation with Kathy Acker." *Review of Contemporary Fiction* 9.3 (1989): 11–22.

Friedman, Susan Stanford. *Mappings: Feminism and the Cultural Geographies of Encounter.* Princeton, NJ: Princeton UP, 1998.

Fussell, Paul. *Class: A Guide Through the American Status System.* New York: Summit, 1983.

Gates, Henry Louis, Jr. *The Signifying Monkey: A Theory of African-American Literary Criticism.* New York: Oxford UP, 1988.

Gehman, Richard. "He's Always Racing His Motor: Why He Rebels Against Society." *TV Guide* 21 Apr. 1962: 17–20.

Gilbert, Sandra M., and Susan Gubar. *The Madwoman in the Attic: The Woman Writer and the Nineteenth-Century Literary Imagination.* New Haven: Yale UP, 1979.

Ginsberg, Allen. "Howl." Ed. Ann Charters. *Portable Beat Reader.* 62–71.

———. *Selected Poems: 1947–1995.* New York: Harper, 1996.

Glassman, Joyce [Joyce Johnson]. *Come and Join the Dance.* New York: H. Wolff (simultaneously in Canada: McClelland), 1961.

"Go Further." *Toronto Star* 31 Aug. 2003. EBSCO*host.* 2 Mar. 04.

Golden, Joseph. "TV's Womanless Hero." *Television Quarterly* 2 (Winter 1963): 13–19.

Gómez-Peña, Guillermo. Epigraph. *Finding Family Stories: An Arts Partnership Project, 1995–1998.* Los Angeles: Japanese American National Museum, 1998. 13.

Goodrich, Chris, and Gayle Feldman. "On the Bus with Kesey, Viking and Thunder's Mouth." *Publisher's Weekly* 237 (15 June 1990): 34–36.

Goodridge, Mike. "The World Run a Monk." *Advocate* 805: 15 Feb. 200l. EBSCO*host.* 19 June 2005.

Goodwin, Michael, and Naomi Wise. *On the Edge: The Life and Times of Francis Coppola.* New York: Morrow, 1989.

Gosney, John W. *Beyond Reality: A Guide to Alternate Reality Gaming.* Boston: Course Technology, 2005.

Gottlieb, Sidney. "*Stranger Than Paradise.*" *Magill's Cinema Annual.* Ed. Frank N. Magill. Englewood Cliffs, NJ: Salem, 1985. 455–60.

Griffin, Farah Jasmine. *"Who Set You Flowin'?" The African-American Migration Narrative.* New York: Oxford UP, 1995.

Grimes, Teresa. "BBS: Auspicious Beginnings, Open Endings." *Movie* 31–32 (1987): 54–66.

Grover, Ronald. "Spike Lee's Magic Bus." *Business Week* 21 Oct. 1996: 6.

Hardin, Nancy, and Marilyn Schlossberg. *Easy Rider: Original Screenplay Plus Stills, Interviews and Articles.* New York: Signet, 1969.

Hark, Ina Rae. "Fear of Flying: Yuppie Critique and the Buddy-Road Movie in the 1980s."

The Road Movie Book. Ed. Steven Cohan and Ina Rae Hark. New York: Routledge, 1997. 204–29.

Harris, William J. *The LeRoi Jones/Amiri Baraka Reader.* In collaboration with Amiri Baraka. New York: Thunder's Mouth, 1991.

Heath, Stephen. *Questions of Cinema.* Bloomington: Indiana UP, 1981.

Herold, Charles. "Pick a Number, It's Sequel Season." *New York Times* 11 Nov. 2004: E1+.

Hesse, Hermann. *The Journey to the East.* 1932. Trans. Hilda Rosner. New York: Picador, 1956.

Hill, Lee. *Easy Rider.* London: BFI, 1996.

Hillier, Jim. *The New Hollywood.* New York: Continuum, 1992.

Hillier, Jim, and Aaron Lipstadt. "The Economics of Independence: Roger Corman and New World Pictures 1970–80." *Movie* 31–32 (1987): 43–53.

Hirsch, Foster. "This Hurts Me More Than It Hurts You." *New York Times* 26 Nov. 1972, sec. 2: 9.

Hoberman, J. "*Pull My Daisy:* The Queen of Sheba Meets the Atom Man." *The American New Wave, 1958–1967.* Walker Art Center/Media Study. Buffalo: Walker Art Center, 1982.

———. "Rev. of *Stranger Than Paradise.*" *Village Voice* 2 Oct. 1984: 49. Rpt. in Jerome S. Ozer, ed. *Film Review Annual 1985:* 1282–84.

———. "Rev. of *Back to the Future.*" *Village Voice* 2 June 1985: 48. Rpt. in Jerome S. Ozer, ed. *Film Review Annual 1985:* 69–70.

Holmes, John Clellon. "The Name of the Game." Nd. *The Beats: Literary Bohemians in Postwar America, Part 2.* Ed. Ann Charters. 627–29.

———. "This is the Beat Generation." 1952. *The Beats: Literary Bohemians in Postwar America, Part 2.* Ed. Ann Charters. 629–31.

———. "The Philosophy of the Beat Generation." 1958. *The Beats: Literary Bohemians in Postwar America, Part 2.* Ed. Ann Charters. 631–36.

hooks, bell. *Black Looks: Race and Representation.* Boston: South End, 1992.

Hopper, Dennis. "Into the Issue of the Good Old Time Movie Versus the Good Old Time." *Easy Rider.* Ed. Nancy Hardin and Marilyn Schlossberg. 7–11.

Hughes, Robert. "The Patron Saint of Neo-Pop." *New York Review of Books* 1 June 1989: 29–32.

Hugo, Chris. "*Easy Rider* and Hollywood in the '70s." *Movie* 31–32 (1987): 67–75.

Hundert, Edward J. "Oswald Spengler: History and Metaphor, the Decline and the West." *Mosaic* 1 (1967): 103–17.

Hunt, Tim. *Kerouac's Crooked Road: The Development of a Fiction.* 1981. Berkeley: U of California P, 1996.

Hutchison, Alice L. *Kenneth Anger.* London: Black Dog, 2004.

Huyssen, Andreas. "Mass Culture as Woman: Modernism's Other." *Studies in Entertainment: Critical Approaches to Mass Culture.* Ed. Tania Modleski. Bloomington: Indiana UP, 1986. 188–207.

James, Caryn. "Rev. of *Candy Mountain.*" *New York Times* 10 June 1988, sec. C6: 5.

James, David. *Allegories of Cinema: American Film in the Sixties.* Princeton: Princeton UP, 1989.

Jameson, Fredric. *Postmodernism, or, The Cultural Logic of Late Capitalism*. Durham: Duke UP, 1991.

Jeffords, Susan. *The Remasculinization of America: Gender and the Vietnam War*. Bloomington: Indiana UP, 1989.

Jeffries, John W. "The 'Quest for National Purpose' of 1960." *American Quarterly* 30 (Fall 1978): 451–70.

Jenkins, Henry. "Media Convergence." Nd. MIT Faculty Page. 28 Dec. 2005. <http://web.mit.edu/cms/People/henry3/converge.html>

———. "Transmedia Storytelling." 13 Jan. 2003. *Technology Review: An MIT Enterprise*. 28 Dec. 2005. <http://www.technologyreview.com/BioTech/wtr_13052,312,pl.html?PM=GO>

Johnson, Robert K. *Francis Ford Coppola*. Boston: Twayne, 1977.

Johnson, William S. *The Pictures are a Necessity: Robert Frank in Rochester, NY: November 1988*. Rochester Film and Photo Consortium Occasional Papers, No. 2. Rochester: Museum of Photography, Eastman House, Jan. 1989.

Jones, LeRoi [see also Amiri Baraka]. *Blues People: Negro Music in White America*. New York: Morrow, 1963.

———. *Home: Social Essays*. New York: Morrow, 1966.

———. Letter. *Evergreen Review* 2 (Spring 1959): 253–56.

———. *The Moderns: An Anthology of New Writing in America*. New York: Corinth, 1963.

———. *The System of Dante's Hell*. New York: Grove, 1965.

Kadohata, Cynthia. *The Floating World*. New York: Ballantine, 1989.

Kael, Pauline. "The Current Cinema." Rev. of *Play It as It Lays,* dir. Frank Perry. *New Yorker* 11 Nov. 1972: 155–58.

———. "Split." Rev. of *Two-Lane Blacktop,* dir. Monte Hellman. *New Yorker* 10 July 1971: 55–56.

———. "Woman on the Road." Rev. of *Alice Doesn't Live Here Anymore,* dir. Martin Scorsese. *New Yorker* 13 Jan 1975: 74–78+.

Kaplan, Fred. Rev. of *Alice Doesn't Live Here Anymore,* dir. Martin Scorsese. *Cinéaste* 7.1 (1975): 32–34.

Kaplan, Caren. *Questions of Travel: Postmodern Discourses of Displacement*. Durham: Duke UP, 1996.

Katz, Ephraim. *The Film Encyclopedia*. New York: HarperCollins, 1994.

Kauffman, Bill. Review of *Cannonball Run II,* dir. Hal Needham. 29 June 1984, sec. 2.7. Rpt. in Jerome S. Ozer, ed. *Film Review Annual, 1985:* 266.

Keller, Ulrich. *Highway as Habitat: A Roy Stryker Documentation, 1943–1955*. Santa Barbara: U Art Museum, 1986.

Kennedy, John F. "John F. Kennedy on Broadcasting." *Telefilm Magazine* Apr. 1960: 13+.

———. "We Must Climb to the Hilltop." *Life* 49 (22 Aug. 1960): 70B–77.

Kerouac, Jack. "Beatific: The Origins of the Beat Generation." 1958. *The Portable Jack Kerouac*. Ed. Ann Charters. 565–73.

———. "Belief and Technique for Modern Prose." *Evergreen Review* 2.8 (1959): 57.

————. *The Dharma Bums.* 1958. New York: Penguin, 1976.

————. "Essentials of Spontaneous Prose." *Evergreen Review* 2.5 (1958): 72–73.

————. Introduction. *The Americans.* Robert Frank. 5–11.

————. "Lamb, No Lion." 1958. *The Portable Jack Kerouac.* Ed. Ann Charters. 562–65.

————. *On the Road.* 1957. New York: Penguin, 1976.

————. "The Vanishing American Hobo." *Holiday* Mar. 1960: 60–61+.

————. *Visions of Cody.* New York: Penguin, 1972.

Kesey, Ken. "Is There Any End to Kerouac Highway?" *Esquire* Dec 1983: 60–63.

Kesey, Zane. Telephone interview. 20 May 2004.

Keyser, Lester J. *Martin Scorsese.* New York: Twayne, 1992.

Key-Z Productions. *Intrepid Traveler and His Merry Band of Pranksters Look for a Kool Place: Episode One: Journey to the East.* Pleasant Hill, OR: Key-Z Productions, n.d.

————. *Intrepid Traveler and His Merry Band of Pranksters Look for a Kool Place: Episode Two: North to Madhattan.* Pleasant Hill, OR: Key-Z Productions, n.d.

Kinder, Marsha. "The Return of the Outlaw Couple." *Film Quarterly* 27.4 (1974): 2–10.

Kingsolver, Barbara. *Barbara Kingsolver.* 28 Dec. 2005. <http://www.kingsolver.com/about/about.asp>

Kingston, Maxine Hong. *Tripmaster Monkey: His Fake Book.* 1987. New York: Vintage, 1990.

Kracauer, Siegfried. *Theory of Film.* Oxford: Oxford UP, 1960.

Lackey, Kris. *Road Frames: The American Highway Narrative.* Lincoln: U of Nebraska P, 1997.

Laderman, David. *Driving Visions: Exploring the Road Movie.* Austin: U of Texas P, 2002.

Leary, Timothy. *The Politics of Ecstasy.* New York: Putnam's, 1968.

Least Heat Moon, William. *Blue Highways: A Journey into America.* New York: Fawcett, 1982.

Lefcowitz, Eric. *The Monkees' Tale.* Berkeley: Last Gasp, 1989.

Lhamon, W. T., Jr. *Deliberate Speed: The Origin of a Cultural Style in the American 1950s.* Washington: Smithsonian, 1990.

Lopez, Erika. *Flaming Iguanas: An Illustrated All-Girl Road Novel Thing.* New York: Simon, 1997.

Lowry, Ed. "The Appropriation of Signs in *Scorpio Rising.*" *Velvet Light Trap* 20 (Summer 1983): 41–46.

Mailer, Norman. "The White Negro." 1959. *The Portable Beat Reader.* Ed. Ann Charters. 582–605.

Man, Glenn. *Radical Visions: American Film Renaissance: 1967–1976.* Westport, CT: Greenwood, 1994.

Mann, Dave, and Ron Main. *Races, Chases and Crashes: A Complete Guide to Car Movies and Biker Flicks.* Osceoloa, WI: Motorbooks, 1994.

Marc, David. *Comic Visions: Television Comedy and American Culture.* 1989. Malden, MA: Blackwell, 1999.

Marriner, Mike, and Nathan Gehard, with Joanne Gordon. *Roadtrip Nation: A Guide to Discovering Your Path in Life.* New York: Ballantine, 2003.

Marsh, Katherine. "What Is Real?" *Rolling Stone* 843 (22 June 2000): 71–78. *ProQuest.* 18 June 2005.

Martelle, Scott. "A Personal Note, from Icon to Icon; In 1957, Jack Kerouac Wrote to Marlon Brando." *Los Angeles Times* 7 May 2005: E1. *ProQuest.* 9 May 2005.

Mason, Bobbie Ann. *In Country.* 1984. London: Fontana, 1985.

Mason, John L. *The Identity Crisis Theme in American Feature Films 1960–69.* New York: Arno, 1977.

Maynard, Richard. "TV's First Road Show." *Emmy Magazine* Sept.-Oct. 1983: 42–47.

McCaffery, Larry. "The Artists of Hell: Kathy Acker and 'Punk' Aesthetics." *Breaking the Sequence: Women's Experimental Fiction.* Ed. Ellen G. Friedman and Miriam Fuchs. Princeton, NJ: Princeton UP, 1989. 215–30.

McClanahan, Ed. *Spit in the Ocean: All About Kesey.* New York: Penguin, 2003.

McLuhan, Marshall. *Understanding Media: The Extensions of Man.* New York: Signet, 1964.

McKeen, William. *Hunter S. Thompson.* Boston: Twayne, 1991.

Mekas, Jonas. *Movie Journal: The Rise of a New American Cinema: 1959–1971.* New York: Collier, 1972.

Modleski, Tania. *Studies in Entertainment: Critical Approaches to Mass Culture.* Bloomington: Indiana UP, 1986.

Morley, David. *Home Territories: Media, Mobility, and Identity.* New York: Routledge, 2000.

Morrison, Toni. Afterword. *The Bluest Eye.* 1970. New York: Penguin, 1994.

———. *Song of Solomon.* 1977. New York: Plume, 1987.

MTV Press Release. "MTV and Cox Communications Hit the Road this Summer with the Ultimate *Road Rules* Promotion." San Francisco: 17 July 1995.

Mulvey, Laura. "Afterthoughts on 'Visual Pleasure and Narrative Cinema' Inspired by King Vidor's *Duel in the Sun* (1946)." *Feminist Film Theory, A Reader.* Ed. Sue Thornham. Edinburgh: Edinburgh UP, 1999. 122–30.

Murray, Lawrence L. "Hollywood, Nihilism, and the Youth Culture of the Sixties: *Bonnie and Clyde* (1967)." *American History/American Film.* Ed. John E. O'Connor and Martin A. Jackson. New York: Ungar, 1988. 237–56.

Murray, Soraya. "High Art/Low Life: The Art of Playing *Grand Theft Auto.*" *PAJ: A Journal of Performance and Art* 27.2 (2005): 91–98.

Musser, Charles. "The Travel Genre in 1903–1904: Moving Towards Fictional Narrative." *Early Cinema: Space, Frame, Narrative.* Ed. Thomas Elsaesser. London: BFI, 1990. 127–32.

Nabokov, Vladimir. *The Annotated Lolita.* Ed. Alfred Appel Jr. New York: McGraw, 1970.

Nafisi, Azar. *Reading Lolita in Tehran: A Memoir in Books.* New York: Random, 2004.

Neaverson, Bob. *The Beatles Movies.* London: Cassell, 1997.

Nicosia, Gerald. *Memory Babe: A Critical Biography of Jack Kerouac.* New York: Grove, 1983.

O'Connor, Flannery. *Collected Works.* New York: Library of America, 1988.

O'Dell, Denis, with Bob Neaverson. *At the Apple's Core: The Beatles from the Inside.* London: Owen, 2002.

Olderman, Raymond. M. *Beyond the Waste Land: A Study of the American Novel in the Nineteen-Sixties.* New Haven: Yale UP, 1972.

O'Malley, Bryan Lee. *Lost at Sea.* Portland: Oni Press, 2005.

"One Tiger to a Hill." Rev. of *Route 66* episode. *Variety* 26 Sept. 1962: 13.

Ozer, Jerome S. *Film Review Annual, 1985.* Englewood, NJ: Film Review Publications, 1985.

Paes de Barros, Deborah. *Fast Cars and Bad Girls: Nomadic Subjects and Women's Road Stories.* New York: Lang, 2004.

Peck, James. *Freedom Ride.* New York: Grove, 1962.

Perloff, Marjorie. *Postmodern Genres.* Norman: U of Oklahoma Press, 1988.

Perry, Paul, and Ken Babbs. *On the Bus: The Complete Guide to the Legendary Trip of Ken Kesey and the Merry Pranksters and the Birth of the Counterculture.* New York: Thunder's Mouth, 1990.

Pirsig, Robert M. *Zen and the Art of Motorcycle Maintenance: An Inquiry into Values.* 1974. New York: Quill, 1979.

Pratt, Mary Louise. *Imperial Eyes: Travel Writing and Transculturation.* London: Routledge, 1992.

Primeau, Ronald. *Romance of the Road: The Literature of the American Highway.* Bowling Green, OH: BGSU Popular Press, 1996.

Pynchon, Thomas. *The Crying of Lot 49.* 1965. New York: Harper, 1990.

Rascaroli, Laura. "New Voyages to Italy: Postmodern Travellers and the Italian Road Film." *Screen* 44 (Spring 2003): 71–91.

Ressner, Jeffrey. "They've Got to Have It: What Spike Lee's film did for African Americans, *Smoke Signals* aims to do for Native Americans." *Time* 29 June 1998: 58. *ProQuest.* 17 Aug. 2005.

Rexroth, Kenneth. "The Commercialization of the Image of Revolt." 1960. *The Beats: Literary Bohemians in Postwar America, Part 2.* Ed. Ann Charters. Dictionary of Literary Biography. 16. Detroit: Gale Research Company, 1983. 643–50.

———. "Disengagement: The Art of the Beat Generation." *A Casebook on the Beat.* Ed. Thomas Parkinson. New York: Crowell, 1961. 179–93.

Rich, Adrienne. *On Lies, Secrets, and Silence: Selected Prose 1966–1978.* New York: Norton, 1979.

Rosenberg, Howard. "Poetry Carries a Big Shtick as PBS Seeks Pulse of America." *LA Times* 12 Feb. 1996: F1+.

———. "To Learn about Teens, Go Along for 'The Ride.'" *LA Times* 1 Nov. 1994: F1+.

"Puts George Maharis in the Driver's Seat." Rev. of *Route 66* episode. *TV Guide,* 18 Feb. 1961: 17–19.

"San Andreas Game a Masterpiece of Mayhem on the Warpath to L.A., Vegas, Frisco." *Toronto Star* 7 Nov. 2004: D01. EBSCO*host.* 18 Jun. 2005.

Sargeant, Jack. *Naked Lens: Beat Cinema.* London: Creation, 1997.

Sargeant, Jack, and Stephanie Watson. *Lost Highways: An Illustrated History of Road Movies.* London: Creation, 2000.

Schatz, Thomas. *Hollywood Genres: Formulas, Filmmaking, and the Studio System.* Philadelphia: Temple UP, 1981.

Schickel, Richard. *Elia Kazan.* New York: Harper, 2005.

Schivelbusch, Wolfgang. *The Railway Journey: Trains and Travel in the 19th Century.* 1977. New York: Urizen, 1979.

Scorsese, Martin. *Scorsese on Scorsese.* Ed. David Thompson and Ian Christie. London: Farber, 1989.

Scott, Joan. "The Evidence of Experience." *The Lesbian and Gay Studies Reader.* New York: Routledge, 1993. 397–415.

Seate, Mike, and Matthew J. Gagnon. *Two Wheels on Two Reels: A History of Biker Movies.* North Conway, NH: Whitehorse, 2000.

Seldes, Gilbert. "Rev. of *Route 66.*" *TV Guide* 10 Feb. 1962: 4.

Shaw, Jessica. "Rich Girls Gone Wild!" *Entertainment Weekly* 11 June 2004: 41.

Sherrill, Rowland A. *Road-Book America: Contemporary Culture and the New Picaresque.* Urbana: U of Illinois P, 2000.

Silk, Gerald. *Automobile and Culture.* Los Angeles: Museum of Contemporary Art, 1984.

Simpson, Mona. *Anywhere But Here.* New York: Vintage, 1986.

Sitney, P. Adams. *Visionary Film: the American Avant-Garde.* 2nd ed. New York: Oxford UP, 1979.

Smith, Cecil. "From Screen Gems: Empire." *TV Times* 8–14 July 1962: 3.

Smith, Lillian. Introduction. *Freedom Ride.* By James Peck. New York: Grove, 1962. 7–10.

Sontag, Deborah. "I Want My Hyphenated-Identity MTV." *New York Times* 19 June 2005, sec. 2: 1+.

Sontag, Susan. *Against Interpretation.* New York: Delta, 1965.

Staiger, Janet. *Perverse Spectators: The Practices of Film Reception.* New York: New York UP, 2000.

Standage, Tom. *The Victorian Internet.* New York: Berkley, 1999.

Sterritt, David. *Screening the Beats: Media Culture and the Beat Sensibility.* Carbondale: Southern Illinois UP, 2004.

Stone, Robert. "The Prince of Possibility: On the Road with Ken Kesey." *New Yorker* 14 & 21 June 2004: 70–89.

Stout, Janice P. *The Journey Narrative in American Literature.* Westport, CT: Greenwood, 1983.

Sturken, Marita. *Thelma and Louise.* London: BFI, 2000.

Suárez, Juan A. *Bike Boys, Drag Queens, and Superstars: Avant-Garde, Mass Culture, and Gay Identities in the 1960s Underground Cinema.* Bloomington: Indiana UP, 1996.

Taylor, John Russell. "Rev. of *Wanda,* dir. Barbara Loden." *Sight and Sound* 40.1 (1970–71): 15.

"The 1980s: A Reference Guide to Motion Pictures, Television, VCR, and Cable." *Velvet Light Trap* 27 (Spring 1991): 78–88.

Thompson, Hunter S. *Hell's Angels.* 1967. New York: Ballantine, 1996.

Trumbo, Sherrie Sonnett. "A Woman's Place is in the Oven." *New York Times* 10 Oct. 1971, sec. 2: 1.

Tuten, Frederick. "Introduction to *Easy Rider*." *Easy Rider*. Ed. Nancy Hardin and Marilyn Schlossberg. 36–40.

Tyler, Parker. *Underground Film: A Critical History*. New York: Grove, 1965.

Van Oostrum, Duco. "Wim Wenders's Euro-American Construction Site: *Paris, Texas* or Texas, Paris." *Social and Political Change in Literature and Film: Selected Papers from the 16th Conference on Literature and Film*. Ed. Richard L. Chapple. Gainesville: UP of Florida, 1994. 7–20.

Walker, Beverly. "Two-Lane Blacktop." *Sight and Sound* 40.1 (1970–71): 34–37.

Wallis, Brian. *Art After Modernism: Rethinking Representation*. New York: New Museum of Contemporary Art, 1984.

Watson, Mary Ann. *The Expanding Vista: American Television in the Kennedy Years*. New York: Oxford UP, 1990.

Wenders, Wim. *Wim Wenders: On Film*. 1997. Trans. Michael Hofman. New York: Faber, 2001.

West, Dennis, and Joan M. West. "Sending Cinematic *Smoke Signals:* An Interview with Sherman Alexie." *Cinéaste* 23.4 (1998): 28–37.

Whitney, Dwight. "And He Hasn't Crumpled a Fender Yet: Glenn Corbett's Diplomatic Driving Has Everyone Purring Along 'Route 66.'" *TV Guide* 6 July 1963: 10–13.

Widmer, E. L. "Crossroads: The Automobile, Rock and Roll, and Democracy." *Roadside America: The Automombile in Design and Culture*. Ed. Jan Jennings. Ames: Iowa State UP, 1990. 82–91.

Widmer, Kinglsey. "The Post-Modernist Art of Protest: Kesey and Mailer as American Expressions of Rebellion." *Centennial Review* 19.3 (1975): 121–35.

Williams, Mark. *Road Movies: The Complete Guide to Cinema on Wheels*. New York: Proteus, 1982.

Williams, Raymond. *Television: Technology and Cultural Form*. 1974. Hanover: Wesleyan UP, 1992.

Willis, Sharon. "Hardware and Hardbodies, What Do Women Want?: A Reading of *Thelma and Louise*." *Film Theory Goes to the Movies*. Ed. Jim Collins, Hilary Radner, and Ava Preacher Collins. New York: Routledge, 1993. 120–28.

Wills, Gary. *Reagan's America*. Garden City: Doubleday, 1987.

Wolfe, Tom. "The Chief and His Merry Pranksters Take a Trip with Electric Kool Aid." *World Journal Tribune: New York* 29 Jan. 1967: 4–7+.

———. *The Electric Kool-Aid Acid Test*. 1968. New York: Bantam, 1981.

———. *The Kandy-Kolored Tangerine-Flake Streamline Baby*. New York: Farrar, 1968.

———. *The New Journalism*. New York: Harper, 1973.

———. "Super-Hud Plays the Game of Power." *World Journal Tribune: New York* 5 Feb. 1967: 12+.

Wolff, Janet. "On the Road Again: Metaphors of Travel in Cultural Criticism." *Cultural Studies* 7.2 (1993): 224–40.

Wright, Stephen. *Going Native*. New York: Delta, 1994.

Wyatt, Justin. *High Concept: Movies and Marketing in Hollywood*. Austin: U of Texas P, 1994.

———. "From Roadshowing to Saturation Release: Majors, Independents, and Marketing/Distribution Innovations." *The New American Cinema,* ed. Jon Lewis. Durham: Duke UP, 1998. 64–86.

Yamamoto, Hisaye. *Seventeen Syllables.* Berkeley: Kitchen Table, 1988.

York, Steven J. *Crossroads (Generation X).* New York: Berkley, 1998.

Index

Katie Mills is a visiting assistant professor at Occidental College in Los Angeles. She earned her PhD in the interdisciplinary film and literature program at the University of Southern California. She served as education coordinator at the Petersen Automotive Museum in Los Angeles. She has published articles about road stories in various journals and in *The Road Movie Book* (1997) and *GenXegesis: Essays on "Alternative" Youth (Sub)Culture* (2003).